International Journal on Advances in Systems and Measurements

2016 vol. 9 nr. 1&2

Printed from e-media with permission by:

Curran Associates, Inc.
57 Morehouse Lane
Red Hook, NY 12571

Some format issues inherent in the e-media version may also appear in this print version.

Printed by Curran Associates, Inc. (2018)

International Academy, Research, and Industry Association (IARIA)
412 Derby Way
Wilmington, DE 19810

Phone: (408) 893-6407
Fax: (408) 527-6351

petre@iaria.org

Additional copies of this publication are available from:

Curran Associates, Inc.
57 Morehouse Lane
Red Hook, NY 12571 USA
Phone: 845-758-0400
Fax: 845-758-2633
Email: curran@proceedings.com
Web: www.proceedings.com

The *International Journal on Advances in Systems and Measurements* is published by IARIA.
ISSN: 1942-261x
journals site: http://www.iariajournals.org
contact: petre@iaria.org

Sponsored by IARIA
www.iaria.org

International Journal on Advances in Systems and Measurements
Volume 9, Number 1 & 2, 2016

Barcelona (ICMAB-CSIC), Spain
Kevin Lee, Murdoch University, Australia
Wolfgang Leister, Norsk Regnesentral (Norwegian Computing Center), Norway
Andreas Löf, University of Waikato, New Zealand
Jerzy P. Lukaszewicz, Nicholas Copernicus University - Torun, Poland
Zoubir Mammeri, IRIT - Paul Sabatier University - Toulouse, France
Sathiamoorthy Manoharan, University of Auckland, New Zealand
Stefano Mariani, Politecnico di Milano, Italy
Paulo Martins Pedro, Chaminade University, USA / Unicamp, Brazil
Don McNickle, University of Canterbury, New Zealand
Mahmoud Meribout, The Petroleum Institute - Abu Dhabi, UAE
Luca Mesin, Politecnico di Torino, Italy
Marco Mevius, HTWG Konstanz, Germany
Marek Miskowicz, AGH University of Science and Technology, Poland
Jean-Henry Morin, University of Geneva, Switzerland
Fabrice Mourlin, Paris 12th University, France
Adrian Muscat, University of Malta, Malta
Mahmuda Naznin, Bangladesh University of Engineering and Technology, Bangladesh
George Oikonomou, University of Bristol, UK
Arnaldo S. R. Oliveira, Universidade de Aveiro-DETI / Instituto de Telecomunicações, Portugal
Aida Omerovic, SINTEF ICT, Norway
Victor Ovchinnikov, Aalto University, Finland
Telhat Özdoğan, Recep Tayyip Erdogan University, Turkey
Gurkan Ozhan, Middle East Technical University, Turkey
Constantin Paleologu, University Politehnica of Bucharest, Romania
Matteo G A Paris, Universita` degli Studi di Milano,Italy
Vittorio M.N. Passaro, Politecnico di Bari, Italy
Giuseppe Patanè, CNR-IMATI, Italy
Marek Penhaker, VSB- Technical University of Ostrava, Czech Republic
Juho Perälä, Bitfactor Oy, Finland
Florian Pinel, T.J.Watson Research Center, IBM, USA
Ana-Catalina Plesa, German Aerospace Center, Germany
Miodrag Potkonjak, University of California - Los Angeles, USA
Alessandro Pozzebon, University of Siena, Italy
Vladimir Privman, Clarkson University, USA
Mohammed Rajabali Nejad, Universiteit Twente, the Netherlands
Konandur Rajanna, Indian Institute of Science, India
Nageswara Rao, Oak Ridge National Laboratory, USA
Stefan Rass, Universität Klagenfurt, Austria
Candid Reig, University of Valencia, Spain
Teresa Restivo, University of Porto, Portugal
Leon Reznik, Rochester Institute of Technology, USA
Gerasimos Rigatos, Harper-Adams University College, UK
Luis Roa Oppliger, Universidad de Concepción, Chile
Ivan Rodero, Rutgers University - Piscataway, USA
Lorenzo Rubio Arjona, Universitat Politècnica de València, Spain
Claus-Peter Rückemann, Leibniz Universität Hannover / Westfälische Wilhelms-Universität Münster / North-German Supercomputing Alliance, Germany
Subhash Saini, NASA, USA
Mikko Sallinen, University of Oulu, Finland
Christian Schanes, Vienna University of Technology, Austria
Rainer Schönbein, Fraunhofer Institute of Optronics, System Technologies and Image Exploitation (IOSB), Germany
Cristina Seceleanu, Mälardalen University, Sweden

Guodong Shao, National Institute of Standards and Technology (NIST), USA
Dongwan Shin, New Mexico Tech, USA
Larisa Shwartz, T.J. Watson Research Center, IBM, USA
Simone Silvestri, University of Rome "La Sapienza", Italy
Diglio A. Simoni, RTI International, USA
Radosveta Sokullu, Ege University, Turkey
Junho Song, Sunnybrook Health Science Centre - Toronto, Canada
Leonel Sousa, INESC-ID/IST, TU-Lisbon, Portugal
Arvind K. Srivastav, NanoSonix Inc., USA
Grigore Stamatescu, University Politehnica of Bucharest, Romania
Raluca-Ioana Stefan-van Staden, National Institute of Research for Electrochemistry and Condensed Matter, Romania
Pavel Šteffan, Brno University of Technology, Czech Republic
Chelakara S. Subramanian, Florida Institute of Technology, USA
Sofiene Tahar, Concordia University, Canada
Muhammad Tariq, Waseda University, Japan
Roald Taymanov, D.I.Mendeleyev Institute for Metrology, St.Petersburg, Russia
Francesco Tiezzi, IMT Institute for Advanced Studies Lucca, Italy
Theo Tryfonas, University of Bristol, UK
Wilfried Uhring, University of Strasbourg // CNRS, France
Guillaume Valadon, French Network and Information and Security Agency, France
Eloisa Vargiu, Barcelona Digital - Barcelona, Spain
Miroslav Velev, Aries Design Automation, USA
Dario Vieira, EFREI, France
Stephen White, University of Huddersfield, UK
Shengnan Wu, American Airlines, USA
Qingsong Xu, University of Macau, Macau, China
Xiaodong Xu, Beijing University of Posts & Telecommunications, China
Ravi M. Yadahalli, PES Institute of Technology and Management, India
Yanyan (Linda) Yang, University of Portsmouth, UK
Shigeru Yamashita, Ritsumeikan University, Japan
Patrick Meumeu Yomsi, INRIA Nancy-Grand Est, France
Alberto Yúfera, Centro Nacional de Microelectronica (CNM-CSIC) - Sevilla, Spain
Sergey Y. Yurish, IFSA, Spain
David Zammit-Mangion, University of Malta, Malta
Guigen Zhang, Clemson University, USA
Weiping Zhang, Shanghai Jiao Tong University, P. R. China

International Journal on Advances in Systems and Measurements
Volume 9, Numbers 1 & 2, 2016

CONTENTS

The Impact of Control Setpoints on Building Energy Use in Different Weather Conditions

Stephen Treado
Department of Architectural Engineering
Pennsylvania State University
University Park, PA, USA
streado@psu.edu

Xing Liu
Department of Architectural Engineering
Pennsylvania State University
University Park, PA, USA
xul121@psu.edu

Abstract - **This paper examines the impact of building Heating, Ventilation and Air Conditioning (HVAC) control system setpoints such as temperature and flow rate on total building energy requirements, for a typical system design and operation in four different weather conditions. Through the simulation and the result sensitivity analysis, the range of energy usage and the potential for minimizing building energy requirements by dynamically adjusting setpoints are presented in this paper.**

Keywords-buildings; cooling; control systems; energy; heating; HVAC; simulation; setpoints

I. Introduction

The increasing demand of air-conditioning and the energy crisis during the last decades have led to a surge of attention and there is no doubt that the improvement of the Heating, Ventilating and Air Conditioning (HVAC) control system is one of the effective solutions to realize sizable energy-saving for the building sector. The aim of HVAC control is to provide a comfortable, safe, healthy and productive environment for occupants using the least energy. Significant energy saving potential exists for building systems during operation with the help of current technology such as intelligent, adaptive or model predictive control. The development of this kind of technology has led to the possibility of the improvement of building operational performance. However, it is difficult to evaluate the potential or effectiveness of the new control strategies without first gaining a better understanding of the range of operating conditions possible for any particular building/HVAC system combination. That is, the amount of energy savings is a function of both the actions of the new control strategy and the fundamental capabilities of the HVAC system. In its most basic form, a building control system can do no more than monitor sensors, apply logic and manipulate actuators. Thus, the main objective of the work described in this paper is to clearly identify and define the space within which the building/HVAC combination is capable of operating in order to enable the determination of both energy saving potential and optimal setpoints and control logic. While this is not specifically an optimization effort, i.e., we are not seeking a single optimal solution since it is understood that setpoints and control logic may need to be adjusted on a dynamic basis, the primary metric utilized, namely total building energy usage, can be considered as an objective function.

The content is organized as follows. Section II reviews the recent studies. Section III presents the models adopted and simulation work. Section IV gives the results and analysis. Lastly, Section V presents the conclusions and possible future work.

II. Literature Rievew

Simulation is taken as one of the oldest but very effective tools to engineers in every discipline. Building simulation began in the 1960s and became the hot topic of the 1970s within the energy research community. For nowadays, computer simulation is not only used for the building design stage like sizing and configuration design, but also adopted for system performance analysis more and more widely. Building simulation can be applied to reveal the inter-actions between the building itself and its occupants, HVAC systems, and the outdoor climate This paper is a further improvement to our previous work [1]. A large amount of work has been done to show how important building simulation is in the study of building energy performance [2]. For examples, Li et al. [3] and Pan et al. [4] analyzed and displayed the building energy break-down with calibrated models in 2007 and 2009, respectively; however, more effort is needed to understand how to obtain optimum operating parameters, particularly for building control systems. Simulation does provide a good opportunity to evaluate the dynamic and energy performance of HVAC system control strategy in a convenient and low cost way. The control strategy can also be pre-tuned before being utilized in the real system with the help of simulation. Recent research also showed performing building simulation analysis enabled diagnosis of malfunctioning or incorrectly commissioned equipment within the building and thus also assisted with future commissioning and tuning of the building performance [5].

Future development and application of information technology in the building industry will lead to a completely new building design philosophy and methodology [6]. In 2003, Mathews and Botha [7] conducted simulation with three cases and proved that simulation does indeed have the

TABLE I. REFERENCE CHARACTERISTICS OF EQUIPMENT

Components	Selected parameters values	
Chiller	33 Capacity (hp)	2.75 COP
	44 T_lcw (°F)	85 T_ecf (°F)
	4.24 V_chw (ft^3/min)	4.87 V_cdw (ft^3/min)
Natural Gas Boiler	0.8 Boiler Efficiency	950 Heat Value (Btu/lb)
Variable Volume Fan	4500 Rated Flow rate (ft^3/min)	3 Rated Power (hp)
	0.087 Pressure Rise (psi)	0.7 Fan Efficiency
Variable Speed Pump	2.54 Rated Flow rate (ft^3/min))	2 Rated Power (hp)
	50 Pump head (ft)	0.66 Pump Efficiency

*T-Temperature, V-Flow Rate, lcw-leaving chilled water, ecf-entering condenser fluid, chw-chilled water, cdw-condenser water

TABLE II. DEFAULT PARAMETER VALUE FOR SIMULATION

Variable	Value
Zone Area	S=750 ft^2
Overall Envelope Heat Transfer Rate	U = 0.064 Btu/h-ft^2-°F
Ambient Temperature	T_a = 90 °F (summer condition)
	T_a = 30 °F (winter condition)
Ambient Pressure	P = 1 atm
Zone Air Temperature	T_z = 75 °F (summer condition)
	T_z = 72 °F (winter condition)
Outdoor Air fraction	F_o = 30%
Solar Heat Gain	q_s=1.5 w/ft^2 (summer condition)
	q_s=0.8 w/ft^2 (winter condition)
Lighting Heat Gain	q_l = 1.0 w/ft^2
Equipment Heat Gain	q_e = 1.5 w/ft^2
Occupants Heat Gain	q_o = 1.0 w/ft^2
Ventilation Air Flow rate	M_v = 1.5 cfm/ft^2
Infiltration Air Flow Rate	M_i = 0.1 cfm/ft^2
Heat Exchanger Effectiveness	U_1 = 75%
Energy Recovery Effectiveness	U_2 = 70%

ability to improve the thermal and energy management of building HVAC systems. A lot of work has been done in the field of building energy consumption simulation but more work remains to be done. Traditionally, less attention has been put on buildings operation compared with the design of a system and its construction/installation. What's more, the simulation software has been evolving steadily over recent years. HVAC component and subsystem models are now generally well understood and have been the subject of a number of researches [8]. Simulation has been extended to the use to the building operation process, although it has been traditionally regarded as a design tool.

III. SIMULATIONS

The simulations were performed in four different cities. They are: State college, Pennsylvania; Miami, Florida; Phoenix, Arizona and Minneapolis, Minnesota. The weather files used in this paper are typical meteorological year (TMY) format, which are widely adopted in the building energy simulation software nowadays and are obtained from the United States Department of Energy website (2010). A typical meteorological year (TMY) is a collation of selected weather data for a specific location, generated from a data bank much longer than a year in duration. It is specially selected so that it presents the range of weather phenomena for the location in question, while still giving annual averages that are consistent with the long-term averages for the location in question. TMY annual weather data information is known to be used in the EnergyPlus program. As the weather data is given for each hour throughout the year, the simulation is run at intervals of one hour. The four different cities were chosen based on their typical weather patterns. Minneapolis was chosen for its cold and dry climate, State college for its mild climate, Phoenix for its hot and dry climate and Miami for its hot, and humid weather. The detail weather profile for these four cities are not presented here but can be found at the United States Department of Energy website.

The simulations that were conducted consisted primarily of quasi steady state determinations of hourly incremental and total building energy requirements for a range of setpoint combinations and exposed to a summer (cooling) or winter (heating) condition. In essence, a grid was established, which represented a collection of setpoints, and annual building energy performance was determined for each grid point. The setpoints were constrained to maintain proper equipment operating conditions (e.g., temperature, mass flow). The primary objective of the simulations was to quantify the range of possible operating points and the maximum potential savings under different weathers, assuming that the control logic could direct the HVAC system to the optimal operating conditions. HVAC Equipment performance was modeled as described below.

Total building energy was determined utilizing performance characteristics of the each component: the chiller, the cooling tower, the chiller water pump and the supply air fan plus the energy input value related to lighting and other electrical equipment. The evaluation metric is:

$$E_{total} = E_{lighting} + E_{equipment} + E_{chiller} + E_{pump} + E_{fan} \quad (1)$$

where:

E_{total} = total energy power density
$E_{lighting}$ = lighting power density input
$E_{equipment}$ = Equipment power density input
$E_{chiller}$ = chiller power density input
E_{pump} = pump power density input
E_{fan} = fan power density input

The first two terms are specified as follows, according to ASHRAE Standard 90.1 IP [9]:

$E_{lighting} = 1.0$ w/ft^2

$E_{equipment} = 1.5$ w/ft^2

The system schematic is presented in Figure 2. As the diagram shows, one zone of a multiple zone Variable Air Volume (VAV) system with energy recovery ventilator was studied for this simulation analysis. For HVAC component energy consumption analysis, polynomial fits were used with representative coefficients, with the important variables being chilled water supply temperature, coil loads, chilled water flow rate, outdoor air fraction, supply airflow rate, supply air temperature and room temperature [10]. These component mathematical equation models are commonly used in similar applications. For the simulation software, Engineering Equation Solver (EES) [11] was selected because of its built–in high-accuracy thermodynamic and heat transfer parameters and capability for solving design problems in which the effects of one or more parameters must be determined. Previous research work also shows that the simplicity of the models and the use of an equation solver to run the simulation ensure good robustness and full transparency [12]. Then Equation-based simulation models were created through the EES and the equation-based simulation models use generalized solution techniques to solve arbitrarily complex sets of differential and algebraic equation, which is another one of the main advantages of this approach: the easiness of developing and maintaining model. Table I summarizes the model parameters.

To minimize the effect from the building itself on the simulation results, the zone is simplified as much as possible. The case that is used in this simulation is assumed to be an office zone has a dimension of 25ft ×30ft with a 9ft high ceiling and 12ft wall height. An overall envelop thermal transfer rate is given. The U value is assumed to be 0.064 Btu/h-ft^2-°F. The infiltration rate through the exterior walls is set at 0.1cfm/ft^2, which is based on information from [13]. This infiltration occurs 24 hours a day. The ventilation rate is assumed to be 1.5 cfm/ ft^2 which is an assumption for the most energy-intensive scenario. For the lighting and occupants heat gain are all assumed equal to 1w/ft^2, the equipment heat gain is assumed at 1.5w/ft^2. Also, the effectiveness of the energy wheel is assumed to be constant throughout the year while it is not true in real word. It should change with the outdoor temperature and humidity changes throughout the year. For this case, the effectiveness is set at 70% constantly and the effectiveness for the heat exchanger is assumed to be 75%. It is worth mentioning that the system efficiency is more important than the efficiency of individual components, when the energy performance of HVAV system is evaluated.

The zone load is defined as the sum of all kinds of loads, internal and external, sensible and latent, which are needed to be balanced from the indoor zone to keep a comfort environment. In other words, the zone load is actually the sum of heat gains transferred from outer space such as sun, occupant, equipment etc. to the zone air. As a result, there are different types of heat gains, solar, heat transmission through the walls, human, lights, ventilation and infiltration. Depending on the building characteristics, these heat gains are converted to loads after some time delay. The latent load, which is produced when moisture in the air goes from a vapor to a liquid state, is not calculated in this paper but will be discussed in the future work. In order to evaluate the objective function as defined, it is necessary to specify some parameters first (Table II).

$$Q_Z = q_s + q_i + q_t + q_o + q_e + q_l \quad (2)$$

where:

q_s = solar load

q_i = infiltration air load

q_t = envelope thermal load

q_o = occupants load

q_e = equipment load

q_l = lighting load

As shown above, for this simulation, the zone load is made up of solar load, lighting load, equipment load, occupants load, infiltration air load and envelope thermal load (heat gains to zone were assumed as positive). The zone heating and cooling loads are met by supplying conditioned air to the zone such that the product of the mass flow rate of the supply air, the specific heat of air and the temperature change of the air from supply (T_s) to return (T_r) are equal to the zone thermal load:

$$q_i = m_i \cdot cp_{air} \cdot (T_z - T_a) \quad (3)$$

$$q_t = UA \cdot (T_z - T_a) \quad (4)$$

Since the heat gain from lighting, equipment occupants and solar was already set up, the load values of infiltration and envelope thermal conduct can be determined from the thermodynamic relationships as described above, the zone load can be figured out for the energy consumption simulation.

$$E_{chiller} = \frac{Q_{avail} \cdot ChillerEIRFTemp \cdot ChillerEIRFPLR}{COP_{ref}} \quad (5)$$

$$E_{pump} = v_{water} \cdot \frac{Pump_{Head}}{Total_{Efficiency}} \quad (6)$$

$$E_{fan} = f_{pl} \cdot m_{design} \cdot \frac{P_{rise}}{e_{tot} \cdot \rho_{air}} \quad (7)$$

where:

$Q_{avail} = Q_{ref} \times$ ChillerCapFTemp

V_{water} = mass flow rate of chilled/hot water

f_{pl} = air part load factor

m_{design} = fan design flow rate

P_{rise} = fan pressure rise

e_{tot} = fan total efficiency

ρ_{air} = density of air

In the heating situation, the fuel input was calculated with this equation [14]:

$$F_{boiler} = m_{hw} \cdot cp_{water} \cdot \left[\frac{T_{hws} - T_{hwr}}{BE \cdot VHI}\right] \cdot 3600 \quad (8)$$

where:

BE = boiler efficiency

VHI = fuel heat value

m_{hw} = hot water mass flow rate

cp_{water} = specific heat capacity of water

T_{hws} = hot water supply temper

T_{hwr}= hot water return temperature

The operating hours are assumed from 6:00 to 22:00. Fan efficiency is selected as 70% as shown in Table I. For the gas boiler energy consumption, the energy consumed in the form of natural gas is converted to electricity by the unit conversion from BTU/h to KW. The heat rate of natural gas is 1000 BTU/ft^3.

For the cooling and heating coils, cooling/heating and dehumidification/humidification of the incoming fresh air is performed here. The temperature effectiveness in a heating or cooling is governed by the effectiveness relationship. An effectiveness of 75% is assumed as presented previously in Table II. In sum, the effectiveness of all the main components are related to design and operating conditions. When the operating conditions fluctuate near design conditions, the effectiveness change is really small. To simplify analysis, effectiveness for various components is assumed to be constant as discussed in the previous part.

Fan and pump energy is an important factor in the annual energy consumption of an HVAC system. Fan (pump) performance can be characterized by its efficiency, which itself is dependent on operational air-flow rate. Mostly, rated volumetric flow rate, pressure rise and efficiency are available from the manufacturer. But for this research, these numbers are assumed as shown in Table I with reasonable values.

Last thing to notice is that HVAC components such as chiller and pumps are composed of a number of sub-components such as engine, evaporator, compressor, condenser and throttling valve, but these sub-components are not included for this study as in the energy balance equation derived for the simulation, only the inter-connections are of interest.

The setpoints were changed as described in Table III. For the summer condition simulation, five parameters, condenser entering temperature, chilled water supply temperature, chilled water mass flow rate, supply air temperature and flow rate are set as variables. Ten different values are selected for each parameter so there are 50 different scenarios in total. As only hot water supply temperature and mass flow rate, supply air temperature and flow rate were changed in the winter condition, 40 group of total power density resulted from the simulation. But here as the whole year total energy consumption is the object of study, the summer cooling and winter heating will be simulated simultaneously with a condition judgment statement coded in EES. To simply simulation, the heating/cooling is assumed to be enabled immediately when the outdoor air temperature below/above corresponding setpoint temperature. For this simulation, when the outdoor air temperature is greater than 80 °F, the cooling will be on and when the outdoor air temperature is less than 55°F, the heating will be simulated.

IV. RESULTS

The simulation figure depicts the one whole year total power density as a function of different setpoint settings. The total power density consumed in each city is shown in figures below. Each city stands for a typical weather conditions.

Figures 3, 4, 5, and 6 illustrate the annual power density for four different weather cases from highest to the lowest for the year around. The different colors present the breakdown of the electricity usage. As we can see, HVAC system (including chiller, cooling tower pump, chiller water pump and supply air fan) is the biggest electric consumer in the model, which accounts for around 60% of total energy consumption, while both lighting and equipment account for around 15% of the total power consumption, respectively. According to Table IV, the maximum annual power density can reach 36.121kwh/sf-year at Miami when the chilled/hot water flow rate at the biggest value and a small supply air flow rate can decrease the energy consumption to 26.712kwh/sf-year at state college. Please note the annual power density is high compared to typical office buildings' numbers due to the high ventilation air flow rate setting in the simulation. The simulation is operated in this way to reflect the possible situation using the most energy.

Figure 7 is the simulated building energy usage breakdown in the four weather conditions. The percentage of the total power that is required by HVAC system to ventilate and condition (fans, pumps, chillers and boilers) is 67% in Minneapolis, 71% in Miami, 68% in Phoenix and 63% in state college. Among the HVAC system energy consumption itself, chiller and boiler is the largest power consumer while the pump consumes the least energy.

To sum up, the energy performance of this particular building/HVAC system combination was evaluated for typical scenarios in order to illustrate the methodology and the energy saving potential of dynamic setpoint manipulation. While the magnitude of the potential energy savings would be expected to vary for different buildings and locations, the methodology would still be applicable and useful provided the proper information was available to accurately model the HVAC system and its components. The methodology could also be used to evaluate the effectiveness of advanced control strategies by comparing

TABLE III. CASE DESCRIPTION FOR THE TWO CONDITIONS

Cases(summer)	Simulation Description
1 (10 numbers)	Increase condenser entering temperature (50-60 °F)
2 (10 numbers)	Increase chilled water flow rate (0.4-0.7 lbm/s)
3 (10 numbers)	Increase chilled water supply temperature (45-55 °F)
4 (10 numbers)	Increase supply air flow rate (500-700 cfm)
5 (10 numbers)	Increase supply air temperature (60-65 °F)

Cases(winter)	Simulation Description
1 (10 numbers)	Increase hot water supply temperature (185-195 °F)
2 (10 numbers)	Increase hot water supply flow rate (0.4-0.7 lbm/s)
3 (10 numbers)	Increase supply air flow rate (500-700 cfm)
4 (10 numbers)	Increase supply air temperature (85-95 °F)

TABLE IV. COMPARISON OF POWER DENSITY IN DIFFERENT SCENARIOS

City	Annual Power Density maximum (Kwh/sf-year)	Annual Power Density minimum (Kwh/sf-year)	Potential Energy Saving (Kwh/sf-year)	Saving Percentage
Minneapolis	34.689	31.723	2.966	8.55%
Phoenix	33.423	31.645	1.778	5.32%
Miami	36.121	35.340	0.781	2.16%
State College	28.644	26.712	1.932	6.75%

TABLE V. RESULT STATISTICAL ANALYSIS

City	Mean Value of Annual Power Density	Standard deviation of Annual Power Density minimum
Minneapolis	32.65	0.45
Phoenix	32.37	0.29
Miami	35.61	0.11
State College	27.63	0.34

TABLE VI. SENSITIVITY ANALYSIS RESULTS FOR: (A) MILD, (B) COOL AND DRY, (C) HOT AND DRY AND (D) HOT AND HUMID WEATHER CONDITION

Parameters	SC(A)	SC(B)	SC(C)	SC(D)
Supply air flow rate	0.51	0.47	0.54	0.38
Chilled/hot water supply flow	0.49	0.51	0.68	0.26
Supply air temperature	0.011	0.73	0.89	0.41
Condenser entering temperature	0.0037	0.012	0.015	0.13
Chilled/hot water supply temperature	0.0021	0.045	0.0092	0.084

the energy savings predicted or realized by those methods to the maximum potential savings identified using the approach described here.

To gain a deeper understanding of the simulation results, statistical analysis was carried out showing the cumulative percent of the total data population described at each yearly energy density value, working from smallest to largest. The distribution of the data is close to a normal cumulative distribution, which agrees with previous assumption that most total energy consumption for buildings has a normal distribution. It can be seen that the considered cases show a significant energy usage difference between the best and worst cases. Thus, there should be a significant savings potential, which can be potentially achieved by adjusting the HVAC system setpoints.

Another thing should be noticed is that the standard deviation and mean numbers for these four conditions as presented in Table V. The mean number stands for the average energy usage during a whole year. So, based on the results, Miami (hot and humid weather) has the largest average power density while state college (mild weather) has the smallest one. Perhaps the difference on the running time of chillers may contribute to such an outcome.

In statistics and probability theory, the standard deviation shows how much variation or dispersion from the average exists. A low standard deviation indicates that the data points tend to be very close to the mean; a high standard deviation indicates that the data points are spread out over a large range of values. So for here, a larger standard deviation means the energy usage is relatively unstable when changing the setpoints, but at the same time it also indicates a larger saving potential. Minneapolis has the biggest standard deviation which is consistent with the results in Table IV. And Miami has a relatively stable data so it is likely in the hot and humid weather condition, changing system setpoints will not bring a significant fluctuation in the energy usage per to this study.

To evaluate the effects of these key parameters on the energy performance in different climate conditions, sensitivity analysis was generated. Sensitivity Analysis (SA) is defined as the study of how uncertainty in the output of a model (numerical or otherwise) can be apportioned to different sources of uncertainty in the model input [15], which provides a good opportunity of giving a hierarchical rating to a large number of energy model inputs based on their relative importance to building energy consumption.

When mentioned the method of sensitivity analysis, [16] documents three SA Techniques: Differential Sensitivity Analysis (DSA), Monte Carlo Analysis (MCA) and Stochastic Sensitivity Analysis (SSA), the DSA is most commonly used due to its simplicity and easy-to-understand. For this research, the DSA method is picked to assess the relative influences of selected inputs on the energy consumption.

The sensitivity coefficient presented below is defined as the percentage change of the output divided by the percentage change of the input. Figure 1 provides a more vivid picture of the proposed procedure.

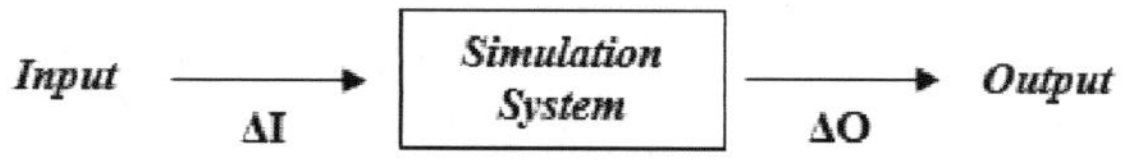

Figure 1. Total Power Density for Winter Condition

The equations used for the sensitivity analysis are shown as below:

$$SensitivityCoeffecient(SC) = \left|\frac{\Delta O}{\Delta I}\right| \quad (9)$$

where:

$$\Delta O = \frac{O_{pert} - O_{base}}{O_{base}} \quad (10)$$

$$\Delta I = \frac{I_{pert} - I_{base}}{I_{base} - I_{\min}} \quad (11)$$

These two terms are the changes of the ouput and input relative to the base model and input, respectively. O_{base} and I_{base} are the base model output and input, respectively. O_{pert}, I_{pert} and I_{min} are the perturbed model output, input and potential minimum value of input, respectively.

In this paper, the interested simulation outputs include whole building annual electricity (lighting, etc.) and boiler gas energy uses, as well as the chiller, the pump and the fan energy uses. And these outputs are connected to certain input parameters. So, to sum up here, for both the cooling and heating conditions, there are five interested input variables, they are condenser entering temperature, chilled/hot water supply temperature, chilled/hot water supply flow rate, supply air flow rate and supply air temperature. Then, the range of each parameter was determined according to the actual building operation situation. But here the range is set as shown in Table III. Perturb one parameter at a time while keeping other parameters constant, the sensitivity coefficient can be calculated based on the simulated output.

So, based on the sensitivity-analysis method described in previous, and pre the simulation results for these four different climates, the sensitivity coefficient (SC) that determined by their relative importance to the annual whole building energy use for the four different climates is demonstrated as in Table VI.

According to the data shown in the previous page, with regards to the mild weather, the supply air flow rate has the largest sensitivity coefficient, which means minimizing the supply air flow rate is shown to be the most effective measure to save the energy usage. On the opposite, chilled/hot water temperature has the smallest value, which indicates the variation on the chilled/hot water temperature settings will have the least influence on the power consumption. While for the rest three outdoor conditions, the supply air setpoint temperature is in the driving position.

V. CONCLUSIONS AND FUTURE WORK

A methodology was developed and demonstrated for determining the impact of HVAC control system setpoints on the total building energy requirements for a typical combination of HVAC system in four different outdoor environment situations in order to quantify the maximum potential energy savings due to dynamic setpoint adjustment. The analysis reveals that a large potential of energy reduction exists in the building. Whole building energy saving from fine tuning HVAC system can be significant in certain condition. According to the simulation result, the energy saving potential through possible optimum control is substantial and more noticeable in winter season. The potential saving can be as high as 8.55% and as low as 2.16% for cold and dry climate and hot and humid climate, respectively, when comparing the best performance with the worst one. Sensitivity analysis shows different control system setpoints provide different degree of energy savings. Minimizing the supply air flow rate is shown to be the most effective measure to save electricity usage in mild weather, while a too high or too low supply air temperature may lead to overwhelm other settings effects on power consumption in other three weather conditions. The results suggest that control strategies that are capable of dynamically adjusting setpoints in response to environmental and occupant conditions can potentially save a substantial amount of energy as compared to fixed setpoints.

What's more, the use of the engineering equation solver computer program to perform simulations on a conditioned zone with various collections of setpoints in four different cities which stand for four different outdoor environments further proofs of the possibility and usability of equation-based simulation methods.

However, there are still some investigations needed. For the future work, the following recommendations are made for future work:

- The number of setpoints studied is limited and the more detailed model could be studied.
- Latent load should be considered in the future work.
- The results should be conducted with cross comparison with other software output.
- More comprehensive climate regions should be further extended and investigated.
- Sensitivity analysis might consider the simultaneous variation of parameters and interaction term.
- The energy recovery system efficiency could include the effects from outdoor air temperature and humidity. Perform an energy consumption simulation with variable effectiveness values of energy recovery system to see the effect of changing effectiveness due to outdoor temperature and humidity on the result.

References

[1] S. Treado and X. Liu, "The Impact of Control Setpoints on Building Energy Use," Proceedings of SIMUL 2013, Venice, Italy, 2013, pp. 187-192.

[2] J. Clarke, J. Cockroft, S. Conner, J.Hand, N. Kelly, R. Moore, T. O'Brien, and P. Strachan, "Simulation-assisted control in building energy management systems," Energy and Buildings, 34, 2002, pp. 933-940.

[3] Y. Li, Y. Pan, and C. Chen, "Study on energy saving retrofitting strategies for existing public building in Shanghai," Proceedings of Energy Sustainability 2009, San Francisco, California, USA, 2009. pp. 301-307.

[4] Y. Pan, Z. Huang, and G. Wu, "Calibrated building energy simulation and its application in a high-rise commercial building in Shanghai," Energy and Buildings 39, 2007, pp. 651-657.

[5] G. Osborne, "The contribution of simulation to the building tuning process for 2 Victoria Avenue," Proceedings of Building Simulation, Sydney, Australia, November 14-16, 2011, pp. 239-246.

[6] T. Z. Hong, S. K. Chou, and T. Y. Bong, "Building simulation: an overview of developments and information sources," Building and Environment 35, 2000, pp. 347-361.

[7] E. H. Mathews and C. P. Botha, "Improved thermal building management with the aid of integrated dynamic HVAC simulation," Building and Environment 38, 2003, pp. 1423-1429.

[8] R. C. Clark, "HVACSIM+ Building Systems and Equipment Simulation Program Reference Manual," Published by the U.S. Department of Commerce, National Bureau of Standards, National Engineering laboratory, Center for Building Technology, Building Equipment Division, Gaithersburg, MD 20899

[9] ASHRAE, 2010. ASHRAE Standard 90.1-2010, Energy standard for buildings except low-rise residential buildings, American Society of Heating, Refrigerating and Air-Conditioning Engineers, Inc.

[10] Energy Plus, Engineering Reference Manual, U.S. Dept. of Energy, 2010.

[11] Engineering Equation Solver, User Manual, F-Chart Software, 1992.

[12] S. Bertagnolio, P. Andre, and V. Lemort, "Simulation of a building and its HVAC system with an equation solver: Application to audit," Building Simulation, Volume 3, Issue 2, pp. 139-152, June 2010.

[13] F.C. McQuiston and J.D. Spitler, Cooling and Heating Load Calculation Manual, 2nd ed., American Society of Heating, Refrigerating and Air-Conditioning Engineers, Inc., Atlanta, Georgia, 1992.

[14] A. Wienese, "Boiler, Boiler Fuel and Boiler Efficiency," Proceedings of South African Technology Association, 2001, pp. 275-281.

[15] A. Saltelli, K. Chan,, Scott, E.M., and others, "Sensitivity analysis," Wiley New York, 2000.

[16] K.J Lomas, H.Eppel, "Sensitivity analysis techniques for building thermal simulation programs," Energy and Buildings 19, 21–44, 1992.

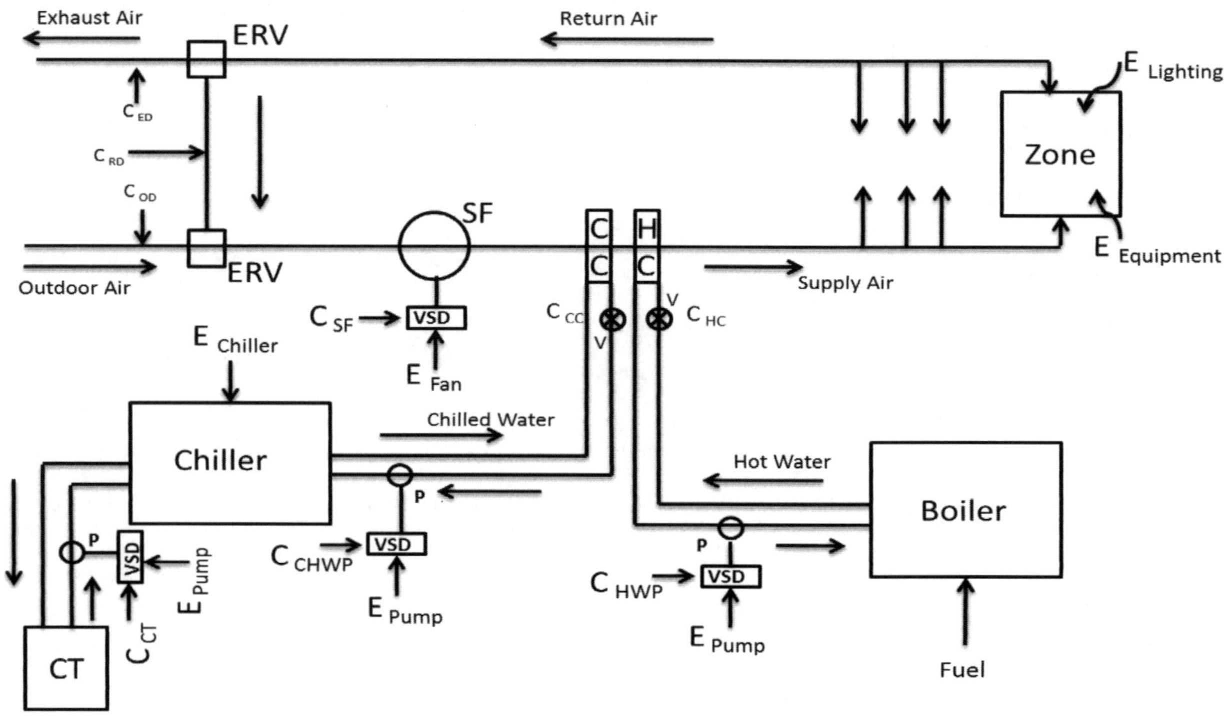

Nomenclature

ERV	Energy Recovery Ventilator
SF	Supply Fan
CC	Cooling Coil
HC	Heating Coil
VSD	Varied Speed Driver
P	Pump
V	Valve

Control Point Lists

C_{ED}	Exhaust Air Damper
C_{RD}	Return Air Damper
C_{OA}	Outdoor Air Damper
C_{SF}	Supply Fan Driver
C_{CC}	Cooling Coil Valve
C_{HC}	Heating Coil Valve
C_{CT}	Cooling Tower Pump
C_{CHWP}	Chilled Water Pump
C_{HWP}	Hot Water Pump

Figure 2. System Schematic

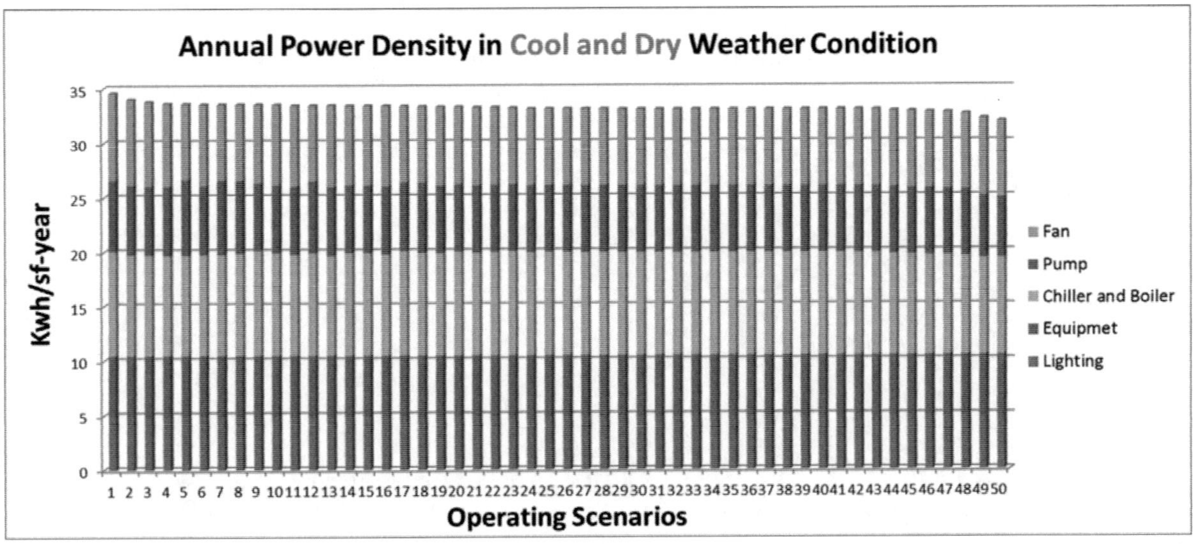

Figure 3. Annual Power Density in Minneapolis

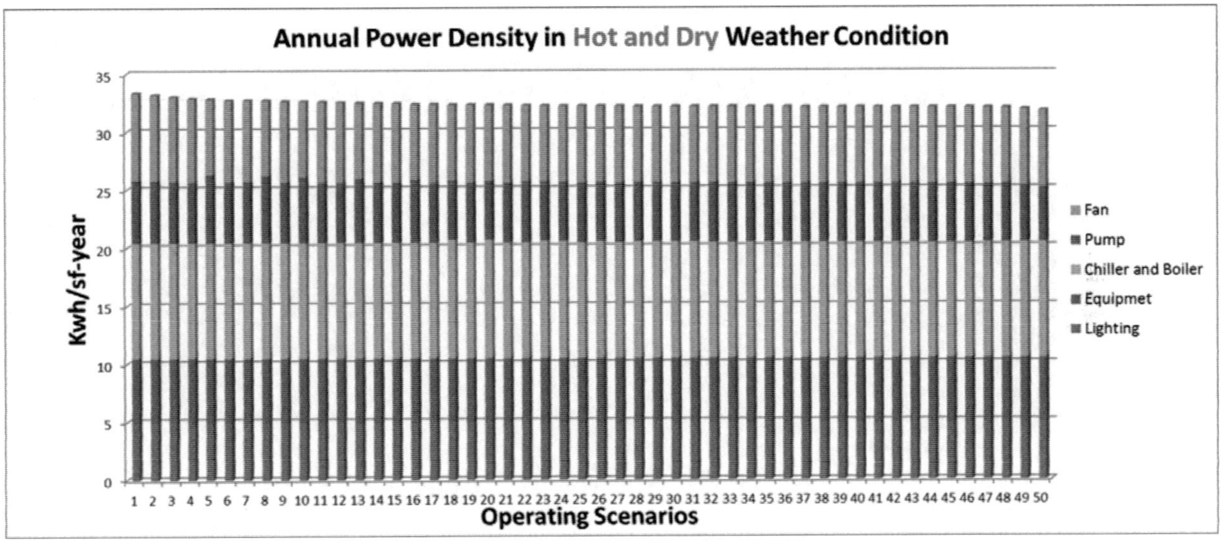

Figure 4. Annual Power Density in Phoenix

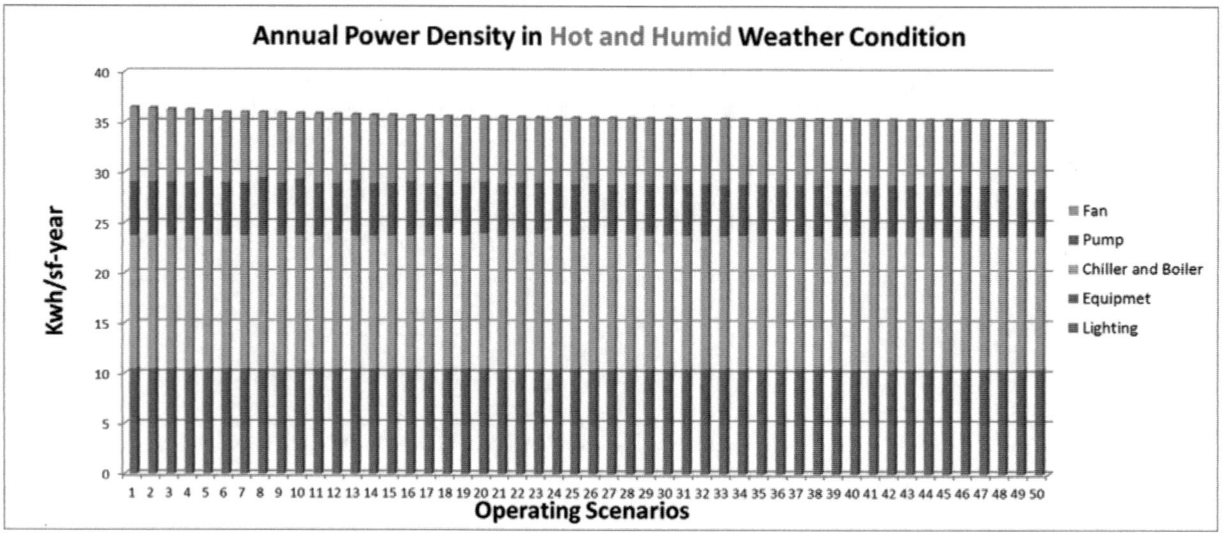

Figure 5. Annual Power Density in Miami

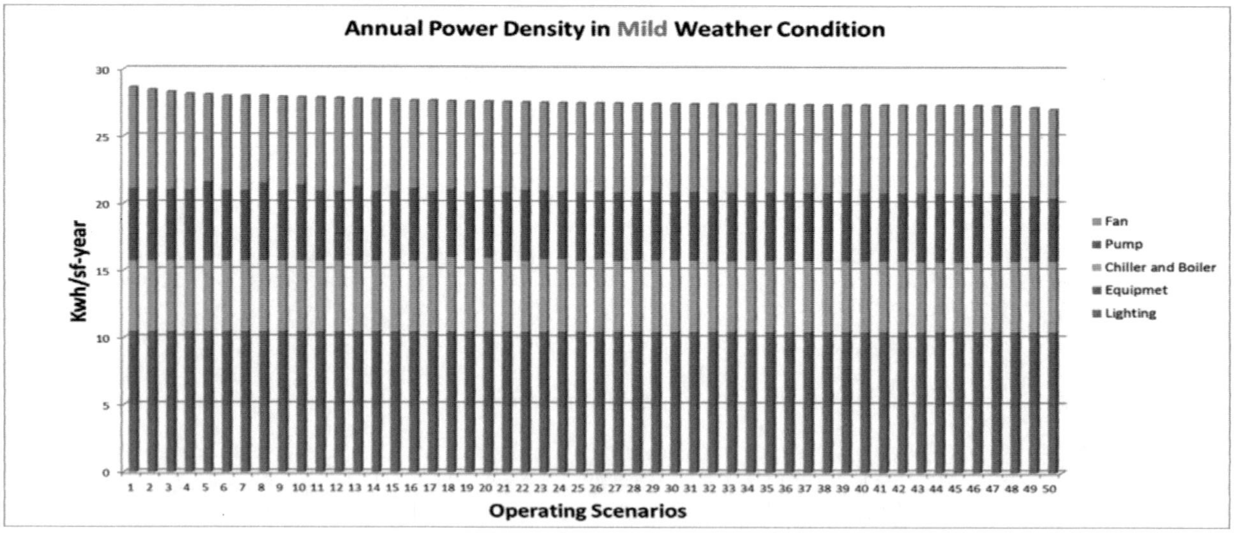

Figure 6. Annual Power Density in State College

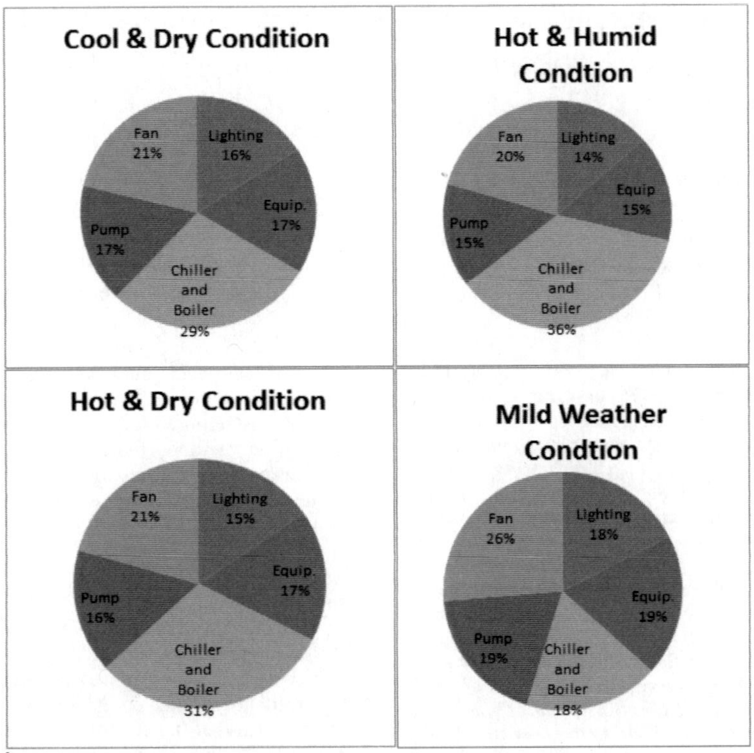

Figure 7. Breakdown of Power Use

Approaches to Cleaning Gas Response Signals from Metal Oxide Sensors

Optimisation and Generalizabilty

Jacqueline Whalley, Philip Sallis
Engineering, Computer and Mathematical Sciences
Auckland University of Technology
Auckland, New Zealand
e-mail: {jwhalley, psallis}@aut.ac.nz

Enobong Bassey
Geography, Environment and Disaster Management
Coventry University
Coventry, England
e-mail: enobong.bassey@coventry.ac.uk

Abstract—**This paper reports on a comparative analysis of techniques – from simple polynomial curve fitting to digital filters, local regression and wavelet denoising – for cleaning thin film composite metal oxide gas sensor response signals. This research expands and extends a preliminary investigation of simple methods for smoothing metal oxide gas sensor response signals. As part of the analysis an extensive series of systematic experiments were conducted in order to tune the parameters, including span or frame sizes and degrees of polynomial as appropriate, for each of the digital filters and to select the appropriate mother wavelet and threshold chooser for the wavelet approach. The signal processing challenge of maintaining a balance between the measured signal variation and the disparity variation in the smoothed signal is outlined and considered in comparing the performance of the signal cleaning methods. The results indicate that a Savitsky Golay filter with a polynomial degree of 3 and a frame size of 9% of a signal's width provides a practical solution for denoising metal oxide gas sensor signals because it was found to consistently give a cleaned signal that is suitable for further processing (feature extraction and pattern recognition). This work provides support for the premise that a generalized method for cleaning metal oxide gas sensor signals, regardless of sensor composition, is possible and suggests that a Savitsky Golay filter is a suitable candidate.**

Keywords-Denoising; Wavelets; Savitsky Golay filter; Frame Size; Polynomial; Metal Oxide Sensors.

I. INTRODUCTION

This research expands and extends a preliminary investigation of simple methods for smoothing metal oxide gas sensor response signals [1]. Precise and reliable measurements of trace gases such as carbon monoxide (CO), nitrous oxide (NO), sulfur dioxide (SO_2) carbon dioxide (CO_2), methane (CH_4) and other hydrocarbons [2] are essential for environmental monitoring. Such gases are harmful not only to the environment but also to human health if present beyond certain concentrations [3]. Local, national and international legislation requires continuous monitoring of air quality and rate of emissions. This emissions data is critical to the decision making and formulation of policies related to climate change. As a consequence, there has been considerable effort focused on the fabrication of low cost, portable, reliable and accurate sensors for monitoring such gases. For the measurements obtained from these sensors to be accurate, reliable and interpretable some processing of the raw signal is required. A useful summary of statistical and optimization methods that have been used to process gas sensor array signals is provided by Gutierrez-Galvez [4].

The signal processing of gas sensor data has four key steps: *pre-processing*, *dimensionality reduction*, *prediction*, and *validation* [5]. This work focuses on the pre-processing phase; which facilitates noise elimination, data smoothing/filtering and signal enhancement; with the sole aim of increasing the signal-to-noise ratio without greatly distorting the original response signal.

In sensor systems noise has several possible sources introduced at various points in the measurement process. Several forms of noise are irreducible because they are inherent to the underlying electronic components or physical properties of the sensor [6]. Other forms of noise originate from processes and include 1/f noise, quantization and transmission noise [7]. The most harmful noise is the noise that is propagated in the early stages of measurement and, therefore, can be propagated and amplified through the later stages in the signal pathway [8].

One approach to producing a clean signal would be to use physical filters. While physical filters have been shown to produce cleaner signals they do not cover the full resolution and shape of the curve [1]. This is problematic because in order to improve the interpretability, sensitivity and selectivity of the measurements from metal oxide (MOX) gas sensor array signals it is preferable to use the full resolution and profile of the signal. An alternate approach to physical filters is to use a digital filter to clean the signal. If taking this approach the choice of signal pre-processing method is critical because it has a significant impact on the overall final quality of the processed signal [7].

This paper reports on a systematic series of experiments that were conducted in order to compare various computational methods for the smoothing or denoising of MOX gas sensor response signals using digital filtering approaches. For each method a comprehensive and systematic set of experiments was conducted in order to tune the parameters for the method. The aim was to establish a general method and guidelines for the signal pre-processing phase (denoising phase) of responses from SnO_2-ZnO devices regardless of composition. The rest of this paper is organized as follows. Section II discusses the relevant background research into the denoising and smoothing of chemical sensor responses. Section III outlines the fabrication and signal acquisition of the SnO_2-ZnO sensor devices. Section IV describes the smoothing and denoising methods used. Section V provides the results of a series of systematic experiments to tune each of these signal preprocessing methods. Section VI addresses the issue of which of these preprocessing methods is most appropriate for the cleaning of MOX sensors by providing a comparison of the output signals for each of the methods using the optimal values for the tuning parameters as identified in Section V. Finally, conclusions are drawn in Section VII.

II. BACKGROUND

While the literature on denoising and smoothing of chemical sensor signals is extensive, very little has been published specifically examining appropriate methods for denoising the gas response signals obtained from MOX sensors.

Guiñón et al. used both moving average (MA) and Savitsky Golay (SG) filters to smooth the photochemical and electrochemical reactor data [9]. They concluded that the SG filter was better than averaging because it tends to preserve data features that are usually attenuated by the MA filter and produce very little distortion in the signal. The SG filter has also been used to smooth electrocardiogram (ECG) signals and the effect of the smoothing parameters was evaluated [10]. Leo at al. [11] reported on the use of SG filters to denoise a large scale chemical sensor array prior to classifying the response signals from a variety of sensors composed of conducting polymer materials. The choice of SG filters was based on our earlier preliminary work on the use of SG filters for denoising pure SnO_2 and pure ZnO thin film gas sensor responses to methanol [1]. In this earlier work the use of local regression, moving average and SG filters were evaluated. Further work using these filters was reported but this time with a number of thin film SnO_2-ZnO composite gas sensor devices [8]. This work resulted in the conclusion that the SG smoothing filter gave the best denoising result regardless of thin film composition, target gas concentration and device operating temperature. However, in both of these studies [1][8], the tuning parameters were not established in a thorough and systematic manner. Instead, they were chosen based on the researcher's knowledge of the data. Therefore, it is necessary to revisit this work with a view to tuning the parameters in order to obtain an optimal result.

In the past two decades much of the research in signal pre-processing of chemical sensor signals has been focused on wavelet transforms because they provide a procedure that has low memory requirements, high precision, and good reproducibility [12][13]. Wavelet based denoising was proposed by Donoho [14]. In 1997 Barclay and Bonner reported on the application of wavelet transforms to experimental spectra in the analytical chemistry domain. They compared discrete wavelet transform (DWT) with other common techniques: smoothing (SG filters) and denoising (Fourier transforms) on liquid chromatograms and electrospray mass spectra. They reported that in this context wavelet filters are superior to the other methods evaluated. DWT has also been used as a technique for removing noise from biosensors [15]. Singh and Tiwari presented an evaluation of mother wavelets for denoising electrocardiogram (ECG) signals [16]. They reported that their wavelet denoising approach, DWT using a Daubechies mother wavelet [17] of order 8 and Donoho's hybrid SureShrink threshold selection procedure [18], effectively removed noise while retaining the necessary diagnostic information in the original ECG signal. One recent effective application of denoising based on wavelet transforms was the cleaning of GPS receiver positioning data [19]. Kim et al. used DWT with hard thresholding and a biorthogonal mother wavelet to denoise synthetically generated response signals [20]. In examining methods for smoothing MOX sensor signals Bassey, Whalley and Sallis [8], proposed that wavelets might be a suitable approach but did not investigate their usefulness. To date there has been little work that systematically compares and evaluates these methods for MOX sensor signal denoising.

As an expansion of our initial results [1][8] this paper aims to identify a general method for SnO_2-ZnO composite gas sensor signal preprocessing that is applicable regardless of the sensor composition. Hence, this paper evaluates a number of potential methods for denoising SnO_2-ZnO composite gas sensor devices including MA, local regression, robust local regression, SG, and wavelet transform methods. The results of extensive experiments to determine the best span sizes and degrees of polynomial for those methods is presented. Additionally, approaches to selecting the appropriate wavelet function are explored. The signal processing challenge of maintaining a balance between the measured signal variation and the disparity variation in the smoothed signals is outlined and considered within a systematic evaluation process.

III. ACQUISITION OF THE RESPONSE SIGNALS

Five sensor devices were fabricated with different SnO_2-ZnO compositions (Table I). Thin films of these composites were deposited on to a silicon wafer using a radio frequency sputtering process (similar to the reported for $BaTiO_3$-CuO mixed oxide sensors [21]) for thirty minutes on a silicon/silicon dioxide substrate [22].

In initial experiments, each of these sensor devices was exposed to 150 parts per million of methanol vapor at 150, 250 and 350 degrees Celsius, respectively. A constant voltage of 5 volts was applied to the sensing elements while recording the sensor response to the target gas as a function of time of exposure to target gas.

TABLE I. MOLAR FRACTION COMPOSITIONS OF THE MOX SENSORS.

	Thin film composition (mole percentage)				
SnO_2	100	75	50	25	0
ZnO	0	25	50	75	100
Sensor	$\mathbb{S}$	$\mathbb{S}_3\mathbb{Z}_1$	$\mathbb{S}\mathbb{Z}$	$\mathbb{S}_1\mathbb{Z}_3$	$\mathbb{Z}$

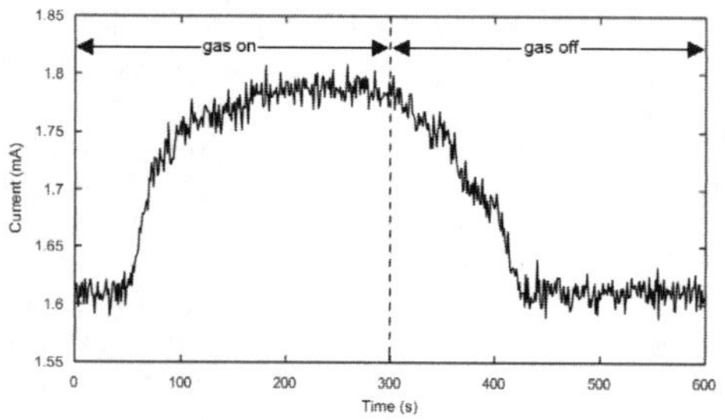

Figure 1. A typical gas sensor signal.

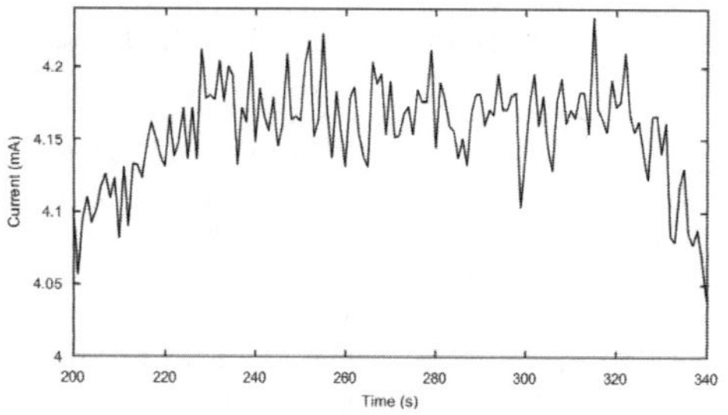

Figure 2. A subregion of the $\mathbb{S}_1\mathbb{Z}_3$ signal illustrating typical pertubations.

Typically for calibration of MOX sensors the response is characterized using a calibration curve of the signal response (current or resistance) [23]. An unprocessed digital response from the S device, as current in milliamperes, is depicted in Fig. 1. The response data was acquired with a sampling rate of one sample per second for ten minutes. Data acquisition commenced when the target gas reached the required flow rate (the rate needed to provide the required concentration of target gas) and the gas flow was turned off after five minutes. The analog signal acquired was converted to a digital signal using a 14 bit analog to digital converter (ADC).

In initial experiments, it was found that at 150 degrees Celsius the gas response was less sensitive and that the optimal temperature of those tested for operation of these sensors was 250 degrees Celsius. For this reason the experiments for signal cleaning (denoising/smoothing) reported here use the raw signal responses obtained from the gas sensing experiments conducted at an operating temperature of 250 degrees Celsius.

Fig. 2 shows the signal noise characteristics of the $\mathbb{S}_3\mathbb{Z}_1$ MOX sensor. Apart from the individual signal profile of each device, the signal noise characteristics did not exhibit any significant variation between devices. Therefore, this paper will focus on the signal processing aspects and optimization of the filter parameters.

IV. METHODS

The following methods, (A) polynomial curve fitting, (B) MA smoothing algorithm (C) local regression smoothing, (D) SG smoothing algorithm, and (E) wavelet denoising, were applied to the sensor response data obtained from the five MOX gas sensor devices.

A. Polynomial curve fitting

Arguably the simplest approach to removing noise and extracting characteristics from the raw sensor signal is to model or approximate the sensor response curve using a polynomial function. The task of selecting an appropriate degree of the polynomial is straight forward and is the only tuning required.

B. Moving average smoothing

One of the simplest digital filters is the MA filter. It is able to reduce random noise, through smoothing the signal, while retaining sharp step responses making it a suitable type of filter for time domain encoded signals [9]. A MA filter that is equivalent to low pass filtering was used to smooth data by replacing each data point with the average of the neighboring data points within a specified span of data points as described by the difference equation (1) where $y_s(i)$ is the smoothed value for the ith data point, N is the number of neighboring data points on either side of $y_s(i)$, and $2N+1$ is the span.

$$y_s(i)=\frac{1}{2N+1}\left(y(i+N)+y(i+N-1)+\ldots+y(i-N)\right) \qquad (1)$$

C. Locally weighted regression

Locally weighted scatterplot smoothing (loess and lowess) are two non-parametric regression methods that combine multiple regression models in a k-nearest-neighbor-based meta-model [24]. For lowess and loess the smoothed values are determined by considering neighboring data points within a span. The process is weighted using a regression weight function that is defined for all the data points contained within the specified span. The span, which specifies the neighborhood as a fraction of the total number of data points, is often referred to as the smoothing parameter or bandwidth. This is the main parameter for these methods and controls the smoothness of the estimated signal in each local surrounds. Lowess and loess are differentiated by the model used in the regression: lowess uses a linear polynomial, while loess uses a quadratic polynomial.

With MA the smoothing parameter defines the span of the moving window. However, for the local regression methods the span size is given in terms of the percentage of data points in the span.

The *robust* local regression methods (rlowess and rloess) differ from lowess and loess in that a lower weight is assigned to outliers in the regression, and a zero weighting is given to data outside six mean absolute deviations. This robust approach typically gives results that are more resistant to outliers.

Experiments using loess, lowess, rloess and rlowess with span sizes of 1, 5, 8, 10, 15, and 20% of the data points were conducted in order to tune each of these methods.

D. Savitsky Golay smoothing

The SG smoothing algorithm is one of many other types of digital smoothing polynomials [25] and has arguably become "an almost universal method to improve the signal-to-noise ratio of any kind of signal" [26]. The SG method [27] is a generalization of the moving average filter and is considered to be both relatively simple and have a low computational cost. It uses polynomial coefficients to determine the best least-squares fit to the points in the span. The procedure consists of replacing the central point p of a frame ($2p$+1) with the value obtained from the polynomial fit. The frame is moved one data point at a time, until the entire signal is scanned, creating a new smoothed value for each data point. The smoothed signal $g(t)$ is calculated by convolving the signal $f(t)$ with a smoothing (or convolution) function $h(t)$ [13] for all observed data points p where $f(m)$ is the curve function at point m and $h(m-t) \neq 0$ (2). The convolution function $h(t)$ is defined for each combination of degree of the polynomial and frame size.

$$g(t) = f(t)\times h(t)=\frac{\sum f(m)h(m-t)}{\sum h(m)} \tag{2}$$

In SG smoothing each data point f_i is replaced with a linear combination of g_i (3) and a number of nearby neighbors n where nL is the number of neighboring points prior to the data point i, nR is the number of neighbors after data point i, and the coefficients c_n are the weights of the linear combination [28].

$$g_i=\sum_{n=-nL}^{nR} c_n f_{i+n} \tag{3}$$

The moving frame average (4) is computed as the average of the data points from $fi - nL$ to $fi + nR$ for some fixed $nL = nR = M$ and the weights $c_n = 1 / (nL + nR + 1)$ [29]:

$$g_i=\sum_{n=-M}^{M} \frac{f_{i+n}}{2M+1} \tag{4}$$

The weights c_n are chosen in such a way that the smoothed data point g_i is the value of a polynomial fitted by least-squares to all ($nL + nR + 1$) points in the moving window. That is, for the group of $2M + 1$ data centered at $n = 0$ the coefficient of the polynomial is obtained by (5) [30].

$$c_n=p(n)=\sum_{k=0}^{N} a_k n^k \tag{5}$$

This minimizes the mean-squared approximation error (6) for the group of input samples centered on $n = 0$.

$$\varepsilon_N=\sum_{n=-M}^{M} (p(n)-x[n])^2=\sum_{n=-M}^{M}\left(\sum_{k=0}^{N} a_k n^k - x[n]\right)^2 \tag{6}$$

Therefore, g_i the smoothed data [29] is given by (7).

$$g_i=\frac{\sum_{n=-nL}^{nR} c_n f_{i+n}}{\sum_{n=-nL}^{nR} c_n} \tag{7}$$

For the SG smoothing algorithm there are two tuning parameters: the frame size $F = (nL + nR + 1)$ and the polynomial order k. The polynomial order k must be less than the frame size F, which must be odd. If $k = F - 1$ then the designed filter produces no smoothing. Frame sizes of 5, 25, 55, 75, and 95 data points with polynomials of order 3, 6, and 9 were evaluated in order to find the optimal tuning parameters for the MOX gas sensor response signals.

E. Wavelet denoising

Where the previously discussed methods smooth the signal by removing high frequencies and retaining low frequencies, denoising attempts to remove whatever noise is present and retain whatever signal is present regardless of the frequency content of the signal. This is essentially denoising by shrinking (nonlinear soft thresholding) in the wavelet transform domain. Third, it consists of three steps: a linear forward wavelet transform (8), a nonlinear shrinkage denoising (9), and a linear inverse wavelet transform (10). This can be defined mathematically assuming that the observed data $x(t)$ consists of the true signal $s(t)$ and noise $n(t)$ as functions in time t to be sampled [31]:

$$y = W(x) \tag{8}$$

$$z = D(y, \lambda) \tag{9}$$

$$\hat{s} = W^{-1}(z) \tag{10}$$

Where $\hat{s}(t)$ is the signal recovered as an estimate of $s(t)$, $W(\cdot)$ and $W^{-1}(\cdot)$ are the forward and inverse wavelet transform operators respectively, and $D(\cdot, \lambda)$ is the denoising operator with soft threshold λ.

One of the main considerations in wavelet denoising involves the selection of an appropriate mother wavelet function at a suitable level N and the subsequent computation of the wavelet decomposition of the signal s down to level N. There are many different types of mother wavelets available and it is important that a suitable mother wavelet is selected. The most common selection method is to visually compare the signal with potential mother wavelets and select a mother wavelet based on the degree of visual similarity. An alternate quantitative approach is to calculate the regularity, vanishing moment and degree of shift variance [32][33]. Other quantitative approaches include Satio's use of the minimum description length (MDL) as a means of selecting the optimal wavelet, from a database of orthonormal bases, for noise suppression [34]. MDL is based on an assumption that the best model is one that provides the shortest description of both the data and the model itself. Another method is to use the maximum cross correlation coefficient as a selection criterion [16][35]. To date there is no accepted standard or generalized method for selecting the mother wavelet function [36]. In the experiments conducted here the mother wavelet was selected using the maximum cross correlation coefficient method. This approach was used after an initial selection of potential mother wavelets by visual inspection in order to ensure that the mother wavelet selected was appropriate.

The next step is to threshold, for each level from *1* to *N*, the detail coefficients. Therefore, the next important consideration is the choice of threshold selection rule [37]. A choice between hard and soft thresholding must also be made. Hard thresholding is the simpler method and results in the sharp signal features being restored but smooth regions within the signal are not always as smooth as desired. On the other hand, soft thresholding can result in over smoothing of sharp transitions but the smooth regions of the signal are restored well. It has been reported that soft thresholding tends to give better denoising results [38] for audio files. Because audio files appear to often have similar noise perturbations to those observed for the MOX sensor data it is reasonable to extrapolate that a soft thresholding approach will prove more appropriate for the preprocessing of MOX sensor gas response signals. Moreover, because we are interested in preserving the overall signal profile and in smoothing the signal more than denoising the signal a soft thresholding chooser seems to be the best option. In order to ensure that the correct thresholding chooser method was selected four commonly used choosers are evaluated:

- universal threshold selection method [14]
- minimax threshold [39]
- Stein's unbiased risk estimator (SURE) [40]
- an heuristic variant of Stein's Unbiased Risk and fixed form thresholding (heurSURE) [41]

V. PARAMETER TUNING RESULTS

This section firstly presents the results for the tuning of the parameters for the smoothing methods and the selection of mother wavelet for wavelet denoising. All the experiments were conducted using MATLAB. All the raw data were in quantized form. The raw data or signals and denoised or smoothed signals each contained 600 data points. The best or optimal signal smoothing method was considered to be the one that best preserves the height, width, amplitude, and overall profile and data features of the signal while also reducing noise in the signal. The process for determination of "best fit" used was a visual examination. Given the data point distribution generated, this method was regarded as both adequate and appropriate. In order to assist in the determination of "best fit" the curves produced were also plotted against the 95% confidence intervals (CIs). CIs are useful in determining the precision of the predicted model and help give an idea of how useful the model is for a particular region of the data.

For the non-parametric methods, MA and the four local regression techniques, it is not possible to directly calculate CIs because the smoothed curve (model) is not based on a specific mathematical model or distribution [42]. Calculating CIs for the nonparametric methods can in principle be achieved by viewing each fitted value as a predictor value from a regression equation and then calculating the pointwise confidence limits for each of the predicted values [43]. To plot the CIs all adjacent upper and lower confidence limits are connected with line segments in order to produce the final confidence band. It should be noted that although pointwise confidence limits do not strictly define the 'global' CIs they are known to work well, in practice, for illustrating the uncertainty in a loess curve [44].

In the following discussions we have not presented exhaustive examples of these experiments but instead have given examples to illustrate key points.

A. *Polynomial curve fitting*

In order to find the best polynomial fit for the sensor response curves 3rd, 6th, and 9th degree polynomials were fitted to the response curves. The aim is to find the lowest degree polynomial that still provides a good fit to the raw signal without attenuation of the data features. The best fit for all sensor devices was that given by the 9th degree polynomial; curve fittings of less than polynomial 9 gave poor results (Fig. 4). In the case of the 𝕊 sensor the fit is largely within the 95% confidence bounds for the entire profile but does not maintain the profile of the signal at the start or end of the signal (Fig. 5). The polynomial curves fit less well with the other sensor devices (e.g., Fig. 6). While the 9th degree polynomial model for the 𝕊ℤ sensor does not fit well in the equilibrated measurement phase (~200-300 seconds) and the initial 'gas off' period (300-400 seconds), it provides a better fit after 400 seconds, when the response returns to the base line 'off' state, than the 6th degree polynomial curve.

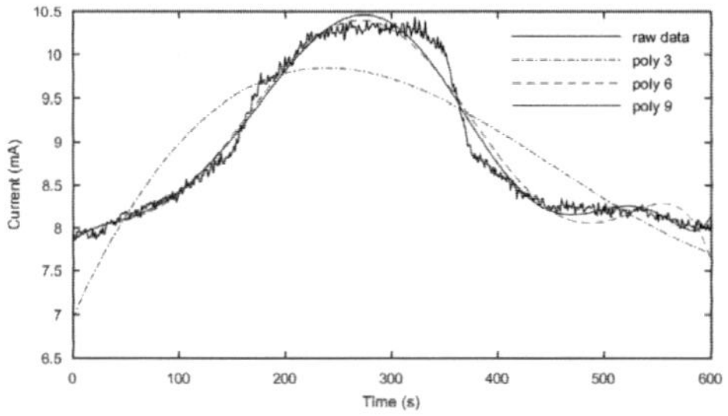

Figure 4. 3rd, 6th and 9th polynomial curve fitting for the 𝕊ℤ sensor response signal.

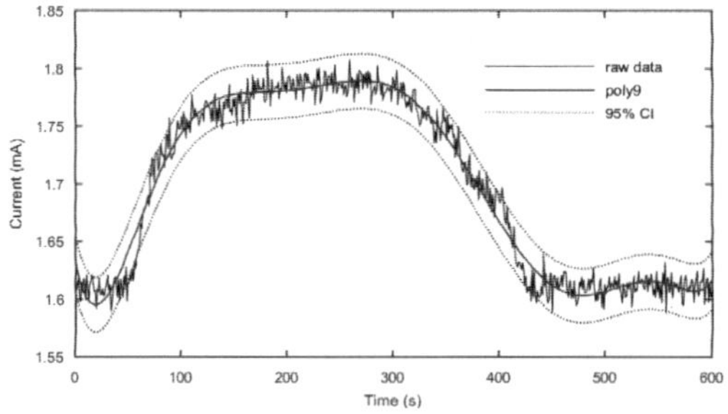

Figure 5. 9th degree fitted polynomial for the 𝕊 sensor response signal.

Fig. 4 and Fig. 6 clearly illustrate that using this approach is not the best solution because it is difficult to fit the polynomial to areas of the signal that exhibit rapid change. Thus, this approach – curve fitting with simple polynomial functions – is not explored further.

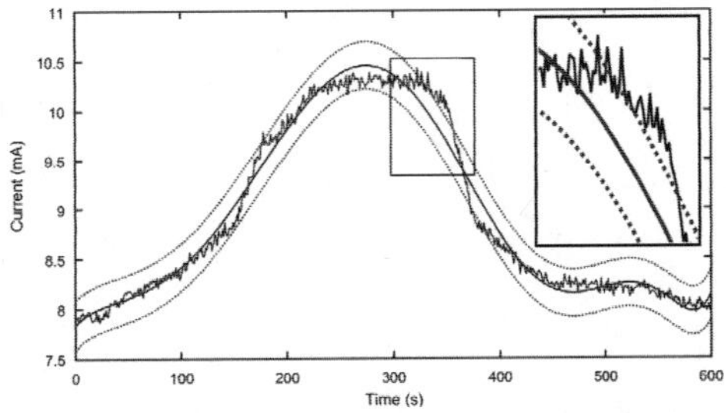

Figure 6. 9th degree fitted polynomial for the $\mathbb{SZ}$ sensor response signal (inset) showing data outside of the 95% CIs for the model.

B. *Moving average*

To establish the optimal smoothing parameter using the MA technique span sizes of 5, 25, 55, 75, 95, and 125 data points were evaluated. Fig. 7 gives the root-mean-square error (RMSE) for each device using the MA filter with varying span sizes. As expected, as the span size increases the RMSE error increases meaning that the smoothed signal is deviating further from the profile of the original signal.

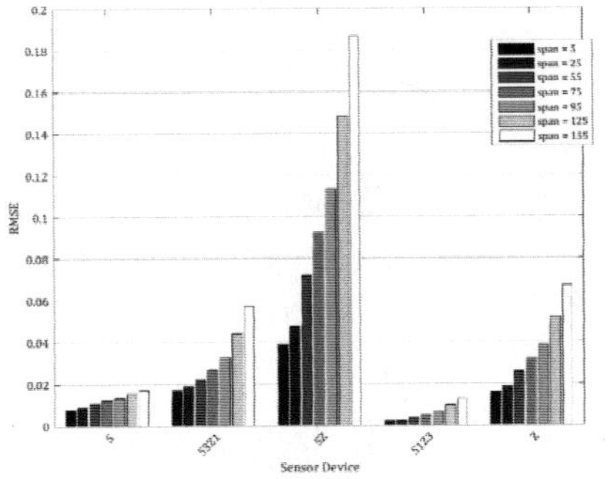

Figure 7. RMSE of the smoothed signals by device and span size.

The optimal smoothing span should therefore be the lowest possible span to ensure preservation of the profile of the raw signal and prevent loss of signal features.

MA smoothing produced the best smoothing using a span size of 25 (e.g., Fig. 8(a) and (b)). The smoothing achieved provided an improvement on the initial reported results (see [1][8]). For all the sensors when a span size of more than 55 was used the MA filter over-smoothed the approximation and, therefore, the approximated curve did not fit as well with the raw signal and response information was lost (e.g., Fig. 8(c) and (d)).

C. *Weighted regression methods*

For loess and rloess the best smoothing result was achieved with a span of 10% (Fig. 9). With a span of 1% the signal still contained perturbations that might obscure the values of the gas response features (see the $ytS1_i$ curves in Fig. 9). As the span size increases the noise in the signal becomes lower; however, using a 25% span shows that as the span size increases distortions in the signal are observed due to the smoothing filter (see the $ytS25_i$ curves in Fig. 9). Using a 20% span the resulting signal was considered to be slightly "over-smoothed", as it did not maintain the resolution of the signal (Fig 10(c)). The other sensor devices also displayed the best loess and rloess smoothing with a 10% span (Fig. 10). This finding confirms earlier work in which a span size of 10% was suggested to be optimal for MOX sensor signal smoothing with loess and rloess filters [1][8].

The lowess filter of the $\mathbb{S}_3\mathbb{Z}_1$, and $\mathbb{S}$ and $\mathbb{Z}$ sensor signals exhibited the best smoothing with a 5% span. Spans of 8% and 10% gave the best smoothing for the $\mathbb{SZ}$ (Fig 11(a)) and $\mathbb{S}_1\mathbb{Z}_3$ sensor signals, respectively. For rlowess the best smoothing was observed, for all the sensor devices, when a 5% span was used (e.g., the $ytS5_i$ curve in Fig. 11(b)).

Generally, above a 10% span all the local regression smoothing methods resulted in "over-smoothed" signals where noise was removed at the expense of the profile of the signal response. This results in a loss of the key diagnostic characteristics of the gas sensing signal. The results of these experiments show that different local regression smoothing methods provide optimal smoothing at different span sizes. For this reason local regression is not a viable option as a generalized method for the smoothing of MOX sensor response signals.

D. *SG smoothing*

In the polynomial curve fitting experiments reported earlier in this section it was found that polynomials of less than 9 gave a poor fit for the gas response signals for all of the sensor devices. In earlier work it had been reported that SG smoothing gave the best result using a frame of size of 55 data points [1][8], with a cubic (3rd order) polynomial but neither of these parameters had been tuned to ensure that these were the optimal values. In fact, the earlier work had been restricted to frame sizes of only 5 and 55.

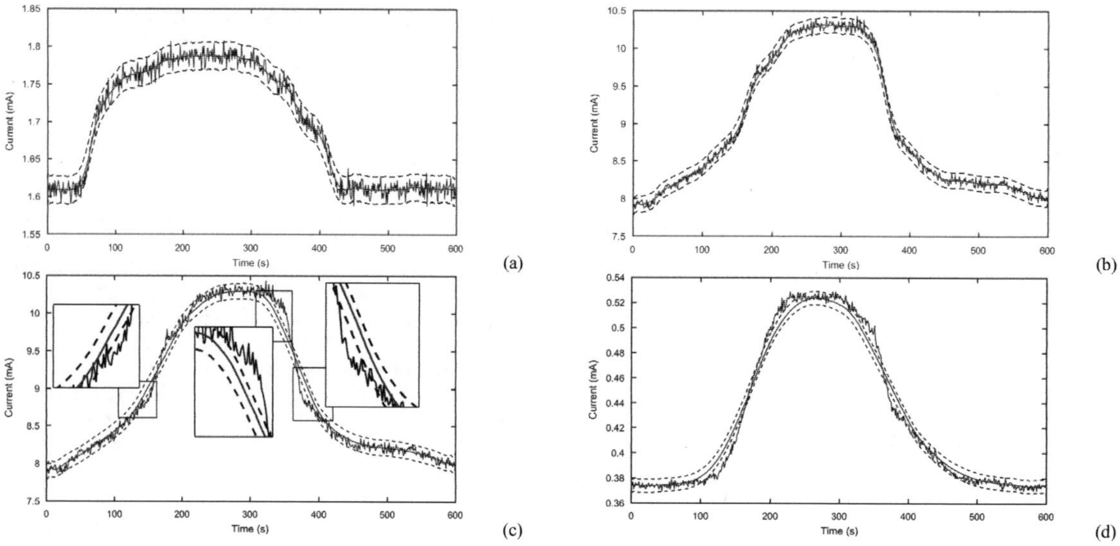

Figure 8. Raw vs smoothed signal using a MA filter: (a) 𝕊 device with a span of 25, (b) 𝕊ℤ device with a span of 25, (c) 𝕊ℤ device with a span of 75 (insets) highlight some of the areas where the model is outside of the 95% confidence bands, and (d) 𝕊3ℤ1 device with a span of 55.

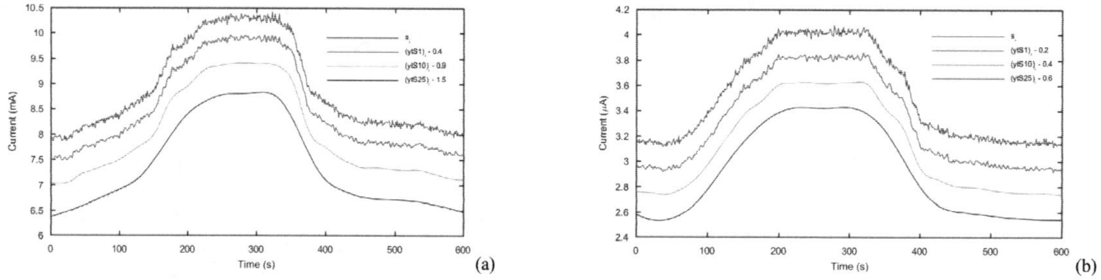

Figure 9. The same signal filtered with 1, 10 and 25% spans respectively, signals are offset for visibility: (a) noisy 𝕊ℤ signal vs. loess curves, (b) noisy ℤ signal vs. rloess curves.

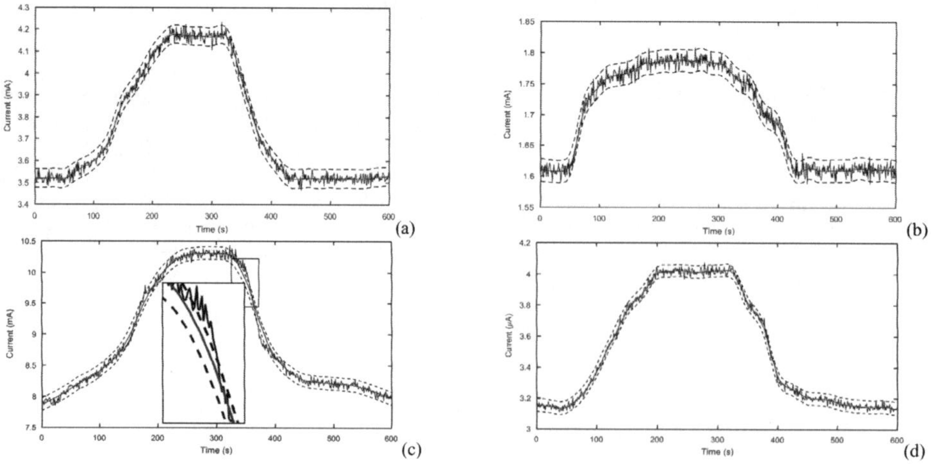

Figure 10. Smoothing with a 10% span using loess: (a) 𝕊3ℤ1 signal and (b) 𝕊 signal and rloess curve filtering (c) 𝕊ℤ device signal filtering using a 20% span, (d) ℤ device signal filtering using a 10% span.

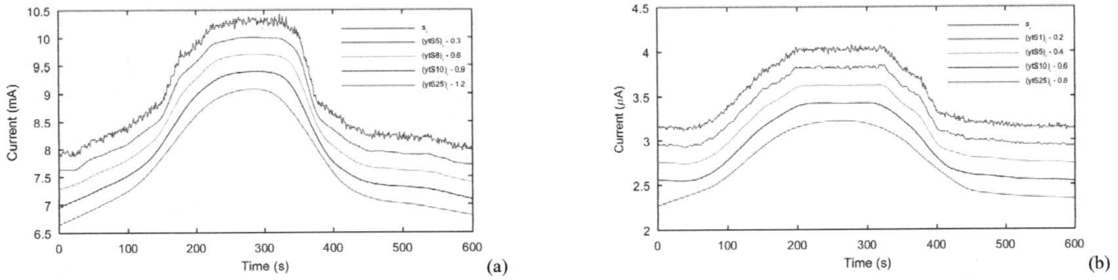

Figure 11. Raw signals vs. filtered curves, signals are offset for visibility: (a) noisy $\mathbb{S}\mathbb{Z}$ signal lowess filtered with 5, 8, 10 and 25% spans, (b) noisy $\mathbb{Z}$ signal rlowess filtered with 1, 5, 10 and 25% spans.

Frame sizes F of 5, 25, 55, 75, and 95 data points with polynomials of order k = 3, 6, and 9 were tested in order to find the optimal tuning parameters for the SG filtering model. As a general rule of thumb it has been suggested that the best value for SG filter is the same as that for MA and that the polynomial order k should be kept as low as possible [45]. Generally, a k value should be chosen that is considerably smaller than F in order to achieve the appropriate level of smoothing and also to ensure numerical stability. Theoretically, the smaller k is in comparison to F, the greater smoothing is achieved. For our purpose, a balance needs to be made between k and F that results in a signal that preserves the raw signal's profile but also sufficiently smooths the spectra. Additionally, we require single values for k and for F that give good smoothing results across all five sensor devices.

Fig. 12 shows the influence of polynomial order k on the smoothing of the $\mathbb{S}$ device's gas response signal with a frame size of 25. Visual inspection shows that an order of 3, cubic, gives the best result. This confirms earlier work suggesting that optimal results are obtained with a cubic polynomial [8]. The remaining experiments therefore use a polynomial order of 3 for the SG filter. Fig. 13 shows the results of altering the frame size while keeping k constant. The smoothed signal obtained using a frame size of 25 results in a smoothed signal that still contains some perturbations, therefore, it was concluded that as reported earlier a frame size of 55 was optimal [8] as it provides a smoother signal but still maintains the profile and features of the signal.

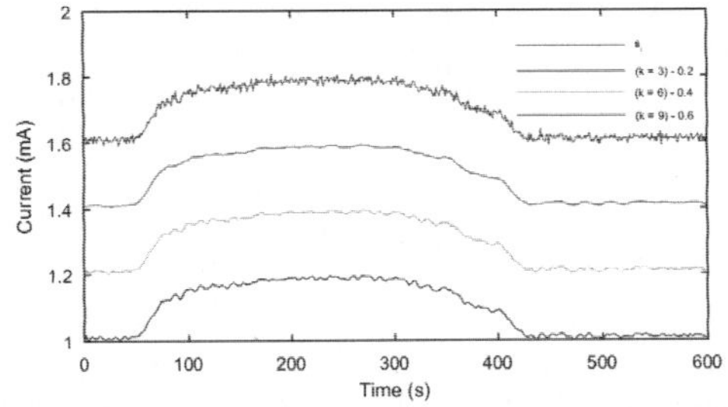

Figure 12. The effect of polynomial order on the degree of SG smoothing of the $\mathbb{S}$ device response signal (s_i). Signals are offset for visibility.

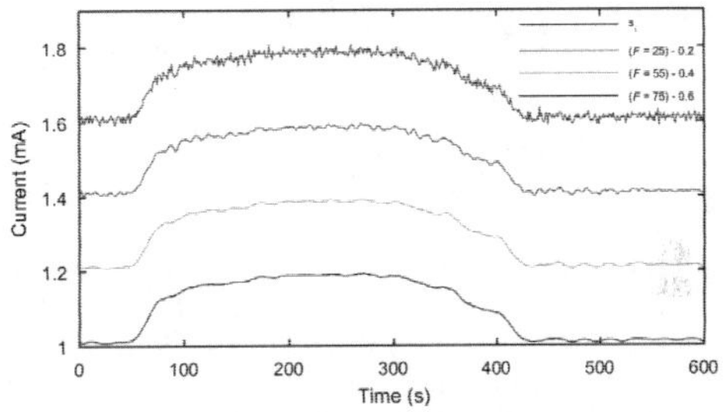

Figure 13. The effect of frame size (F) on the level of smoothing for the $\mathbb{S}$ signal using a cubic polynomial. Signals are offset for visibility.

Fig. 14 depicts the SG smoothed curves for the $\mathbb{S}\mathbb{Z}$ and $\mathbb{S}_1\mathbb{Z}_3$ devices using the optimal tuning parameter values (k = 3, F = 55) showing that this method is suitable for all five of the MOX sensors.

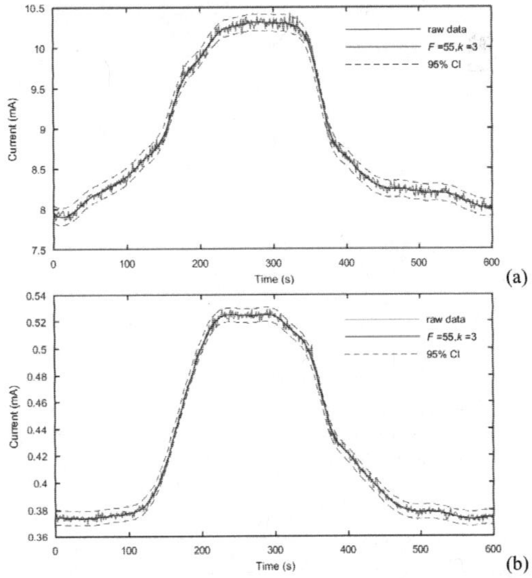

Figure 14. Plot of raw signal vs. SG smoothed signals (k =3, F = 55) with pointwise 95% confidence bands: (a) $\mathbb{S}\mathbb{Z}$ device, (b) $\mathbb{S}_1\mathbb{Z}_3$ device.

E. Wavelet denoising

Visual inspection of the perturbations in the signal show that similar perturbations can be seen in the Daubechies, Symlet, and Coiflet biorthogonal families of wavelets and, therefore, they are all potential mother wavelet candidates. The cross correlation between the 𝕊 gas sensor signal and the selected wavelet filter was calculated for selected wavelets from these four wavelet families (Fig. 15).

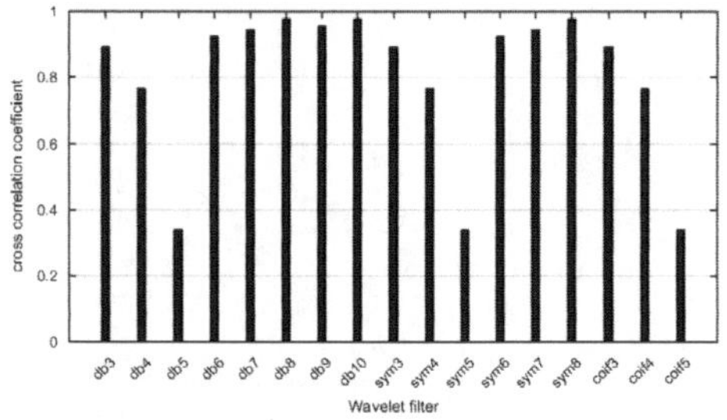

Figure 15. .Comparative plot of cross correlation coefficients with selected mother wavelet filters for the 𝕊 signal.

The optimum wavelet filter is one that maximizes the cross correlation coefficient [16]. Based on this cross correlation coefficient criterion, for the 𝕊 gas sensor signal a Daubechies filter of order 8 (decomposition level 10) is considered to be the optimal filter. Fig. 16 is a plot of the RMSE of the denoised signals for all five devices, using a Daubechies 8 (db8) basis function with various thresholding schemes.

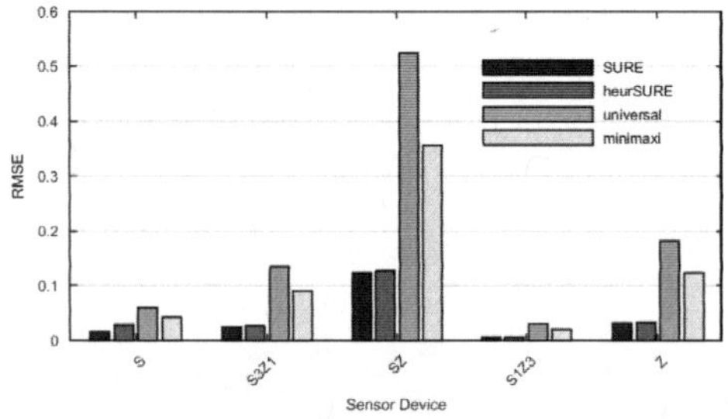

Figure 16. .Comparative plot of SURE, heurSURE, universal and minimaxi thresholding schemes for all five MOX gas sensor response signals.

With the exception of the 𝕊 gas sensor response signal SURE and heurSURE gave the same RMSE and performed the best as a thresholding chooser for wavelet denoising of the signals. Fig. 16 shows that for the 𝕊 signal the SURE threshold chooser resulted in less difference between the denoised signal and the original signal. Therefore, the optimal wavelet denoising method for all five SnO_2-ZnO composite devices sensing methanol vapor was found to be a discrete wavelet denoising approach that employed a Daubechies basis function of order 8 at a decomposition level of 10. The detail coefficients were thresholded using soft thresholding and the SURE threshold chooser with the noise scaled using a single estimation of the level of noise based on the first-level coefficients. Fig. 17(a) and (b) compare the denoised and the original (raw) signals for the 𝕊 and ℤ sensor devices.

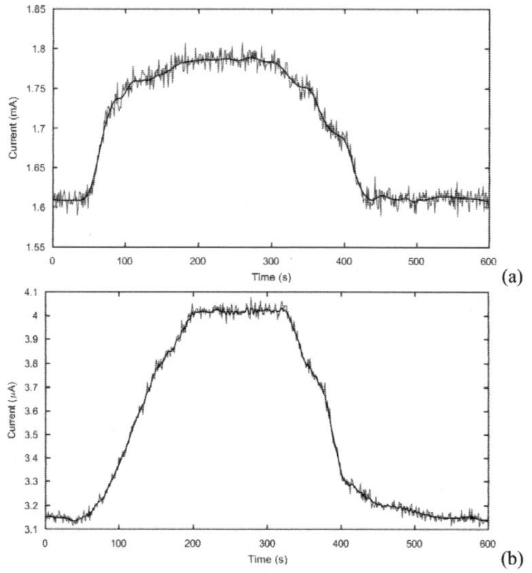

Figure 17. .Plot of raw vs. wavelet denoised 𝕊 (a) and ℤ (b) sensor signals with optimal mother wavelet (db8) and soft thresholding (with SURE).

VI. Empirical Method Evaluation

In order to compare the smoothing performance of the signal pre-processing methods evaluated, the coefficient of determination (R^2) and the RMSE were calculated for each method using the near-optimal generalized parameter values identified by this research.

R^2 measures the "goodness of fit" or how well the smoothed signal approximates the original signal where *SSE* is the sum of squared error, *SSR* is the sum of squared regression, and *SST* is the sum of squared total (11).

$$R^2 = \frac{SSR}{SST} = 1 - \frac{SSE}{SST} \tag{11}$$

The RMSE measures the differences between values estimated by the signal processing method and the values actually observed (the original signal). The RMSE represents the sample standard deviation of the differences between estimated values and the actual values (12).

$$\text{RMSE} = \sqrt{\frac{1}{n}\sum_{i=1}^{n}(s(n) - \hat{s}(n))^2} \tag{12}$$

For all methods and devices over 95% of the variance between the original and smoothed signals can be explained by the pre-processed model.

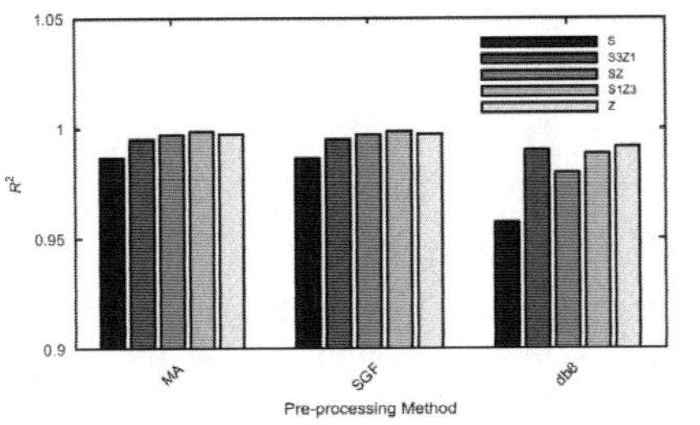

Figure 18. . Coefficient of determination for the best signal pre-processing methods using the near-optimal generalized tuning parameter values.

Based on the R^2 statistic the tuned MA and SG methods gave the best processed signals for all devices (Fig. 18) while the wavelet denoising approach performed slightly less well.

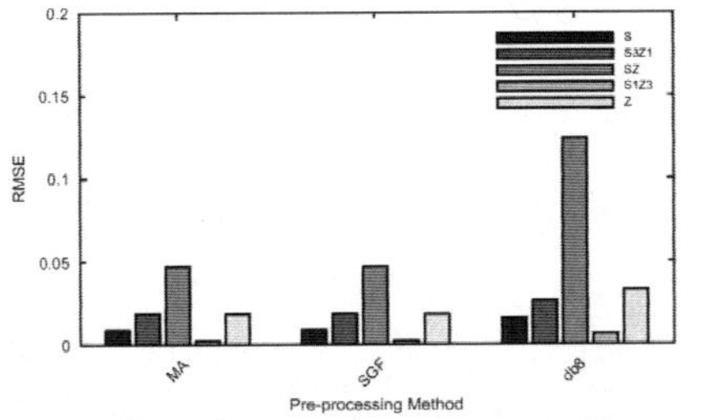

Figure 19. . RMSE for the best signal pre-processing methods using the near-optimal generalized tuning parameter values.

Fig. 19 shows that for all the methods similar RMSEs were observed for each of the devices and methods with the exception of the $\mathbb{SZ}$ device with wavelet denoising. Denoising the $\mathbb{SZ}$ sensor using the db8 wavelet method resulted in the greatest difference between original and processed signal observed of all sensor/method combinations evaluated.

In determining which method holds the most promise as a generalised approach for MOX gas response signal pre-processing a balance must be found between the goodness of fit of the processed signal to the actual raw signal, the simplicity and practicality of the method, and the degree to which the method preserves the features and profile of the original signal. As discussed, the best way to determine the quality of the signal pre-processing (smoothing or denoising) is to use a visual inspection of the processed signal. If we used a purely statistical approach (R^2 and RMSE) then the best approach appears to be either SG smoothing or MA. Given that a moving average approach is simpler than SG, it is tempting to assume that MA offers the most promising generalized approach. However, visual examination of the results of smoothing showed that the SG gives a better smoothing result than MA because it maintains the features and profile of the signal better when considering the consistency in the quality of the smoothing regardless of device composition (as discussed in Section V).

While wavelet denoising appears to lack sufficient consistency in results across the different sensor devices' MOX compositions, visual inspection of the denoised signals suggests that wavelet denoising is a plausible alternative to SG smoothing. It should also be noted that even though wavelet denoising of the $\mathbb{SZ}$ sensor has a lower R^2 and a higher RMSE, the difference in fit and error between it and the other sensors is actually minimal.

Fig. 20 shows plots for the wavelet denoising of the $\mathbb{SZ}$ sensor signal (the worst wavelet denoising result) and the $\mathbb{S}_3\mathbb{Z}_1$ sensor (the best wavelet denoising result).

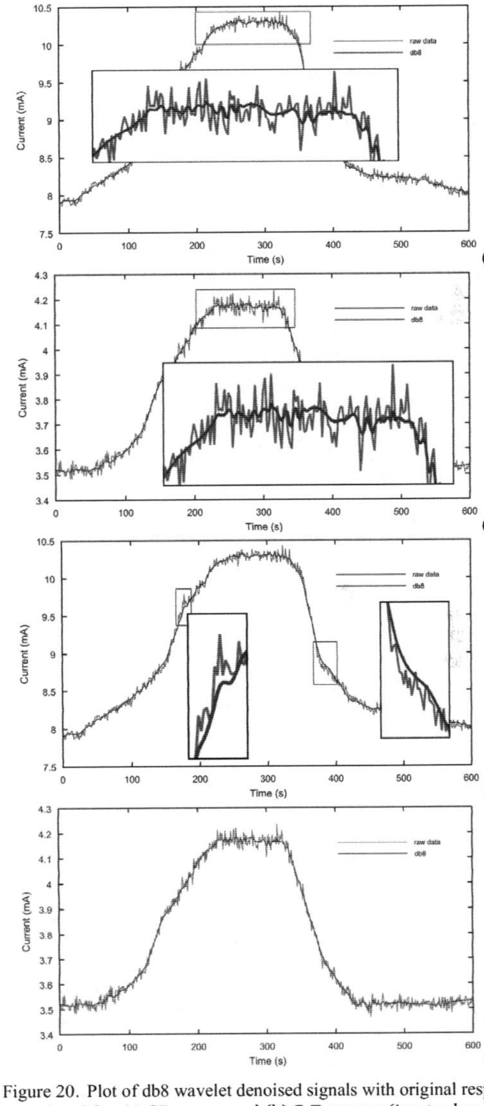

Figure 20. Plot of db8 wavelet denoised signals with original response signal for: (a) $\mathbb{SZ}$ sensor and (b) $\mathbb{S}_3\mathbb{Z}_1$ sensor (insets show perturbations), (c) $\mathbb{SZ}$ sensor (insets highlight regions where the profile of the original curve is not maintained) and (d) the full $\mathbb{S}_3\mathbb{Z}_1$ signal.

The insets provided in Fig. 20(a) and (b) show an enlarged view of the perturbations remaining in the denoised signals. Fig. 20(c) contains insets that highlight some of the regions in the denoised signal where it deviates from the profile of the original raw response signal. If the $\mathbb{S}\mathbb{Z}$ signal is compared with the $\mathbb{S}_3\mathbb{Z}_1$ signal it can be seen that the denoised $\mathbb{S}\mathbb{Z}$ signal has a poorer fit than the denoised $\mathbb{S}_3\mathbb{Z}_1$ signal. Both denoised signals appear to have a very similar degree of smoothing. Less smoothing of the signal is observed using the wavelet approach than when using a SG filter (Fig. 14) but the wavelet denoised signal preserves the features and the profile of the original signal well.

VII. Conclusion and Future Work

In this paper, an optimal wavelet basis function was applied to a set of MOX gas sensor response signals generated by exposing the sensor devices to methanol. The results revealed that a Daubechies mother wavelet of order 8 gives a reasonable compromise solution across all the sensor device compositions, suggesting that this might be a suitable method for other metal oxide sensor responses and for devices exposed to other gases as a signal pre-processing step. In order to establish whether or not such an approach is appropriate in practice further study is required to determine how generalizable the method is. Even if wavelets proved to be suitable there may still be complications in the implementation due to the need to select the order of the mother wavelet, level of decomposition of the wavelet coefficients, and thresholding method because these may differ for different MOX sensor compositions and gases.

While the wavelet denoising approach gives good results, it is a more complex process than the other more traditional moving average and regression approaches evaluated in this paper.

The alternative methods investigated do not pose the same degree of challenge in implementation and tuning that denoising using wavelets does. Among these approaches, SG smoothing looks to be the most promising as it resulted in a smoothed signal that maintained the profile of the original signal, and yielded near-optimal tuning parameter values that could be used regardless of sensor composition. SG smoothing was also found to give more consistent results than the wavelet approach, resulting in the removal of more of the perturbations in the signal. These perturbations have the potential to make subsequent feature extraction and pattern recognition difficult. Moreover, because SG is a much simpler approach and the tuning of the parameters is relatively straightforward it should be possible to automate the tuning process. Some work has already been reported in the literature towards automating tuning of the smoothing parameters [26]. This makes the SG smoothing approach (using a frame size of 55 data points/9% of the signal and a polynomial of 3) a more pragmatic solution to the pre-processing of MOX gas sensor response signals than wavelet denoising.

In order to substantiate further the usefulness of the SG approach the methods future work should include an evaluation of the method using signals produced by MOX sensors of different compositions and various gases (e.g., ethanol vapor). Finally, the Daubechies wavelet approach is also worth investigating further in order to see if an automated approach to selecting the mother wavelet and tuning of parameters is possible to simplify the practical application of the method.

Acknowledgment

We thank the School of Computer and Mathematical Sciences for the postgraduate summer internship funding that, in part, supported this research.

References

[1] E. Bassey, J. Whalley, and P. Sallis, "An Evaluation of Smoothing Filters for Gas Sensor Signal Cleaning," The Fourth Int. Conf. Adv. Commun. Comput. (INFOCOMP 2014) IARIA, pp. 19–23, 2014.

[2] C. Wang, L. Yin, L. Zhang, D. Xiang, and R. Gao, "Metal Oxide Gas Sensors: Sensitivity and Influencing Factors," Sensors, vol. 10, no. 3, pp. 2088–2106, 2010.

[3] S. Sharma and M. Madou, "A new approach to gas sensing with nanotechnology," Philos. Trans. A. Math. Phys. Eng. Sci., vol. 370, no. 1967, pp. 2448–73, 2012.

[4] A. Gutierrez Galvez, "Coding and learning of chemosensor array patterns in a neurodynamic model of the olfactory system," Texas A&M University, Texas, United States, 2006.

[5] R. Gutierrez-Osuna, "Pattern analysis for machine olfaction: A review," IEEE Sens. J., vol. 2, no. 3, pp. 189–202, 2002.

[6] V. J. Barclay, R. F. Bonner, and I. P. Hamilton, "Application of Wavelet Transforms to Experimental Spectra: Smoothing, Denoising, and Data Set Compression," Anal. Chem., vol. 69, no. 1, pp. 78–90, Jan. 1997.

[7] I. Garcia-Perez, M. Vallejo, A. Garcia, C. Legido-Quigley, and C. Barbas, "Metabolic fingerprinting with capillary electrophoresis," J. Chromatogr. A, vol. 1204, no. 2, pp. 130–139, Sep. 2008.

[8] E. Bassey, J. Whalley, P. Sallis, and K. Prasad, "Wavelet Transform Smoothing Filters for Metal Oxide Gas Sensor Signal Cleaning," The 8th Int. Conf. Sens. Technol., pp. 2–4, 2014.

[9] J. L. Guiñón, E. Ortega, J. García-Antón, and V. Pérez-herranz, "Moving Average and Savitzki-Golay Smoothing Filters Using Mathcad," The Int. Conf. Eng. Educ., no. 1, pp. 1–4, 2007.

[10] M. Awal, S. Mostafa, and M. Ahmad, "Performance Analysis of Savitzky-Golay Smoothing Filter Using ECG Signal," Int. J. Comput. Inf. Technol., vol. 01, no. 02, pp. 90–95, 2011.

[11] M. Leo, C. Distante, M. Bernabei, and K. Persaud, "An efficient approach for preprocessing data from a large-scale chemical sensor array," Sensors (Basel)., vol. 14, no. 9, pp. 17786–806, 2014.

[12] L. Bao, J. Mo, and Z. Tang, "The Application in Processing Analytical Chemistry Signals of a Cardinal Spline Approach to Wavelets," Anal. Chem., vol. 69, no. 15, pp. 3053–3057, Aug. 1997.

[13] C. Perrin, B. Walczak, and D. L. Massart, "The Use of Wavelets for Signal Denoising in Capillary Electrophoresis," Anal. Chem., vol. 73, no. 20, pp. 4903–4917, Oct. 2001.

[14] D. L. Donoho, "De-noising by Soft-thresholding," IEEE Trans. Inf. Theor., vol. 41, no. 3, pp. 613–627, May 1995.

[15] A. V Jagtiani, R. Sawant, J. Carletta, and J. Zhe, "Wavelet transform-based methods for denoising of Coulter counter signals," Meas. Sci. Technol., vol. 19, no. 6, p. 65102, 2008.

[16] B. N. Singh and A. K. Tiwari, "Optimal selection of wavelet basis function applied to ECG signal denoising," Digit. Signal Process. A Rev. J., vol. 16, no. 3, pp. 275–287, 2006.

[17] I. Daubechies, Ten Lectures on Wavelets. Philadelphia, PA, USA, PA, USA: Society for Industrial and Applied Mathematics, 1992, doi: 10.1137/1.9781611970104.

[18] D. Donoho and I. Johnstone, "Adapting to Unknown Smoothness via Wavelet Shrinkage," J. Am. Stat. Assoc., vol. 90, no. 432, pp. 1200–1224, 1995.

[19] M. R. Mosavi and I. Emamgholipour, "De-noising of GPS Receivers Positioning Data Using Wavelet Transform and Bilateral Filtering," Wirel. Pers. Commun., vol. 71, no. 3, pp. 2295–2312, Aug. 2013.

[20] H. Kim, B. Konnanath, P. Sattigeri, J. Wang, A. Mulchandani, N. Myung, M. a. Deshusses, A. Spanias, and B. Bakkaloglu, "Electronic-nose for detecting environmental pollutants: Signal processing and analog front-end design," Analog Integr. Circuits Signal Process., vol. 70, no. 1, pp. 15–32, 2012.

[21] S. B. Rudraswamy, P. K. Basu, and N. Bhat, "Sensitivity characteristics of Ag doped BaTiO<inf>3</inf>-CuO mixed oxide as carbon-dioxide sensor," Electronics, Computing and Communication Technologies (IEEE CONECCT), 2014 IEEE International Conference on. pp. 1–4, 2014.

[22] E. Bassey, P. Sallis, and K. Prasad, "Analysis of Methanol Sensitivity on SnO_2-ZnO Nanocomposite," in Characterization of Minerals, Metals, and Materials, Hoboken, NJ, USA: John Wiley & Sons, Inc., 2016, doi: 10.1002/9781119263722.ch35

[23] G. Neri, A. Bonavita, G. Micali, G. Rizzo, E. Callone, and G. Carturan, "Resistive CO gas sensors based on In2O3 and InSnOx nanopowders synthesized via starch-aided sol–gel process for automotive applications," Sensors Actuators B Chem., vol. 132, no. 1, pp. 224–233, May 2008.

[24] W. S. Cleveland, "Robust Locally Weighted Regression and Smoothing Scatterplots," J. Am. Stat. Assoc., vol. 74, no. 368, pp. 829–836, 1979.

[25] H. Ziegler, "Properties of Digital Smoothing Polynomial (DISPO) Filters," Appl. Spectrosc., vol. 35, no. 1, pp. 88–92, 1981.

[26] G. Vivó-Truyols and P. J. Schoenmakers, "Automatic Selection of Optimal Savitzky−Golay Smoothing," Anal. Chem., vol. 78, no. 13, pp. 4598–4608, Jul. 2006.

[27] A. Savitzky and M. J. E. Golay, "Smoothing and Differentiation of Data by Simplified Least Squares Procedures," Anal. Chem., vol. 36, no. 8, pp. 1627–1639, Jul. 1964.

[28] W. H. Press, S. A. Teukolsky, W. T. Vetterling, and B. P. Flannery, Numerical Recipes 3rd Edition: The Art of Scientific Computing, New York, NY, USA: Cambridge University Press, 2007.

[29] M. Zuppa, "Drift counteraction with multiple self-organising maps for an electronic nose," Sensors Actuators B Chem., vol. 98, no. 2–3, pp. 305–317, Mar. 2004.

[30] R. W. Schafer, "What is a savitzky-golay filter?," IEEE Signal Process. Mag., vol. 28, no. 4, pp. 111–117, 2011.

[31] C. Taswell, "The what, how, and why of wavelet shrinkage denoising," Comput. Sci. Eng., vol. 2, no. 3, pp. 1–11, 2000.

[32] S. Fu, B. Muralikrishnan, and J. Raja, "Engineering Surface Analysis With Different Wavelet Bases," J. Manuf. Sci. Eng., vol. 125, no. 4, pp. 844–852, Nov. 2003.

[33] S.-Y. Wang, X. Liu, J. Yianni, T. Z. Aziz, and J. F. Stein, "Extracting burst and tonic components from surface electromyograms in dystonia using adaptive wavelet shrinkage," J. Neurosci. Methods, vol. 139, no. 2, pp. 177–184, Oct. 2004.

[34] N. Saito, "Simultaneous noise suppression and signal compression using a library of orthonormal bases and the minimum description length criterion," Wavelets Geophys., vol. 4, pp. 299–324, 1994.

[35] W. Li, "Research on Extraction of Partial Discharge Signals Based on Wavelet Analysis," Electronic Computer Technology, 2009 International Conference on. pp. 545–548, 2009.

[36] W. K. Ngui, M. S. Leong, L. M. Hee, and A. M. Abdelrhman, "Wavelet Analysis: Mother Wavelet Selection Methods," Appl. Mech. Mater., vol. 393, pp. 953–958, 2013.

[37] G. Nason, "Choice of the Threshold Parameter in Wavelet Function Estimation," Wavelets Stat. Lect. Notes, vol. 103, pp. 261–280, 1995.

[38] R. Aggarwal and S. Rathore, "Noise Reduction of Speech Signal using Wavelet Transform with Modified Universal Threshold," Int. J. Comp. App., vol. 20, no. 5, pp. 14–19, 2011.

[39] D. L. Donoho and I. M. Johnstone, "Minimax estimation via wavelet shrinkage," Ann. Stat., vol. 26, no. 3, pp. 879–921, 1998.

[40] C. Stein, "Estimation of the Mean of a Multivariate Normal Distribution," Ann. Stat., vol. 9, no. 6, pp. 1135–1151, 1981.

[41] S. G. Chang, B. Yu, and M. Vetterli, "Adaptive wavelet thresholding for image denoising and compression," IEEE Trans. Image Process, vol. 9, no. 9, pp. 1532–1546, 2000.

[42] M. Nicolich and G. Jorgensen, "Graphical Presentation of a Nonparametric Regression with Bootstrapped Confidence Intervals," 23rd Annual SAS Users Group International, Statistics, Data Analysis, and Modeling, no. 1979, pp. 1–5, 1989.

[43] W. G. Jacoby, "Loess: A nonparametric, graphical tool for depicting relationships between variables," Elect. Stud., vol. 19, no. 4, pp. 577–613, 2000.

[44] N. Beck and S. Jackman, "Getting the mean right is a good thing: generalized additive models," Soc. Polit. Methodol.. [Online]. Available from: http://polmeth.wustl.edu/files /polmeth/beck97.pdf 2016.05.26

[45] D. Wilson, "The black art of smoothing," Electr. Autom. Technol., June/July Issue, pp. 35–36, 2006.

Dynamics in Carbon Nanotubes for In-Materio Computation

Stefano Nichele, Johannes Høydahl Jensen, Dragana Laketić, Odd Rune Lykkebø and Gunnar Tufte

Department of Computer and Information Science
Norwegian University of Science and Technology
Trondheim, Norway
Email: {nichele, johannj, draganal, lykkebo, gunnart}@idi.ntnu.no

***Abstract*—In-materio computation exploits physical properties of materials as substrates for computation. Evolution-In-Materio (EIM) uses evolutionary search algorithms to find such configurations of the material for which material physics yields desired computation. New unconventional materials have been recently investigated as potential computational mediums. Such materials may intrinsically possess rich physical properties, which may allow a wide variety of dynamics. However, how to access such properties and exploit them to carry out a wanted computation is still an open question. This article explores the dynamics in one particular type of nanomaterials which is used to solve computational tasks. Nanocomposites of Single-Walled Carbon Nanotubes (SWCNTs) and PolyButyl MethAcrylate (PBMA) are configured so as to undergo evolutionary processes with the goal of performing certain computational tasks. Early experiments showed that rich dynamics may be achieved, which may yield complex computations. Some indications of chaotic behavior were observed so further work was carried out with the aim of examining the dynamics achievable by such nanocomposites. Since it is not an easy task to access the physics at the very bottom of the material, investigation of the material dynamics is kept within the limits imposed by our measurement equipment and the level of observability enabled by it. Presented results show that interesting, complex dynamics is achievable by examined nanocomposites and that it depends on the type of signals used for the material configuration as well as on the material intrinsic properties such as percentage of SWCNTs in the nanocomposite.**

Keywords–Computation-in-Materio; Evolution-in-Materio; Evolvable Hardware; Carbon Nanotubes; Dynamical Systems; Complexity.

I. INTRODUCTION

Computations result from perturbations of some dynamical system. The observable output of the system is the result of its dynamics. Dependent on the type of dynamics exhibited by the system, computations of various complexity levels may be achieved. The type of dynamics depends on the physics of the system and on the way in which the system is manipulated. Our work considers novel nanoscale materials [1] and was carried out within the EU-funded NASCENCE (NAnoSCale Engineering for Novel Computation using Evolution) project [2]. The nanomaterials investigated within the project are nanocomposites of Single-Walled Carbon Nanotubes (SWCNTs) and polymer molecules (PBMA), and networks of gold nanoparticles. The investigation of nanocomposites is performed under the Evolution-In-Materio (EIM) scenario [3], [4].

EIM is a novel approach to designing computing devices where various materials are used as computational substrates. It is one approach that may emerge as an answer to the challenges of today's widely accepted semiconductor technology. Digital computers based on silicon technology are designed using a conventional top-down process by human engineers. Engineering of such processors poses technological challenges due to scaling down. Various design techniques are applied in order to sustain scaling down of the semiconductor technology but it is becoming increasingly difficult to fabricate transistors at the nanoscale.

This has motivated efforts towards novel technologies that will assume not only new computational substrates but also novel principles of the design of computing devices and their usage. EIM is a bottom-up approach in which the physics of a computing substrate is used to produce computations of interest. Different computational substrates have been previously explored such as liquid crystals and Field Programmable Gate Arrays (FPGAs) [5]–[7]. The configuration of the computing substrate, i.e., some material, undergoes evolutionary changes until some desired response of the material is achieved according to the computational task at hand. The digital computer accesses the material via a special board, which allows the Evolutionary Algorithm (EA) to apply configuration and input signals and read the material response which will guide the evolutionary search.

Figure 1 illustrates an EIM system. Three main entities can be distinguished: a digital computer, the material and the interface between the two. The system clearly shows the separation of an analog/physical domain in which materials operate and a digital domain in which the computer responsible for input/output mapping and configuration operates. In all such systems an interface is needed for bidirectional translation of signals between digital signals of the computer and analog signals in the physical domain of the material. As mentioned, the digital computer is used for running the EA, which generates a population of genomes, and translates each genome into suitable analog signals which can be sent to the interface board.

Further, the response of the material for a given configuration and input signals is translated from analog form as produced by the material to its corresponding digital value so that the computer can calculate the fitness value of the genome. The fitness value guides evolutionary search towards a solution to the problem at hand.

In order to produce interesting behavior under the EIM scenario, it is required that the material is able to exhibit rich dynamics. The richness of the exhibited dynamics can be attributed to the physical properties of the material. In a

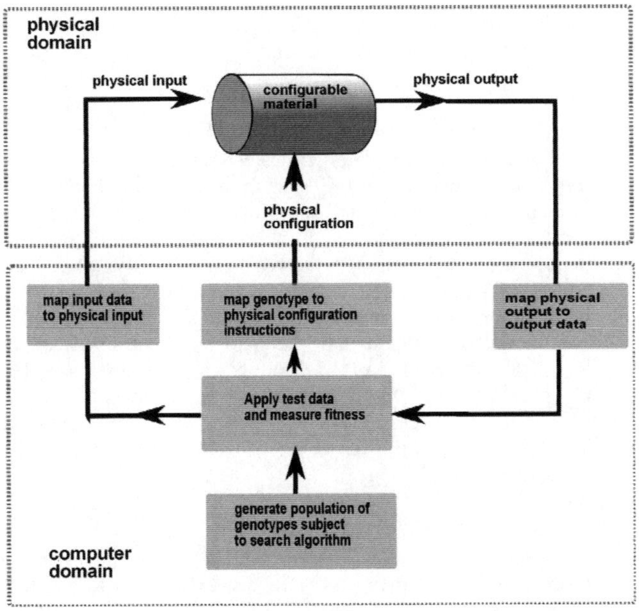

Figure 1. Principle of EIM illustrating the separation of an analog/physical domain where the material operates and the digital domain of computers, from [3].

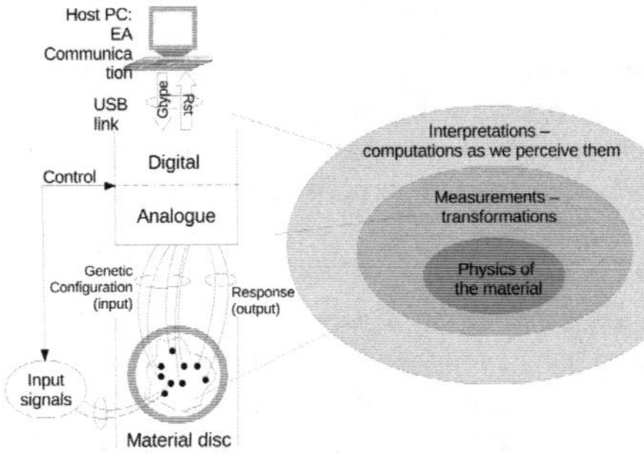

Figure 2. Conceptual domains of the computing system.

way it can be said that EIM manipulates the material so as to produce rich dynamics. The material blob is treated as a black box and EAs are used to "program" the material to solve a problem at hand.

Such a black box hybrid approach has been shown successful for a number of computational problems [8]–[13]. At the current state of research, it is not clearly understood what the exploited physical properties are and what the best way of exploring them is, e.g., what number of inputs and outputs and which types of signals - electrical (static voltages, sinusoidal waves, square waves) or even of some other kind such as temperature or light. The solved problems serve as a proof of concept that an EIM approach may be used for solving computational problems and indicates that it may be competitive in terms of computational time, size, and energy consumption. However, scaling-up to solve larger instances of a problem requires a better understanding of the dynamics exhibited by the material. In other words, the black box needs to be opened so that the underlying physical properties of the material are well understood. The number of used input electrodes, configuration signals available, etc. will directly affect the evolutionary search space.

Observing dynamics and its emergent complexity in computational materials is not an easy pursuit. Observability is limited by what output can be measured from the material and at which scale. At some scales we are not able to directly observe physical effects present in the materials, e.g., quantum effects due to mechanisms of electron transmission through carbon nanotubes. Therefore, we are limited to use signals which can be observed and measured. Figure 2 illustrates the taken approach to observe, exploit and gain an understanding of the dynamics of EIM systems. At the lowest level we have the physics of the material where computations happen, but due to nanoscale and even quantum effects, what is captured by our instruments will at best be just an approximation. In other words, the lowest level is inaccessible and must be treated as a black box. At the second level, the level of measurements and transformations, physical properties and dynamics are observable in the analog domain. This level can be explored to gain insight into the electrical properties of the material. The top level is the level of interpretations, i.e., computations as we perceive them. So, as shown in Figure 2, the dynamics of the analog signals are interpreted and transferred to data, i.e., the computational input – output mapping is performed. The top level is the level which is explored for computation. Here, it is important to note that the observations on the top level emerge as a result of all underlying dynamics.

The work presented in this paper includes a specific approach, as illustrated in Figure 2, to investigate the dynamics of the material at hand. The approach considers the complexity of the input - output mapping performed by the material for computation. Complexity is hard to measure even when well defined as, for example, Kolmogorov complexity [14]. Some approximations are needed if we want to obtain quantitative measures. In this work, we adopt *compressibility* as a measure of complexity.

This paper, which is an extended version of [1], is organized as follows: Section II provides background on EIM and position of the NASCENCE project within the field. Section III presents experimental platform Mecobo, which was developed within NASCENCE project, and which is used in our EIM experiments. Also, an experimental setup is explained as well as the material which was used in the experiments. Moreover, the section provides some background on different computational domains which can be distinguished under EIM computing scenario. Further, Section IV provides some initial results, presented in [1], which demonstrate interesting behaviors of the investigated material. Section V presents experiments which were conducted with the aim of investigating material dynamics in a greater detail. A measure of complexity is introduced which is used as the description of material behavior, the three sets of experiments are described followed by the results and the discussion which relates results to theoretical foundations. Finally, Section VI provides conclusion about the presented experiments and exhibited material dynamics within EIM computing.

II. Background – Evolution-in-Materio

The term Evolution-in-Materio was introduced by Julian Miller and Keith Downing in 2002 [4]. The general concept of EIM is that physical systems may intrinsically possess properties which may be exploited for computation.

A. Pioneering work

Early work on manipulation of physical systems for computation is related to the work of Gordon Pask [15], a classical cyberneticist whose pioneering work dates back to the 1950s. He tried to grow neural structures, dendritic wires, in a metal-salt solution by electrical stimulation [7]. His goal was to self-assemble a wiring structure within the material in order to carry out some sort of signal processing embedded in the material. He was able to alter the position and structure of the wiring filaments, and thus the behavior of the system. This was achieved by external influence, which consisted in applying different currents on electrodes in the metal-salt solution. This early version of material manipulation was done without aid of computers and different electrical configurations were tested manually. Stewart [16] later defined such a process as manufacturing logic "by the pound, using techniques more like those of a bakery than of an electronics factory".

B. Analog computers, FPGAs and liquid crystal

Later, Mills constructed an analog computer which he called Kirchhoff-Lukasiewicz Machine (KLM) [17]. The construction was done by connecting a conductive polymer material to logical units. The analog computation was carried out by placing current sources and current sinks into the conductive foam layer and reading the output from the logical units. One could argue that such machines were not easy to program due to the manual placement of connections into the material. On the other hand, some advantages of performing computation directly in the material substrate became obvious, e.g., a large number of partial differential equations were solved within nanoseconds.

In 1996, Thompson used intrinsic evolution to produce electrical circuits in FPGAs [5]. In his well-known experiment, he demonstrated that artificial evolution can be used to exploit physical properties of FPGAs to build working circuits, e.g., a frequency discriminator circuit. He found out that placing the circuit in a different part of the chip or disconnecting some unused modules would result in a non-working solution. Moreover, he was unable to replicate the chip behavior in simulation because evolution had exploited underlying physical properties of the FPGA. In fact, changing the FPGA with a similar model from the same producer would result in slightly different behavior. Thompson described such a process as "removing the digital design and letting evolution do it".

In [4], Miller and Downing suggested several materials which may be suitable for EIM, liquid crystals being among them. Simon Harding [18] later demonstrated that it was indeed possible to apply EIM on liquid crystals to evolve several computational devices: a tone discriminator [19], logic gates [20], and robot controllers [6]. Liquid crystal is a movable material where voltages affect orientation of the crystals. The movability was problematic since the material would undergo permanent changes during evolution. This led to unstable solutions that worked only once. Nevertheless, he showed that it was possible to quickly reach a working solution again by re-running the evolutionary algorithm for a couple of generations [19].

C. The NASCENCE project and recent work

Recently, the NASCENCE project [2] addressed nanomaterials and nanoparticles for EIM with the long term goal to build information processing devices exploiting such materials without the need to reproduce individual components. In particular, investigated nanomaterials included nanocomposites made of SWCNTs and polymer molecules and nanoparticle networks, in particular gold coated nanoparticles. Several hard-to-solve computational problems have been solved as proof of concept, e.g., Traveling Salesman [8], logic gates [9], bin packing [10], machine learning classification [11], frequency classification [12], function optimization [13] and robot controllers [21]. The SWCNT materials from the project are the subject of our investigation in this paper.

D. Interpretation and computation

As stated, EIM has been used to solve a variety of problems. However, these results are all limited to a specific problem domain. To assess the potential computational power available in a material, we need a more general measurement. One way is to view *complexity* as indication of potential computational power [22].

Kolmogorov complexity [14], [23] is well-defined but incomputable in theory. However, it is possible to use measures such as compressibility to approximate complexity to some extent [24]–[27]. In fact, strings that are hardly compressible have a presumably high Kolmogorov complexity. Complexity is then proportional to the compression ratio.

High measurable complexity of output data or a high complexity ratio between input and output data may not always be a desired property. In classifier systems, such as Thompson's frequency discriminator [5], the output may be a binary response to a complex input signal. In this case the complexity ratio between output and input is very low. However, the computation, i.e., internal state transitions in the underlying physics of the material, is still a complex process but the complexity is unobservable since we only observe the input and output signals.

III. A Platform for Experiments and Understanding of EIM Systems

The conceptual idea of exploiting physics for computation requires a physical device, i.e., the material. In most EIM works, an intrinsic approach has been taken – computation is a result of real physical processes and the evaluation is a result of the performance of a physical system. An intrinsic approach allows access to all inherent physical properties of the material [3]. An analog computation [28] is a possibility, however, in this work a hybrid approach is taken. The hybrid approach includes the computational matter in a mixed signal system using a digital computer to configure and communicate with the material. Such an approach enables the computational power of the material with the ease of programmability of digital computers [2]. In a hybrid approach, observability is an issue, i.e., ensuring that the data from the material is observable and sound without using more computational power for the observation than the actual computation [29].

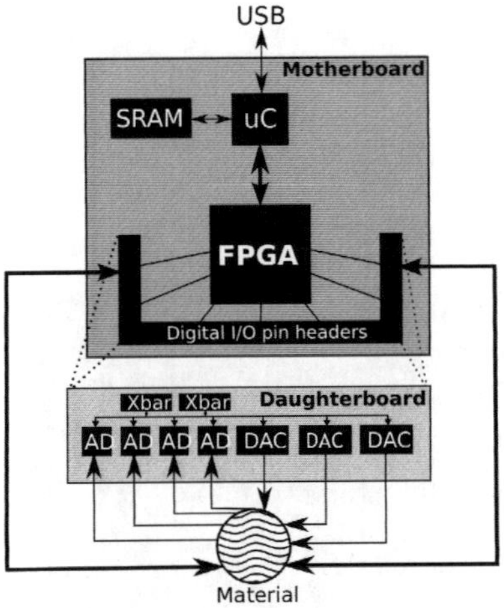

(a) Block diagram of the Mecobo hardware interface.

(b) Picture of the Mecobo motherboard with mixed signal daughter board.

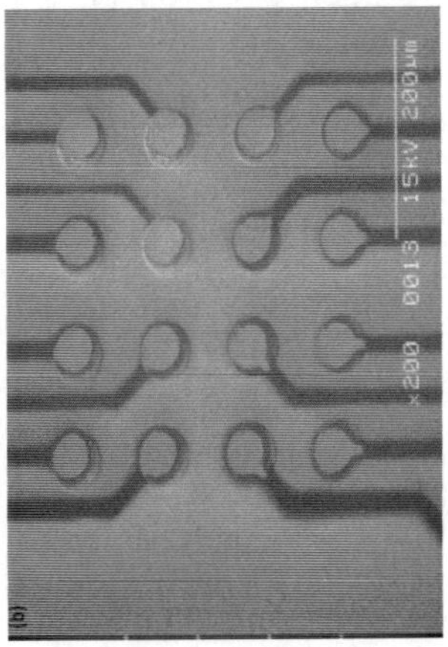

(c) Electrode array, microscopic view. (Source: documentation of the NASCENCE project).

Figure 3. Overview of the Mecobo hardware interface.

A. *NASCENCE's Mecobo: an experimental platform for EIM*

A hybrid approach requires an interface between the digital world of computers and the analog world of materials. The Mecobo experimental platform [30] from the NASCENCE project is a hardware/software platform implementing the conceptual Evo-Materio-system shown in Figure 1.

Figure 3 shows an overview of the hardware interface: a Mecobo platform and microelectrode array on the material slide. A block diagram of the Mecobo platform is shown in Figure 3a. Configuration specification, i.e., genotypes, are loaded from a PC to Mecobo over a USB port. A micro-controller communicates with the USB interface and with an FPGA via an internal bus. The FPGA can be interfaced to the materials directly or, as shown in the figure, use a daughter board to extend the range of possible signals.

A picture of the Mecobo hardware is presented in Figure 3b. In the picture, the Mecobo is shown with a mixed signal daughter board and a material sample on a glass slide plugged in. Electrical connection between the material on the slide and the board is realized by the microelectrode array. A microscopic view of the microelectrode array before material disposition is shown in Figure 3c.

Mecobo is capable of controlling close to 100 individually configurable input/output signals (pins), which can be connected to the material. Each signal is described by parameters at a given point in time. For example, a pin can be programmed as a recording pin from time 0 to $100ms$, or as an output pin of square waves of some frequency from 0 to $1000ms$, or as an output pin of a constant voltage level, e.g., $2.7V$ from time 0 to $1500ms$ etc. Mecobo is connected to a host PC over USB and communicates via a Thrift server [31]. Communication based on Thrift technology also enables access to Mecobo remotely over the Internet. The maximum analog sampling frequency of the Mecobo board is $500kHz$. Input signals may be static voltages or periodic (e.g., square, sinusoidal) waves ranging in frequency between $400Hz$ and $25MHz$. For more details on Mecobo and an overview of the full range of programmable properties of the platform, see [30].

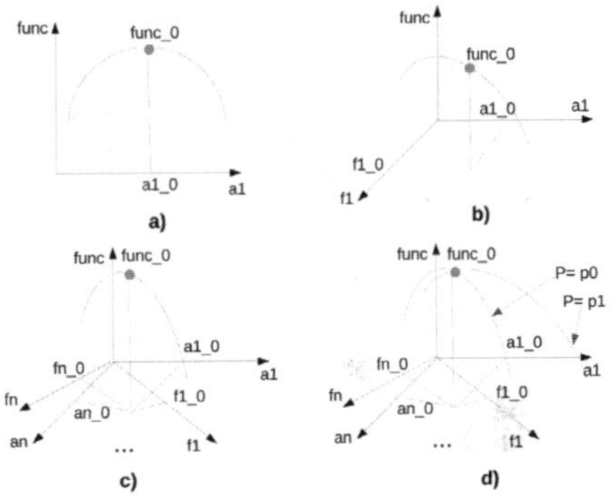

Figure 4. CNT computing system within a system theory framework.

B. *Explaining computations within EIM*

It can be said that computations are based on transformations of a system, so that the system input(s) and output(s) are related in some functional way. This functional relation can be expressed by a simple formula:

$$y = F(x) \qquad (1)$$

where x and y correspond to an input and output of the system, respectively, and, in general, they are considered to be multidimensional and represented by vectors.

One way of analysis, more formally addressed within the system theory [32], [33] assumes that the system state is described by a set of variables that move through a state space.

For an EIM scenario, a better look into the state space of the system needs clarification of what is meant by system variables [34]. According to the explanation of different domains of computation as described in Section I, the variables of the system belong to the *domain of measurements* as schematically shown in Figure 2. The voltages and the set of properties which define them in this domain, i.e., amplitude, frequency and phase, can be represented with:

$$v_i = a_i \cdot func_p(f_i, \phi_i) \quad (2)$$

where v_i is voltage on the i-th electrode, a_i the amplitude, $func_p$ some periodic function, f_i frequency of the function $func_p$ and, finally, ϕ_i the phase of the voltage, all referring to the i-th electrode. The symbols are left lower case to remind that all of these values can be time varying.

Let us now consider an example in which for a system to perform functionality $func\_0$, for the input x_0, an output value y_0 is desired (Figure 4 a)). For simplicity, the variables on each of the axes are assumed to be scalars. When different configuration voltages are applied to the material, they change the system variables so that it passes through various states in the state space along some trajectory. Further, let us assume that only one electrode is used for configuration voltage and only one voltage parameter is changed, for example amplitude. By changing the amplitude along the a_1 axis different input-output mappings will be performed by the system. EIM would then search through the space until $func\_0$ point is reached. If also the frequency of the voltage v_1 is changed, then the state space could be searched along two axes as shown in Figure 4 b)). And even further, if more than one electrode is used for configuring the material, then, in general, the space would look something like in Figure 4 c) and would be searchable along high number of axes, the limitation being only the physical number of electrodes in the system. Moreover, the state space may grow due to the change in some parameter, like temperature or light, as shown in Figure 4 d), which may all increase the size of the state space to search for the solution.

IV. A Detailed View of Material Dynamics

Experiments are performed on SWCNT mixed with PBMA on a micro electrode array supplied by Durham University. Material samples and micro electrode arrays are produced in a process where SWCNT-PBMA mixture is dissolved in anisole (methoxy benzene). The material samples are prepared on $4x4$ grids of gold micro-electrode arrays with pads of $50\mu m$ and pitch of $100\mu m$, see Figure 3c. The preparation is done by dispensing $20\mu L$ of the material onto the electrode area. The concentration of SWCNTs varies as shown in Table I where the material samples used in our experiments are listed. The SWCNT mixed with PBMA material dispersed over electrode array is baked for $30min$ at $90C^{\circ}$. The solvent dries out and leaves a thick film of immovable SWCNTs supported by polymer molecules. The substrate is cooled slowly over a period of 1h. This process leaves a variable distribution of nanotubes across the electrodes. Typically, carbon nanotubes are 30% metallic and 70% semi-conducting, while PBMA creates insulation areas within nanotube networks. Such electrical properties of the material may allow non-linear current versus voltage characteristics.

The coverage of gold microelectrodes with randomly dispersed nanotubes varies and some of the electrodes may even be left with little or no coverage, as visible in the Scanning Electron Microscope (SEM) image in Figure 5.

TABLE I. Different materials used in the experiments.

Material	SWCNT Concentration, $wt\%$
B09S12	0.53%
B15S03	1.25%
B15S04	1.50%
B15S08	5.00%

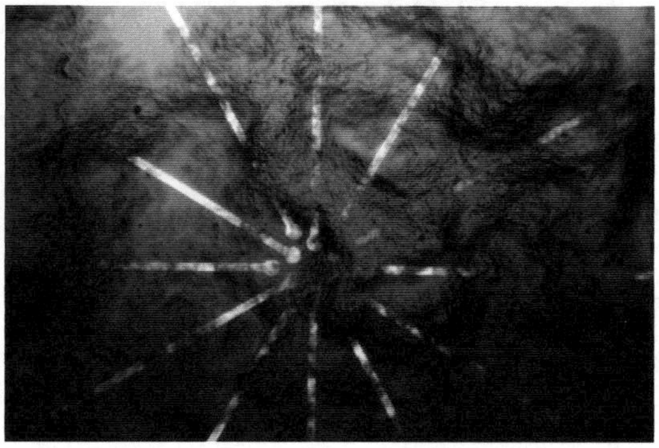

Figure 5. SEM image of gold electrode array with different coverage of nanotubes. Adopted from [9].

Initial investigation of the material response to various input signals showed several interesting behaviors in the material [1]. The goal was to gain insight into the material dynamics to identify suitable ways in which the material can be manipulated to perform computation.

As mentioned, EIM requires an interface between a digital computer which runs the EA and the material whose physics undergoes analog processes. This interface is typically provided by the Mecobo board. However, in order to better understand the underlying properties of the material and its responses, it is necessary to use more precise instruments. In these experiments, oscilloscopes and signal generators were used to get a more detailed view of the material dynamics.

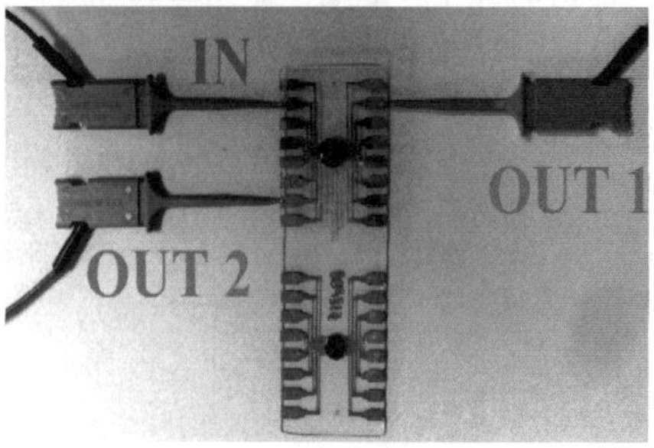

Figure 6. Material slide and pins connected to signal generator (IN) and oscilloscope (OUT).

A. Experimental Setup

In the experiments herein, we connect a material slide to a Hewlett Packard 33120A $15MHz$ function / arbitrary waveform generator (used as input) and an Agilent 54622D $100MHz$ mixed signal oscilloscope (used as output). Input signals are square waves at different frequencies from the signal generator and the output signals are recorded on the oscilloscope.

The input / output pins were chosen so that there would be an equal distance between microelectrode pads within the microelectrode array (Figure 3c). The placement of input and output signals on the material slide is shown in Figure 6, where the input probe (from the signal generator) is placed on pin #2 (IN) and the two output probes (to the oscilloscope) are connected to pins #9 (OUT1) and #7 (OUT 2).

B. Results and discussion

Figure 7 presents the experimental results. In particular, Figures 7a) show several snapshots of the material response on two different pins at different frequencies, ranging from $1KHz$ (Figure a1) to $14MHz$ (Figure a12). At $1KHz$ the signals may seem similar (a1), where the material charges-up and subsequently discharges, but in a zoomed in snapshot, i.e., where a part of the response is shown at a higher resolution (a2), a voltage spike is visible on the second probe which is not present on the first probe. This is better visible at $5KHz$ (a3), $30KHz$ (a4) and $100KHz$ (a5), where it is possible to notice that on the rising front there is a sudden voltage increase/drop. The material behavior is capacitor-like. Starting from $500KHz$ (a6), which is also zoomed in (a7), the second probe signal is similar to a square wave (most of the harmonic frequencies are passed) while the first probe acts more like a filter. The difference is caused by different concentrations of CNTs between the IN-OUT electrodes, i.e., different paths the current is enabled to follow between the electrodes. In both cases, there is a resonance phase which results in a deterministic yet semi-chaotic waveform. This may be the effect of some conducting sub-networks in the material that are enabled at specific frequencies and disabled at others. At 2, 5 and $8.5MHz$ the measured voltage decreases while frequency increases. At $10MHz$ (a11) a strange phenomenon is observed where both signals show a voltage increase. The effect is more prominent on the first output. We ascribe such behavior to be due to a feedback effect where harmonics of some frequencies are fed again into the material by some nanotube sub-networks. At $14MHz$ (a12) the signal on the second probe is sinusoidal, i.e., only one harmonic is present. As such, it may be concluded that with a single square wave input it is possible to observe a rich variety of behaviors while the frequency spectrum is traversed.

As the system produces uniform, stable, and semi-chaotic behaviors, it is of particular interest to visualize input-output responses and output-output relations in order to better understand traversed trajectories and attractors. For this purpose, XY plots are shown in Figure 7b), where OUT1 is plotted against OUT2 and Figure 7c), where IN is plotted against OUT1. In Figure 7b1), some orbits are present at $30KHz$. Similar orbits are visible at $60KHz$ (b2) and $100KHz$ (b3), moving towards opposite corners to those where the impulse is. After each impulse, there is a semi-chaotic orbit that relaxes before the next impulse arrives, as the semi-chaotic behavior is annihilated by the lack of energy in the material, until the arrival of the next impulse. This suggests that chaotic behavior may be present, yet particularly difficult to observe.

XY plots between input and output are shown in Figure 7c). These figures represent the phase space of the system (input-output pin pair). Figure 7c1) is obtained at $350Khz$. Several oscillating orbits are present, which are zoomed-in at $2MHz$ (c2). The same effect is observed for frequencies up to $5MHz$ (c3) while for frequencies around $10MHz$ and higher we observe a hysteresis loop, which indicates that some saturation may have been reached in the material. Some sort of non-linearity seems present, which is always a good indicator that the system may achieve complex behavior.

To summarize this set of results, even if a single square wave input signal is used, the resulting output shows a variety of behaviors. Square waves [35] produce richer dynamics than what may be achieved by a single static voltage or by a sinusoidal wave. Such richness of the response is due to the rich spectrum of the square waves which contains a variety of harmonics. In particular, some of the nanotube sub-networks may be sensitive to certain frequencies. Therefore, square waves may be better suited to penetrate the material and exploit the nanocomposite's intrinsic properties.

V. A COMPLEXITY VIEW OF MATERIAL DYNAMICS

The initial experiments with the oscilloscope measurements gave valuable insight into the different dynamics available in the material. However, such detailed measurements only give a very narrow view of the possible behaviors of the system. In order to get a broad picture of the space of possible material dynamics, one has to sacrifice some amount of detail. By using the Mecobo hardware platform (Section III) we are able to explore material dynamics at a higher level.

Mecobo allows us to scan a much wider range of signal frequencies, explore a myriad of different material locations and easily analyze the results on a PC. For these experiments we use the digital signal generator on Mecobo to generate square waves as input signals. The output signal is sampled as analog voltage using the on-board AD converter (Figure 3).

Complexity of the input/output signal is used as metric to classify different types of material dynamics. We use compressibility as an estimate of complexity as described in Section II-D. Since we are primarily interested in the complexity contribution of the material (and not the complexity of the input signal itself), we adapt the *complexity ratio*:

$$C_r = \frac{C_o}{C_i}$$

where C_o is the complexity of the output signal and C_i is the complexity of the input signal.

We present three sets of experiments where the computational complexity of the material is explored:

1) Complexity as number of input signals are increased
2) Complexity as function of one input frequency
3) Complexity as function of two input frequencies

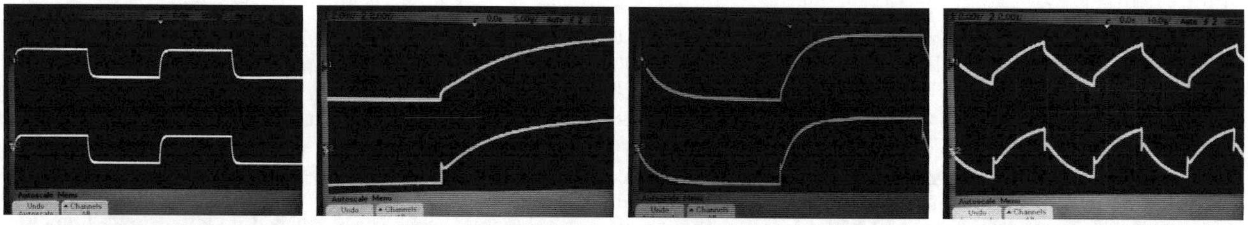

(a1) $1kHz$ (scale: $5V, 200\mu s$) (a2) $1kHz$ (zoom, $2V, 5\mu s$) (a3) $5kHz$ (scale: $2V, 20\mu s$) (a4) $30kHz$ (scale: $2V, 10\mu s$)

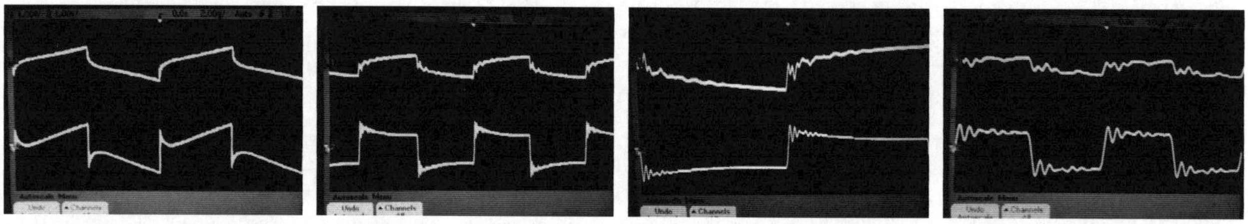

(a5) $100kHz$ (scale: $1V, 2\mu s$) (a6) $500kHz$ (scale: $1V, 500ns$) (a7) $500kHz$ (zoom, $500mV, 200ns$) (a8) $2MHz$ (scale: $1V, 100ns$)

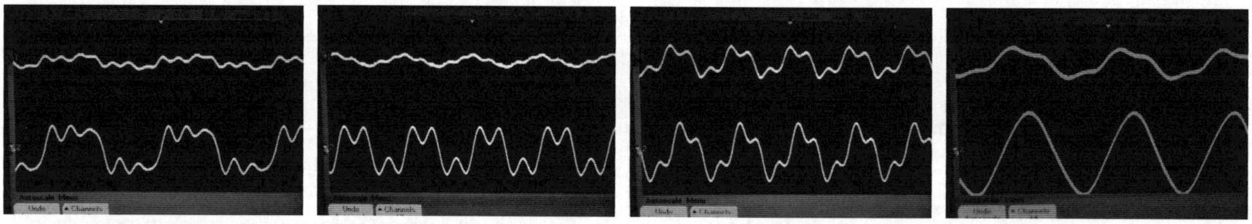

(a9) $5MHz$ (scale: $1V, 50ns$) (a10) $8.5MHz$ (scale: $1V, 50ns$) (a11) $10MHz$ (scale: $1V, 50ns$) (a12) $14MHz$ (scale: $500mV, 20ns$)

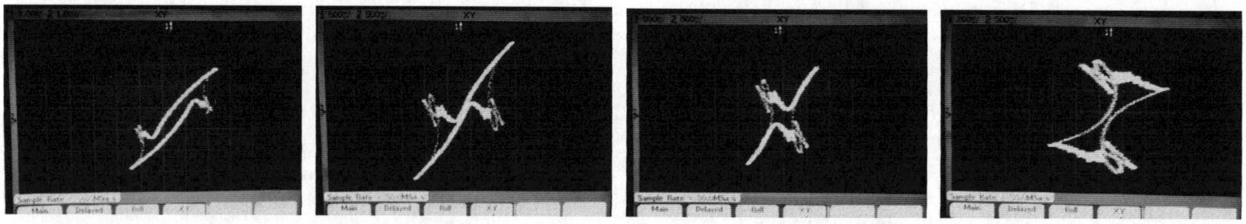

(b1) $30kHz$ (scale: $1V, 1V$) (b2) $60kHz$ (scale: $500mV, 500mV$) (b3) $100kHz$ (scale: $500mV, 500mV$)(b4) $500kHz$ (scale: $200mV, 200mV$)

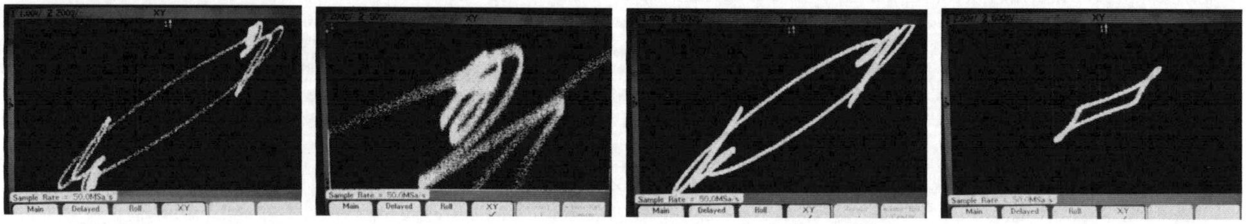

(c1) $350kHz$ (scale: $1V, 1V$) (c2) $2MHz$ (zoom, $200mV, 50mV$) (c3) $5MHz$ (scale: $1V, 200mV$) (c4) $10MHz$ (scale: $2V, 500mV$)

Figure 7. Oscilloscope screenshots. The resolution is indicated in parentheses. The resolutions have been chosen so as to be able to show interesting results at different scales.
(a) Voltage responses on 2 different pins with input square wave at different frequencies.
(b) XY plots, X (OUT1) is plotted against Y (OUT2) at different frequencies.
(c) XY plots, X (IN) is plotted against Y (OUT1) at different frequencies.

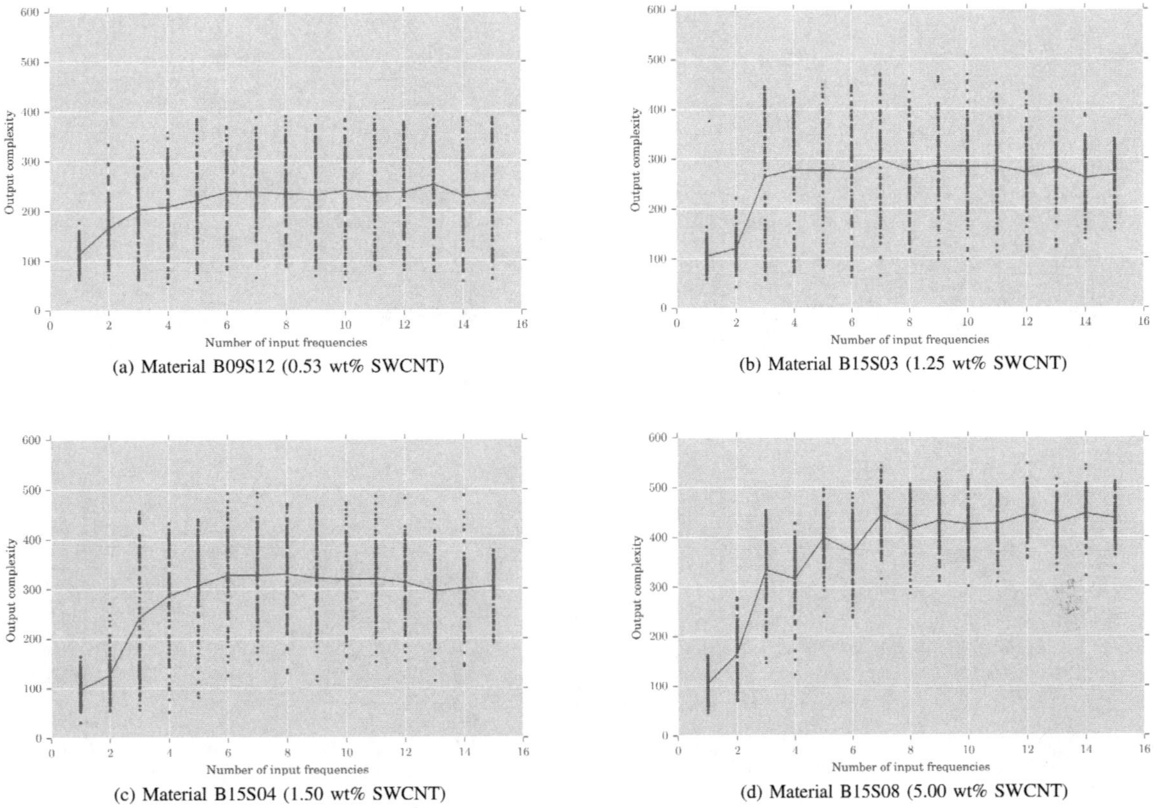

(a) Material B09S12 (0.53 wt% SWCNT)

(b) Material B15S03 (1.25 wt% SWCNT)

(c) Material B15S04 (1.50 wt% SWCNT)

(d) Material B15S08 (5.00 wt% SWCNT)

Figure 8. Output complexity as the number of input frequencies are increased from 1 to 15 for four different material samples. The red scatter plot shows individual measurements while the blue line indicates the mean values for each of the 100 data points.

A. Experimental Setup

For all the experiments, a set of input signals are sent through the material and a single output signal is recorded. The input signals are digital square waves in the range $400Hz$ to $25kHz$. The amplitude of the square waves is $0 - 3.3V$, which means that the material is exposed to a sharp rise and fall of the signal in this range. The duty cycle is held constant at 50%.

The output signal is recorded as analog voltage over time and sampled at a frequency of $500kHz$ for 10ms resulting in an output buffer of 5000 samples.

In order to compare the analog output signal to the digital input signal, we digitize the output signal by using the mean voltage as digital threshold. In other words, samples above the mean correspond to logical 1 and samples below the mean correspond to logical 0. To reduce sensitivity to noise, we apply hysteresis so that transitions between logic levels happen only if the analog voltage crosses the mean by a noise margin.

Complexity is estimated by compressing the sample buffer with zlib (zlib is based on LZ77 [36]) and calculating the length of the compressed string. Input complexity C_i is calculated based on a set of ideal square waves sampled at the same frequency as the output signal ($500kHz$).

All the experiments are repeated for the different material samples listed in Table I.

1) Complexity as number of input signals are increased: In the first experiment, the number of input pins are increased from 1 to 15. Input pins are selected at random and for each input pin a random frequency is chosen in the range of $400Hz - 25kHz$. The output signal is recorded from pin #0. The experiment is repeated 100 times for each number of input pins resulting in 1500 output signals.

2) Complexity as function of one input frequency: The second set of experiments provides a more detailed view of a subset of the first experiment by traversing the input frequency spectrum. Frequencies are increased from $400Hz - 25kHz$ in steps of $1000Hz$ resulting in 25 different input frequencies. The number of input pins are again increased from 1 to 15 but the same frequency is now applied to all input pins. In addition, both input pins and output pins are selected at random. For each number of input pins and for each frequency, the experiment is repeated 100 times resulting in 37500 output signals.

3) Complexity as function of two input frequencies: In the third experiment, we again traverse the same input frequency spectrum ($400Hz - 25kHz$), but this time for two input pins. In other words, the frequency spectrum is traversed in

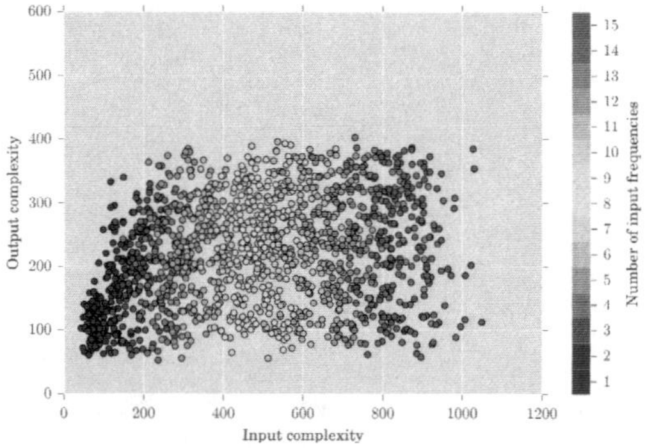

(a) Material B09S12 (0.53 wt% SWCNT)

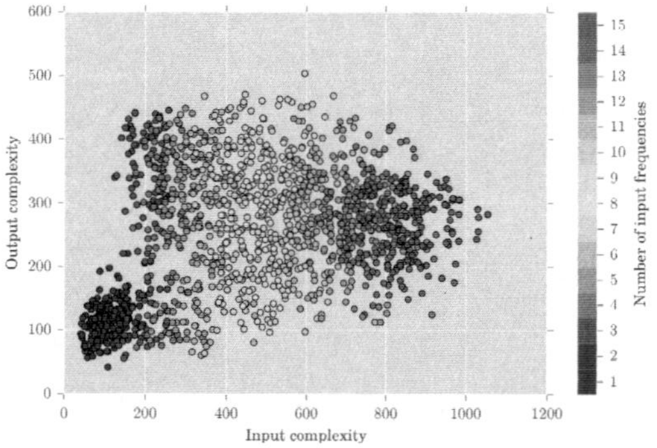

(b) Material B15S03 (1.25 wt% SWCNT)

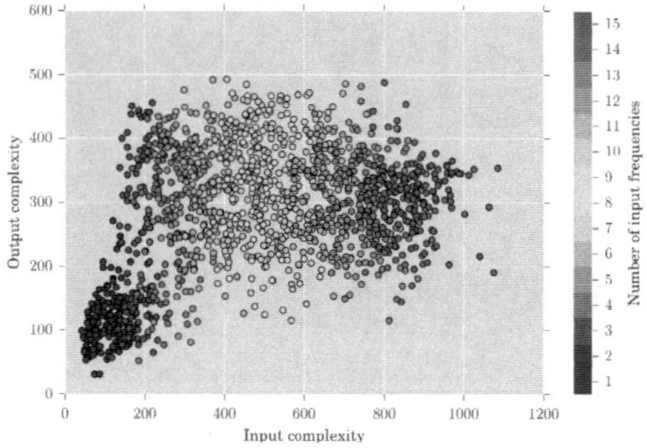

(c) Material B15S04 (1.50 wt% SWCNT)

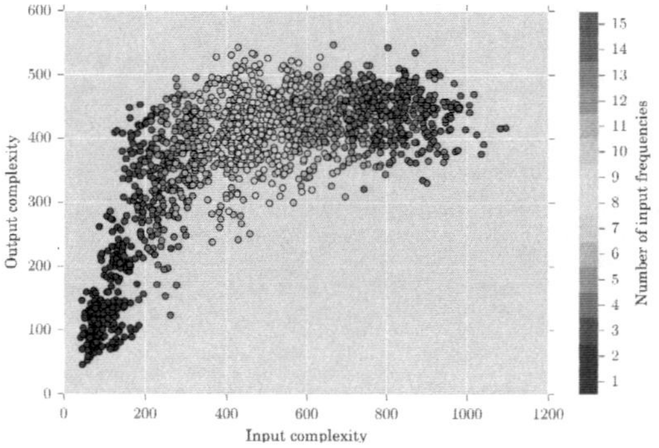

(d) Material B15S08 (5.00 wt% SWCNT)

Figure 9. Input vs output complexity as number of input frequencies are increased from 1 to 15 for four different material samples. The dots are colored according to the number of input frequencies used.

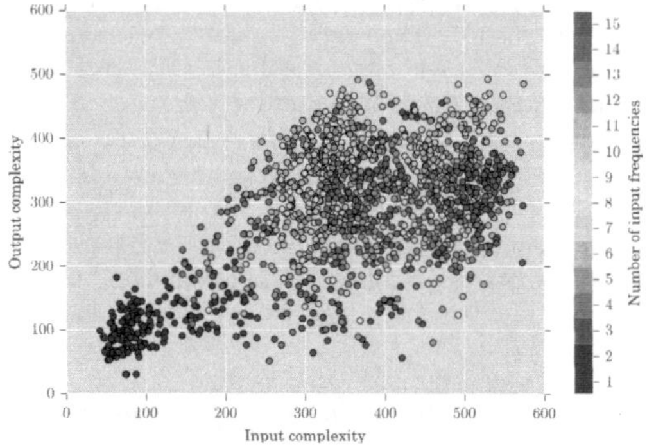

(a) Material B15S04 (1.50 wt% SWCNT)

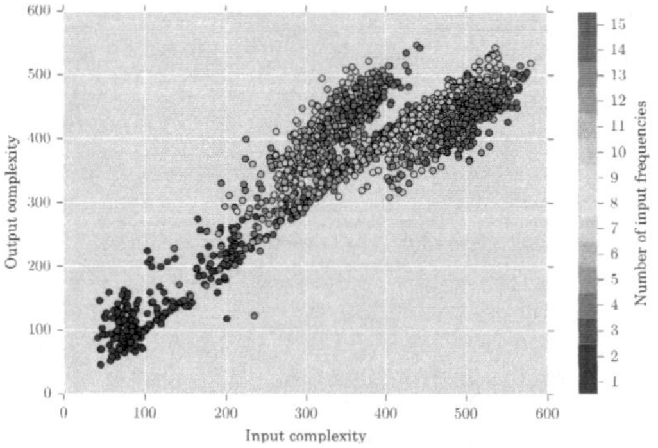

(b) Material B15S08 (5.00 wt% SWCNT)

Figure 10. Input vs output complexity when the input signals are summed together before input complexity is estimated. Results from two material samples with different SWCNT concentrations are shown. The dots are colored according to the number of input frequencies used.

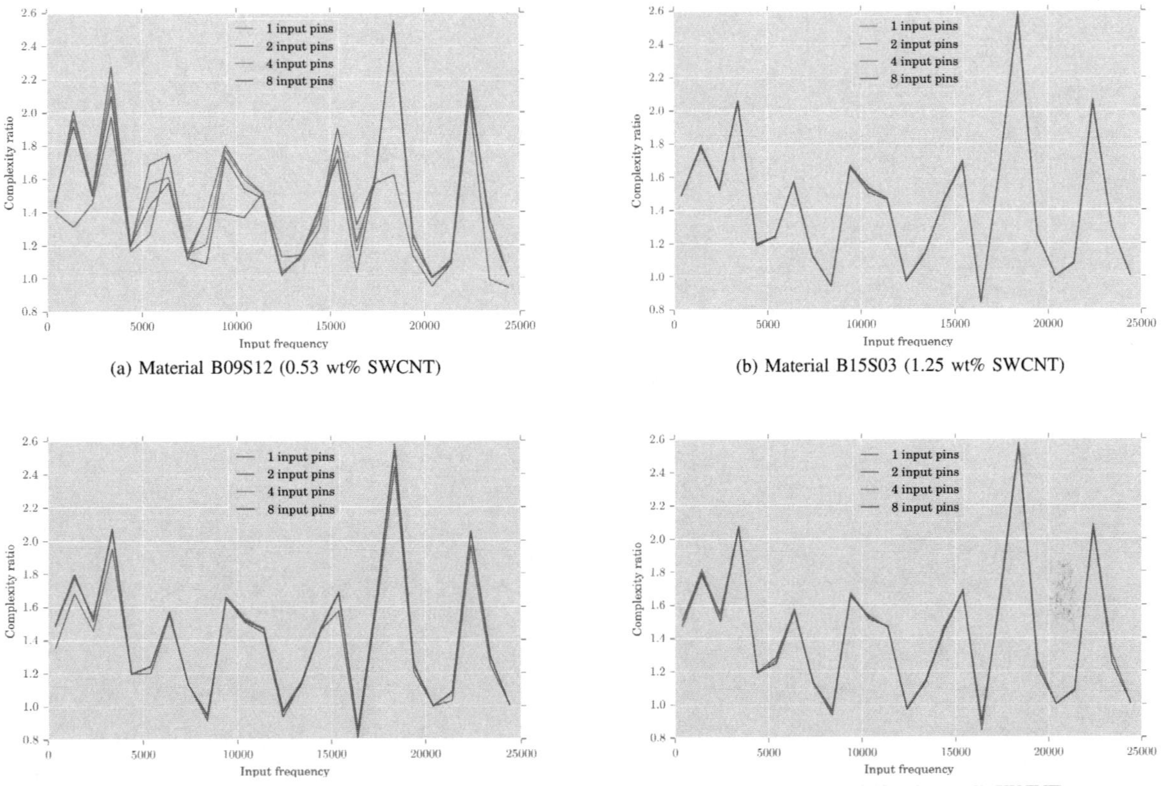

(a) Material B09S12 (0.53 wt% SWCNT)

(b) Material B15S03 (1.25 wt% SWCNT)

(c) Material B15S04 (1.50 wt% SWCNT)

(d) Material B15S08 (5.00 wt% SWCNT)

Figure 11. Mean complexity ratio as function of input frequency for 1, 2, 4 and 8 input pins. The same frequency is applied to all input pins. Results from four different material samples are shown.

two dimensions resulting in 25^2 pairs of input frequencies. Both input pins and output pins are selected at random. The experiment is repeated 10 times for each set of input/output pins.

B. Results and discussion

1) Complexity as number of input signals are increased: Figure 8 shows output complexity C_o measured over the range of 1-15 input frequencies. The blue line shows the mean output complexity value for each of the 100 data points. As shown in the plots, the output complexity increases with the number of input signals. There appears to be a fairly sharp rise in complexity as the number of square wave inputs are increased from 1 to 4. After this point the output complexity appears to saturate.

The scatter plot shows a fairly high variation in output complexity when the number of input signals exceeds one. This indicates that the materials exhibit a rich variety in output depending on the frequency and/or the choice of input pins.

A more detailed view is obtained when output complexity is plotted against input complexity (Figure 9). In these plots, it becomes clear that the input complexity C_i increases almost linearly with the number of input signals. Output complexity, however, saturates quickly above 3-4 input signals. In other words, above this level the added complexity from the input signal is not observed at the output.

Again the richness of output complexity can be observed. The output signal is generally less complex than the input signal, which indicates that the material acts as a filter or stable attractor. However, there are situations where the complexity of the output signal exceeds that of the input signal. The input complexity is estimated from *ideal* square waves, which are not directly comparable to the signals generated by the hardware platform. However, the estimate does give an indication that the materials exhibit rich dynamics.

From Figures 8 and 9 it appears as if higher concentrations of SWCNTs result in higher output complexity. Such a trend is counter-intuitive, since as concentration increases the electrical resistance of the material is reduced. As resistance goes towards zero the material should act more like a wire, which means that the input signals should pass through unaltered. If multiple input signals are sent through a wire, the output signal would simply be the sum of the input signals. Therefore, it would be interesting to investigate how closely the output signal resembles the sum of the input signals.

Figure 10 plots input vs output complexity when the input signals are summed together before C_i is estimated. For the material with high SWCNT concentration (B15S08, Figure

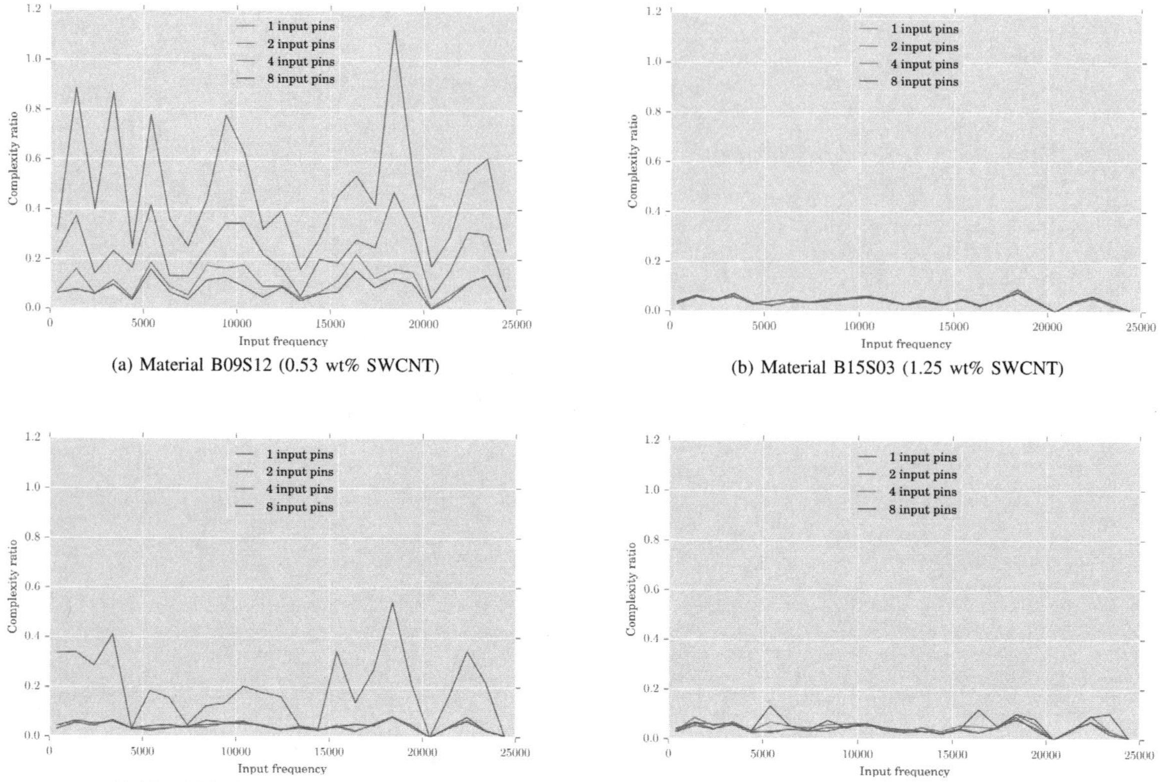

(a) Material B09S12 (0.53 wt% SWCNT)

(b) Material B15S03 (1.25 wt% SWCNT)

(c) Material B15S04 (1.50 wt% SWCNT)

(d) Material B15S08 (5.00 wt% SWCNT)

Figure 12. Standard deviation of complexity ratio as function of input frequency for 1, 2, 4 and 8 input pins. The same frequency is applied to all input pins. Results from four different material samples are shown.

10b) there is now a clear linear relationship between input complexity and output complexity. In other words, this material appears to behave much like a wire that simply sums the input signals together in some way. Lower SWCNT concentrations, however, display more diverse behavior as can be seen in Figure 10a, where there is no clear linear relationship between C_i and C_o.

2) Complexity as function of one input frequency: Figure 11 shows the mean *complexity ratio* C_r over the range of input frequencies applied to the four material samples. From the plots it is evident that C_r is highly dependent on the input frequency with spikes at certain frequencies. Complexity appears to be fairly consistent across the four material samples, i.e., the materials are sensitive to the same frequencies.

Applying the input frequency to more pins does not seem to affect the mean complexity by much. However, there is a clear reduction in complexity variation, as can be seen from Figure 12, where standard deviation of the complexity ratio is shown. One possible explanation is that the input signal is effectively amplified as it is applied to more input pins.

Another trend that can be seen from the plots in Figure 12 is an inverse relationship between complexity variation and the SWCNT concentration, i.e., more uniform output complexity with increased SWCNT concentration. This may be due to the fact that higher SWCNT concentration leads to a lower electrical resistance in the material and thus more pathways for the input signal to reach the output pin. However, one exception can be observed for the B15S04 sample where a higher variation is found when the frequency is applied to only one input pin. This likely indicates that one electrode is only partially connected to the material in this particular sample.

3) Complexity as function of two input frequencies: By sweeping the two input frequencies applied to the material we get a more detailed view of some of the results from the first experiment. Figure 13 depicts complexity ratio as a heat map where the two input frequencies are swept in the X and Y axes and color represents complexity. The colors range from dark purple (low complexity) to bright yellow (high complexity). As with one input signal, the heat maps show clearly that the complexity landscape is dependent on the selection of input frequencies.

Figures 13a and 13b depict complexity for the same material sample B09S12, but with different selection of input and output pins. As can be seen, the two heat maps display clear differences in complexity ratio, where the latter pin configuration (13b) generally exhibits more complex output. However, this is not always the case, as can be seen in Figures 13c and 13d, where different input locations result in quite

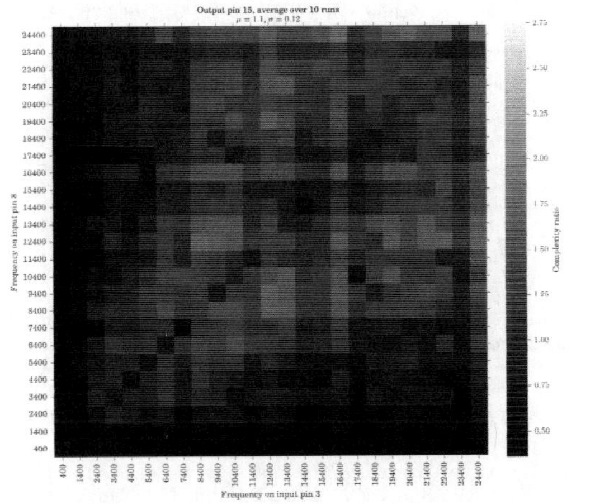

(a) Material B09S12 (0.53 wt% SWCNT), input pins 3 and 8, output pin 15

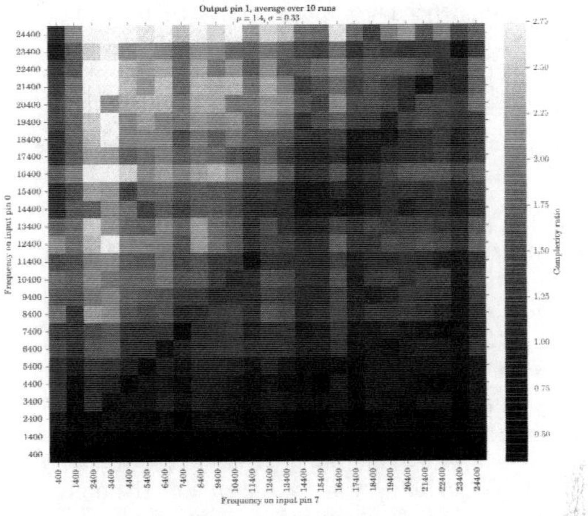

(b) Material B09S12 (0.53 wt% SWCNT), input pins 7 and 0, output pin 1

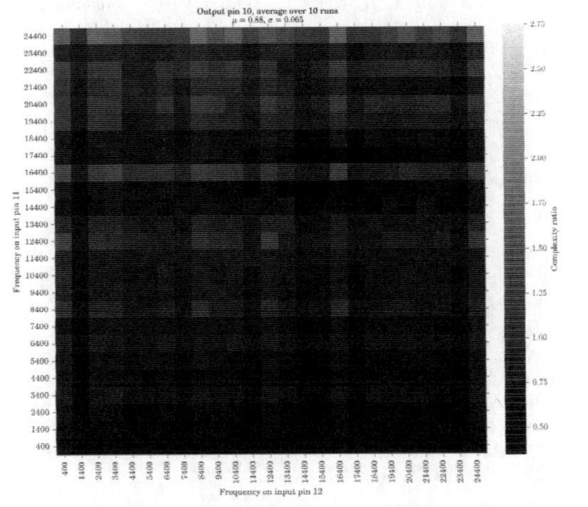

(c) Material B15S08 (5.00 wt% SWCNT), input pins 12 and 11, output pin 10

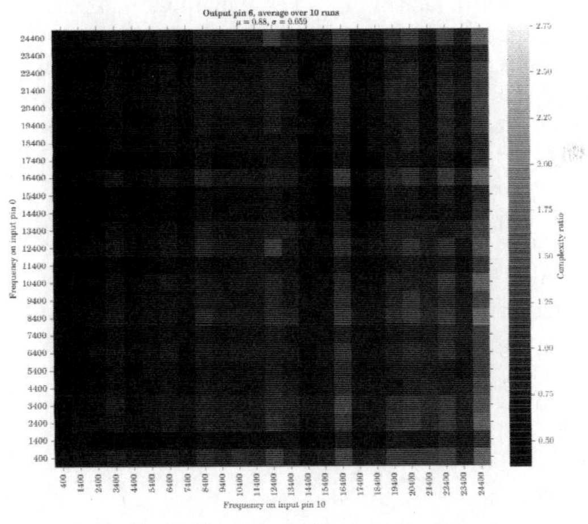

(d) Material B15S08 (5.00 wt% SWCNT), input pins 10 and 0, output pin 6

Figure 13. Complexity ratio as function of two input frequencies (X and Y axes). The heat maps shows complexity ratio C_r averaged over 10 runs. Colors range from dark purple (low complexity) to bright yellow (high complexity). Four heat maps are shown for two material samples: B09S12 (13a-13b) and B15S08 (13c-13d). Each heat map shows complexity when input is applied to different input/output pins.

similar complexity landscapes.

VI. Conclusion

The general ideas, experiments, and results presented relates to dynamics performed by SWCNT and PBMA nanocomposites, which may be exploited by EIM. The materials and experimental system (as presented in Section II) has shown promising computational behavior on a variety of problems. In this work, the behaviors are related to measurable dynamic behavior. That is, the experiments are designed to capture dynamic properties of the materials as to gain an understanding of what inherent dynamics are observable in an EIM setting. The approach taken is to view the material, i.e., physical system, as a hierarchical information processing device (Figure 2). At the bottom level the physical dynamics, i.e., quantum effects due to mechanisms of electron transmission through carbon nanotubes, are not observable within a reasonable resource usage. As such, the lowest level is treated only at a conceptual level. Dynamics at the bottom level are only observed as resulting voltages in the analogue domain. The information available at this level is exploited to gain insight into the electrical properties of the material when exposed to dynamic input stimuli. At the top level the material is interpreted as a discrete dynamical system. However, the observable dynamics at this discrete level is a result of all the underlying physics.

As stated by Miller et al. [3]: "...exploit the intrinsic properties of materials, or "computational mediums", to do computation, where neither the structure nor computational properties of the material needs to be known in advance". The statement may indicate that any material can be looked at as a black-box. However, insight into what properties are available for evolution provides knowledge on how to construct a successful EIM system. Our findings show that the materials exhibit rich dynamical properties observable at the analogue level. Figure 7 shows the behavior at an (close to) analogue time and voltage scale. The properties of these behaviors are available for exploitation by evolution, even if not explicitly controllable from the top discrete digital domain.

At the top level, the abstract measurements of complexity shows how such a measurement can indicate what computational problems the EIM system may handle. Especially, the experimental results from Figure 13 show that the materials tested include behavior found in classifier systems, such as Thompson's frequency discriminator [5] (generally a trend of reduced complexity as illustrated in Figure 13d). From the same experiment, Figure 13b shows an increase in complexity generated by the dynamics of the material. A clear indication of a system which has more internal (observable) states than of the input data.

Our results also reveal several specific properties of the SWCNT materials used. In particular, as the number of input signals grows, a saturation of output complexity is reached. From an EIM perspective this is interesting, since it implies that information is filtered when many input signals are applied. The results also show a wide variety in output complexity depending on input frequency and selection of input/output pins. An indication that the materials are capable of many different modes of operation.

Acknowledgment

The research leading to these results has received funding from the European Community's Seventh Framework Programme (FP/2007-2013) under grant agreement number 317662.

References

[1] S. Nichele, D. Laketić, O. R. Lykkebø, and G. Tufte, "Is there chaos in blobs of carbon nanotubes used to perform computation?" in FUTURE COMPUTING 2015, The Seventh International Conference on Future Computational Technologies and Applications. ThinkMind, 2015, pp. 12–17.

[2] H. Broersma, F. Gomez, J. Miller, M. Petty, and G. Tufte, "Nascence project: nanoscale engineering for novel computation using evolution," International journal of unconventional computing, vol. 8, no. 4, 2012, pp. 313–317.

[3] J. Miller, S. Harding, and G. Tufte, "Evolution-in-materio: evolving computation in materials," Evolutionary Intelligence, vol. 7, no. 1, 2014, pp. 49–67.

[4] J. Miller and K. Downing, "Evolution in materio: Looking beyond the silicon box," in The 2002 NASA/DoD Conference on Evolvable Hardware, A. Stoica, J. Lohn, R. Katz, D. Keymeulen, and R. S. Zebulum, Eds., Jet Propulsion Laboratory, California Institute of Technology. Alexandria, Virginia: IEEE Computer Society, 15-18 July 2002, pp. 167–176.

[5] A. Thompson, Hardware evolution - automatic design of electronic circuits in reconfigurable hardware by artificial evolution. CPHC/BCS distinguished dissertations, 1998.

[6] S. Harding and J. Miller, "Evolution in materio : A real-time robot controller in liquid crystal," in Proceedings of the 2005 NASA/DoD Conference on Evolvable Hardware, J. Lohn, D. Gwaltney, G. Hornby, R. Zebulum, D. Keymeulen, and A. Stoica, Eds. Washington, DC, USA: IEEE Press, 29 June-1 July 2005, pp. 229–238.

[7] P. Cariani, "To evolve an ear: epistemological implications of Gordon Pask's electrochemical devices," Systems Research, vol. 10, no. 3, 1993, pp. 19–33.

[8] K. Clegg, J. Miller, K. Massey, and M. Petty, "Travelling salesman problem solved "in materio" by evolved carbon nanotube device," in Parallel Problem Solving from Nature - PPSN XIII, ser. Lecture Notes in Computer Science, T. Bartz-Beielstein, J. Branke, B. Filipic, and J. Smith, Eds. Springer International Publishing, 2014, vol. 8672, pp. 692–701.

[9] A. Kotsialos, K. Massey, F. Qaiser, D. Zeze, C. Pearson, and M. Petty, "Logic gate and circuit training on randomly dispersed carbon nanotubes." International journal of unconventional computing., vol. 10, no. 5-6, September 2014, pp. 473–497.

[10] M. Mohid, J. Miller, S. Harding, G. Tufte, O. R. Lykkebø, K. Massey, and M. Petty, "Evolution-in-materio: Solving bin packing problems using materials," in The 2014 IEEE Conference on Evolvable Systems - ICES, IN PRESS. IEEE Computer Society, 2014.

[11] M. Mohid, J. Miller, S. Harding, G. Tufte, O. Lykkebø, M. Massey, and M. Petty, "Evolution-in-materio: Solving machine learning classification problems using materials," in Parallel Problem Solving from Nature PPSN XIII, ser. Lecture Notes in Computer Science, T. Bartz-Beielstein, J. Branke, B. Filipic, and J. Smith, Eds. Springer International Publishing, 2014, vol. 8672, pp. 721–730.

[12] M. Mohid, J. Miller, S. Harding, G. Tufte, O. R. Lykkebø, K. Massey, and M. Petty, "Evolution-in-materio: A frequency classifier using materials," in The 2014 IEEE Conference on Evolvable Systems - ICES, IN PRESS. IEEE Computer Society, 2014, pp. 46–53.

[13] M. Mohid, J. Miller, S. Harding, G. Tufte, O. Lykkebo, M. Massey, and M. Petty, "Evolution-in-materio: Solving function optimization problems using materials," in Computational Intelligence (UKCI), 2014 14th UK Workshop on, D. Neagu, M. Kiran, and P. Trundle, Eds. IEEE, September 2014, pp. 1–8.

[14] A. N. Kolmogorov, "Three approaches to the quantitative definition of information," Problems of information transmission, vol. 1, no. 1, 1965, pp. 1–7.

[15] G. Pask, "Physical analogues to growth of a concept," Mechanisation of Thought Processes, 1959, pp. 877–922.

[16] R. Stewart, "Electrochemically active field-trainable pattern recognition systems," Systems Science and Cybernetics, IEEE Transactions on, vol. 5, no. 3, 1969, pp. 230–237.

[17] J. W. Mills, "Polymer processors," Technical Report TR580, Department of Computer Science, University of Indiana, Tech. Rep., 1995.

[18] S. L. Harding and J. F. Miller, "Evolution in materio: Computing with liquid crystal," Journal of Unconventional Computing, vol. 3, no. 4, 2007, pp. 243–257.

[19] S. Harding and J. F. Miller, "Evolution in materio: A tone discriminator in liquid crystal," in Evolutionary Computation, 2004. CEC2004. Congress on, vol. 2. IEEE, 2004, pp. 1800–1807.

[20] ——, "Evolution in materio: Evolving logic gates in liquid crystal," in In Proceedings of the workshop on unconventional computing at ECAL 2005 VIIIth European. Beckington, UK, 2005, pp. 133–149.

[21] M. Mohid and J. Miller, "Evolving robot controllers using carbon nanotubes," in The 2015 European Conference on Artificial Life. The MIT Press, 2015.

[22] T. Kowaliw, "Measures of complexity for artificial embryogeny," in Proceedings of the 10th annual conference on Genetic and evolutionary computation. ACM, 2008, pp. 843–850.

[23] M. Li and P. Vitányi, An introduction to Kolmogorov complexity and its applications. Springer Science & Business Media, 2013.

[24] S. Nichele and G. Tufte, "Measuring phenotypic structural complexity of artificial cellular organisms," in Innovations in Bio-inspired Computing and Applications. Springer, 2014, pp. 23–35.

[25] M. Hartmann, P. K. Lehre, and P. C. Haddow, "Evolved digital circuits and genome complexity," in Evolvable Hardware, 2005. Proceedings. 2005 NASA/DoD Conference on. IEEE, 2005, pp. 79–86.

[26] P. K. Lehre and P. C. Haddow, "Developmental mappings and phenotypic complexity." in IEEE Congress on Evolutionary Computation (1). Citeseer, 2003, pp. 62–68.

[27] H. Zenil and E. Villarreal-Zapata, "Asymptotic behavior and ratios of complexity in cellular automata," International Journal of Bifurcation and Chaos, vol. 23, no. 09, 2013, p. 1350159.

[28] B. J. MacLennan, "A review of analog computing. technical report ut-cs-07-601," University of Tennessee, Knoxville, Tech. Rep., 2007.

[29] H. J. Bremermann, Self-Organizing Systems-1962. Spartan Books, 1962, ch. Optimization through Evolution and Recombination, pp. 93–106.

[30] O. R. Lykkebø, S. Harding, G. Tufte, and J. Miller, "Mecobo: A hardware and software platform for in materio evolution," in Unconventional Computation and Natural Computation - 13th International Conference, UCNC 2014, London, ON, Canada, July 14-18, 2014, Proceedings, 2014, pp. 267–279.

[31] A. S. Foundation, "Apache thrift," accessed: 2016-06-07. [Online]. Available: https://thrift.apache.org/

[32] W. R. Ashby, Design for a Brain, the origin of adaptive behaviour. Chapman & Hall Ltd., 1960.

[33] L. von Bertalanffy, General System Theory. George Braziller, Inc., Revised edition, Fourth printing, 1973.

[34] D. Laketić, G. Tufte, S. Nichele, and O. R. Lykkebø, "An explanation of computation - collective electrodynamics in blobs of carbon nanotubes," in Proceedings of the 9th EAI International Conference on Bio-Inspired Information and Communications Technologies (formerly BIONETICS). EAI, ACM Digital Library, 2015.

[35] O. R. Lykkebø, S. Nichele, and G. Tufte, "An investigation of square waves for evolution in carbon nanotubes material," Proceedings of the European Conference on Artificial Life, 2015, pp. 503–510.

[36] J. Ziv and A. Lempel, "A universal algorithm for sequential data compression," IEEE Transactions on Information Theory, vol. 23, no. 3, May 1977, pp. 337–343.

Near-wall Thermometry Using Brownian Motion of PIV Particle Tracers

Kanjirakat Anoop
Mechanical Engineering Program
Texas A&M University at Qatar
Education City, Doha, Qatar
anoop.baby@qatar.tamu.edu

Reza Sadr
Mechanical Engineering Program
Texas A&M University at Qatar
Education City, Doha, Qatar
reza.sadr@qatar.tamu.edu

Abstract— **The present work reports an application of near-wall (on the order of 100 nm) thermometry utilizing Brownian motion of nano-particle image velocimetry (nPIV) tracer particles within a solid-fluid interface. Initially, a Monte Carlo simulation of Brownian particle movement in the evanescent wave region in the fluid-wall interface was employed to optimize the relevant measurement parameters. The results of the numerical simulation showed that the ratio of peak-width to peak-height of the nPIV correlation function could be successfully used as a temperature measurement index in the flow. Furthermore, the percentages of the particles remaining in the visible depth of the evanescent wave region may be considered as another thermometric parameter. Experimental studies using an objective-based evanescent wave technique were conducted to verify the results of the numerical simulations and to establish the experimental uncertainty of the temperature measurement. The experimental results verify the feasibility of temperature measurement within ±2.5°C accuracy bond and an out-of-plane resolution of O (100 nm) within the wall region. Variations of the evanescent wave thickness, i.e., out-of-plane resolution of thermometry, did not affect the sensitivity of the temperature measurement. However, the temperature range measured using the objective-based total internal reflection technique was limited due to changes in the optical characteristics of the imaging setup at higher temperatures.**

Keywords- Evanescent wave; Near-wall thermometry; nano-PIV; PIV.

I. INTRODUCTION

This paper is an extension of our previous work reported in ICQNM 2012 [1]. Temperature measurement, or thermometry, is of paramount significance in many industrial applications as well as in scientific research [2]. Recently, advancements in micro fabrication techniques have made it possible to miniaturize fluidic devices to the micro scale [3]. In this fluid transport regime, or microfluidics, fluid flows through small channels with overall dimensions on the order of 10 to 100 μm. Micro-heat exchangers, micro-mixers, polymerase chain reaction (PCR) microchips, microfluidic incubators, and Lab-on-a-chip devices are some examples of microfluidic applications. Microfluidic platforms are the main structure of the so-called Lab-on-a-chip systems that have helped to reduce not only the testing sample size but also the process time and component cost in biochemistry.

Thermometry at the microscale is an important requirement in the design and operation of micro-thermal devices for a wide range of applications, such as biological reactions, chemical processing fuel cells, and heat exchangers. [4]. Temperature-induced control of gene expressions and tumor metabolism, for example, requires accurate thermometry inside living cells for implementation [5]. Kucsko et al. [6] developed a nanometer-scale thermometry method in living cells utilizing the coherent manipulation of the electronic spin associated nitrogen-vacancy color centers in diamond. Temperature variations as small as 1.8 mK were detected using this technique. Chaudhari et al. [7] demonstrated the use of transient liquid crystal thermometry of micro fabricated PCR vessels for DNA replication. The reflected wavelengths of light from these excited liquid crystals are strongly dependent on the sample temperature. PCR processes require an accurate cycling of sample temperature, and the measurement of temperature uniformity in a micro-fabricated vessel array using encapsulated liquid crystal was demonstrated. Temperatures were measured with a resolution of ±0.5°C. Thermo-chromic liquid crystal–based slurries and paints have been reported to measure surface temperatures with a maximum spatial resolution of 1 μm [8].

Thermometry also plays a crucial role in electronic cooling inside miniaturized devices. In micro-electronic device systems, the exponential growth of component density has generated challenging thermal management issues for implementation. The present local chip heat fluxes are much higher for forced-air cooling techniques to effectively dissipate heat from the hotspots [9]. Single-phase forced-liquid and two-phase evaporative cooling techniques are currently designed for the microprocessors for better efficiencies. These cooling devices consist of mini or micro channels for maintaining a coolant flow through the microprocessors. Accurate measurements of the wall surface and bulk fluid temperatures would help to better estimate the heat transfer coefficients. Measurements with micron-scale spatial resolution without disturbing the flow would further assist in the better design of these channels.

With the available measurement methodologies, micro-scale thermometry techniques that can measure wall surface and bulk fluid temperatures can be broadly classified as invasive or non-invasive thermometry [2]. The invasive technique, for example, includes micro- or nano-thermocouples, resistance temperature detectors (RTD), scanning thermal probes, and atomic force microscope (AFM) temperature probes. Non-invasive thermometry includes optical thermometry, liquid crystal thermometry, infrared thermometry, and Raman thermometry [10] .

Invasive, or contact-based, methods use standard CMOS (complementary metal-oxide semiconductor) technologies in the installation of conventional temperature sensors inside micro- or mini-channels. In small-scale applications, an array of diode sensors was used for surface temperature measurement at small scale [11]. However, the spatial resolution was relatively low because it depended on the dimensions of the diodes used. Additionally, this technique required intricate fabrication procedures for both the sensor array and the control unit. Han and Kim measured the surface temperature of a square area using a 32x32-diode array with a spatial resolution on the order of one hundred microns. Watanabe et al. [12] investigated the use of micro thermocouple probes for measuring cellular thermal responses. Williams and Wickramasinghe [13] introduced the concept of scanning thermal microscopy (SThM) by fabricating a 1000nm nm thermocouple at the end of a scanning tunneling microscope tip. The AFM-based thermal probe also works under similar principles [14]. Kim et al [15] used the SThM technique to measure temperature fields in a vacuum with a spatial resolution of 10 nm and a temperature resolution of 15 mK. The above measurement methods were not suitable for whole-field temperature measurement. In addition, these methods required electrical connections that could produce electromagnetic noise along with possible sparks. These effects could deter their use in corrosive environments. However, these sensors are intrusive, and their application can affect the micro-scale flow structure. Because of this limitation, non-invasive methods are generally preferred.

For the past few decades, many attempts have been made to measure the temperature field at the microscale with non-invasive or non-contact modes. Non-invasive thermometric methods such as molecular tagging thermometry (MTT), infrared thermometry (IRT), laser-induced fluorescence thermometry (LIFT) and particle image velocimetry (PIV)-based thermometry are generally preferred for micro-scale flow investigations [16-18]. Infrared thermography has been used to measure the surface temperature of microchannel heat sinks [19]. However, the emissivity values of the tested medium need to be known to accurately predict the temperature in this technique. LIFT is based on the temperature dependence of fluorescent dye intensity dissolved in the fluid and has been widely used in micro-fluidics thermometry. Ross et al. [20] demonstrated an application of the LIF method using a single dye and measured temperatures with a maximum uncertainty of 3.5°C. A two-color LIF method was suggested to overcome the uncertainties caused by possibly non-uniform illumination [21]. Rayleigh-Bernard convection was investigated using two-color laser-induced fluorescence by Sakakibara and Adrian [22]. Kim and Yoda [23] used a dual-tracer fluorescence thermometry technique at the microscale and showed a measurement uncertainty of ± 1.1°C at a spatial resolution of 3.7 μm in their work. Thompson and Maynes [24] utilized phosphorescence tracer dyes to simultaneously quantify fluid temperature and fluid velocity fields using MTT and molecular tagging velocimetry (MTV), respectively. Hu and Koochesfahani [25] conducted a simultaneous whole-field measurement of velocity and temperature using the MTT technique and were able to measure temperature with an uncertainty of 0.23°C.

Fluorescent particle tracers seeded in the fluid for micro- or nano-PIV are small and undergo Brownian motion [26] This motion can introduce a bias in PIV fluid velocity measurements at low velocity when using a cross-correlation method by increasing the width and reducing the height of the correlation peak. This is an undesirable effect in velocimetry as it reduces the signal-to-noise ratio of the results and increases the uncertainty of determining the average particle displacement. Olsen and Adrian [27] proposed that such spreading of the correlation peak width could be utilized for thermometry because the Brownian motion of the seeded particles has a direct dependence on the fluid temperature. Hohreiter et al. [28] demonstrated the use of a cross-correlation-based micro-PIV (μPIV) technique utilizing the Brownian motion of seeded particles to determine the temperature. Their results showed temperature measurement with an experimental accuracy of ± 3°C inside a microchannel. In a separate study, Chamarthy et al. [29] noted that a low image density PIV tracking method to process particle images performed better than the cross-correlation method for thermometry. The average difference between the predicted and measured fluid temperature was recorded to be ± 2.6°C with an out-of-plane resolution of approximately 20 μm.

Park et al. [30] showed the potential application of optical serial sectioning microscopy method (OSSM) for temperature measurement utilizing Brownian motion of nanoparticles in a fluid away from the wall. OSSM uses diffraction patterns of particle images to track its full three-dimensional Brownian motion. They used a dry objective lens to detect the diffraction patterns of 500 nm polystyrene fluorescent nanoparticles suspended in water at a low volume concentration of 4×10^{-6}. Their experiments for a fluid temperature range of 5 to 70°C showed a correlation between the Brownian diffusivity and the mean square displacement (MSN) of nanoparticles that could potentially be used in a non-intrusive and micro-scale thermometry for nanoparticle suspension fluids. However, in the near-wall region, the Brownian motion of nanoparticles is non-isotropic and hindered, and the estimated diffusion will not be same as that in the bulk flow. Moreover, in the micro-scale measurements discussed above, volume illumination is commonly used, which makes the measurements more complicated.

nPIV is an extension of μPIV, where illumination is provided only in the region very close to the wall on the order of O (100 nm) [31-36]. nPIV is based on evanescent-wave illumination created by the total internal reflection (TIR) of a laser beam at the fluid-solid interface. At the sub-micron scale, Brownian displacement is of the same length scale as that of the fluid convection and can therefore greatly affect fluid velocimetry when using particle tracers. The effect of hindered Brownian motion in the near-wall region is prominently visible in nPIV measurements as particles move in and out of visible depth during the nPIV imaging time interval [36-38]. This movement could cause the cross-correlation peak-widths in nPIV measurements to behave in a different manner than that in μPIV measurements. We reported a simple numerical investigation of the effect of fluid temperature variation on the nPIV correlation function in the evanescent wave region in the near-wall region [1]. We showed that the PIV correlation function characteristics of the hindered Brownian motion of tracer particles in the near-wall region could be utilized for temperature measurements. However, the effect of the variation in fluorescence intensity of tracer particles and surface forces caused by the temperature change, which occurs in practical thermometry with fluorescence particles, were not considered.

The present work aims to extend and apply our earlier study [1] for near-wall temperature measurements, or nano-particle image thermometry (nPIT), to a wider temperature range and implement it in a real experimental setup. Prior to actual nPIV experimentation, the feasibility of the technique for non-intrusive near-wall temperature measurement is initially investigated using a Monte Carlo simulation to study the effect of temperature on the cross-correlation function peak-width and peak-height in the near-wall hindered Brownian motion. Artificial nPIV images are generated for fluids at stationary conditions and varying temperatures to include experimental effects such as non-uniform illumination, hindered Brownian motion, particle-wall surface forces, and temperature dependence of particle fluorescent intensity. Experiments are then performed under similar conditions to verify the results of the simulations and establish the applicability of nPIT and its experimental uncertainties and to demonstrate the practicability of using an objective-based nPIT setup for near-wall temperature measurement.

The remainder of this paper is organized as follows. In Section II the methods used in our analysis are described. Theoretical background for the thermometric method is also presented, and we describe our experimental setup and methodology used in the experimental measurements. The results are presented in Section III. Finally, we present our conclusions and ideas for future work in Section IV.

II. METHOD

A. Theoretical

As mentioned earlier, the nPIV method makes use of the evanescent wave generated at the glass-water interface to illuminate particles only in the near-wall region. Fig. 1 shows a schematic of the experimental setup for the present study. Here, the light beam passes through a microscope objective and microscope slide, with refractive index n_1 into the transparent fluid (water) with a lower refractive index, n_2, at an angle exceeding the critical angle, causing total internal reflection at the interface.

$$\theta_c = \sin^{-1}(n_2/n_1) \tag{1}$$

The electromagnetic field enters into the lower refractive index region and propagates parallel to the interface, creating an evanescent wave close to the interface. This evanescent wave excites the fluorescent particles in this region, while the particles further away in the bulk liquid remain unexcited. Intensity of the evanescent wave decays exponentially with distance normal to the wall (z),

$$I = I_o e^{\left(-\frac{z}{z_p}\right)} . \tag{2}$$

I_0 is the maximum intensity at the wall and z_p is the penetration depth, given as:

$$z_p = \frac{\lambda_0}{4\pi n_1}\left[sin^2\theta - \left(\frac{n_2}{n_1}\right)^2\right]^{-\frac{1}{2}} . \tag{3}$$

Here λ_0 is the wavelength of the light and θ is the incident angle. For visible light at a glass-water interface, z_p is on the order of O (100 nm). However, the effective depth of the visible region z_v depends on the optical features of the imaging system: penetration depth, intensity of the incident laser beam, fluorescent particle properties, and characteristics of the imaging camera. In an actual experiment, z_v typically ranges from 300 to 400 nm. In an nPIV setup, the objective lenses generally have a larger focal depth than the penetration depth of the evanescent wave, and all of the particles in the image are in focus [36].

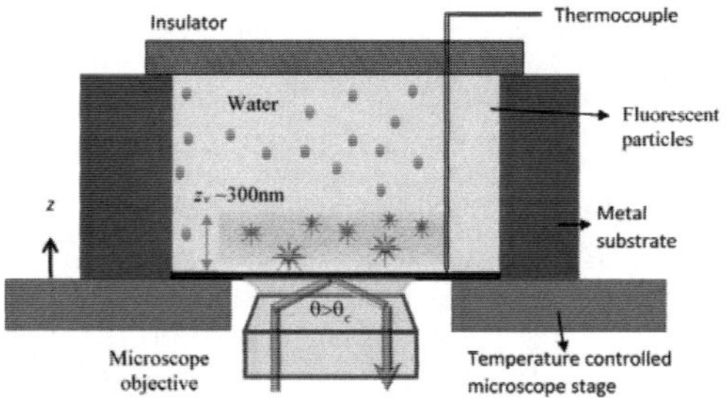

Figure 1: Schematic of nPIV measurement technique and the experimental setup used (not to scale)

For a stationary fluid, Brownian motion and surface forces govern the particle movement in the wall region. Brownian motion is usually characterized in terms of its diffusion coefficient. In an unconfined flow, the Stokes-Einstein equation represents the Brownian diffusion coefficient in the form given below [34].

$$D = \frac{kT}{6\pi\mu a} \tag{4}$$

Here k is the Boltzmann constant and T, a and μ are the temperature, diameter of particle and viscosity of the fluid, respectively. In addition to the direct dependence of the diffusion coefficient on temperature, the absolute viscosity of liquids also decreases with temperature. In the region close to the wall where nPIT is performed, the diffusion coefficient is hindered due to the additional hydrodynamic effects at the wall. The diffusion coefficient in this region is different from the value in Equation (1) and is different in the directions parallel and normal to the wall [34]. In the near-wall region, where nPIT is interrogating, the diffusion coefficient is hindered due to the additional hydrodynamic effects at the wall and the Brownian diffusion coefficient, β, can be expressed in the tensor form as:

$$D = \begin{bmatrix} D_x & 0 & 0 \\ 0 & D_y & 0 \\ 0 & 0 & D_z \end{bmatrix} = \mathrm{D}\begin{bmatrix} \beta_{\parallel} & 0 & 0 \\ 0 & \beta_{\parallel} & 0 \\ 0 & 0 & \beta_{\perp} \end{bmatrix}. \quad (5)$$

$\beta_{\perp}$ and $\beta_{\parallel}$ are the wall correction factors for movement perpendicular and parallel to the wall, respectively [11]:

$$\beta_{\parallel} = \left[1 - \frac{9}{16}\left(\frac{a}{z}\right) + \frac{1}{8}\left(\frac{a}{z}\right)^3 - \frac{45}{256}\left(\frac{a}{z}\right)^4 - \frac{1}{16}\left(\frac{a}{z}\right)^5\right] \quad (6)$$

and

$$\beta_{\perp} = \left[\frac{2h \cdot (3h + a)}{6h^2 + 9ah + 2a^2}\right], \quad (7)$$

where a is the particle radius and $h=(z-a)$. As the particles move away from the wall, the correction factors tend to unity and the diffusion coefficient tends to that of the Stokes-Einstein value. In the present simulation, this anisotropic nature of Brownian diffusion coefficient is considered. Quantifying the relative changes in particle movement due to Brownian motion is the key principle used in nPIT. In the present simulation, this anisotropic nature of the Brownian diffusion coefficient is considered. Quantifying the relative changes in particle movement due to Brownian motion is the key principle used in nPIT. Details of the numerical simulation are presented next.

In the numerical simulation, particle displacement over a time period Δt due to Brownian motion $\Delta\vec{r} = \Delta x.\hat{\imath} + \Delta y.\hat{\jmath} + \Delta z.\hat{k}$ (where i, j, k are unit vectors in Car tesian co-ordinate system) is obtained from the Langevin equation [31, 35]. For a stationary fluid with no external forces acting on the particle, the Langevin equation in the direction parallel to the wall reduces to

$$\Delta x = \Delta y = \sum_{t=0}^{t=\Delta t} \{\chi \delta r\} \quad (8)$$

where χ is white noise and $\delta r = \sqrt{2D\delta t}$. Here, diffusion (D represents diffusion coefficient) is considered in the direction parallel to the wall. In the z direction perpendicular to the wall, the Langevin equation reduces to

$$\Delta z = \sum_{t=0}^{t=\Delta t} \left\{\frac{D_z}{kT} F_z \delta t + \frac{dD_z}{dz} \delta t + \chi \delta r\right\} \quad (9)$$

where D_z is the diffusion coefficient normal to the wall and t represents time. The presence of the wall has a significant effect on the distribution of particles in the near-wall region through surface-induced forces on the particles. The external forces (F_z) acting on the particles in the direction perpendicular to the wall include electrostatic (*el*) and van der Waals (*vdw*) forces caused by the presence of the wall as well as the buoyancy force (*b*). The sum of these forces results in a non-uniform particle distribution within the suspending medium in the wall region. The total force acting on a particle in the direction normal to the wall would be the summation of all of these forces, $Fz = F_{el} + F_{vdw} + F_b$, which generates a net repulsive force that pushes the tracers away from the wall.

From DLVO (Derjaguin, Landau, Vervey, and Overbeek) theory, the electrostatic repulsive force, F_{el}, is expressed as [39]

$$F_{el} = 4\pi\varepsilon_0\varepsilon a \left(\frac{kT}{e}\right)^2 \left(\frac{\hat{\zeta}_p + 4\gamma_p \Psi a\kappa}{1 + \Psi a\kappa}\right)(4\gamma_w)\kappa e^{-\kappa(z-a)} \quad (10)$$

where $\kappa = 1/\lambda$, $\hat{\zeta}_p = e\zeta_p / kT$, $\hat{\zeta}_w = e\zeta_w / kT$,

$\gamma_p = \tanh(\hat{\zeta}_p/4)$, $\gamma_w = \tanh(\hat{\zeta}_w/4)$, $\Psi = (\hat{\zeta}_p - 4\gamma_p)/2\gamma_p^3$ and ε_0 is the vacuum electrostatic permeability. ε is the dielectric constant of the fluid, e is the elementary charge, λ is the wall's Debye length, and ζ_p and ζ_w are the zeta potentials of the particle and wall, respectively.

The van der Waals forces, F_{vdw}, can be expressed as [39]:

$$F_{vdw} = \frac{A}{6}\left[\frac{1}{(z-a)} - \frac{a}{(z-a)^2} - \frac{1}{(z+a)} - \frac{1}{(z+a)^2}\right] \quad (11)$$

where Hamaker's constant, A, is of order $O(10^{-20})$ for a spherical particle near a flat wall [33].

The buoyancy force acting on a particle suspended in a fluid is due to the difference in weight between the particle and the displaced fluid and is expressed as:

$$F_b = \frac{4\pi}{3} a^3 g(\rho_p - \rho_f) \quad (12)$$

where ρ_p and ρ_f are the particle and fluid densities, respectively, and g is the gravitational acceleration. This force is observed to be negligible when compared to the electrostatic and van der Waals forces. The effects of temperature on viscosity, Debye length, zeta potential [40], and the dielectric constant value of water [41] are also included in the simulation.

For Monte Carlo simulations, artificial images of tracer particles at time t = 0 and later at time $t = \Delta t$ are generated. Particle Brownian displacements in the x, y, and z directions are calculated for different time steps of $\Delta t = \sum\delta t$ using Equations (2) and (3) by including all the above-mentioned forces. The time step used in this work, $\delta t = 5\ \mu$s, is much smaller than Δt and is orders of magnitude larger than the particle momentum relaxation time [36]. Particle–wall collisions are considered perfectly elastic, preventing any particles from going 'through' the wall.

Particles were assumed to be circular with intensity values following a Gaussian distribution profile. The peak intensity values were selected from the experimental observations. In the present work, an illumination with exponential decaying intensity was considered in artificial images. The level of decay intensity was similar to the evanescent wave illumination in the described experiments. For a given optical setup undergoing total internal reflection, the brightness (or size) of a particle in the image is an inverse function of its distance from the wall, where particles near the wall look bigger and brighter than those farther away. This variation in particle sizes in the field is created by implementing the exponentially decaying intensity of illumination normal to the wall combined with a fixed image noise level. An effective particle image diameter of four pixels with an airy disk pattern was employed for the brightest particle in the simulation.

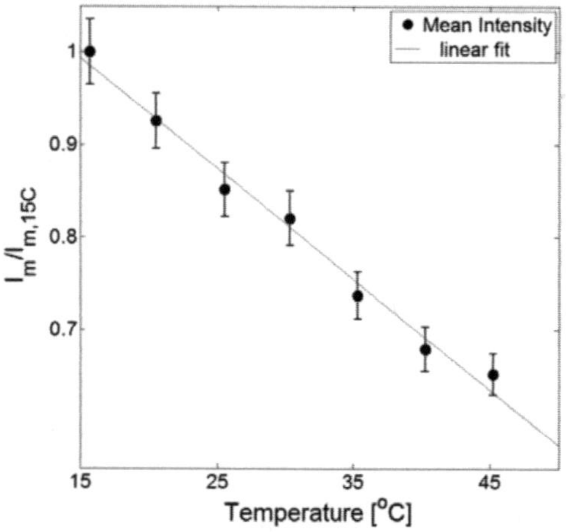

Figure 2: Variation of mean intensity of particles with temperature in experimental images

The excitation intensity of most fluorescent dyes varies with temperature. Initial experimental observations revealed that the mean particle intensity of the tracer beads also decreased with increasing temperature. Such variations can affect the PIT processing results to obtain temperature information from the obtained experimental images. The seeded particles used in this experiment were 100 nm (±5%) diameter polystyrene fluorescent particles (F8803, Invitrogen). Experiments were performed to quantify this effect, and Fig. 2 shows the results of the mean intensity of particles averaged over 100 images and normalized by their intensity at 15°C. This figure shows that the tracer particle intensity drops approximately 1.2 percent/°C for the temperature range tested. This effect is considered in the simulation of the generated nPIT images. Electronic noise and shot noise were also added to images using a combination of white and Gaussian distribution noise, respectively, to mimic real image characteristics [31].

A total of 1,200 particles with a radius of 50 nm were initially distributed over a distance of 875 nm normal to the wall in the fluid for the simulation. This resulted in a particle density of ~2.83 particles/μm^3 and an image size of (200x180 pixels (corresponding to 50μmx45μm), in the (x, y) directions, similar to the actual experimental images. Particles are initially uniformly distributed in the flow and then surface forces move the particles to their final steady state distribution. The final Probability Distribution Function (PDF) of the particles location throughout the visible region, z_v, at this stage is shown in Fig. 3 for two cases: a) with no surfaces forces, and b) with surface forces for ζ-potentials of $\zeta_{particle}$ = 100mV and ζ_{wall} = 80mV, respectively [35, 42]. The surface forces and zeta potential of the particles and surface contribute significantly to the distribution of particles near the wall. As the figure shows, when the surface force effects are considered, the particles are pushed away from the wall region, creating a sparse particle density near the walls. The probability distribution function of the particles, for a given surface force, can adequately be modeled by a Boltzmann profile for the steady state condition [35]

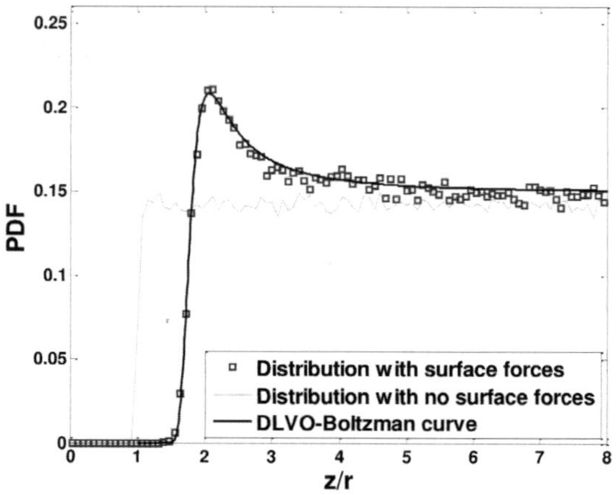

Figure 3: Probability distribution function of particle distribution throughout z_v

The image pairs were then processed using a standard FFT-based cross-correlation program to determine the width and height of the correlation peaks [31]. This program used a 3D Gaussian peak-finding algorithm based on a surface fit of 13 points in the peak region,

$$G(x,y) = A \cdot e^{\frac{-(x-x_0)}{2\sigma_x^2}} \times e^{\frac{-(y-y_0)}{2\sigma_y^2}}, \qquad (13)$$

where A is the peak height , σ_x and σ_y are representative peak widths in x and y directions, respectively. For a stationary fluid, the widths in both the x and y directions were similar in magnitude [29], therefore, the average peak-width value of x and y is presented.

Figure 4: Typical experimental (left) and simulation (right) nPIT images

B. Experimental setup

An objective-based nPIV experimental setup [43] shown in Fig. 1 was used to obtain experimental images at a constant fluid temperature. A constant temperature condition was achieved by placing a small fluid cell made of aluminum, the measurement cell, on top of a temperature-controlled inverted microscope stage. The measurement cell was made of an aluminum substrate with a glass coverslip (0.13 mm thick) pasted below it to provide optical access for the total internal reflection and imaging of the surface of the coverslip in the confined fluid. The fluid cell and microscope stage was insulated on the top. The microscope stage temperature and that of the fluid cell on it were maintained at a constant value by circulating water through the microscope stage from a constant-temperature supply tank (F25-ED Julabo). Prior to each experiment, the fluid was preheated to the temperature of the microscope stage to achieve a faster steady state condition. The fluid temperature in the fluid cell and in contact with the glass cover slip was recorded using precision K-type thermocouples. Experiments were conducted at a steady state condition where the fluid temperature was measured with an accuracy of ±0.1°C during each experiment.

The near-wall region was illuminated using an Ar-Ion continuous wave laser beam to excite the fluorescent particles. An EMCCD camera (ProEM 512, Princeton) attached to the microscope (Leica DMI6000B) captured images via a 63x1.47 NA oil immersion objective. The pixel resolution obtained from this imaging setup was 4,106 (pixels/meter). The seeded fluorescent particles had peak excitation and emission wavelengths of 505 nm and 515 nm, respectively. In all of experimental runs, the particle concentration was maintained at a constant volume fraction of 0.02%. Evanescent wave illumination was generated on the lower glass-water interface of the fluid cell with a laser beam incident angle of 63°. The depth of the visible region (z_v) was estimated to be z_v=350±25 nm based on the penetration depth (z_p of approximately 150 nm) and the intensity value of background noise in the captured images. Fig. 4 shows a typical experiment and simulated nPIT images obtained at 20°C.

For each experiment at varying fluid temperatures, 1,500 image pairs of 200x170 pixels were acquired with an inter-frame time delay of 1.6 ms. The interrogation window size was set to 180×150 pixels with a search radius of 20 pixels to ensure sufficient numbers of matched tracer particles in the interrogation windows. The images were then post-processed using the same cross-correlation program used in the simulation section to determine the correlation peak-widths and peak-heights.

III. RESULTS AND DISCUSSION

Equation (3) shows that Brownian displacement for a given fluid and particle size depends on the temperature and the inter-frame time delay Δt. Monte Carlo simulation was used to establish the effect of inter-frame time delay on PIV cross-correlation peak characteristics for different fluid temperatures. Synthetic images at different inter-frame time delays matching those of a typical nPIT experiment (1, 2, and 4 ms) were generated for the analysis. Image processing and analysis parameters were also kept equal to those used for experimental images.

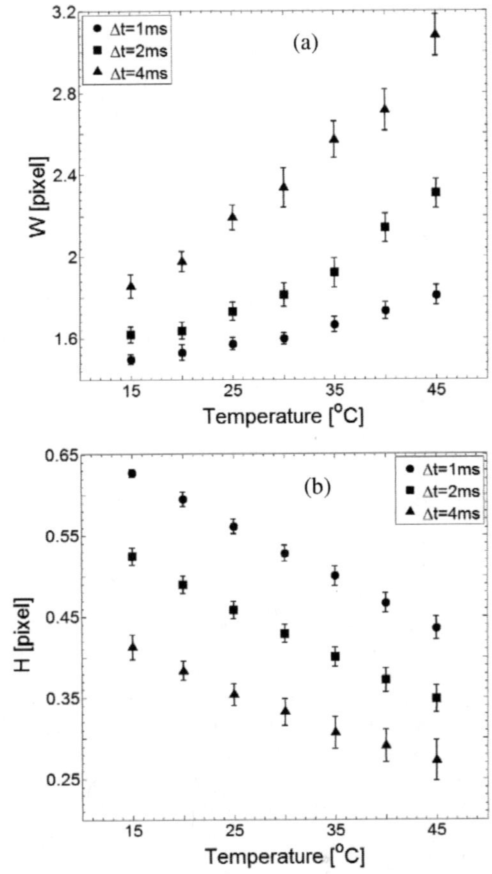

Figure 5: Peak-width variation with temperature (top) and peak-height variation (bottom) with temperature

Fig. 5a shows the variation of the calculated cross-correlation function peak-widths (W) for synthetic nPIT images for the three inter-frame time delays, with error bars representing 95% confidence intervals [44]. This figure shows a semi-linear increase in the width of the nPIT correlation function with temperature for all of the time delays considered. Fig. 5b shows the variation of the peak-height (H) with temperature for the same time delays given in Fig. 5a. The correlation peak value shows a decreasing trend with temperature due to the increase in Brownian motion of the particles. Fig. 5 shows that in addition to an increase in the magnitude of the error bars with temperature, the calculated uncertainty at a given temperature increases when the time delay increases from 1 ms to 4 ms. The increase in experimental uncertainty due to an increase in inter-frame time delay may be associated with levels of the tracer particle mismatch caused by particle drop off due to Brownian motion [36].

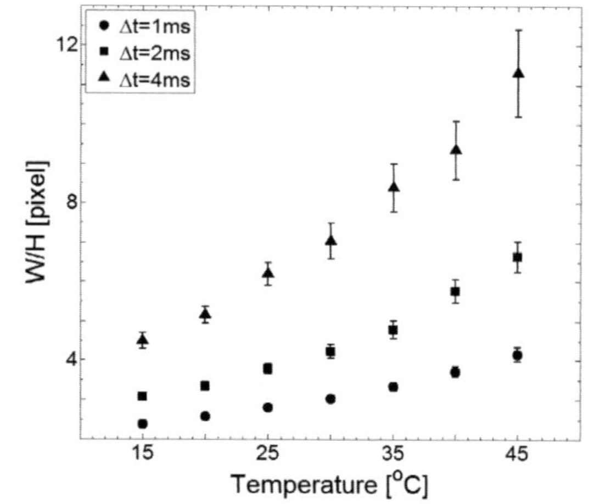

Figure 6: Variation of peak-width-to-height ratio with temperature obtained from the numerical simulation

Because the peak-width and peak-height variations seem to have opposite trends, the ratio of peak-width to peak-height is proposed as a better parameter for thermometry that offers a higher level of sensitivity than temperature measurement. The peak-width to peak-height ratio variation for various temperatures is depicted in Fig. 6. The temperature measurement sensitivity increases with increasing time delays, which can be attributed to a stronger effect of temperature on Brownian displacement of particle-tracers for longer time delays. However, measurement uncertainty also increases as the inter-frame time delay increases due to the deterioration of cross-correlation estimates. Considering additional experimental uncertainties, a smaller inter-frame time delay is preferable for an experiment, even though it has a slightly lower sensitivity to temperature variations.

After verifying the feasibility of using the nPIT technique based on Monte Carlo simulations, experiments were conducted to validate the results of the simulation. The nPIT images of the stationary fluid sample at varying bulk temperatures were collected using the objective-based illumination technique discussed earlier. Due to the small thickness of illumination in the evanescence region, Brownian motion caused the tracer particles to drop in and out of the visible region during the PIV inter-frame time delay Δt [36]. Because Brownian motion is a function of temperature, the number of particles staying in the visible region is expected to decrease with increasing fluid temperature.

Experimental images were analyzed to quantify this effect by measuring the percentage of the particles remaining within the visible depth (Ω) of the image, or "matched" particle, after a specified time delay Δt=1.6 ms. Fig. 7 depicts the percentage of particles that stayed within the visible region of z_v in an image pair, where error bars indicate a 95% confidence level of the presented data [44]. The experimental values are determined by searching for the particles in an image pair that stayed within a given observation window of five pixels. This figure shows that as the fluid temperature increased, the number of particles that stayed in the visible depth during the time interval decreased. This result is caused by an increase in Brownian motion at higher temperatures, pushing more particles out of the visible depth.

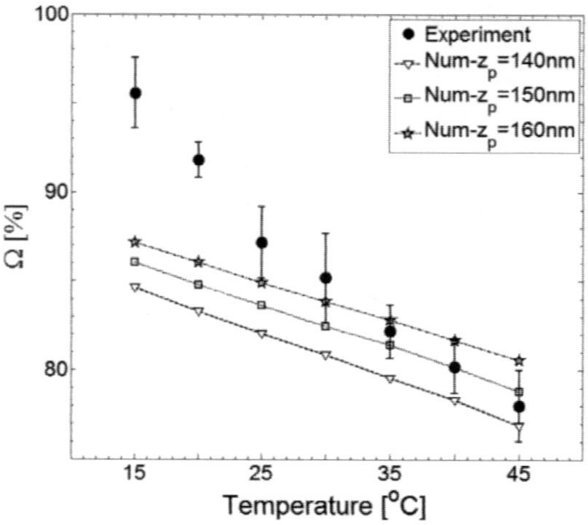

Figure 7: Percentage of particles remaining in the visible depth during nPIT experimentation

The results of the numerical simulation for the calculated values of Ω are also presented in Fig. 7 for three different evanescent wave thicknesses. Num-z_p in the figure represents the numerical prediction for the corresponding penetration depth. For these data, the number of the particles staying within the visible depth was determined based on the exact z position of the particles calculated from the numerical simulation. The numerical results also showed a systematic decreasing trend for the number of particles remaining in the visible region, confirming that this parameter could be used as an assessment tool in thermometry. This figure also shows that the percentage of particles remaining in the visible depth increases with increasing penetration depth of the evanescent wave, with similar decreasing trends with temperature increase. Fig. 7 shows that for a 30°C temperature increase, Ω predicts a 23% and 8% reduction for experimental and numerically estimated values, respectively. This difference may be attributed to other experimental factors, such as variations of particle size, fluorescence, and image noise with temperature, which affect detection of particles in the image. Further detailed experimental data are required to quantify this parameter as a tool for direct temperature measurement. In the present work, focus is given only to characterizing the effects of this particle "mismatch" on the standard cross-correlation function obtained from nPIT images for fluid thermometry. In an additional note, the above method also serves as a metrological self-check on the basis of functional redundancy [45].

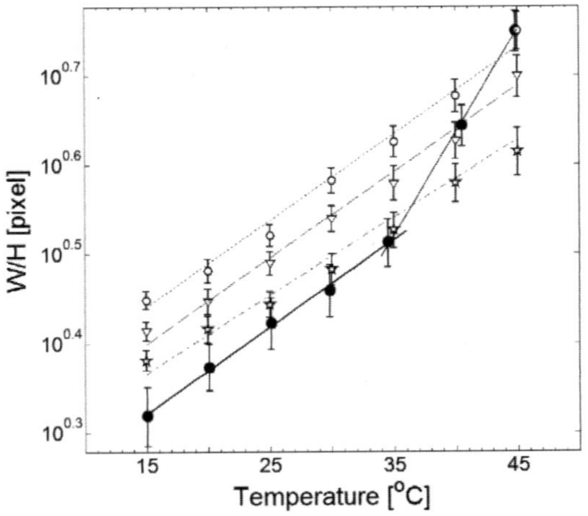

Figure 8: Correlation peak width-to-height ratio comparison for simulation and experiments at Δt=1.6 ms

Fig. 8 compares the peak-width to peak-height ratio obtained from the experiment for different temperatures at a Δt value of 1.6 ms and simulations performed at the same time delay on a semi-log plot. Numerical results are presented for three different penetration depths in the range of the estimated experimental depth. The temperature measurement sensitivity is not significantly influenced by the variation in penetration depth (or incident angle of TIR). The experimental data follows two trends: the initial slope of the data up to 35°C matches well with that of the simulations but deviates beyond 35°C. One reason for this deviation could be the change in optical characteristics of the objective used in the measurement, which was factory-corrected for working up to a temperature limit of 35°C. In addition, the optical properties of the contact oil used with the objective may also have varied at higher temperatures. These parameters could adversely affect measurements at higher temperatures and be cited as major drawbacks to the measurement technique using an objective-based system. There is a good agreement the between experimental and numerical trends for the peak-width to peak-height ratio for temperatures up to 35°C regardless of the assumed penetration depth. The ratio decreases with increasing penetration depth of the evanescent wave. At larger penetration depths, more particles remain in the visible region (imaged), resulting in higher correlation peak-height values. From the spread of uncertainty in the width-to-height ratio of the experimental data depicted in Fig. 8, the maximum uncertainty in the temperature measurement was estimated to be ±2.5°C for the case with z_v of approximately 350 nm.

The peak-width and peak-height values depend on the experimental and image processing parameters such as interrogation window size, number of particles, surface forces, and image noise level. Therefore, a calibration test to estimate the peak-width to peak-height ratio needs to be conducted prior to a practical near-wall temperature measurement.

IV. Conclusion

The feasibility of near-wall thermometry using evanescent wave illumination, or nano-particle image thermometry (nPIT), was investigated. Monte Carlo simulation was used to generate artificial nPIT images of the Brownian motion of fluorescent particle tracers in a stationary fluid with exponentially decaying illumination intensity from the wall. The results of simulations show that the cross-correlation peak-width increases while the peak-height decreases with increasing fluid temperature. The peak width-to-height ratio is determined to be the parameter of choice for quantifying temperature using the nPIT technique. Although higher temperature sensitivity was observed with larger inter-frame time delays, smaller time delays are preferred due to lower uncertainty values. Experiments were conducted, and the results were compared to the simulation results. The reduction in fluorescent intensity values with increasing temperature was observed to be significant and cannot be neglected in the Brownian-based thermometry using fluorescence particle tracers. The experimental results show a maximum uncertainty of ± 2.5°C in the temperature measurement with an out-of-plane measurement depth of approximately 350 nm from the wall. In addition, the objective-based near-wall thermometric method was imperfect at higher temperatures due to the changes in the optical characteristics of the imaging setup.

This work presents the application of Brownian motion analysis for near-wall thermometry in a stationary fluid. However, real applications often have fluid flow in the system. Detailed analysis for near-wall thermometry in the evanescent wave region together with velocimetry has not yet been reported. When there is no flow, the cross-correlation function (of image pairs) has similar widths in both the x and y directions. However, with the flow, the width in one direction of the flow will be different from the width perpendicular to it. The effect caused by the variation in temperature needs to be detected by further analyzing additional effects of the particle convection due to the fluid flow on the cross-correlation function [29]. In the future, we intend to conduct experimental studies on this aspect. In addition, in the present work fluorescent particles with a mean diameter of 100nm was only considered, as it was optimal for the measurement system. The effect of particle size distribution on near-wall thermometry was not investigated and would be an important factor to be considered for further studies.

Acknowledgment

This publication was made possible by NPRP grant # 08-574-2-239 and 9-1183-2-241 from the Qatar National Research Fund (a member of Qatar Foundation). The statements made herein are solely the responsibility of the authors.

REFERENCES

[1] K. Anoop and R. Sadr, "Evanescent wave-based near-wall thermometry utilizing Brownian motion," in *The Sixth International Conference on Quantum, nano and Micro Technologies*, Rome, Italy, 2012, pp. 12-17.

[2] P. Childs, J. Greenwood, and C. Long, "Review of temperature measurement," *Review of Scientific Instruments,* vol. 71, pp. 2959-2978, 2000.

[3] L. H. Fischer, G. S. Harms, and O. S. Wolfbeis, "Upconverting nanoparticles for nanoscale thermometry," *Angewandte Chemie International Edition,* vol. 50, pp. 4546-4551, 2011.

[4] M. M. Kim, A. Giry, M. Mastiani, G. O. Rodrigues, A. Reis, and P. Mandin, "Microscale thermometry: A review," *Microelectronic Engineering,* vol. 148, pp. 129-142, 2015.

[5] Y. Kamei, M. Suzuki, K. Watanabe, K. Fujimori, T. Kawasaki, T. Deguchi, Y. Yoneda, T. Todo, S. Takagi, and T. Funatsu, "Infrared laser–mediated gene induction in targeted single cells in vivo," *Nature methods,* vol. 6, pp. 79-81, 2009.

[6] G. Kucsko, P. Maurer, N. Y. Yao, M. Kubo, H. Noh, P. Lo, H. Park, and M. D. Lukin, "Nanometre-scale thermometry in a living cell," *Nature,* vol. 500, pp. 54-58, 2013.

[7] A. M. Chaudhari, T. M. Woudenberg, M. Albin, and K. E. Goodson, "Transient liquid crystal thermometry of microfabricated PCR vessel arrays," *Microelectromechanical Systems, Journal of,* vol. 7, pp. 345-355, 1998.

[8] T. Nozaki, T. Mochizuki, N. Kaji, and Y. Mori, "Application of liquid-crystal thermometry to drop temperature measurements," *Experiments in Fluids,* vol. 18, pp. 137-144, 1995.

[9] R. Mahajan, C.-p. Chiu, and G. Chrysler, "Cooling a microprocessor chip," *Proceedings of the IEEE,* vol. 94, pp. 1476-1486, 2006.

[10] K. L. Davis, K. L. K. Liu, M. Lanan, and M. D. Morris, "Spatially resolved temperature measurements in electrophoresis capillaries by Raman thermometry," *Analytical chemistry,* vol. 65, pp. 293-298, 1993.

[11] Y. M. Shwarts, V. Borblik, N. Kulish, E. Venger, and V. Sokolov, "Limiting characteristics of diode temperature sensors," *Sensors and Actuators A: Physical,* vol. 86, pp. 197-205, 2000.

[12] M. S. Watanabe, N. Kakutal, K. Mabuchi, and Y. Yamada, "Micro-thermocouple probe for measurement of cellular thermal responses," in *Engineering in Medicine and Biology Society, 2005. IEEE-EMBS 2005. 27th Annual International Conference of the*, 2005, pp. 4858-4861.

[13] C. C. Williams and H. K. Wickramasinghe, "Scanning thermal profiler," *Applied Physics Letters,* vol. 49, pp. 1587-1589, 1986.

[14] S. Gomès, A. Assy, and P.-O. Chapuis, "Scanning thermal microscopy: A review," *physica status solidi (a),* vol. 212, pp. 477-494, 2015.

[15] K. Kim, W. Jeong, W. Lee, and P. Reddy, "Ultra-high vacuum scanning thermal microscopy for nanometer resolution quantitative thermometry," *Acs Nano,* vol. 6, pp. 4248-4257, 2012.

[16] P. Chamarthy, S. V. Garimella, and S. T. Wereley, "Measurement of the temperature non-uniformity in a microchannel heat sink using microscale laser-induced fluorescence," *International Journal of Heat and Mass Transfer,* vol. 53, pp. 3275-3283, 2010.

[17] S. Someya, D. Ochi, Y. Li, K. Tominaga, K. Ishii, and K. Okamoto, "Combined two-dimensional velocity and temperature measurements using a high-speed camera and luminescent particles," *Applied Physics B,* vol. 99, pp. 325-332, 2010.

[18] V. Natrajan and K. Christensen, "Two-color laser-induced fluorescent thermometry for microfluidic systems," *Measurement Science and Technology,* vol. 20, p. 015401, 2009.

[19] G. Hetsroni, A. Mosyak, and Z. Segal, "Nonuniform temperature distribution in electronic devices cooled by flow in parallel microchannels," *Components and Packaging Technologies, IEEE Transactions on,* vol. 24, pp. 16-23, 2001.

[20] D. Ross, M. Gaitan, and L. E. Locascio, "Temperature measurement in microfluidic systems using a temperature-dependent fluorescent dye," *Analytical chemistry,* vol. 73, pp. 4117-4123, 2001.

[21] M. Coolen, R. Kieft, C. Rindt, and A. Van Steenhoven, "Application of 2-D LIF temperature measurements in water using a Nd: YAG laser," *Experiments in Fluids,* vol. 27, pp. 420-426, 1999.

[22] J. Sakakibara and R. Adrian, "Whole field measurement of temperature in water using two-color laser induced fluorescence," *Experiments in Fluids,* vol. 26, pp. 7-15, 1999.

[23] M. Kim and M. Yoda, "Dual-tracer fluorescence thermometry measurements in a heated channel," *Experiments in Fluids,* vol. 49, pp. 257-266, 2010.

[24] S. Thomson and D. Maynes, "Spatially resolved temperature measurements in a liquid using laser induced phosphorescence," *Journal of fluids engineering,* vol. 123, pp. 293-302, 2001.

[25] H. Hu and M. M. Koochesfahani, "Molecular tagging velocimetry and thermometry and its application to the wake of a heated circular cylinder," *Measurement Science and Technology,* vol. 17, p. 1269, 2006.

[26] W. L. Cheng and R. Sadr, "Induced flow field of randomly moving nanoparticles: a statistical perspective," *Microfluidics and Nanofluidics,* vol. 18, pp. 1317-1328, 2015.

[27] M. G. Olsen and R. J. Adrian, "Brownian motion and correlation in particle image velocimetry," *Optics & Laser Technology,* vol. 32, pp. 621-627, 2000.

[28] V. Hohreiter, S. Wereley, M. Olsen, and J. Chung, "Cross-correlation analysis for temperature measurement," *Measurement Science and Technology,* vol. 13, p. 1072, 2002.

[29] P. Chamarthy, S. V. Garimella, and S. T. Wereley, "Non-intrusive temperature measurement using microscale visualization techniques," *Experiments in Fluids,* vol. 47, pp. 159-170, 2009.

[30] J. Park, C. Choi, and K. Kihm, "Temperature measurement for a nanoparticle suspension by detecting the Brownian motion using optical serial sectioning microscopy (OSSM)," *Measurement Science and Technology,* vol. 16, p. 1418, 2005.

[31] R. Sadr, K. Anoop, and R. Khader, "Effects of surface forces and non-uniform out-of-plane illumination on the accuracy of nPIV velocimetry," *Measurement Science and Technology,* vol. 23, p. 055303, 2012.

[32] K. Kihm, A. Banerjee, C. Choi, and T. Takagi, "Near-wall hindered Brownian diffusion of nanoparticles examined by three-dimensional ratiometric total internal reflection fluorescence microscopy (3-D R-TIRFM)," *Experiments in Fluids,* vol. 37, pp. 811-824, 2004.

[33] A. Banerjee and K. D. Kihm, "Experimental verification of near-wall hindered diffusion for the Brownian motion of nanoparticles using evanescent wave microscopy," *Physical Review E,* vol. 72, p. 042101, 2005.

[34] R. Sadr, C. Hohenegger, H. Li, P. J. Mucha, and M. Yoda, "Diffusion-induced bias in near-wall velocimetry," *Journal of fluid mechanics,* vol. 577, pp. 443-456, 2007.

[35] P. Huang, J. S. Guasto, and K. S. Breuer, "The effects of hindered mobility and depletion of particles in near-wall shear flows and the implications for nanovelocimetry," *Journal of fluid mechanics,* vol. 637, pp. 241-265, 2009.

[36] R. Sadr, H. Li, and M. Yoda, "Impact of hindered Brownian diffusion on the accuracy of particle-image velocimetry using evanescent-wave illumination," *Experiments in Fluids,* vol. 38, pp. 90-98, 2005.

[37] A. Goldman, R. G. Cox, and H. Brenner, "Slow viscous motion of a sphere parallel to a plane wall—I Motion through a quiescent fluid," *Chemical engineering science,* vol. 22, pp. 637-651, 1967.

[38] M. G. Olsen, "Depth of correlation reduction due to out-of-plane shear in microscopic particle image velocimetry," *Measurement Science and Technology,* vol. 21, p. 105406, 2010.

[39] M. R. Oberholzer, N. J. Wagner, and A. M. Lenhoff, "Grand canonical Brownian dynamics simulation of colloidal adsorption," *The Journal of chemical physics,* vol. 107, pp. 9157-9167, 1997.

[40] B. J. Kirby and E. F. Hasselbrink, "Zeta potential of microfluidic substrates: 1. Theory, experimental techniques, and effects on separations," *Electrophoresis,* vol. 25, pp. 187-202, 2004.

[41] M. Uematsu and E. Frank, "Static dielectric constant of water and steam," *Journal of Physical and Chemical Reference Data,* vol. 9, pp. 1291-1306, 1980.

[42] J. A. Fagan, P. J. Sides, and D. C. Prieve, "Calculation of ac electric field effects on the average height of a charged colloid: Effects of electrophoretic and Brownian motions," *Langmuir,* vol. 19, pp. 6627-6632, 2003.

[43] K. Anoop and R. Sadr, "nPIV velocity measurement of nanofluids in the near-wall region of a microchannel," *Nanoscale Research Letters,* vol. 7, pp. 1-8, 2012.

[44] L. Benedict and R. Gould, "Towards better uncertainty estimates for turbulence statistics," *Experiments in Fluids,* vol. 22, pp. 129-136, 1996.

[45] R. Taymanov and K. Sapozhnikova, "Metrological self-check and evolution of metrology," *Measurement,* vol. 43, pp. 869-877, 2010.

Impact of the Entering Time on the Performance of MPI Collective Operations

Christoph Niethammer, Dmitry Khabi, Huan Zhou, Vladimir Marjanovic, and José Gracia
High Performance Computing Center Stuttgart (HLRS), University of Stuttgart
70569 Stuttgart, Germany
Email: {niethammer,khabi,zhou,marjanovic,gracia}@hlrs.de

Abstract—**Collective operations strongly affect the performance of many MPI applications, as they involve large numbers, or frequently all, of the processes communicating with each other. One critical issue for the performance of collective operations is load imbalance, which causes processes to enter collective operations at different times. The influence of such late-arrivals is not well understood at the moment. Earlier work showed that even small system noise can have a tremendous effect on the collective performance. Thus, although algorithms are optimized for large process counts, they do not seem to tolerate noise or consider delay of involved processes and even a small perturbation from a single process can already have a negative effect on the overall collective execution. In this work, we show a first detailed study about the effect of late arrivals onto the collective performance in MPI. For the evaluation a new, specialized benchmark was designed and a new metric, which we call delay overlap benefit, was used. Our results show that there is already some potential tolerance to late arrivals for the most common collective operations - namely barrier, broadcast, allreduce and alltoall - but there is also a lot of room for future optimizations.**

Keywords–collectives; late-arrivals; benchmarking; MPI collective operations

I. Introduction

Collective operations strongly affect the performance of many Message Passing Interface (MPI) applications, as they involve large number, usually all, of processes communicating with each other. One critical issue for the performance of collective operations is load imbalance, which causes processes to enter collective operations at different times. The influence of such delayed processes is not well understood at the moment. The results in this paper extend our initial work [1] on this topic. Earlier studies showed that even small system noise can have a tremendous effect on the collective performance [2] [3]. So, though algorithms are optimized for large process counts [4], they do not seem to tolerate noise or consider delay of involved processes and thus even a small perturbation from a single process can already have a negative effect on the overall collective execution.

The MPI 3.0 standard introduced non-blocking collective operations, which give the opportunity to speed up applications by allowing overlap of communication with computation [5], reducing the synchronisation costs of delayed processes as well as the effects of system noise. Many MPI programs are written using non-blocking point-to-point communication operations and application developers are familiar with managing this process using request and status objects. Extending this to include collectives allows programmers to straightforwardly improve application scalability.

In contrast to the already existing blocking collectives, the non-blocking counterparts require the MPI implementations to progress the communication task in parallel to computations. This is a non-trivial task, even if the network hardware provides support for offloading network operations from the CPU, e.g., message buffers may have to be refilled for large messages or more complex collective operations need multiple communication steps. The Cray XE6 and XC30 platforms feature a special "asynchronous process engine" for this, which uses spare hyperthreads (XC30) or dedicated CPU cores (XE6) for the required operations [6].

This work analyses and emphasizes the effect of late arrivals on collective operation in MPI for large number of processes. Therefore, a benchmark and metric for evaluation and detection of effects caused by late arrivals are introduced. The obtained results show the tolerance of state of the arty MPI collective operations used in the latests Cray XC30 and XC40 systems and may point to potential for improving performance by solving the issue of late arrivals in the future.

This work is structured as follows. Section III describes the testing methodology and the micro benchmark suite, which we designed specifically to study the impact of late arrivals, i.e., delay on collective performance. At the begin of Section IV, we define a metric to quantify the amount of tolerated delay. Then, the results for different application relevant collective operations are presented and evaluated on basis of absolute times as well as the delay overlap metric.

II. Background

Since long time, message passing is the standard when it comes to the programming of high performance computing (HPC) applications on distributed memory systems. Since its beginnings many different benchmarks have been developed to measure the performance of the underlying hardware, or to test the efficiency of the MPI library implementation. The most well known of them are the OSU Micro-Benchmarks, Ohio MicroBenchmark suite, Intel MPI Benchmarks and the Effective Bandwidth (b_eff) Benchmark [7]. All of these benchmarks test bandwidth and latency of the various MPI communication functions for different number of processes and data size. These benchmarks assume that communication happens in a perfect environment and all operations are well synchronized. While this allows to figure out the best performance reachable with the various MPI calls for the used hardware and MPI library, it does not represent the majority of real world applications.

At first, real world applications are influenced by system noise. So, compute nodes run services in parallel to the application, as for instance, time synchronization or node health checker, which interrupt the execution of the application. Also, there are shared resources like I/O or the network itself, which are used by other applications running at the same time. This noise can have a tremendous effect on the collective performance [2].

A second point, which is not taken into account by existing benchmarks are load imbalances inside the application. These load imbalances lead to different entering times of different processes at communication points. So called late arrivals will cause other processes to wait on them. The more processes are involved in the communication the more this becomes a problem, as equal load distribution becomes more complicated and the number of processes, which may have to wait on a single late arrival, increases.

Algorithms implementing collective operations use different strategies to optimize the network use and achieve the best possible performance [4]. Common technique here are tree based communication structures and ring sends to match the underlying network hardware on the one hand, as well as to reduce the number of send messages or reduce the bandwidth requirements on the other hand. Late arrivals in these communication schemes will affect the performance badly at this point due to the internal communication dependencies. Though there is potential for optimizations, e.g., deferring the dependence to communicate with a late arrival to the end of the communication scheme inside the collective, can hide some of the delay from this process. However, not much is known about the effects of the entering time on MPI collective performance at the moment; to our knowledge there is no benchmark specific on this topic so far.

III. Methodology and Benchmark description

To study MPI collective operations with respect to late arrivals, a micro benchmark suite was designed. The central point for the analysis therein is a global clock. The global clock is chosen to be the one of process with MPI rank 0. To obtain this global clock the micro benchmark suite determines the clock offsets between process zero and all other processes. Based on the global time, the benchmark performs then the following tasks for a collective benchmark:

- Measures start and end times of all involved MPI processes.
- Determines earliest start and latest end time over all involved MPI processes.

Each benchmark is run with different number of processes and if the collective exchanges data, different data sizes. Initially, a warm-up for the network, CPUs, etc. is performed running the benchmark several times before the real measurement is started. Then, the times for the real benchmark runs are recorded.

The design of the benchmark suite allows for easy extendibility and addition of new benchmarks. Table III lists all currently implemented MPI collective benchmarks. Within this work, results for blocking and non-blocking barrier, allreduce and alltoall operations are reported.

Table I. List of currently implemented MPI collective benchmarks.

benchmark	blocking	non-blocking
barrier	x	x
bcast	x	x
reduce	x	x
allreduce	x	x
alltoall	x	x

A. Clock offset determination

The local clocks of different processors across a distributed system report different times as they are not perfectly synchronized. They may even run at slightly different speeds [8] [9], which is not taken into account by the benchmark suite at the moment. This simplification is acceptable because the benchmarks run only for a relatively short time. Nevertheless, a verification step validating this assumption is performed at the end of the benchmark. It shows that there is no significant change in the time differences over the benchmark runs.

Hence, for the comparison of the times from the different clocks in the benchmark, the error between the clocks has to be taken into account. For this purpose, a simple linear approximation model is used [10]. Because of the short runtime only the clock offset σ—defined as the constant difference between the locally measured reference time t and the remote time t'—is of interest:

$$t' = t + \sigma \; . \tag{1}$$

The offset is determined at the start of the benchmark and checked at its end.

A modified ping pong experiment is used to determine the clock offset following Cristian's algorithm [11]: A root process sends a request to another process after determining his local clock value t_0. The other process answers with his current local time t'_r and the root process recognizes the time t_1 after receiving the response. We improve the accuracy by adding a second timer t_2 directly after taking t_1 allowing to determine the timer delay Δ, which is the time required to read out the clock itself. From this experiment the ping pong latency λ_p and timer delay Δ are obtained, see Figure 1.

To obtain the clock offset σ between local clock t and remote clock t' defined in (1), both messages in the ping-pong are assumed to have the same message latency. In this case, the remote time t'_r is at the mid of the ping pong. The clock offset is then given by

$$\sigma = t'_r - t_0 - (\lambda_p + \Delta)/2 \; , \tag{2}$$

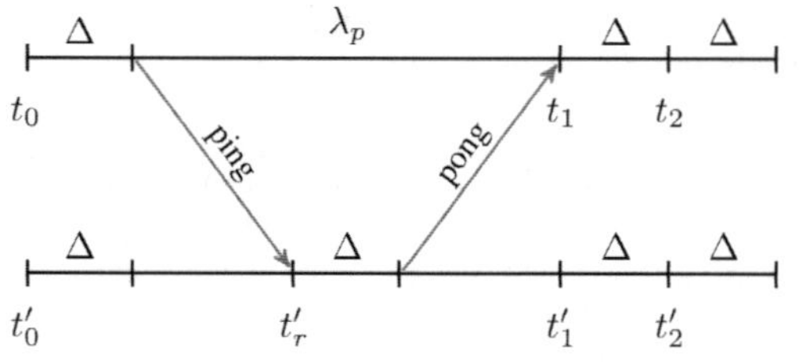

Figure 1. Modified ping pong experiment to determine ping pong latency λ_p, timer delay Δ and clock offset on the basis of the remote time t'_r, which is assumed to be taken at the mid of the ping pong.

where the timer delay Δ is obtained via

$$\Delta = t_2 - t_1 \ . \tag{3}$$

The accuracy of the obtained clock offset is increased by using the statistical value over 100 measurements.

To verify the correctness and to obtain an estimate for the error in the obtained clock offsets intra node times can be compared, which should not vary much. As can be seen in Table II, the clock offsets between rank 0 and all processes residing on one node are the same with a standard deviation of not more than $\pm 2\,\mu s$. In contrast, the clocks of different nodes vary by more than $10\,ms$ between each other.

Table II. DETERMINED AVERAGE CLOCK OFFSET $\bar{\sigma}$ AND STANDARD DEVIATION σ_σ FOR A BENCHMARK RUN WITH 12 PROCESSES AND 4 PROCESSES PER NODE BASED ON A SET OF 100 MEASUREMENTS. (RESULTS OBTAINED ON HERMIT SYSTEM AT HLRS, SEE SECTION IV)

rank	$\bar{\sigma}$ [s]	σ_σ [s]
0	+0.000000	0.000000
1	+0.000000	0.000000
2	+0.000000	0.000000
3	+0.000000	0.000000
4	−0.017258	0.000002
5	−0.017258	0.000001
6	−0.017258	0.000001
7	−0.017258	0.000002
8	−0.011140	0.000002
9	−0.011140	0.000002
10	−0.011140	0.000002
11	−0.011140	0.000002

B. Initial synchronization

A synchronization of all processes is done at the beginning of each benchmark run. Two different synchronization methods are available: One using MPI barrier, and another using clock based synchronization [12]. The interface and implementation of the synchronization function already includes the application of a delay time, which we will describe in more detail in Section III-D.

a) Barrier based synchronization: The barrier based synchronization makes use of the `MPI_Barrier` to synchronize processes as shown in listing 1. The barrier based synchronization may not be perfect as can be seen from the trace in Figure 2 where the processes finish the barrier at slightly different times. The time difference between the processes at the exit of the barrier is there in the order of $4\,\mu s$ for 32 processes over two nodes of hermit. The observed exit time pattern there shows the behaviour of a tree algorithm [13].

One idea to improve the barrier based synchronization is to measuring the time differences at its exit and to improve the sync using delays to compensate them afterwards. This succeeds only if the barrier algorithm works always in the same way, producing the same exit time pattern. But, testing the compensation approach with a delay granularity of $1\,\mu s$, resulted in even worse synchronization.

```
double synchronizeViaBarrier(MPI_Comm comm,
                             double delaytime) {
        MPI_Barrier(comm);
        double r = delay(delaytime);
        return r;
}
```

Listing 1: Implementation of barrier based synchronisation.

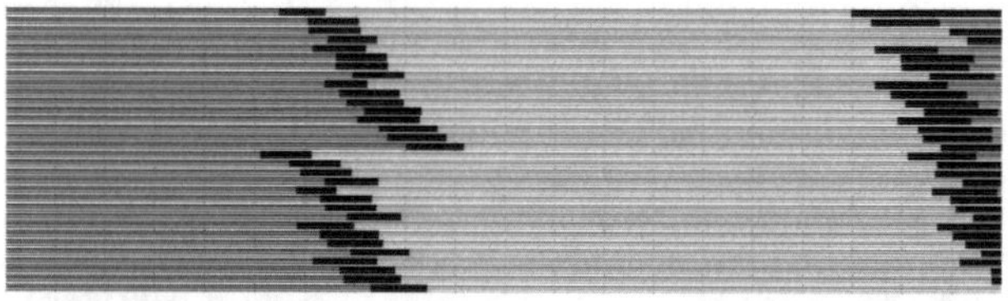

(a)

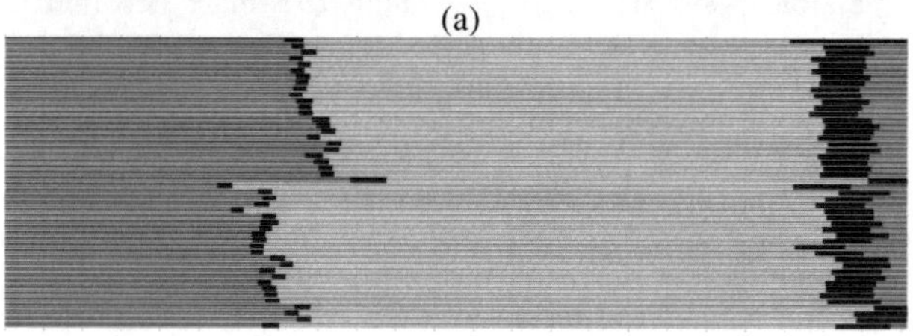

(b)

Figure 2. Time line trace images of synchronization barrier (red) before actual benchmark (orange) separated by timer calls (blue). Traces were obtained with Score-P and Vampir for (a) 32 PEs on 2 nodes of Hornet (Cray XE6) and (b) 48 PEs on 2 nodes of Hazel Hen (Cray XC40).

b) Clock based synchronisation: The clock based synchronisation allows a very precise time synchronization of events across processes [12]. It uses a global clock and local busy waiting until a defined start time point. The start time point is exchanged beforehand between all processes removing the dependence on sending messages over the network for the actual synchronisation step. Therefore, it is not affected by interconnect latencies, which may vary due to network contention. The accuracy of this method is limited by two things:

- the frequency and duration of clock read outs, which are required to monitor the current time
- the accuracy of the clock synchronisation, which is essential to define the global synchronisation time point.

With the current implementation of the clock based synchronisation in listing 2, using internally the POSIX `gettimeofday` for the `timer()`, the quality of the synchronization is already much better as the latest Barrier based synchronization front on Cray XC40 as can be seen in Figure 3.

```
double synchronizeViaClock(MPI_Comm comm,
                           double delaytime) {
        int syncRoot = 0;
        double synctime =
                0.01 - clockOffsetsAvg[comm_rank];
        double endtime =
                synctime + delaytime + timer();
        MPI_Bcast(&endtime, 1,
                  MPI_DOUBLE,
                  syncRoot,
                  comm);
        double r = timer() - endtime;
        while(r < 0) {
                r = timer() - endtime;
        }
        return r;
}
```

Listing 2: Implementation of clock based synchronisation.

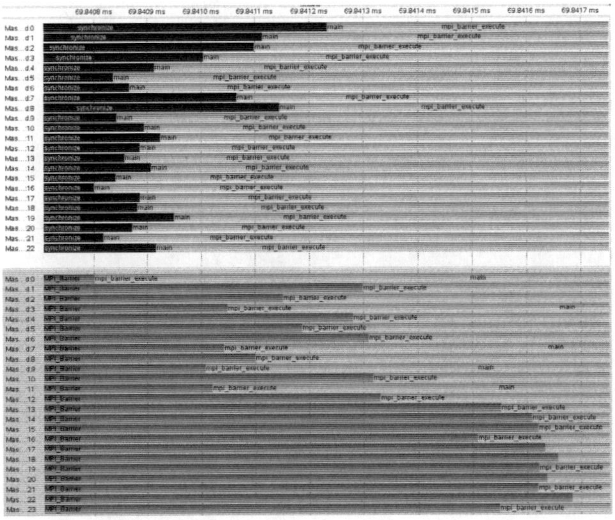

Figure 3. Time line trace image comparing the clock based (blue) with MPI barrier (red) synchronization before actual benchmark (orange). Traces were obtained with Score-P and Vampir for 24 PEs on 1 node of Hazel Hen (Cray XC40).

C. Collected data

For each measurement the process id as well as its start and end time are stored. The results can be output as ASCII text or in binary format using exchangeable data representation (XDR).

In the binary format time values are stored as double precision floating point values, which has 53 significant bits, corresponding to 15 decimal digits, which is more than sufficient for our purpose, as we collect times with no more than nano second resolution over a time frame of several minutes. The stored times are times corrected on the basis of the initially collected clock offsets.

If not mentioned otherwise explicitly, global times for the collective operations are reported, which is the time between the start time of the first process entering and the end time of the last process finishing the collective.

D. Delaying of single process

Load imbalances in programs cause some processes to enter collectives later than the rest. To study the influence of such late-arrivals on the overall collective time, the benchmark suite allows to delay processes by a given amount of time, see Figure 4.

The delay is implemented differently for the different synchronization methods:

For the barrier based synchronisation the delay is implemented indirectly by a separate delay function. The delay function busy loops for the specified time on the bases of the POSIX `gettimeofday` function, providing a microsecond accuracy.

The clock based synchronisation implements the delay directly shifting the internal start time point by the desired delay time. Therefore, the accuracy of the delay is the same as he the one for the synchronisation.

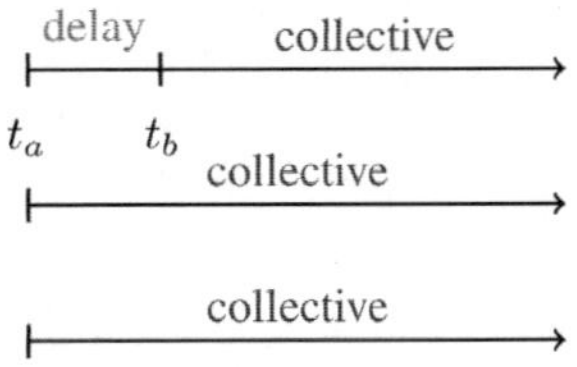

Figure 4. Processes are except one synchronized at time t_a and enter the collective. The one delayed process enters the collective at time $t_b = t_a + \delta$.

IV. RESULTS

In the following, the influence of different delay times and different number of processes on the collective execution time is studied. Within the study blocking collectives and their non-blocking counterparts are compared side by side as they may be implemented in different ways. Here the call of the non-blocking MPI collectives are directly followed by an `MPI_Waitall` mimicing the blocking behaviour.

Two metrics are used within the examination of the results: The global collective time t_{global} and the overlap benefit b.

Global collective time: The global collective time is defined as the time between the earliest start time and the latest end time of the collective operation by any process:

$$t_{\text{global}} = \max(t_{\text{end}}) - \min(t_{\text{start}}) \,. \tag{4}$$

Delay overlap benefit: The overlap benefit metric gives a measure for the potential of internal overlap of the delay with communication in the collectives itself. The delay overlap benefit is defined as the fraction of overlapped execution time:

$$b = \frac{t_0 + \delta - t_\delta}{t_\delta} \,, \tag{5}$$

with t_0 being the collective time when the collective is called without any delayed processes and t_δ being the collective time when a process starts with delay δ.

A positive overlap benefit is found when there is overlap potential within the collective operation. A value of 1 indicates that the collective can hide a delay perfectly up to the time required for the undelayed collective. A value of zero can be observed when the delay just adds to the execution of a non delayed collective call without positive or negative side effects. A negative value means that the delay even results in additional cost compared to a synchronized collective, which is started after waiting delay time.

In the following, results for different collective operations on the Hermit and Hazel Hen systems at HLRS are reported. Hermit was a Cray XE6 system with 3552 dual-socket compute nodes and a total of 113 664 cores, which were connected via the Gemini 3D Torus network. Its successor Hazel Hen is a Cray XC40 system with 7712 dual-socket compute nodes and a total of 185 088 cores, which are connected in dragonfly topology via the Aries interconnect. The native Cray MPI implementations optimized for these system in combination with the GNU compiler were used for all tests.

All benchmarks were run during normal operation mode of the system so that other jobs on the system influenced the process placement and network usage. Benchmark runs were performed up to a maximum of 16 384 processes and were grouped into jobs with the same processor count. We report the found minimum values for the global times within 100 measurements. We use the minimum, as we are not interested in the average behaviour of the collectives but in the best we can get out of them on a system. This is responsible for some outlying data points, as we cannot guarantee to catch the best result even if multiple measurements were performed to reduce this effect. Obtaining the accurate minimum time for an operation under workload conditions is not always possible—especially for the longer benchmark runs using more processes, which get easily disturbed by other jobs.

For all measurements the MPI process with rank 0 was delayed. Most tree based algorithms—usually using rank 0 as tree root—should be badly affected by this choice, if they do not switch over using another process as the tree root.

A. Barrier

The first collective studied is the barrier. As the barrier is used for synchronization within the benchmark suite, the understanding of this operation is essential. While the time for `MPI_Barrier` is measured straightforward, the time for `MPI_Ibarrier` includes the time for the corresponding `MPI_Wait`.

A wide variety of different barrier algorithms exists [13]. Depending on the algorithm and the hardware support used within the implementation, different algorithms may profit differently. On the one hand, for example, the Central Counter barrier may hide the delay of a late arrival easily by concept, or the Binomial Spanning Tree Barrier could intelligently assign the delayed process to a node, which is involved in later communication steps. On the other hand, for example, the Dissemination Barrier requires a ring like communication in each step—which will not tolerate a late arrival.

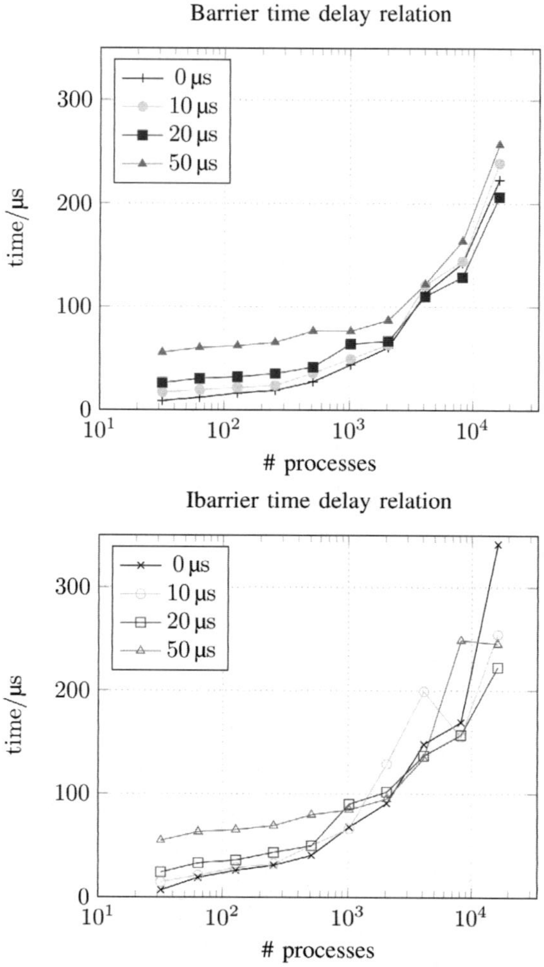

Figure 5. MPI_Barrier and MPI_Ibarrier global times for different delay times on Hornet.

The results in Figure 5 show a nearly logarithmic scaling of the blocking and non-blocking barrier operation up to approximately 2048 processes. For higher process counts, the behaviour seems to have a linear scaling. But we note here that a single cabinet of the Hermit system has 96 nodes with a total of 3072 cores. Jobs exceeding this number of processes are more likely to be spread around the system and therefore affected by network contention caused by other applications. So, finding the minimum time for the barrier operation with our benchmark may not have provided the correct result in this case.

The delay benefit as defined in (5) of the `MPI_Barrier` and `MPI_Ibarrier` for different delay times, where the delayed rank was always rank 0, is shown in Figure 6. As

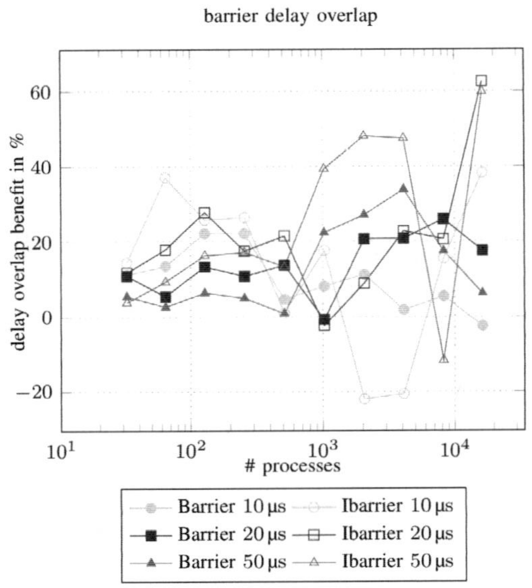

Figure 6. Delay benefit of the `MPI_Barrier` and `MPI_Ibarrier` as defined in (5) for different delay times on Hornet.

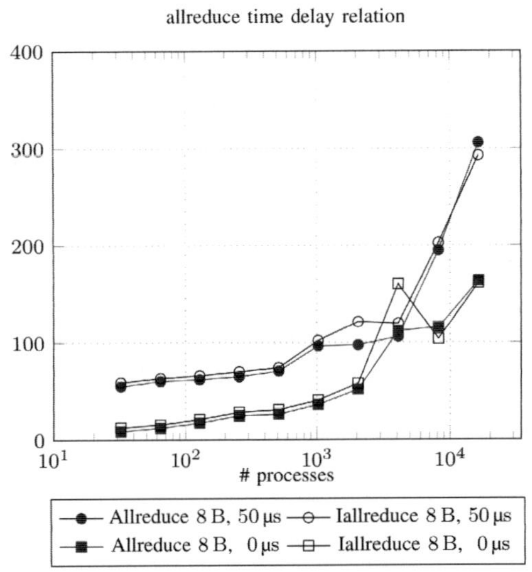

Figure 7. Hornet: `MPI_Allreduce` (circles) and `MPI_Iallreduce` (squares) global times for 8 B message size and a delay time of 50 µs (blue) together with perfectly synchronized reference data (black).

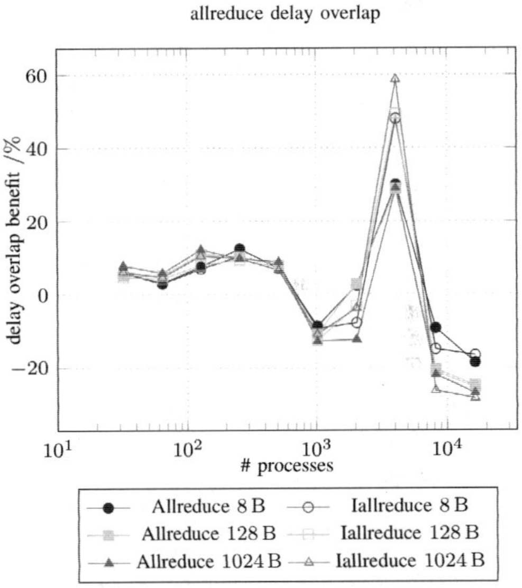

Figure 8. Hornet: Delay benefit of the allreduce collective for different message sizes at a delay time of 50 µs).

the benefit is mostly positive the implemented blocking and non-blocking barrier algorithm already seem to tolerate smaller delays. The non-blocking version `MPI_Ibarrier` seems to perform slightly better than the blocking variant here. Figure 6 shows an change in behaviour at 1024 processes: While at the beginning smaller delays have a higher overlap benefit, for more processes a larger benefit can be seen for longer delays. It is unclear if at this point an algorithm switch occurs within the MPI implementation.

B. Allreduce

An important collective to aggregate data of multiple processes into a single value is the allreduce operation. It may be used to determine, e.g., global energies in molecular simulations, time step lengths in finite element based programs or residues in linear solvers. While the time for `MPI_Allreduce` is measured straightforward, the time for `MPI_Iallreduce` includes the time for the corresponding `MPI_Wait`.

Again, the influence of delaying the process with rank 0 for different number of processes is studied. Results for 8 B messages and a delay of 50 µs are presented in Figure 7 for Hornet and in Figure 9 for Hazel Hen.

For Hornet, we see perfect logarithmic scaling up to 1024 processes, adding less than 5 µs when doubling the number of processes. For larger process counts the scaling is worse and adds up to 100 µs when doubling the number of processes. The behaviour for larger message sizes is similar. It is unclear how the synchronization barrier influences the behaviour, as we showed earlier that the processes do not exit from it perfectly at the same time. Also, the barrier itself does not scale well for larger process counts according to our benchmark results, too, see Figures 2 and 5.

We have to mention a data outlier for the non-delayed Allreduce/Iallreduce benchmark runs with 4096 processes—which were grouped within one job. The job collecting these data was likely disturbed by other jobs and seems not to have been able to find an accurate value for the minimum collective time.

The delay benefit of the blocking and non-blocking allreduce operations presented in Figure 8 shows slight overlap for smaller number of processes. For more than 1024 processors the delay has a negative effect onto the overall performance. The message size does not have an influence on the delay benefit for the chosen values. The peak for 4096 processes is caused by too high values for the perfectly synchronized collectives time t_0.

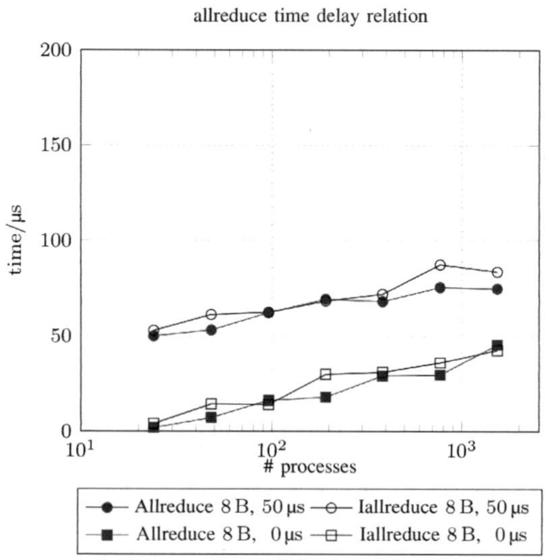

Figure 9. Hazel Hen: `MPI_Allreduce` (circles) and `MPI_Iallreduce` (squares) global times for 8 B message size and a delay time of 50 µs (blue) together with perfectly synchronized reference data (black).

The results for Hazel Hen shown good scaling up to over 1000 PEs in Figure 9. The delay benefit is positive in nearly all cases as can be seen from Figure 10.

C. Alltoall

The alltoall operation is another important collective pattern used in many parallel codes to distribute data in an application. It is the most time consuming collective operation but it may benefit a lot from intelligent algorithms, taking into account delayed processes.

The same measurements as that for the allreduce operation were performed. Results in Figure 11 show a nearly perfect linear scaling for the alltoall algorithm up to the maximum of 16 384 processes used during the benchmarks on Hornet. The message size has a strong influence on the execution time of the alltoall collective but does not affect the overall scaling behaviour.

The results for the delay benefit for the alltoall collective on Hornet, presented in Figure 12, show zero effect for small messages and an inconclusive behaviour for larger messages, which may be caused by the fact, that our benchmark does not find the minimum time as already mentioned before. So, we find slight decreases as well as huge gains in performance.

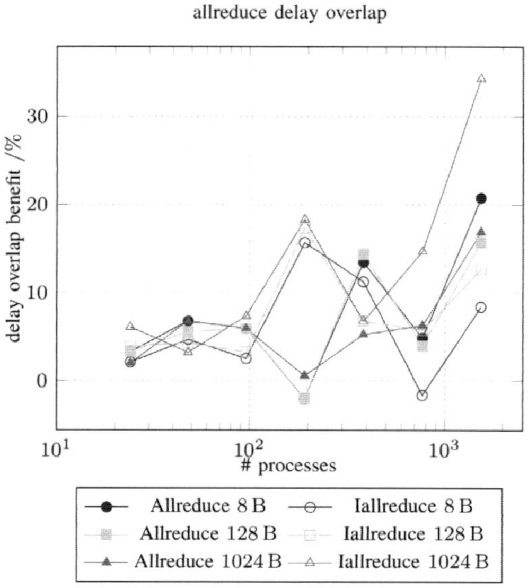

Figure 10. Hazel Hen: Delay benefit of the allreduce collective for different message sizes at a delay time of 50 µs).

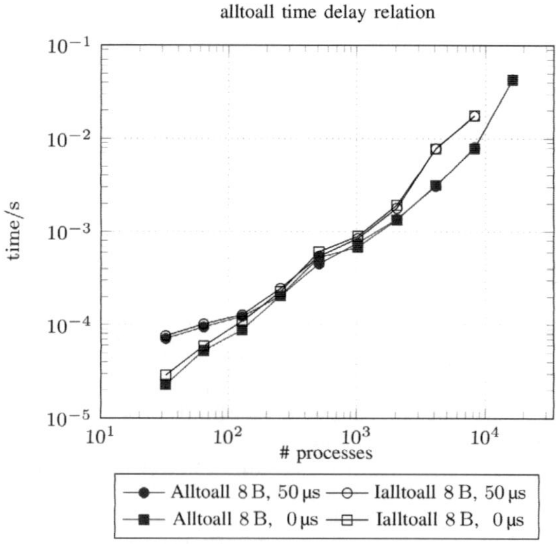

Figure 11. Hornet: `MPI_Alltoall` (circles) and `MPI_Ialltoall` (squares) global times for 8 B message size and a delay time of 50 µs (blue) together with perfectly synchronized reference data (black).

The allreduce results on Hazel Hen show that the delay benefit is nearly zero for small messages there as well. What is interesting here, is the fact that the delay benefit for the blocking versions is better than for their non blocking counterparts, as well as the execution times.

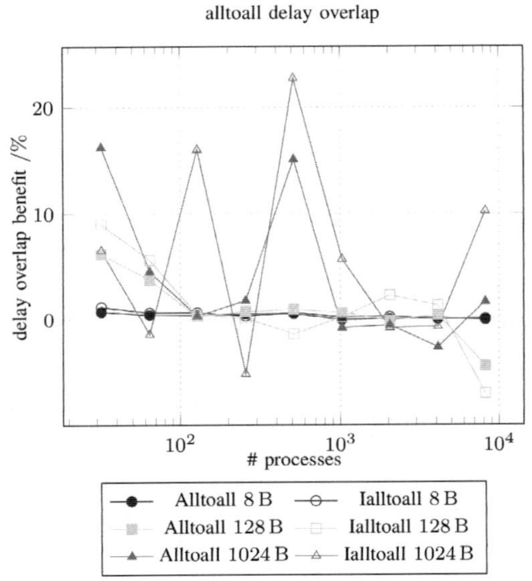

Figure 12. Hornet: Delay benefit for the alltoall collective for different message sizes at a delay time of 50 µs.

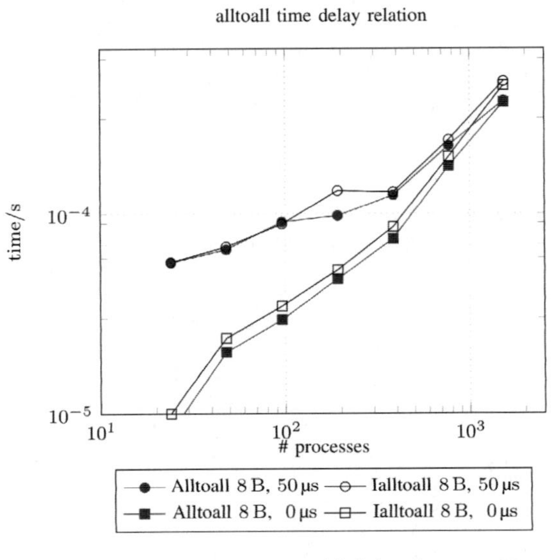

Figure 13. Hazel Hen: MPI_Alltoall (circles) and MPI_Ialltoall (squares) global times for 8 B message size and a delay time of 50 µs (blue) together with perfectly synchronized reference data (black).

D. Broadcast

The broadcast (bcast) operation is another collective pattern found frequently for any kind of initial or intermediate data distribution. For example, it is used to distribute configuration parameters from an input file, which should be not opened and read by all processes at the same time on today's HPC file systems. It is also an operation, which is used within optimized

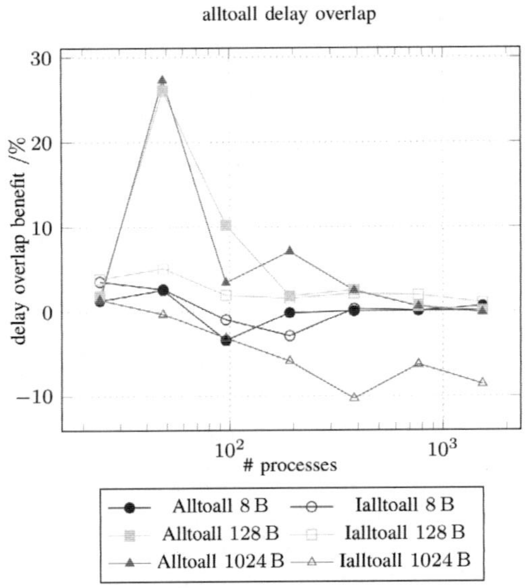

Figure 14. Hazel Hen: Delay benefit for the alltoall collective for different message sizes at a delay time of 50 µs.

versions of more complicated collective operations as part of the underlying communication patterns and algorithms.

The same measurements as before were performed. Results from the Hazel Hen system are presented in Figure 15.

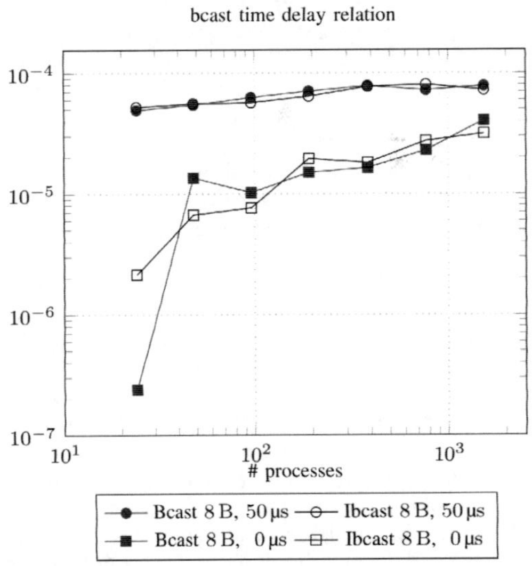

Figure 15. Hazel Hen: MPI_Bcast (circles) and MPI_Ibcast (squares) global times for 8 B message size and a delay time of 50 µs (blue) together with perfectly synchronized reference data (black).

The results for the delay benefit for the bcast collective, presented in Figure 16, show zero effect for small messages and an inconclusive behaviour for larger messages, which may be caused by the fact that our benchmark does not find the minimum time as already mentioned before. So we find slight decreases as well as huge gains in performance.

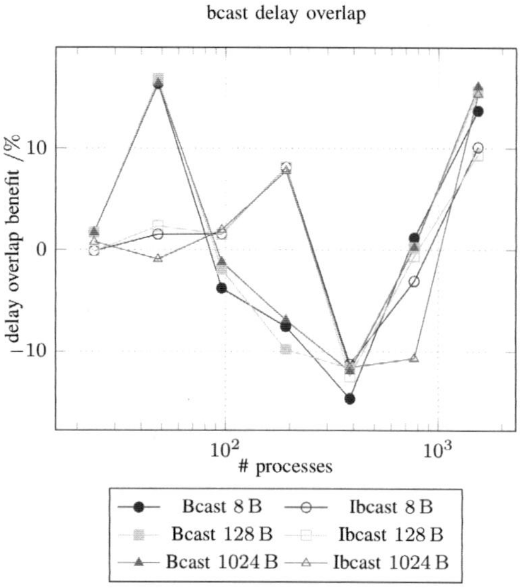

Figure 16. Hazel Hen: Delay benefit for the bcast collective for different message sizes at a delay time of 50 µs.

V. CONCLUSION AND OUTLOOK

In this paper, we have evaluated the impact of late arrivals, i.e., a delayed process, on the performance of the collective operations `MPI_(I)Barrier`, `MPI_(I)Allreduce` and `MPI_(I)Alltoall` on Cray XE6 and `MPI_(I)Bcast` on Cray XC40.

For the detail study we introduce a new benchmark, which allows to delay single MPI process out of a synchronized set. For the process synchronisation we show the effectiveness of a simple Barrier and compare it to the approach of a time based synchronisation scheme. Our findings show that the time based synchronization has better potential to achieve a flat synchronization then a simple barrier, which we find to show the structure of a tree based implementation.

For the evaluation of the results we make use of the global time and the newly defined delay overlap benefit metric. The first specifies the time span from the first process entering the collective to the finishing time of the last process leaving the collective. The overlap benefit metric is the fraction of delay time, which can be overlapped by the collective when comparing the collective times of a collective under a late arrival process with a collective executed starting with well synchronized processes.

The results show that blocking and non-blocking collective barriers can tolerate small delays, i.e., hide a part of the load imbalance within an application. The collectives `MPI_(I)Allreduce` tolerate small delays for up to 1024 processes but is badly affected for larger processes counts. The `MPI_(I)Alltoall` operations tolerate small delays well for up to 1024 processes and the delays have no negative effects for large processes counts. The alltoall operation can profit a lot in some cases for larger message sizes, while we see no negative effects for small messages. The broadcast operation on the Cray XC40 scales well, but shows an inconclusive behaviour when it comes to the tolerance of late arrivals.

We have shown that the overlap availability of non-blocking collectives and benefit of the overlapping depends on the type of the collective operations, size of the communicator and the amount of data to be communicated.

This work shows that the state of the art implementation of the relatively new MPI 3.0 non-blocking collective specification in Cray MPI is mostly head up or better than their blocking counterparts. We expect new algorithms and hardware with better overlapping capabilities and communication offloading support in the future. Our preliminary work in this area shows already some potential to hide small delays of single processes for barrier, allreduce and alltoall operations. The techniques for overlapping communication may also improve collective operations in the case of system noise.

Future studies about other important collectives are planed as well as detailed analysis of delaying other processes than rank 0. Studies are planed to evaluate other MPI library implementations. Here open source implementations can provide insights into the algorithms as well as the cross over points between them for different message sizes and process counts, allowing better understanding of the results.

ACKNOWLEDGEMENT

This work has been supported by the European Community's FP7 programme through the project CRESTA (Grant Agreement no. 287703) and H2020 programme through the project Mont Blanc 3 (Grant Agreement no. 671697). We gratefully acknowledge funding by the German Research Foundation (DFG) through the German Priority Programme 1648 Software for Exascale Computing (SPPEXA). This work made use of computational resources provided by the High Performance Computing Center Stuttgart (Hermit). We thank P. Manninen (Cray Finnland) and R. W. Nash (EPCC) for valuable discussions and assistance.

REFERENCES

[1] C. Niethammer, D. Khabi, H. Zhou, V. Marjanovic, and J. Gracia, "Impact of Late-Arrivals on MPI Collective Operations," in INFOCOMP 2015: The Fifth International Conference on Advanced Communications and Computation, 2015, pp. 60–65.

[2] T. Hoefler, T. Schneider, and A. Lumsdaine, "The Effect of Network Noise on Large-Scale Collective Communications," Parallel Processing Letters, Dec. 2009, pp. 573–593.

[3] K. B. Ferreira, P. G. Bridges, R. Brightwell, and K. T. Pedretti, "The impact of system design parameters on application noise sensitivity," Cluster Computing, vol. 16, no. 1, 2013, pp. 117–129.

[4] R. Thakur and R. Rabenseifner, "Optimization of collective communication operations in mpich," International Journal of High Performance Computing Applications, vol. 19, 2005, pp. 49–66.

[5] T. Hoefler, A. Lumsdaine, and W. Rehm, "Implementation and performance analysis of non-blocking collective operations for mpi," in Proceedings of the 2007 ACM/IEEE Conference on Supercomputing, ser. SC '07. New York, NY, USA: ACM, 2007, pp. 52:1–52:10.

[6] H. Pritchard, D. Roweth, D. Henseler, and P. Cassella, "Leveraging the Cray Linux Environment Core Specialization Feature to Realize MPI, Asynchronous Progress on Cray XE Systems," in Proc. Cray User Group, 2012.

[7] R. Rabenseifner and A. E. Koniges, "Effective communication and file-i/o bandwidth benchmarks," in PVM/MPI, ser. Lecture Notes in Computer Science, Y. Cotronis and J. Dongarra, Eds., vol. 2131. Springer, 2001, pp. 24–35.

[8] L. Lamport, "Time, clocks, and the ordering of events in a distributed system," Commun. ACM, vol. 21, no. 7, Jul. 1978, pp. 558–565.

[9] S. J. Murdoch, "Hot or not: Revealing hidden services by their clock skew," in 13th ACM Conference on Computer and Communications Security (CCS 2006). ACM Press, 2006, pp. 27–36.

[10] D. Becker, R. Rabenseifner, and F. Wolf, "Implications of non-constant clock drifts for the timestamps of concurrent events," in Cluster Computing, 2008 IEEE International Conference on, Sept 2008, pp. 59–68.

[11] F. Cristian, "Probabilistic clock synchronization," Distributed Computing, vol. 3, no. 3, 1989, pp. 146–158.

[12] S. Hunold and A. Carpen-Amarie, "MPI benchmarking revisited: Experimental design and reproducibility," CoRR, vol. abs/1505.07734, 2015. [Online]. Available: http://arxiv.org/abs/1505.07734

[13] T. Hoefler, T. Mehlan, F. Mietke, and W. Rehm, "A Survey of Barrier Algorithms for Coarse Grained Supercomputers," Chemnitzer Informatik Berichte, vol. 04, no. 03, Dec. 2004.

International Journal on Advances in Systems and Measurements, vol 9 no 1 & 2, year 2016, http://www.iariajournals.org/systems_and_measurements/

Data Persistency for Fault-Tolerance Using MPI Semantics

José Gracia,* Nico Struckmann,* Julian Rilli,†‡ Rainer Keller‡
*High Performance Computing Center Stuttgart (HLRS), University of Stuttgart, Germany
†University of Tübingen, Tübingen, Germany
‡University of Applied Sciences, HfT Stuttgart, Germany
Email: gracia@hlrs.de, struckmann@hlrs.de, julian@rilli.eu, rainer.keller@hft-stuttgart.de

***Abstract*—As the size and complexity of high-performance computing hardware, as well as applications increase, the likelihood of a hardware failure during the execution time of large distributed applications is no longer negligible. On the other hand, frequent checkpointing of full application state or even full compute node memory is prohibitively expensive. Thus, application-level checkpointing of only indispensable data and application state is the only viable option to increase an application's resiliency against faults. Existing application-level checkpointing approaches, however, require the user to learn new programming interfaces, etc. In this paper we present an approach to persist data and application state, as for instance messages transfered between compute nodes, which is seamlessly integrated into Message Passing Interface, i.e., the de-facto standard for distributed parallel computing in high-performance computing. The basic idea consists in allowing the user to mark a given communicator as having special, i.e., persistent, meaning. All communication through this persistent communicator is stored transparently by the system and available for application restart even after a failure. The concept is demonstrated by prototypical implementation of the proposed interface.**

Keywords–Message Passing Interface; MPI; fault-tolerance; application-level checkpointing; data persistency

I. Introduction

This paper builds on top of work presented in [1].

Numerical simulation on high-performance computing (HPC) systems is an established methodology in a wide range of fields not only in traditional computational sciences as physics, chemistry, astrophysics, but also becoming more and more important in biology, economic sciences, and even humanities. The total execution time of an application is rapidly approaching the mean time between failures of large HPC systems. Commonly, only a small part of the system will be affected by the hardware fault, but usually all of the application will crash. Application developers can therefore no longer ignore system faults and need to take fault-tolerance and application resiliency into account as part of the application logic. A necessary step is to store intermediate result as well as the current internal state of the application to allow restarting the application at a later time, which is commonly referred to as checkpointing.

In practice, however, the sheer size of simulation data and the limited I/O bandwidth prohibit dumping checkpoints of the full application state or even full compute node memory at high frequency [2]. Checkpointing frequency is therefore chosen to satisfy requirements of the scientific analysis of the simulation data without any safety net for system failure. It is noted, however, that most computational experiments, i.e., simulations, are by definition sufficiently robust to allow drawing similar or equal scientific conclusions if initial or boundary conditions – and by extension intermediate results – are changed slightly within use-case specific limits. Application-level checkpointing of suitably aggregated intermediate results is therefore being considered as a promising technique to improve the resiliency of scientific applications at relatively low cost of resources. The application developer or end user, purposefully discards most of the intermediate data and checkpoints only those data which are absolutely essential for later reconstruction of a sane simulation state. An example would be to store mean values of given quantities, other suitable higher-order moments of the distribution of the quantities, or leading terms of a suitable expansions. Note however, that the nature of the reconstruction data is fully application and even use-case specific. The application at its restart will use this data to reconstruct the state in the part of the application that was lost to the failure, while keeping the full, precise data in the reset of system which was not affected by the fault.

Previous work in [1] suggests a method for persisting intermediate results and internal application state. The method uses idioms and an interface borrowed from the Message Passing Interface (MPI) [3], which is the most widely used programming model for distributed parallel computing in HPC. This allows users of MPI to integrate our method seamlessly into existing applications at minimal development cost.

This paper is organised into a brief overview of related work in Section II, followed by brief review of our approach to data persistency through MPI semantics in Section III, the demonstration and evaluation of the concepts through a prototypical implementation in Section IV and Section V, respectively, and finally, a short summary of this work in Section VI.

II. Related work

SafetyNet [4] is an example of checkpointing at the hardware level. It keeps multiple, globally consistent checkpoints of the state of a shared memory multiprocessor. This approach has the benefit of lower overhead of runtime but it as additional power and monetary cost. Right now, this approach provides checkpointing solution for a single node only.

In the kernel-level approach, the operating system is responsible for checkpointing, which is done in the kernel space context. It uses internal kernel information to capture the process state and further important information required for a process restart. Berkeley Lab Checkpoint/Restart (BLCR) [5][6] and Checkpoint/Restore In Userspace (CRIU) [7] are two examples of this class. This approach provides a transparent solution for checkpointing but files generated by this approach are large and moving checkpoint files to stable storage takes more time. Another problem associated with this approach is that it requires considerable maintenance and development effort as internals of process state, etc. vary greatly from one OS to another and are prone to change over time.

Checkpointing at the user-level solves the problem of high maintenance effort due to kernel diversity. In this case, checkpointing is done in user-space. All relevant system calls are trapped to track the state of a given process. However, due to the overhead of intercepting system calls it takes more time to complete. Similar to kernel-level, user-level checkpointing needs to save complete process state. So, this approach also suffers from the problem of large file size.

In contrast to the schemes mentioned above, which are transparent to user, application-level checkpointing requires explicit user action. The application developer provides hints to the checkpointing framework. By means of these hints, additional checkpoint code is added to the application. This additional code saves required information and restarts the application in case of failure. Application level checkpointing normally creates smaller size checkpoints as they have knowledge about program state.

One such application-level checkpointing scheme is the library Scalable Checkpoint/Restart (SCR) [8][9]. SCR stores checkpoints temporarily in the memory of neighboring compute nodes before writing them to stable storage. It also includes a kind of scheduler which determines the exact checkpointing time according to system health, resource utilisation and contention, and external triggers. SCR is designed to interoperate with MPI. The application developer uses SCR functions to acquire a special file-like handle. Any data written through this SCR handle is replicated in memory across network neighbours for redundancy and checkpointed to storage transparently in the background at a suitable point in time. The drawback is that application developers have to learn yet another programming interface and add additional, possibly complex, code which is not related to their numerical algorithm. Nonetheless, SCR is a powerful scalable checkpointing tool and thus used in the backend of our prototypical implementation as described in later sections of this work.

Previous extensions to MPI, such as FT-MPI [10] offered the application programmer several possibilities to survive, e.g., leave a hole in the communicator in case of process failure. This particular MPI implementation has been adopted in Open MPI [11]. The Message Passing Interface standard in its current form, i.e., MPI-3 [3], does not provide fault-tolerance. Typically, if a single process of a distributed application fails due to, for instance, catastrophic failure of the given compute node, all other processes involved will eventually fail as well in an unrecoverable manner. Recently, several proposals [12][13][14] have been put forward to mitigate the issue by allowing an application to request notification about process failures and by providing interfaces to repair vital MPI communicators. The application, in principle, can use this interface to return the MPI stack to a sane state and continue operation. However, any data held by the failed process is lost. Notably, this includes any messages that have been in flight at the time of the failure.

III. Persistent MPI communication

In this paper, we present an approach that allows application developers to persist, both, essential locally held data and the content of essential messages between processes. Unlike other models, we use idioms that are familiar to any MPI developer. In fact, we add a single function which returns a MPI communicator with special semantic meaning. Then, the programmer continues to use familiar send and receive MPI calls or collective operations to store data and messages persistently or to retrieve them during failure recovery.

A. Background

In MPI, any process is uniquely identified by its *rank* in a given *communicator*. A communicator can be thought of a ordered set of processes. At initialisation time, MPI creates the default communicator, `MPI_COMM_WORLD`, which includes all processes of the application. New communicators can created as subset of existing ones to allow logically grouping processes as required by the application. Collective MPI operations, as for instance a broadcast or scatter, take a communicator as argument and necessarily require the participation of all the processes of the given communicator. In addition, some collective operation single out one processes which is identified by its rank in the respective communicator. Also, point-to-point communication routines take a communicator as argument. In send operations, the target of a message is passed as rank relative to the given communicator argument. The destination of receive operations is given analogously.

In addition, most MPI communication routines require the specification of the so-called *tag* which allows the programmer to classify different message contents. A tag may be thought of as a P. O. Box or similar. Finally, MPI messages are delivered in the same order they have been issued by the sender. Any MPI message can thus be uniquely identified by the signature tuple `(comm, src, dst, tag)` and a sequence number that orders messages with the same signature. The signature is composed of a communicator, `comm`, the rank of the message source, `src`, the rank of the destination, `dst`, and the message tag `tag`.

B. Persistent communicators and proposed idioms

The basic idea of our approach is very simple. The user marks a communicator as having a special, i.e., persistent, semantics. Any communication issued through a persistent communicator is stored transparently by the MPI library and is available for application restart even after failure (see Figure 1). In contrast to no-persistent communicators, the message is not immediately delivered. An MPI process may thus persist any data and application state by sending it to itself through a persistent communicator. In case of failure the data is simply restored by posting a receive operation on the persistent communicator. Moreover, a process may persist data for any other process by sending a message targeted to the other process through a persistent communicator.

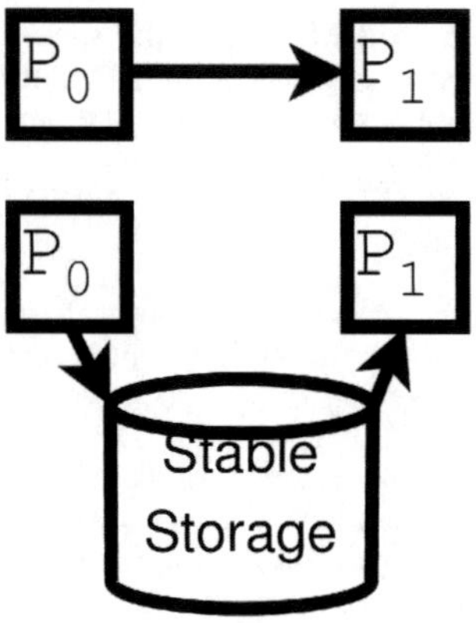

Figure 1. Illustration of communication between two processes, P0 and P1, through regular communicators (top) versus through persisten communicators (bottom).

```
1  #define VALUE_TAG
2  const char mykey[] = "Run␣A,␣June␣6␣2015";
3  MPI_Comm persistent;
4  int value = 3;
5
6  MPI_Comm_persist(MPI_COMM_SELF, info,
7      mykey, persistent);
8
9  if (failure())
10   MPI_Recv(&value, 1, MPI_INT, rank,
11     VALUE_TAG, persistent, &status);
12 else
13   MPI_Send(&value, 1, MPI_INT, rank,
14     VALUE_TAG, persistent);
```

Figure 2. Simple example of data persistency

A communicator is marked as persistent by calling the routine **MPI_Comm_persist**, which has the following signature

```
int MPI_Comm_persist(MPI_Comm comm, char *key,
  MPI_Info info, MPI_Comm *persistentcomm)
```

Here, `persistentcomm` is a pointer to memory, which will hold the newly created persistent communicator. It is derived from the existing communicator `comm` and will consist of the same processes, etc. A user-provided string `key` shall uniquely identify this particular application run or instance in case part of it needs to be restarted after a fault occurred. Essentially this serves as a kind of session key. Finally, the info object `info` may hold additional information for the MPI library, as for instance hints where to store data temporarily, or the size of the expected data volume.

A simple example how to persist data is shown in Figure 2. On line 6, the persistent communicator `persistent` is derived from `MPI_COMM_SELF` which is a pre-defined communicator consisting of just the given process. The routine `failure()` shall return `TRUE` if this process is being restarted after a fault. If this is not the case, the application will persistently store the content of the variable `value` by sending a message to itself on line 13. If a fault occurred the application instead will restore the content of the variable `value` by receiving it from itself on line 10.

Our approach also allows to replay or log communication between processes in the case of faults. The programmer simply derives persistent communicators from all relevant communicators and then mirrors every send operation done on a non-persistent communicators with the persistent one. Receive operations are posted on the persistent communicator as necessary by the failed process only. The reduce the amount of additional code one could also allow transparent persistency. In this case a persistent communicator would persist data and also actually deliver data as expected from a non-transparent one. For simplicity, we will not use this facility for the rest of the paper and use persistent communication explicitly.

The core of a somewhat more elaborated example is shown in Figure 3. For the sake of simplicity, we assume that the application is executed with only two processes. This fictitious algorithm evolves for several iterations a very large array of data through a complex calculation `compute` (line 35). At any given point in time, one can however `aggregate` the data into a single value `seed` (line 45). In turn, `seed` can be used to reconstruct the data array with sufficient accuracy by calling `init_data(seed)` (line 25). The algorithm requires to exchange boundary conditions between processes. The first element of the local array is send to the other process, where it replaces the last element (line 38). The system shall provide a function `failure()`, which notifies fault conditions.

The state of the application is given by the iteration counter `i` of the for loop on line 34. This value is persisted by sending a message to oneself (line 50) at the end of each iteration. The algorithm requires the persistence of the `seed`, again by a message to oneself on line 49. Finally, the exchange of boundary conditions is logged on line 42.

In case of failure, the failed process is restarted and restores its internal state (line 22) and the aggregate (line 21) that is used to reconstruct the data array (line 25). The same initialisation operation had been executed by the surviving process with initial values at the original start of the application. The failed process also retrieves the last boundary value received from the other process (line 29). Then it enters the main loop with the correctly restored iteration counter and resumes normal operation in parallel to the surviving process.

IV. PROTOTYPICAL IMPLEMENTATION

In this section, we briefly outline a prototypical implementation of the proposed interface.

A. *Implementation concerns*

Our proposed persistent communicator semantics is relatively easy to implement. As explained in Section III-A, any given MPI message is uniquely identified by its signature and the sequential ordering. In addition, the user has specified a unique session key at the time of creation of the persistent communicator. Together these are used to store any persistent message content in a suitable stable storage. This could be for instance the memory of a neighbor MPI process (or several for redundancy), remote network filesystems, or any data base. After the failure, the application is restarted with the same session key and thus able to map messages to the state before the fault. In our prototype, we persist messages using the SCR library and leave the details to its automatics.

```
#define SIZE VERY_LARGE
#define SESSION 1001

int rank, other;
float data[SIZE], boundary, seed=321;
int iter = 0;
MPI_Comm persistent, world;

MPI_Init();
world = MPI_COMM_WORLD;
MPI_Comm_rank(world, &rank);
if (rank==0)
  other = 1;
else
  other = 0;
MPI_Comm_persist(world, &info, SESSION,
    &persistent)

if (failure()) {
  // retrieve seed and iter
  MPI_Recv(&seed, rank, SEEDTAG, persistent);
  MPI_Recv(&iter, rank, ITERTAG, persistent);
}

init_data(data, seed);

if (failure()) {
  // retrieve boundary conditions
  MPI_Recv(data[SIZE-1], other, BNDTAG,
    persistent);
}


for (int i = iter; i<10, i++) {
  compute(data);

  boundary = data[0];
  MPI_Sendrecv(&boundary, other, BNDTAG,
     data[SIZE-1], other, BNDTAG,
     MPI_COMM_WORLD);
  // store boundary for recovery
  MPI_Send(&boundary, other, BNDTAG,
    persistent);

  seed = aggregate(data);
  printf("%i␣%i␣%f\n", rank, i, seed);

  // store state and aggregate for recovery
  MPI_Send(&seed, rank, SEEDTAG, persistent);
  MPI_Send(&i, rank, ITERTAG, persistent);
}

printf("Final:␣%i␣%f", rank, seed);
MPI_Finalize();
```

Figure 3. A simple MPI program with persistency for 2 processes

```
#include "scr.h"

int MPI_Init(int *argc, char ***argv) {
  int scr_rc;

  // Regular MPI_Init stuff.
  // Assumes success so far.

  scr_rc = SCR_Init();

  if (SCR_SUCCESS != scr_rc) {
    // and error occurred,
    // delegate to OpenMPI for abort.
    return MPI_ERROR_HANDLER();
  }
  return MPI_SUCCESS;
}

int MPI_Finalize() {
  int scr_rc;

  // shutdown SCR first
  scr_rc = SCR_Init();
  if (SCR_SUCCESS != scr_rc) {
    // and error occurred,
    // delegate to OpenMPI for abort
    return MPI_ERROR_HANDLER();
  }

 // Regular MPI_Finalize stuff.
}
```

Figure 4. Illustrative code for initialisation and shutdown of SCR inside the respective MPI methods

Incoming persistent messages with the same signature, and thus different sequence number, shall overwrite the previously stored one. However, one could also implement a stack of user-defined depth and store a history of messages, which are retrieved in order of storage or in reverse. Such schemes could be facilitated by additional parameters provided in the info object at the time of creation of the persistent communicator. For the sake of simplicity of our prototypical implementation, we have chosen the first approach: incoming messages on a persistent communicator overwrite any received previously message with same signature.

We have implemented our prototype on top of OpenMPI v1.10.0. OpenMPI is a very modular implementation of the MPI standard and thus very easy to extend. We have further used the latest version of SCR.

B. Initialisation & shutdown

Users of our persistent message logging shall not have to invoke any method for initialisation or shutdown other than the usual MPI interfaces, i.e., `MPI_Init()` and `MPI_Finalize()`, respectively.

However, any application wishing to use SCR needs to invoke the method `SCR_Init()` to initialise the library before invoking any other SCR method. Further, such initialisation of SCR needs to happen after MPI initialisation. Similarly, SCR expects to be shut down by invocation of the method `SCR_Finalize()` before invocation of `MPI_Finalize()`.

```
// extend communicator object
struct ompi_communicator_t {
  // Regular OpenMPI code.
  int persistFlg;          // >0 if persistent
  char *key;               // session key
  ompi_info_t persistInfo; // arguments
};

int MPI_Comm_persist(MPI_Comm comm,
    char *key,
    MPI_Info info,
    MPI_Comm *newcomm) {

  int rc;

  // duplicate communicator
  rc = MPI_Comm_dup(comm, newcomm);

  // flag as persistent and attach info
  (*(*newcomm)).persistFlg  = 1;
  (*(*newcomm)).key         = key;
  (*(*newcomm)).persistInfo = info;

  if (MPI_SUCCESS != rc) {
    // and error occurred,
    // delegate to OpenMPI for abort
    return MPI_ERROR_HANDLER();
  }
  return MPI_SUCCESS;
}
```

Figure 5. Illustrative code of the method to create a communicator with persistency semantics.

In order to hide this from the user, we have modified the respective MPI methods to take care of SCR initialisation and shutdown as shown schematically in Figure 4. SCR Initialisation is done at the very end of the MPI initialisation method; similarly, SCR shutdown is done right at the beginning of the MPI initialisation method.

An alternative initialisation scheme, is to delay SCR initialisation up to the point where the first communicator is marked for persistency, i.e., the first call to the method **MPI_Comm_persist**(), or even delayed further to the point where the persistent communicator is used for the first time for sending or receiving a message. The advantage of both these approaches is that SCR is only initialised if persistent message logging is actually used in the application. On the other side, the overhead of repeatedly checking if SCR has been initialised already is presumably non-negligible. In any case, SCR needs to be shutdown together with MPI, as there is no other way to infer the last usage of any persistent communicator.

C. Setting up persistent communicators and passing additional arguments

Our proposed scheme is based on using communicators that have been marked by the user as being special. Setting up such a special communicator with persistent semantics is done through the method **MPI_Comm_persist**(). Figure 5 shows a sketch of our implementation of this routine. In order to designate a given communicator as persistent we have extended the definition of OpenMPI's internal communicator data-structure **struct ompi_communicator_t** and added the flag `persistFlg`. We also added a further field `key` to hold the user-specified session key. The meaning of the last additional field `persistInfo` will be explained a little further down this section.

Essentially, setting up a persistent communicator is down by first duplicating the user-provided non-persistent communicator `comm` using the standard MPI functionality **MPI_Comm_dup**(). Then the communicator is marked as persistent by setting the flag `persistFlg` and storing the session key `key` in the communicator object. Finally, if any of the previous steps produced an error, the implementation delegates to OpenMPI's error handler, otherwise it returns successfully.

In addition, the user shall be able to pass additional arguments or hints during setup of persistent communicators. We have decided to follow the same approach for user-hints as in other parts of MPI and exploit the so-called **MPI_Info** objects. Basically, these info objects are a set of user-defined, arbitrary key-values pairs which have semantic significance only in specific context and ignore otherwise. Note that this is also intended as a way to introduce future extensions to our proposal. To that end the method **MPI_Comm_persist**() also takes an argument `info` of type **MPI_Info**. This argument is stored in the corresponding field of the communicator object for later use. In principle, an advanced implementation of our proposal might check the contents of this object at setup time; our prototype just ignores them at this point.

D. Message logging and retrieval

Most of the programme logic required for our scheme sits in the actual communication primitives. As our prototype is intended only as proof-of-concept, we have implemented our proposal only for the two main communication routines **MPI_Send**() and **MPI_Recv**(), as shown schematically in Figure 6. It is trivial to extend the implementation to non-blocking communication primitives or the other communication modes such as buffered and synchronous.

The first thing the communication routines do, is check if the communicator for this messaging request is flagged as persistent. If it is not, processing of the message is delegated to the regular MPI routine. If the communication takes place on a persistent communicator, though, we construct an unambiguous envelope address from the MPI message signature `(comm, src, dest, tag)` (which uniquely identifies a MPI message, see Section III-A), and the user specified session key, which is retrieved from the communicator. The envelope can be something like a string concatenation or a hash function. The next step consists in calculating the total message volume from size of the given MPI datatype `dtype`, which is determined by calling internal MPI services, and the number of such data items `count`. Finally, we pass control to the method `persist()` and `unpersist()`, for **MPI_Send**() and **MPI_Recv**(), respectively, which takes care of actually persisting and retrieving data.

Figure 7 illustrates the implementation of the routines which are used to persist and retrieve a given message buffer through SCR, respectively. In order to persist messages! we register a checkpoint with SCR by calling

```
#include "scr.h"

int MPI_Send(const void *buf, \
      int count, MPI_Datatype dtype, \
      int dest, int tag, MPI_Comm comm) {

  if (!comm->persistentFlg) {
    // normal send request
    return _MPI_Send(buf, count, \
          dtype, dest, tag, comm);
  }

  // persistent send request from here

  // construct envelope
  src = MPI_Rank(comm);
  key = comm->key;
  env = envelope(comm, src, dest, tag, key);

  // calculate message size
  msize = count * _OMPI_sizeof(dtype);

  // persist buffer
  scr_rc = persist(buf, msize, env);

  if (SCR_SUCCESS != scr_rc) {
    // and error occurred,
    // delegate to OpenMPI for abort.
    return MPI_ERROR_HANDLER();
  }
  return MPI_SUCCESS;
}

int MPI_Recv(void *buf, \
      int count, MPI_Datatype dtype, \
      int src, int tag, MPI_Comm comm, \
      MPI_Status *status) {

  if (!comm->persistentFlg) {
    // normal receive request
    return _MPI_Recv(buf, count, \
          dtype, src, tag, comm, \
          status);
  }

  // persistent recv request from here

  // construct envelope
  dest = MPI_Rank(comm);
  key = comm->key;
  env = envelope(comm, src, dest, tag, key);

  // calculate message size
  msize = count * _OMPI_sizeof(dtype);

  // unpersist buffer
  scr_rc = unpersist(buf, msize, env);

  if (SCR_SUCCESS != scr_rc) {
    // and error occurred,
    // delegate to OpenMPI for abort.
    return MPI_ERROR_HANDLER();
  }
  return MPI_SUCCESS;
}
```

Figure 6. Illustrative code for dealing with persistent communicators inside MPI communication methods.

```
int persist(void *buf, int msize, \
            char *env) {
  char filename[SCR_MAX_FILENAME];
  FILE *fh;

  // register checkpoint with SCR
  SCR_Start_checkpoint();

  // ask SCR for full filename and open
  SCR_Route_file(env, filename);
  fh = open(filename, "w");

  // hand data over to SCR
  fwrite(buf, 1, msize, fh);

  // disengage from SCR
  fclose(fh);
  SCR_Complete_checkpoint();

  return success();
}

int unpersist(void *buf, int msize, \
              char *env) {
  char filename[SCR_MAX_FILENAME];
  FILE *fh;

  // ask SCR for full filename and open
  SCR_Route_file(env, filename);
  fh = open(filename, "r");

  // retrieve message buffer and disengage
  fread(buf, 1, msize, fh);
  fclose(fh);

  return success();
}
```

Figure 7. Illustrative code to persist communication buffers through SCR.

`SCR_Start_checkpoint()` at the beginning of `persist()`. Next, we ask SCR for a full filename path, which is constructed from the unique envelope string described in the previous paragraph. All (write) operations on this file are routed through SCR and form part of the register checkpoint. We use this facility to store the message buffer. The final call to `SCR_Complete_checkpoint()` commits all data and initiates replication across neighbour nodes as well as storage to disk. The routine for retrieving messages from persistent storage, i.e., `unpersist`,is a bit simpler. SCR is involved only to get the SCR filename as above. The message buffer is than read directly via POSIX file operations without intervention by SCR.

V. Experimental Evaluation

In this section, we present a demonstration that our proposed idioms are sufficient to implement user-level fault-tolerance in applications. To that end, we developed a small scientific application, namely heat transfer, and implemented that with Python on top of our MPI prototype. Further, we use this demonstrator to show that the overheads incurred by persisting data through MPI semantics behave as expected.

```
1  import mpi4py
2  from heat import Heat2D
3
4  comm = MPI.COMM_WORLD
5  persist = MPI.Comm_persist(world)
6
7  myself = persist.Get_rank()
8
9  task = Heat2D()
10
11 while time < end_time:
12   # check for failure
13   if task.failure():
14     persist.Recv(state, myself, STATE_TAG)
15     task.restore_local_state(state)
16
17   # normal operation
18   task.exchange_boundaries(comm)
19   task.solver()
20
21   # save state for fault-tolerance
22   if time%interval == 0:
23     state = task.get_local_state()
24     persist.Send(state, myself, STATE_TAG)
25
26   # progress time
27   time += time_step_size
```

Figure 8. Illustration of the python implementation of the heat transfer problem used for evaluation.

A. Experimental setup

We have tested our prototypical implementation on a Cray XC40 supercomputing system running the Cray programming environment CCE 8.4.3. The application code was implemented with Python 2.7.8, and used NumPy 1.9.0 as well as MPI4Py 2.0.0. The prototype was built on top of OpenMPI 1.10.0 and the latest SCR commit 1e8358f from GitHub. The nodes of the Cray XC40 consists of two Intel Haswell E5-2680v3 sockets with 12 cores each. For the experiments we ran OpenMPI over the TCP conduit, as stock OpenMPI does not support the native Cray interconnect.

The application code solves the well known heat diffusion equation. The schematic code in Figure 8 illustrates the parts relevant to this paper only. Most of the programmes business logic is encapsulated in the class `Heat2D` and instantiated as object `task`. The application uses two distinct communicators: the regular communicator `comm`, and a persistent communicator `persist` which is derived from `comm` on line 5. To complete the initialisation, each MPI process stores its own rank in the variable `myself`. The main part of the application consists of the time integration loop starting at line 11. In its original, i.e., non-persistent, version the time loop would consist only of exchanging boundary conditions with neighbour process through the communicator `comm` and the actual solver step on lines 18–19, as well as increment of time on line 27.

To achieve fault-tolerance, the local state is determined and stored periodically through the persistent communicator as illustrated on lines 21–24. Note that the definition of a local state, which is suitable for application restart is completely up to the use case. Here, we have take a straightforward average over the temperatur on the grid. Saving the state is accomplished simply by sending a message to `myself` on the persistent communicator. The user may choose to do this for every times step or at intervals specified through the variable `interval`. In case of failure, the application retrieves the state by receiving a message from `myself` on the persistent communicator. This message is used to restore the local state as shown on lines 12–15.

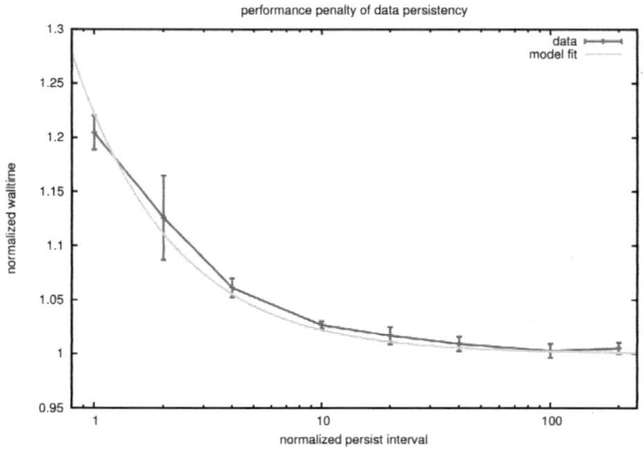

Figure 9. Overhead of our implementation as a function of length of interval between two data persist events.

Clearly, achieving fault-tolerance incurs a runtime overhead for the application. Additional time is spent, in particular, determining if the application state needs saving, aggregating the application state, and the actual cost of persisting it. Part of these overheads are beyond the responsibility of our implementation. However, for the sake on simplicity, we have benchmarked the fault-tolerant code against a version where lines 5, 14–15, and 23–24 were commented out, essentially. So, the measured overhead includes the calculation of the local state, which however should be small.

The overhead should depend on the frequency of persisting the local state, and on the duration of doing so. In our experiment, we have varied the persistency interval, i.e., the variable `interval` in the code above. As we cannot directly control the duration of the persistency operation, we have varied the time taken to calculate a single iteration of the time loop by increasing the problem size. We have expressed the problem size in such a way, that the execution time for a single iteration depends linearly on it. All benchmark experiments have been repeated at least 10 times. The values reported correspond to the average over all runs. The error bars are calculated from the sample variance; error propagation calculus is used for all values calculated from the basic measurements.

B. Results and discussion

In order to study the overheads of our implementation, we have varied the interval at which the local state is persisted. Figure 9 shows the ratio of execution time of the code with persist logic over the original non-fault-tolerant version as a function of the interval. Note that larger interval values correspond to less frequently saved states. As expected, the

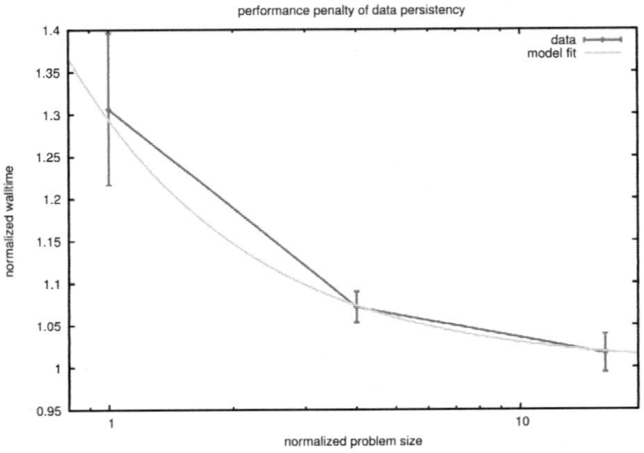

Figure 10. Overhead of our implementation as a function of the application's problem size.

overhead is largest for small intervals and decreases with increasing interval length. We have fitted the experimental data to the expected model curve $T(i) = (i + c_i)/i$. Here, T is the normalised execution time, i the interval length, and c_i a fit parameter. The experimental data is described very well by model; the standard error on the fit parameter c_i is less than 5%. This shows that for large values of the interval the overhead becomes negligible and vanishes asymptotically.

In a second series of experiments, we fixed the interval to unity and varied the problem size as shown in Figure 10. At small problem sizes, the overhead is large, as persisting data takes more time compared to the calculation of an iteration of the algorithm. With increasing problem size, the time taken to persist the application state decreases in relation to the time spent in calculations and the overhead decreases. Again, this can be modelled with a function of the form $T(s) = (s + c_s)/s$. As shown in the figure, the model describes the data very accurately. The error on the fit parameter c_s is less than 3%. From this model, we can again expect that the overhead becomes negligible at sufficiently large problem size.

VI. Conclusions

In this paper, we have presented work in progress on the a method to allow persisting of application data and internal state for fault recovery. Unlike other methods, our approach uses well known MPI semantics. The only addition to MPI is a routine that allows to mark a communicator as persistent. All messages to such a communicator are stored on a stable storage for later usage during failure recovery. We have shown basic idioms of storing and retrieving not only application data, but also internal state of the application and to use message logging to recover messages that have been exchanged with other MPI processes just prior to the fault. To verify that the proposed idioms are sufficient to realise user-level data persistency for fault-tolerance, we have done a prototypical implementation of our interface and demonstrated the concept with a typical scientific application. Finally, we have shown that the overheads of prototypical become negligible for sufficiently large problem sizes or sufficiently large data persistency intervals.

Acknowledgment

This work was supported by the German Research Foundation (DFG) through the German Priority Programme 1648 Software for Exascale Computing (SPPEXA) and the EC H2020 programme through the project MIKELANGELO under Grant Agreement no. 645402.

References

[1] J. Gracia, M. W. Sethi, N. Struckmann, and R. Keller, "Towards data persistency for fault-tolerance using MPI semantics," in Proceedings of International Conference on Advanced Communications and Computation (INFOCOMP 2015). IARIA, 2015, pp. 26–29.

[2] Y. Ling, J. Mi, and X. Lin, "A variational calculus approach to optimal checkpoint placement," IEEE Trans. Computers, vol. 50, no. 7, 2001, pp. 699–708.

[3] MPI Forum, "MPI: A Message-Passing Interface Standard. Version 3.0," September 21st 2012, available at: http://www.mpi-forum.org [retrieved: May, 2016].

[4] D. J. Sorin, M. M. K. Martin, M. D. Hill, and D. A. Wood, "Safetynet: Improving the availability of shared memory multiprocessors with global checkpoint/recovery," SIGARCH Comput. Archit. News, vol. 30, no. 2, May 2002, pp. 123–134.

[5] J. Duell, P. Hargrove, and E. Roman, "The Design and Implementation of Berkeley Lab's Linux Checkpoint/Restart," Future Technologies Group, white paper, 2003.

[6] J. Cornwell and A. Kongmunvattana, "Efficient system-level remote checkpointing technique for blcr," in Proceedings of the 2011 Eighth International Conference on Information Technology: New Generations, ser. ITNG '11. Washington, DC, USA: IEEE Computer Society, 2011, pp. 1002–1007.

[7] CRIU project, "Checkpoint/Restore In Userspace – CRIU," 2015, available at: http://http://www.criu.org/Main_Page/ [retrieved: May, 2016].

[8] A. Moody, G. Bronevetsky, K. Mohror, and B. R. d. Supinski, "Design, modeling, and evaluation of a scalable multi-level checkpointing system," in Proceedings of the 2010 ACM/IEEE International Conference for High Performance Computing, Networking, Storage and Analysis, ser. SC '10. Washington, DC, USA: IEEE Computer Society, 2010, pp. 1–11.

[9] K. Mohror, A. Moody, and B. R. de Supinski, "Asynchronous checkpoint migration with mrnet in the scalable checkpoint / restart library," in IEEE/IFIP International Conference on Dependable Systems and Networks Workshops, DSN 2012, Boston, MA, USA, June 25-28, 2012. IEEE, 2012, pp. 1–6.

[10] G. E. Fagg et al., "Fault tolerant communication library and applications for high performance," in Los Alamos Computer Science Institute Symposium, Santa Fe, NM, Oct. 2003, pp. 27–29.

[11] E. Gabriel et al., "Open MPI: Goals, concept, and design of a next generation MPI implementation," in Proceedings of the 11th European PVM/MPI Users' Group Meeting, ser. LNCS, D. Kranzlmüller, P. Kacsuk, and J. Dongarra, Eds., vol. 3241. Budapest, Hungary: Springer, Sep. 2004, pp. 97–104.

[12] W. Bland, A. Bouteiller, T. Hérault, J. Hursey, G. Bosilca, and J. J. Dongarra, "An evaluation of user-level failure mitigation support in MPI," in Recent Advances in the Message Passing Interface - 19th European MPI Users' Group Meeting, EuroMPI 2012, Vienna, Austria, September 23-26, 2012. Proceedings, 2012, pp. 193–203.

[13] W. Bland, A. Bouteiller, T. Hérault, G. Bosilca, and J. Dongarra, "Post-failure recovery of MPI communication capability: Design and rationale," IJHPCA, vol. 27, no. 3, 2013, pp. 244–254.

[14] J. Hursey, R. Graham, G. Bronevetsky, D. Buntinas, H. Pritchard, and D. Solt, "Run-through stabilization: An mpi proposal for process fault tolerance," in Recent Advances in the Message Passing Interface, ser. Lecture Notes in Computer Science, Y. Cotronis, A. Danalis, D. Nikolopoulos, and J. Dongarra, Eds. Springer Berlin Heidelberg, 2011, vol. 6960, pp. 329–332.

Modeling the Evolution of Terrestrial and Water-rich Planets and Moons

Lena Noack, Attilio Rivoldini, Tim Van Hoolst
Department of Reference Systems and Planetology
Royal Observatory of Belgium (ROB)
Brussels, Belgium
Email: lena.noack@oma.be, attilio.rivoldini@oma.be, tim.vanhoolst@oma.be

***Abstract*—We completed the numerical code CHIC (short for *Coupling Habitability, Interior, and Crust*) for thermo-chemical simulations of the evolution of both terrestrial and water-rich planets and moons. The study focusses on the numerical aspects of the code implementations and their validation. The thermal evolution of the mantle is calculated either by solving the energy conservation equation supplemented by boundary-layer theory (1D parameterized thermal evolution model) or by solving the energy, mass, and momentum conservation equations (2D/3D convective thermal evolution). For the latter setting, the equations can be solved in both incompressible and compressible formulations and can include chemical buoyancy effects for an inhomogeneous mantle by applying a particles-in-cell method. The code provides a user updatable library of thermodynamic properties of core, mantle and water/ice materials derived from the associated equations of state. CHIC has been benchmarked with different convection codes, and has been compared to published interior-structure models and 1D parameterized models. CHIC is an advanced simulation code that can be applied to a diverse range of geodynamic problems and questions.**

Keywords–fluid dynamics; convection; numerical modeling; thermal evolution; planetology.

I. Introduction

To understand geophysical processes in a planet like Earth including convection, surface processes as plate tectonics or volcanism, and the evolution of mantle and atmosphere, numerical models are essential tools [1] and have been applied in the past decades to investigate various planets and moons. Numerical simulations are especially needed for the investigation of feedback cycles between the interior and the surface, as, for example, the CO_2-cycle (where subduction of carbonates helps to regulate surface temperatures over geophysical timescales), the subduction cycle (delivering volatiles to the mantle and releasing volatiles by volcanic outgassing), the evolution of continents (stabilizing plate tectonics) and the possible maintenance of a magnetic field by strong cooling of the core. These processes are likely important for the habitability of Earth, i.e., for the ability to host life, and may also play an important role for other planets [2], [3].

Different numerical models have been applied to study the evolution of terrestrial planets or moons in the literature, either focussing on the mantle convection pattern in 2D or 3D geometries, or investigating the general thermal evolution with 1D parameterized models.

In this study, we couple both methods in one simulation code CHIC together with a library of thermodynamic properties that can be applied to self-consistently determine the interior structure of a planet and its later evolution depending on key factors as, for example, the planet mass, composition, and initial temperature profile.

The paper is organized as follows: Section II gives an overview of the state of the art and the progress in numerical modelling via the CHIC code. In Section III, we describe the different modules of CHIC, followed by the validation of the correctness of the models in Section IV. Finally, in Section V, we summarize the possibilities of a coupled 1D - 2D/3D code and the planned future work.

II. State of the Art

Several 2D and 3D convection codes have been developed over the past decades to investigate Earth-like planets. They typically concentrate solely on either the thermal evolution or do steady-state snapshots of the mantle and crust. Some models include the simplified evolution of the core [4] or of the atmosphere [5], [6] as boundary conditions to the mantle convection simulation. In such a convection model, lateral variations in the mantle can be investigated, including mantle plumes, local melt regions, and plate motions.

On the other hand, a 1D model assumes a laterally averaged profile for temperature and material properties. As a result, simulations of, for example, the volcanic history of a terrestrial planet may differ between 1D and 2D/3D models.

1D thermal evolution models also have several advantages over 2D/3D convection models. Parameterization models [7] are applicable over a large parameter space (applicable also at high convection velocities, where convection models suffer from numerical problems), and include the simulation of both liquid and solid materials. Especially, strongly convecting systems (e.g., liquid core or ocean) can be simulated, which is generally infeasible for planetary convection codes, as they will either produce numerical instabilities or require an unacceptably large amount of computational power. 1D models are very fast compared to convection models. Depending on the specific application, a 1D thermal evolution model runs in the order of seconds or minutes, whereas 2D/3D models (that typically need a high resolution to avoid numerical errors) may run for days or weeks.

To understand different geophysical processes and feedback cycles on Earth-like or water-rich planets, a coupled model

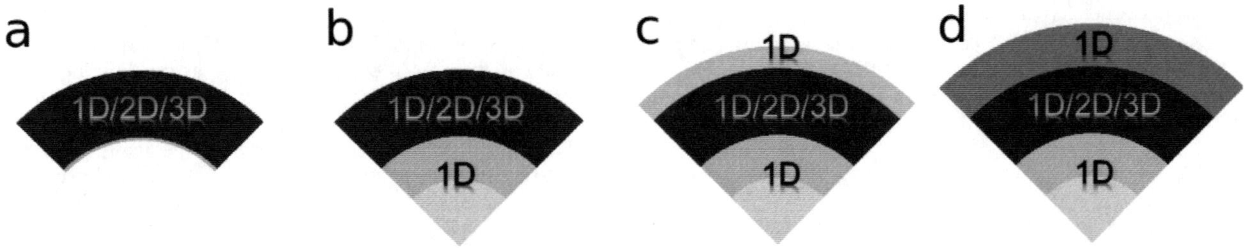

Figure 1. Possible configurations that are investigated with CHIC: a) mantle with variable CMB temperature, b) mantle with core evolution and inner core freezing, c) mantle and core with an atmosphere, d) mantle and core with a deep ocean on top (we neglect here a possible atmosphere).

is needed that can combine 1D parameterized models (for example for the treatment of the water-layer or the core) with 2D mantle convection models.

We therefore developed a new code CHIC at the Royal Observatory of Belgium, that combines different numerical models in one toolbox. The code is written in Fortran, which allows for fast simulations (either running on one processor or in parallel) on standard high-performance clusters.

The CHIC code is able to treat both 1D parameterized models (using the thermal boundary layer theory to determine the temperature evolution in a terrestrial planet [7], [8] or ocean planet [9]) and 2D/3D models to investigate the detailed convection pattern in a silicate mantle or ice layer over time.

In our implementation, the planets are assumed to consist of several different spherical layers (shells). The lowermost shell represents the core and is overlain by a silicate shell (mantle and crust) and a potential water-ice layer. The uppermost shell represents the planets atmosphere. All shells are thermally coupled, i.e., the heat flux and temperature are continuous at each interface between the different layers. The surface temperature is allowed to vary with time depending on the greenhouse gases in the atmosphere, or is taken constant if changes in the atmosphere are neglected.

CHIC allows the user to apply different 1D or 2D/3D modules as needed: for the core, either only changes in the core-mantle boundary (CMB) temperature are investigated, or a 1D parameterized model of the iron core including inner core freezing is applied (Figures 1(a) and 1(b)); the thermal state of the mantle and high-pressure ice layers are investigated either via a convection model or a 1D parameterized model; the atmosphere and a potential water ocean (Figures 1(c) and 1(d)) are investigated with a 1D module, whereas ice layers could be investigated also with the 2D/3D convection module. CHIC is therefore a powerful tool for the investigation of the evolution of terrestrial or ocean planets - from interior to atmosphere - and their possible habitability.

III. Models

CHIC uses various modules for modelling different shells of a terrestrial or ocean planet. The basic modules provided by CHIC are listed below. The density of the material and other physical properties are determined as described in Section III-A, and can be applied to both 1D and 2D/3D modules. The input file used for the simulations is similar for all modules, which simplifies comparison of the 1D model with the 2D mantle model.

A. Interior structure model and material properties

Within CHIC, simple interior structure models can be generated to assess the radius of a terrestrial planet for given mass, composition, and temperature profile. Those models assume a spherical planet that is differentiated into an iron core, a silicate shell, and an optional ocean layer. For the silicate mantle we assume an Mg-end member olivine system. We neglect high pressure olivine polymorphs but allow for the disassociation of olivine to perovskite and Mg-wstite and the occurrence of post-perovskite at high pressure and temperature. Material properties (density ϱ, thermal expansion coefficient α and heat capacity c_p) are computed from equations of state for variable pressure and temperature [10], [11].

The gravitational acceleration $g(r)$ as a function of radius r is determined from the Poisson equation, it depends on the gravity value at the surface of the planet,

$$dg/dr = 4\pi G\varrho - 2g/r \quad (1)$$

where G is the gravitational constant.

The pressure as a function of depth is calculated by assuming hydrostatic equilibrium and depends on the atmospheric pressure at the surface:

$$dp/dr = -g\varrho \quad (2)$$

The mass $m(r)$ is

$$dm/dr = 4\varpi r^2 \varrho \quad (3)$$

B. Core evolution model

The 1D core evolution module determines the variation of upper core temperature with time via the energy conservation equation

$$\rho_c c_{p,c} V_c \varepsilon_c dT_c/dt = -q_c A_c \quad (4)$$

where the index c denotes core values, V_c is the core volume and A_c the core surface area, ε_c is a constant relating the average core temperature to the CMB temperature, t is the time and q_c is the heat flux from the core into the mantle (defined via the heat flux that the mantle can take up, e.g., [8]),

$$q_c = -k_m dT/dr|_{r=R_c} \quad (5)$$

where k_m is the mantle thermal conductivity. We neglect radioactive heat sources in the core, as well as tidal heating effects. If the freezing of an inner core is considered, additional terms for latent heat and gravitational energy release have to be added in Eq. (4) [12]. For 2D/3D convection models, temperature is calculated at pre-defined grid points, and the average temperature gradient at the CMB is calculated over the two bottom shells of the mantle grid; in the 1D parameterized model, the heat flux is computed from the boundary-layer theory.

For the thermal evolution, either a pure iron core or an iron-rich core containing lighter elements like sulfur is considered. In the latter case, core freezing can be modelled if the core temperature falls below the melting temperature. This model, however, only works if the freezing of the core starts at the core center (leading to a solid inner core as on Earth). This may not be the case for Mercury or Ganymede, where iron may solidify in the upper part of the core and sink down as (so-called) iron snow.

We only model planets without the iron snow regime and adopt the model of [4], which determines latent heat released by iron solidification and gravitational energy produced by differentiation of the core into an inner and outer core. Both mechanisms have an influence on the thermal evolution of the mantle. For super-Earths (i.e., planets up to 10 Earth masses), we neglect lighter elements in the core, as material properties for those are only known for a limited pressure range.

C. Mantle: 1D parameterized model

The 1D module assesses the thermal evolution of the mantle based on [7], [8], [9]. We refer to these references for full details. The model determines the evolution of the upper mantle temperature T_m over time by considering that the loss of energy due to mantle cooling and heat flux out of the mantle is balanced by the heat flux from the core into the mantle and the radioactive heat production in the mantle (we neglect heat produced by tidal friction):

$$\varrho_m c_{p,m} V_l \varepsilon_m dT_m/dt = -q_l A_l + q_c A_c + Q_m V_l \quad (6)$$

The index m denotes mantle values. V_l is the volume of the mantle from core to the base of the lithosphere, and A_l is the area at the boundary between mantle and lithosphere. The constant ε_m relates the average mantle temperature with T_m. The mantle temperature decreases due to heat flux out of the mantle into the lithosphere q_l, increases due to inflowing heat flux from the core q_c and increases with heat released by radioactive heat sources Q_m.

CHIC also allows to model possible melting events and crust formation over time. This leads to additional terms in (6). For details on the crustal evolution, as well as the definition of the thermal boundary layers and calculation of the temperature in the lithosphere, we refer to [8]. Note that the 1D parameterized model only considers the evolution of the temperature over time, and assumes effective convection. To understand the convection mechanism and its strength depending on mantle parameters and planet size (possibly triggering plate tectonics at the surface), a more sophisticated 2D/3D convection model is needed.

D. Mantle: 2D / 3D convection model

The CHIC code uses a finite volume (FV) field approach to solve the conservation equations of mass, momentum and energy. A finite grid is placed in the mantle, with shells from the CMB to the planet surface, and a predefined number of grid points per shell. We then define Voronoi cell volumes around each grid point and solve the system of equations on each cell volume considering the flux in and out of the cell and the energy production in the cell. We employ a staggered grid, see Figure 2, where the scalar values like temperature (T) and pressure (p) are defined at the cell center (i,k), whereas the lateral and radial velocities u, w are defined at the cell faces. The viscosity η is calculated at the cell centers (CV) and is interpolated at the cell nodes (N) and cell faces (A,B,C in x-,y- and z-direction) with a geometric averaging scheme.

The grid is either defined in Cartesian coordinates in a 2D or 3D box or in polar coordinates for a 2D cylindrical sphere (a cut through the planet at the equator representing the temperature profile of a cylinder with the 2D plane as a basis) or a 2D spherical annulus (an equatorial cut or polar section that approximates the temperature profile of a sphere in 3D, [13]), see Figure 3. For the 2D models with spherical or cylindrical geometry, it is often useful to employ a regional sector of the 2D spherical model (as shown in Figure 6). In addition to the grid, randomly distributed particles (also called tracers) are used to transport local information as for example density variations or water content, see Section III-D3.

In CHIC, the thermal (or thermochemical, see Section III-D3) evolution can be modelled either for an incompressible medium with the Boussinesq approximation (BA) or the Extended-Boussinesq approximation (EBA), or for a compressible medium with the (truncated) anelastic liquid approximation (TALA/ALA).

1) (Extended) Boussinesq approximation: We solve the equation system for an incompressible medium either with the Boussinesq approximation (BA), which neglects the influence of compressibility on the mantle, or we apply the Extended-Boussinesq approximation (EBA), which yields an adiabatic temperature increase with depth depending on the dissipation number $Di = \alpha g D/C_p$, where D is the mantle thickness (see [7] for details on the model). For a dissipation number Di of zero, the formulation reduces to the Boussinesq approximation (BA). We therefore concentrate on the EBA model below.

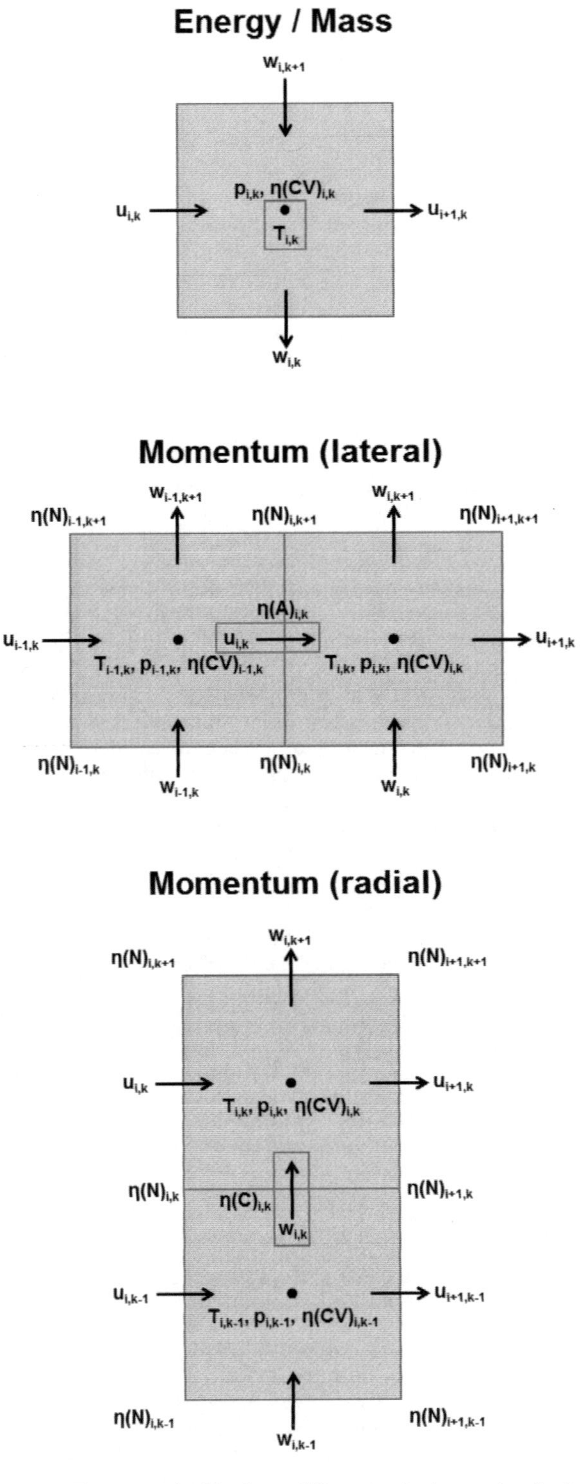

Figure 2. The staggered grid enforces different local solver meshes for the energy, mass and momentum conservation equations. The center of each local mesh is highlighted with a red box.

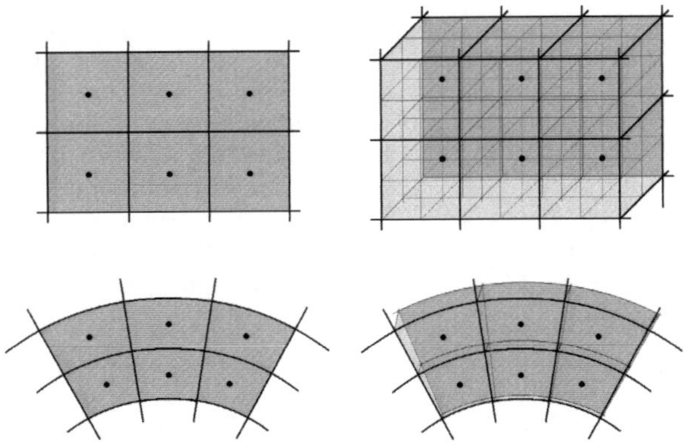

Figure 3. Geometries implemented in CHIC. Top: 2D Cartesian box and 3D Cartesian box. Bottom: 2D cylinder and 2D spherical annulus.

In the EBA approximation, the non-dimensional conservation equations of energy, mass and momentum can be expressed as (e.g., [14]):

$$\frac{\partial T}{\partial t} + \vec{v} \cdot \nabla T + Di(T + T_0)\vec{v}_r = \nabla^2 T + \frac{Di}{Ra}\Phi + H \quad (7)$$

$$\nabla \cdot \vec{v} = 0 \quad (8)$$

$$-\nabla p + \nabla \cdot \sigma = RaTe_r \quad (9)$$

$$\sigma = \eta \left(\nabla \vec{v} + \nabla \vec{v}^{\mathrm{T}} \right) \quad (10)$$

Here, T is temperature, T_0 surface temperature, t time, and Di the dissipation number. The convective pressure is denoted by p; $\vec{v}$ is the velocity and $\vec{v}_r$ the radial velocity, whereas e_r is the radial unit vector. H is the heat source (e.g., radioactive heat source). σ the convective stress tensor, η is the viscosity, and T indicates a transposed matrix. The Rayleigh number Ra is a measure for the convective vigour

$$Ra = \frac{\rho g \alpha D^3 \Delta T}{\kappa \eta_{ref}} \quad (11)$$

where ΔT is the mantle temperature contrast, $\kappa = k/(\rho C_p)$ the thermal diffusivity and η_{ref} a reference viscosity defined at a reference temperature, pressure and stress (for non-Newtonian viscosity), see Section III-D5. Φ is the viscous dissipation [7], [13], [14]

$$\Phi = \frac{1}{2}\sigma : \dot{\varepsilon} = \eta \dot{\varepsilon} : \dot{\varepsilon} \quad (12)$$

with strain rate tensor $\dot{\varepsilon} = \partial v_i / \partial x_j$.

Equations (7)-(9) are written in a non-dimensional form [15]. The non-dimensionalization is obtained by dividing the dimensional value of each variable by a reference value as given in [15]. The quantities given in Section IV are also non-dimensional values.

2) Anelastic liquid approximation: While the (Extended) Boussinesq approximation models a constant density in the mantle, in reality the density increases with depth due to pressure-induced compression. In Mars' and Mercury's mantle the compressiblity effect is small and is typically neglected. For Earth-size and larger planets the density increases significantly within the mantle and is typically addressed in mantle convection codes via the (truncated) anelastic liquid approximation (short TALA or ALA), see [7] and [14].

Reference profiles are employed for the pressure, density and temperature $(\bar{p}, \bar{\rho}, \bar{T})$, as well as lateral variation fields due to convection (p', ρ', T'):

$$\begin{aligned} T &= \bar{T} + T' \\ p &= \bar{p} + p' \\ \rho &= \bar{\rho} + \rho' \end{aligned}$$

In addition, we apply reference profiles for the gravitational acceleration, thermal expansion coefficient, heat capacity at constant volume or pressure, bulk modulus and Grüneisen parameter $(\bar{g},\bar{\alpha},\bar{C_v},\bar{C_p},\bar{K_T},\bar{\gamma})$.

The conservation equations of mass and momentum for the ALA formulation are solved together in a coupled system and read in non-dimensional quantities [7]

$$\nabla \cdot (\bar{\rho}\vec{v}) = 0 \tag{13}$$

$$-\nabla p' + \nabla \cdot \sigma + Di \frac{\bar{\rho}\bar{g}p' C_p}{\bar{\gamma}\bar{K_T} C_v} \vec{e_r} = Ra\bar{\rho}\bar{g}\bar{\alpha}(T - \bar{T})\vec{e_r} \tag{14}$$

$$\sigma = \eta \left(\nabla \vec{v} + \nabla \vec{v}^{\mathrm{T}} - \frac{2}{3} \nabla \cdot \vec{v} I \right) \tag{15}$$

I is the identity tensor. C_p and C_v are the specific heat at constant pressure and volume, K_T is the isothermal bulk modulus.

In the truncated anelastic liquid approximation (TALA), the third term in equation (14) is neglected

$$-\nabla p' + \nabla \cdot \sigma = Ra\bar{\rho}\bar{g}\bar{\alpha}(T - \bar{T})\vec{e_r} \tag{16}$$

The TALA formulation is a simplified compressible formulation that is favoured by several codes to avoid numerical problems due to the additional ALA term (third term in Eq. (14)). Furthermore, this term is often neglected as it requires knowledge of several material properties (as Gruneisen parameter or isothermal bulk modulus) depending on pressure, which requires the usage of an equation of state.

The energy conservation equation for the composite temperature field $(T = \bar{T} + T')$ can be expressed as

$$\begin{aligned} \bar{\rho}\bar{C_p} \left(\frac{\partial T}{\partial t} + \vec{v} \cdot \nabla T \right) &= \nabla \cdot \left(\bar{k} \nabla T \right) + Di \bar{\alpha} \bar{\rho} \bar{g} v_r (T + T_0) \\ &+ \frac{Di}{Ra} \Phi + \bar{\rho} H. \end{aligned} \tag{17}$$

3) Thermochemical formulation: Chemical inhomogeneities influence the convective behaviour. Buoyancy results from both thermal and compositional variations. The buoyancy term in Equation (9) changes to

$$Ra \left[(T - \bar{T}) - B \ (1 - d) \right] \vec{e_r} \tag{18}$$

for the BA and EBA formulation, for the TALA and ALA formulation it changes to

$$Ra\bar{\rho}\bar{g} \left[\bar{\alpha}(T - \bar{T}) - B \ (1 - d) \right] \vec{e_r}, \tag{19}$$

where B is the buoyancy number defined here as $1/(C_{p,0}\alpha_0)$ and $d = C_{ref} - C$ is the nondimensional density variation (a value of 0 denotes reference mantle material density C_{ref} and a positive d value a decreased local density). Such a chemical density variation can occur for example from partial melting or subduction of crustal material. Note that the chemical density variation is different from the compressible density increase with depth. The conservation of the chemical field C is modelled similarly to the energy conservation

$$\frac{\partial C}{\partial t} + \vec{v} \cdot \nabla C = \frac{1}{Le} \nabla^2 C \tag{20}$$

where Le is the Lewis number, which is a dimensional number defined as the ratio of thermal diffusivity κ to chemical diffusivity κ_c. For rocks, the chemical diffusivity is negligibly small and often set to zero. However, solving Eq. (20) without the diffusion term leads to numerical problems. In convection codes therefore either large Lewis numbers are used, or the particle are used instead of a chemical field to trace local density variations. In that approach, the particles are advected along the convective stream lines at the end of each time step via a Runge-Kutta method of fourth order. Averaged cell values are obtained by arithmetic averaging of particle values of all particles in the cell weighted by the reciproce distance of the particle to the cell centre.

4) Solver routines: The energy equation is solved with a second-order implicit Euler method. To solve the conservation equation of mass and momentum, we either use a direct solver or a coupled mass and momentum solver. The direct solver uses one solver matrix for (8) and (9) and applies a penalty formulation following [16]. The iterative, coupled solver employs a pressure correction algorithm called SIMPLER following [16], [17]. In this paper, we apply the direct solver.

The resulting linear equations (for mass, momentum and energy) are solved iteratively with either the Pardiso solver [18] or a biconjugate gradient (BiCG) solver with an under-relaxation scheme. The BiCG solver is slower compared to the Pardiso solver, but is advantageous for parallelization in combination with the SIMPLER pressure correction.

5) Viscosity formulations: The equations above depend on the viscosity of the material η. The viscosity depends on several factors including the temperature, pressure, grain size, water content and strain rate of a material. In the mantle of the Earth, creep is typically described by dislocation creep (motion of dislocations through the crystal lattice) and diffusion creep (deformation of crystalline solids by the diffusion of vacancies through their crystal lattice). The latter is largely independent of the strain-rate, whereas dislocation creep does not depend on the grain size. In CHIC, the user can choose between a dislocation viscosity, a diffusion viscosity and a mix of both formulations. The smaller viscosity is the dominant viscosity for material motion.

The general equation used in CHIC for the viscosity follows an Arrhenius law [19], [20]

$$\eta = A\dot{\varepsilon}_{II}^{\frac{1-n}{n}} d^{\frac{p}{n}} C_{OH}^{\frac{-r}{n}} \exp\left(\frac{E+pV}{nRT}\right) \tag{21}$$

A is a material-dependent constant, n is the stress exponent, d is the grain size, C_{OH} is the concentration of water (for dry materials r=0), r is the water exponent, E the activation energy and V the activation volume. p is the pressure and R the gas constant. Note that the pressure p is the hydrostatic pressure and not the convective pressure as in (9). The parameters for both diffusion and dislocation creep are taken from [19], [20] for both wet and dry materials. The concentration of water C_{OH} is traced via particles and does not only influence the viscosity, but also the local melt temperature, which is smaller in the presence of water than for dry materials [21].

Even though the Arrhenius viscosity (21) is preferentially used for simulations of terrestrial planets, for benchmarks and basic convection simulations typically an approximated viscosity is used, the so-called Frank-Kamenetskii approximation (FKA), given by

$$\eta = A\exp\left(-\theta_T T + \theta_p z\right) \tag{22}$$

Here, θ_T and θ_p are either the logarithm of a pre-defined viscosity contrast with respect to temperature or pressure, respectively, or they are derived from the parameters in (21) [22]. z is the non-dimensional depth (0 at the surface and 1 at the CMB). Note that for the application to plate tectonics simulations, the FKA (22) may not be suitable as shown in [22] and the Arrhenius viscosity (21) should be applied.

E. OpenMP and MPI parallelisation

The Pardiso solver [18], that can be used to solve the linear equations for the mass-momentum and energy equations (see Section III-D4), can employ an automatic OpenMP parallelization. In addition, we implemented an MPI domain decomposition for the mesh. The domain is separated into several subdomains, on which the conservation equations of mass, momentum and energy are solved individually. However, the solution on each subdomain depends on the neighbouring domains. For this reason, additional boundary cells (ghost cells) are added at the boundary between subdomains, which contain the corresponding values (for example, temperature or velocity) from the neighbour domain and serve as boundary cells for their respective MPI domain. After the equation system is solved, ghost cells are updated with the new values from their neighbour domain and the conservation equations are re-solved. This iteration continues until convergence occurs for the root-mean-square velocity.

Figure 4 shows the domain decomposition for four CPUs using either non-periodic or periodic boundary conditions at the left and right side of the box. The bottom and top boundaries are free-slip boundaries (the temperature values are either pre-set boundary values or evolve over time at the 1D model interface for core or ocean/atmosphere). Grey stars denote boundary cells, boxes with coloured boundaries are ghost cells, and black dots denote the cells, for which the mass, momentum and energy equations are solved.

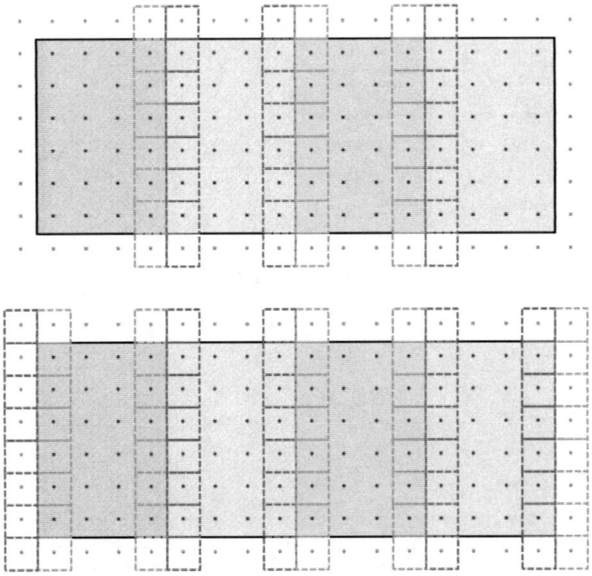

Figure 4. Schematic mesh decomposition for a 2D Cartesian box using four CPUs. Additional cells at the domain boundaries are highlighted in the respective domain color. The upper plot uses a free-slip, reflective side boundary condition, the lower plot applies a periodic boundary condition.

The MPI speed-up factor and simulation times are plotted in Fig. 5 for different grid sizes (shells) and amounts of CPU for a 2D Cartesian box and aspect ratio 1 (i.e., same number of grid points in lateral directions as number of shells) for the first 10 time steps, where the simulation parameters are taken from the first benchmark case in Blankenbach et al. [23]. Here, the Pardiso solver is applied (see Section III-D4). The high-performance SGI cluster, on which the simulations were executed, contains nodes with 24 CPU cores and two Xeon E5-2680V3 processors per node.

The speed-up factor is based on simulations with two CPUs instead of one. The update of the ghost cells (boxes with coloured boundary in Fig. 4) demands at least two iterations to solve the coupled mass-momentum equation system. When using only one CPU, no update of ghost cells and thus no additional iteration is needed. The parallel version can therefore never show a perfect speed-up behaviour when using one CPU as reference. The effect of parallelization on the simulation time can also be observed in the right plot in Fig. 5.

For small grid sizes with 20, 40 or 80 shells, the speed-up

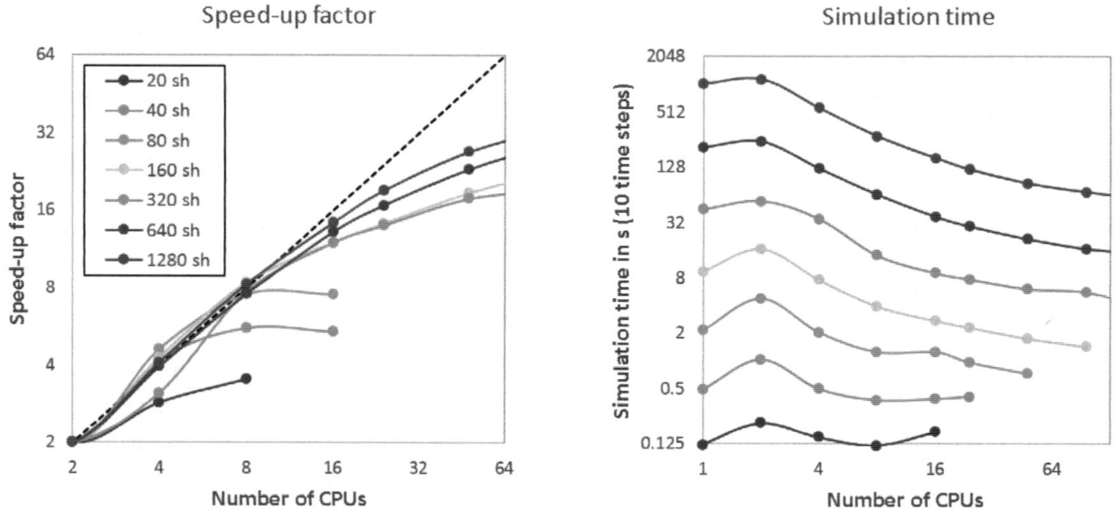

Figure 5. Left: scaling factor for MPI parallelization using different grid sizes (20sh stands for 20x20 grid points plus boundary cells) based on a reference time obtained for 2CPUs. Right: simulation time in seconds for different amounts of CPU for the same simulations.

factor decreases to non-optimal behaviour (i.e., curve drops below the black dotted line) when using more than 2, 4 and 8 CPUs, respectively. For larger grids the simulations show an optimal speed-up behaviour up to approximately 24 CPUs, which is the number of CPUs per node on the used HPC architecture. The simulation time is still steadily reduced with increasing number of CPUs.

When employing a larger 2D grid size with doubled resolution, the number of grid points is four times larger. The right plot in Fig. 5 shows that the simulation time also increases by a factor ~4 for doubled resolution.

IV. Code Validation Results

In this section, we present several benchmark tests that have been applied to validate the code.

A. Incompressible model

To validate our 2D Cartesian box implementation of the thermal convection simulation in the incompressible approximation we compare it to the standard benchmark by Blankenbach [23]. The benchmark assumes either isoviscous convection or temperature- and pressure-dependent viscosity in the Boussinesq approximation. A free-slip boundary condition is applied to the walls of the box. The non-dimensional temperature at the surface of the box is set to 0 and at the bottom to 1. The simulations are run until steady-state is reached (i.e., variations of the non-dimensional temperature drop below a tolerance value of 10^{-10}).

In Table I, we compare our results (for a fixed resolution of 80(200)x80 cells for aspect ratio 1 or 2.5) to the published

TABLE I. Benchmark comparison of CHIC (CH) to [23] (BL).

	RMS velocity		*Max temperature*		*Nusselt number*	
	CH	BL	CH	BL	CH	BL
1a	42.92	42.74-42.87	0.425	0.421-0.427	4.920	4.864-4.896
1b	194.3	192.4-198.0	0.432	0.415-0.437	10.60	10.42-10.69
1c	835.1	823.7-842.5	0.440	0.431-0.446	21.81	21.08-22.07
2a	496.6	458.3-503.3	0.725	0.716-0.741	10.43	10.04-10.07
2b	183.1	166.7-193.1	0.390	0.385-0.403	7.271	6.806-7.409

Case 1: isoviscous material, ℓ=1, a) Ra=1e4, b) Ra=1e5, c) Ra=1e6.
Case 2: FKA (11), a) Rasurf=1e4, θ_T=ln(1000), θ_p=0, ℓ=1,
b) Rasurf=1e4, θ_T=ln(16384), θ_p=ln(64), ℓ=2.5.

results. Note that in [23] different resolutions have been used, therefore we give the min and max values for resolutions of at least 33x33 cells. Here, we provide only the three most important quantities: the root-mean-square (RMS) velocity, the maximum of the upper mantle temperature profile at the middle of the box (0.5ℓ, where ℓ is the length divided by height, i.e., the aspect ratio) and the surface Nusselt number, which is a measure of the ratio of convective to conductive heat transport at the surface of the box. For more information on the benchmark setup we refer the reader to [23]. CHIC yields results that are in good agreement with all cases published in [23], see Table I. They are either within the range of published results or differ by less than 4 %.

A comparison between different geometries (Cartesian box in two or three dimensions, 2D cylindrical shell and 3D sphere) for the Boussinesq approximation has been published by Noack and Tosi [24] using the convection code GAIA [25]. To verify our implementation of the different geometries, we compare the CHIC code to the published results with respect to RMS velocity, average mantle temperature and surface Nusselt number. For the 2D box, we apply a resolution of

TABLE II. BENCHMARK COMPARISON OF CHIC (CH) TO [24] (NT)

Case	*RMS velocity*		*Average temperature*		*Surface Nusselt number*	
	CH	NT	CH	NT	CH	NT
2D box, ℓ=1, RBC [a]	54.59	53.81	0.689	0.6872	1.987	1.956
2D box, ℓ=2, RBC [a]	54.59	53.79	0.689	0.6871	1.987	1.956
2D box, ℓ=1, PBC [b]	55.61	54.62	0.7016	0.6993	2.047	2.014
3D box, ℓ=1, RBC	61.91	57.21	0.7092	0.6927	2.259	2.363
2D full cylinder [c]	35.93	35.25	0.5734	0.5711	1.444	1.439
2D half cylinder	35.30	34.84	0.574	0.5725	1.439	1.440
2D quarter cylinder	35.31	34.87	0.574	0.5725	1.439	1.440
2D cylinder, CV [d]	17.39	17.11	0.4394	0.4377	0.993	0.995
2D cylinder, CR [e]	14.62	14.51	0.4046	0.4039	0.909	0.914
3D sphere / 2D spherical annulus [f]	15.5	16.19	0.3635	0.3374	0.796	0.744

We apply a surface Rayleigh number of Ra=10 and a FKA (22) viscosity contrast of 1e5.
[a] RBC stands for reflective boundary condition at the side wall with free-slip boundary.
[b] PBC stands for periodic boundary conditions.
[c] The sphere uses a radius ratio of 2, i.e., the core radius is half the planet radius.
[d] CV means corr. volume: ratio of core area divided by mantle volume is as in 3D.
[e] CR means corr. radius: ratio of core area divided by surface area is as in 3D.
[f] We use a 2D spherical annulus for CHIC with 4 initial plumes; a 3D sphere was used for GAIA.

80(160 for ℓ=2)x80 cells, for the 3D box 40x40x40 cells and for the 2D shells we use 80 shells in radial direction with 754, 377, 189, 440, 419 and 754 points per shell for the six considered cylindrical/spherical cases. Note that we compare the 2D spherical annulus of CHIC to the case of 3D sphere of GAIA.

The results obtained with CHIC are in good agreement with those obtained with GAIA, with deviations below 2 % apart from the 3D box (7.6 % deviation for the velocity) and the spherical annulus (7.2 % deviation for the temperature), where we compare to the 3D sphere in [24], see Table II. The plots in Figure 6 show the steady-state for all cases.

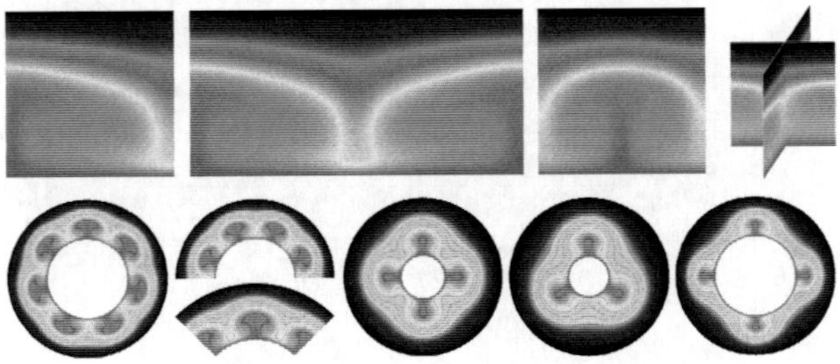

Figure 6. Convection patterns obtained with CHIC for different available geometries. See text and Table II for more details.

We do a further validation of our 2D spherical annulus implementation for isoviscous material by comparing it to the results in [13] for bottom-heated (i.e., constant bottom temperature) and internally heated convection (i.e., zero heat flux at bottom and internal heat sources), see Figure 7.

The non-dimensional radius of the core is 1.2222 and the planet radius is 2.2222. We use a resolution of 32 shells with 256 points on each shell. The CHIC results are in good agreement with the published results. The differences are less than 5 %, see Table III.

The largest deviations appear for time-dependent simulations (indicated by $\sim$). For these cases averaged values depend

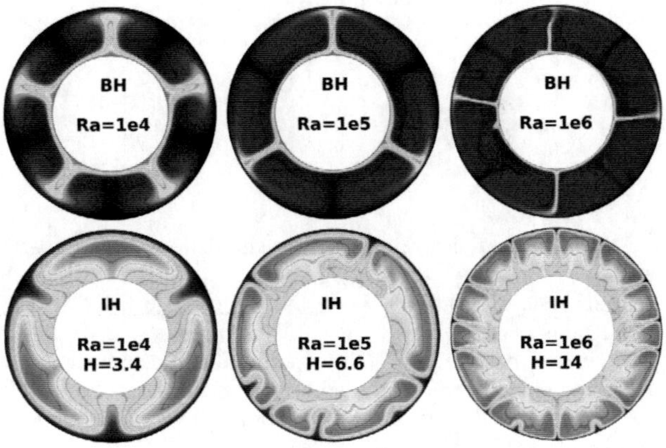

Figure 7. Temperature fields obtained for the isoviscous spherical annulus models from [13].

TABLE III. BENCHMARK COMPARISON OF CHIC (CH) TO [13] (HT)

Ra	*Average RMS velocity*		*Nusselt number*	
	CH	HT	CH	HT
1e4	38.22	37.7	4.13	4.18
1e5	157.2	$\sim$160	7.06	$\sim$7.39
1e6	$\sim$622	$\sim$640	$\sim$14.1	$\sim$14.4
Ra/H	*Average RMS velocity*		*Average mantle temperature*	
1e4 / 3.4	24.3	23.5	0.3	0.308
1e5 / 6.6	$\sim$76.6	$\sim$78.5	$\sim$0.36	$\sim$0.349
1e6 / 14	$\sim$252.4	$\sim$265	$\sim$0.35	$\sim$0.35

Isoviscous material, case 1: bottom-heated convection, case 2: internally-heated convection.

on the size of the averaging time domain (in this study an interval of up to $\sim$0.2 diffusion times is applied). For this reason, typically only steady-state simulations are used in community benchmarks. Recently, an increasing attention has been drawn to benchmarks for time-dependent simulations, for example for plastic deformation and episodic overturn [26].

B. 2D compressible model

The 2D compressible implementations TALA and ALA (see Section III-D1) are compared to a benchmark published by King et al. [14]. The benchmark includes compressible simulations in a 2D Cartesian box using different dissipation numbers and Rayleigh numbers. For the comparison we apply a resolution of 80x80 cells and a dissipation number of $Di = 1$. No viscosity variation is considered. The Rayleigh number is varied between 10^4 and the maximal value that still leads to a steady-state solution.

TABLE IV. BENCHMARK COMPARISON OF CHIC (CH) TO [14] (KI)

	RMS velocity		*Average temperature*		*Nusselt number*	
	CH	KI	CH	KI	CH	KI
EBA, Ra=1e4	24.2	23.9-24.2	0.47	0.47-0.47	2.19	2.15-2.19
EBA, Ra=2e4	39.4	39.1-39.5	0.47	0.47-0.47	2.65	2.60-2.65
EBA, Ra=5e4	71.5	70.8-71.7	0.47	0.47-0.47	3.36	3.30-3.36
EBA, Ra=1e5	107.9	107.1-108.2	0.48	0.48-0.48	3.95	3.89-3.97
EBA, Ra=2e5	146.7	147.0-148.0	0.49	0.49-0.49	4.42	4.40-4.44
TALA, Ra=1e4	26.0	26.0-26.1	0.51	0.51-0.51	2.56	2.51-2.57
TALA, Ra=2e4	40.2	40.2-40.5	0.51	0.51-0.52	3.01	2.96-3.02
TALA, Ra=5e4	66.9	66.8-68.7	0.52	0.52-0.52	3.63	3.61-3.64
TALA, Ra=1e5	84.6	84.9-91.1	0.53	0.52-0.53	3.91	3.89-3.98
ALA, Ra=1e4	24.3	24.7-25.0	0.51	0.51-0.51	2.42	2.44-2.47
ALA, Ra=2e4	37.9	38.5-39.0	0.52	0.52-0.52	2.86	2.88-2.92
ALA, Ra=5e4	64.1	64.9-65.9	0.52	0.52-0.52	3.50	3.51-3.55
ALA, Ra=1e5	84.0	84.6-85.6	0.53	0.53-0.53	3.86	3.86-3.88

We validate the accuracy of the simulations by comparing the RMS velocity, the average mantle temperature and the Nusselt number in Table IV to the value range listed in [14]. CHIC compares well with the published results with deviations below two percent. Note that these small deviations appear only for some of the TALA and ALA cases, where less codes contributed to the original study, leading to a narrower value range in [14].

C. Chemical buoyancy

Density variations in the mantle occur due to temperature influences (the thermal buoyancy term in the momentum equation), chemical influences (inhomogeneous mantle due to crust subduction, local melt depletion, etc.), and compressibility effects. CHIC traces chemical density variations either via particles or with a field approach, see Section III-D3.

We compare our implementation of the chemical advection (i.e., buoyancy forces driven by chemical density variations) to the benchmark by van Keken et al. [27]. Three cases for chemical advection have been investigated in the study modelling a light layer at the bottom of a Cartesian box below a dense layer. In addition, a viscosity contrast between the two layers of 1 (case a), 10 (b) and 100 (c) is applied. The density field of all three cases is shown in Fig. 8 at a non-dimensional time of 500. For the simulations we use a spatial resolution of 200x200 grid points and 50 tracer per cell for the particle approach and a Lewis number of 10^{10} for the field approach.

The benchmark study [27] calculates the following control parameters: the growth rate of the interface at the beginning of the simulation, the maximal rms velocity and the time when the

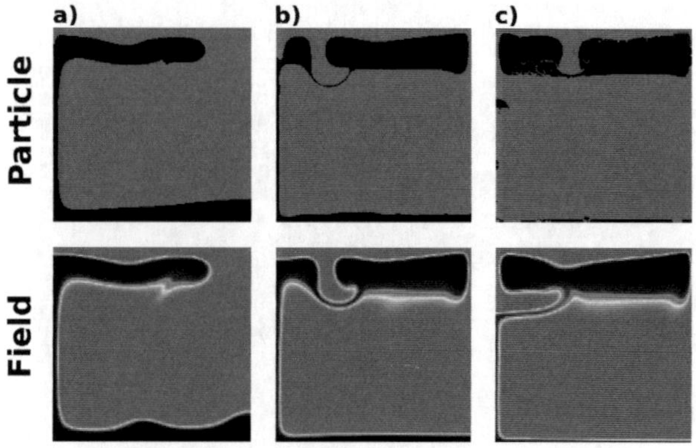

Figure 8. Chemical convection initiated by the chemical buoyancy of light material (black) below a layer of dense material (red) from benchmark [27] at non-dimensional time 500 for the particle approach (top) and the field approach (bottom).

maximal value is reached. The growth rate is calculated from the initial rms velocity increase via the following formula (we use t=100):

$$\Gamma = \ln \left(v_{rms}(t) / v_{rms}(0) \right) / \Delta t \tag{23}$$

Table V lists the growth rate, maximal rms velocity and time for both the particle (P) and the field (F) approach for the three cases. Our results reproduce the benchmark case almost exactly.

TABLE V. BENCHMARK COMPARISON OF CHIC (CH) TO [27] (VK)

	Growth rate Γ		*Max RMS velocity*		*Time (Max RMS v.)*	
	CH	VK	CH	VK	CH	VK
a	0.0117 (P) 0.0115 (F)	0.011- 0.0125	0.00303 (P) 0.00308 (F)	0.00289- 0.0031	213.3 (P) 208.3 (F)	206.4- 215.7
b	0.0472 (P) 0.0429 (F)	0.0392- 0.0482	0.00944 (P) 0.00917 (F)	0.00908- 0.00959	72.7 (P) 72.6 (F)	71.9- 77.1
c	0.1058 (P) 0.099 (F)	0.096- 0.1052	0.01457 (P) 0.01371 (F)	0.01385- 0.01506	50.2 (P) 49.4 (F)	48.8- 51.3

D. 1D parameterized model

To our knowledge, unlike for the mantle convection calculation, benchmark results for the 1D parameterized model have not been published. Therefore, we have validated our code by reproducing results of [8]. The results are very similar [28], but differ in detail because not all parameters used in the studies are known. The module has been integrated into the CHIC code and has been extended to include a regolith layer and compared to [29], yielding again comparable results.

We do a further validation of our 1D parameterized thermal evolution implementation by comparing it to a 2D convection calculation in a spherical annulus. The simulations are done for a Mars-like planet. We assume a Newtonian viscosity law and apply the Boussinesq approximation. The initial mantle temperature is 2000 K and the CMB temperature is 2300

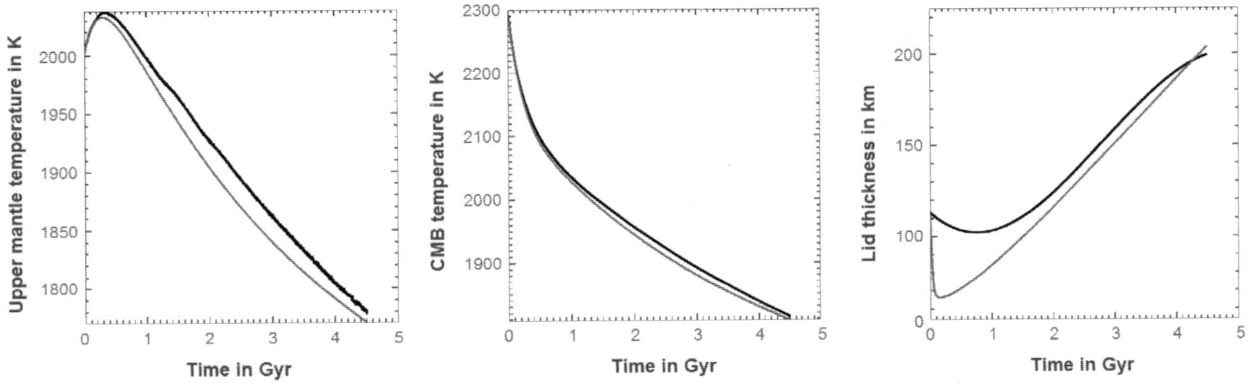

Figure 9. Upper temperature, CMB temperature and lid thickness for a thermal evolution of Mars applying either the 2D spherical annulus (black curve) or the 1D parameterized model (red).

K, the surface temperature is set to 220 K. Heat sources are homogeneously distributed in the mantle and are taken Earth-like [7]. For the 2D model, we use a quarter sphere with a radial resolution of 80 shells.

In the convection model, we define the lid over the depth where the conductive heat transport is more efficient than the convective heat transport. The lid thickness is then fitted by a third-order polynomial since the lid is strongly time-dependent and oscillations occur. The lid thickness is in the beginning larger than that of the 1D model (where we plot the total conductive layer thickness including both the lid and the upper thermal boundary layer), but shows a similar increase with time after 2 Gyr (see Figure 9). The different lid thicknesses at the beginning of the evolution can be explained by a delayed on-set of convection in the 2D model, which also leads to a slightly weaker mantle cooling at the beginning and hence a shift in the upper mantle temperature compared to the 1D model, see see Figure 9.

Our results show that the 1D parameterized model leads to a thermal evolution comparable to the results obtained with convection models.

V. CONCLUSION

We developed a new, advanced numerical code that couples different models that are needed for the investigation of habitability-relevant processes and feedback mechanisms for Earth-like or water-rich planets or moons. The code can be used with 1D and 2D/3D geometries for the silicate mantle or ice shells. The thermal state of the core, the ocean and atmosphere layer are simulated with a parameterized approach.

We have extended our earlier study [1] by a compressible formulation, which is especially of interest for planets of Earth size or larger. Chemical convection has been included to investigate buoyancy effects from density variations due to for example partial melting or subducted crust. Particles have been implemented to transport local information like the water content through the mantle. Both OpenMP and MPI parallelisation are available to allow the usage of CHIC on standard high-performance clusters.

We have validated our implementations for the parameterized model and 2D/3D convection model by comparing CHIC to published results and by running a set of standard benchmarks. For all benchmarks, CHIC is in good agreement with literature values.

The code can be applied to investigate the possible habitability of terrestrial or water-rich planets [9] and moons, including the simulation of feedbacks between the interior and surface for stagnant-lid and plate tectonics planets.

ACKNOWLEDGMENT

L. Noack has been funded by the Interuniversity Attraction Poles Programme initiated by the Belgian Science Policy Office through the Planet Topers alliance. A. Rivoldini was supported by the PRODEX program managed by the European Space Agency in collaboration with the Belgian Federal Science Policy Office. This work results within the collaboration of the COST Action TD 1308. We thank Clemens Heistracher, Nastasia Zimov, François Labbé, and Thomas Boiveau for their contributions to the project.

REFERENCES

[1] L. Noack, A. Rivoldini, and T. Van Hoolst, "CHIC - Coupling Habitability, Interior and Crust," INFOCOMP 2015, Brussels, Belgium, vol. ISBN: 978-1-61208-416-9, 2015, pp. 84–90.

[2] P. van Thienen et al., "Water, life, and planetary geodynamical evolution," *Space Sci. Rev.*, vol. 129, 2007, pp. 167–203, doi: 10.1007/s11214-007-9149-7.

[3] L. Noack and D. Breuer, "Interior and surface dynamics of terrestrial bodies and their implications for the habitability," in Habitability on other planets and satellites: The quest for extraterrestrial life, J.-P. de Vera and F. Seckbach, Eds. Springer, Dordrecht, 2013, pp. 203–233, doi: 10.1007/978-94-007-6546-7_12.

[4] G. Schubert, M. N. Ross, D. J. Stevenson, and T. Spohn, "Mercurys thermal history and the generation of its magnetic field," Mercury, 1998, pp. 429–460, iSBN 9780816510856.

[5] L. Noack, D. Breuer, and T. Spohn, "Coupling the atmosphere with interior dynamics: Implications for the resurfacing of venus," *Icarus*, vol. 217, 2012, pp. 484–498, doi:10.1016/j.icarus.2011.08.026.

[6] C. Gillmann and P. Tackley, "Atmosphere/mantle coupling and feedbacks on venus," *J. Geophys. Res. Plan.*, vol. 119, 2014, pp. 1189–1217, doi:10.1002/2013JE004505.

[7] G. Schubert, D. L. Turcotte, and P. Olson, Mantle convection in the Earth and planets. Cambridge University Press, Cambridge, UK, 2001, doi:10.1017/CBO9780511612879.

[8] A. Morschhauser, M. Grott, and D. Breuer, "Crustal recycling, mantle dehydration, and the thermal evolution of Mars," *Icarus*, vol. 212, no. 2, 2011, pp. 541–558, doi:10.1016/j.icarus.2010.12.028.

[9] L. Noack et al., "Water-rich planets: how habitable is a water layer deeper than on Earth?" *Icarus*, in press, doi:10.1016/j.icarus.2016.05.009.

[10] L. Stixrude and C. Lithgow-Bertelloni, "Thermodynamics of mantle minerals–i. physical properties," *Geophys. J. Int.*, vol. 162, no. 2, 2005, pp. 610–632, doi:10.1111/j.1365-246X.2005.02642.x.

[11] J. Bouchet, S. Mazevet, G. Morard, F. Guyot, and R. Musella, "Ab initio equation of state of iron up to 1500 GPa," Physical Review B, vol. 87, no. 094102, 2013, pp. 1–8, doi:10.1103/PhysRevB.87.094102.

[12] D. J. Stevenson, T. Spohn, and G. Schubert, "Magnetism and thermal evolution of the terrestrial planets," *Icarus*, vol. 54, 1983, pp. 466–489, doi:10.1016/0019-1035(83)90241-5.

[13] J. W. Hernlund and P. J. Tackley, "Modeling mantle convection in the spherical annulus," *Physics of the Earth and Planetary Interiors*, vol. 171, no. 1, 2008, pp. 48–54, doi:10.1016/j.pepi.2008.07.037.

[14] S. D. King et al., "A community benchmark for 2-d cartesian compressible convection in the earth's mantle," *Geophys. J. Int.*, vol. 180, no. 1, 2010, pp. 73–87, doi:10.1111/j.1365-246X.2009.04413.x.

[15] U. R. Christensen, "Convection with pressure- and temperature-dependent non-newtonian rheology," *Geophys. J. R. astr. Soc.*, vol. 77, 1984, pp. 343–384, doi:10.1111/j.1365-246X.1984.tb01939.x.

[16] S. Zhong, D. A. Yuen, and L. N. Moresi, "Numerical methods in mantle convection," Treatise on Geophysics, vol. 7, 2007, pp. 227–252, doi:10.1016/B978-044452748-6.00118-8.

[17] S. V. Patanker, "A calculation procedure for two-dimensional elliptic situations," Numerical Heat Transfer V, 1981, pp. 409–425, doi:10.1080/01495728108961801.

[18] O. Schenk and K. Gärtner, "On fast factorization pivoting methods for symmetric indefinite systems," Elec. Trans. Numer. Anal., vol. 23, 2006, pp. 158–179, iSSN 1068-9613.

[19] S. Karato and P. Wu, "Rheology of the upper mantle: A synthesis," *Science*, vol. 260, 1993, pp. 771–778, doi:10.1126/science.260.5109.771.

[20] G. Hirth and D. Kohlstedt, "Rheology of the upper mantle and the mantle wedge: A view from the experimentalists," Inside the subduction Factory, 2003, pp. 83–105, doi:10.1029/138GM06.

[21] R. Katz, M. Spiegelman, and C. Langmuir, "A new parameterization of hydrous mantle melting," *Geochem. Geophys. Geosyst.*, vol. 4, no. 9 - 1073, 2003, pp. 1–19, doi:10.1029/2002GC000433.

[22] L. Noack and D. Breuer, "First- and second-order Frank-Kamenetskii approximation applied to temperature-, pressure- and stress-dependent rheology," *Geophys. J. Int.*, vol. 195, 2013, pp. 27–46, doi:10.1093/gji/ggt248.

[23] B. Blankenbach et al., "A benchmark comparison for mantle convection codes," *Geophys. J. Int.*, vol. 98, 1989, pp. 23–38, doi:10.1111/j.1365-246X.1989.tb05511.x.

[24] L. Noack and N. Tosi, "High-performance modelling in geodynamics," in Integrated Information and Computing Systems for Natural, Spatial, and Social Sciences, C.-P. Rückemann, Ed. IGI Global, 2013, pp. 324–352, doi:10.4018/978-1-4666-2190-9.ch016.

[25] C. Hüttig and K. Stemmer, "Finite volume discretization for dynamic viscosities on voronoi grids," *Physics of the Earth and Planetary Interiors*, vol. 171, 2008, pp. 137–146, doi:10.1016/j.pepi.2008.07.007.

[26] N. Tosi et al., "A community benchmark for viscoplastic thermal convection in a 2-d square box," *Geochem. Geophys. Geosyst.*, vol. 16, 2015, pp. 2175–2196, doi:10.1002/2015GC005807.

[27] P. E. van Keken et al., "A comparison of methods for the modeling of thermochemical convection," *J. Geophys. Res.: Solid Earth*, vol. 102, no. B10, 1997, pp. 22 477–22 495, doi:10.1029/97JB01353.

[28] T. Boiveau, "Convection mantellique dans les plantes telluriques," Rapport de stage, unpublished.

[29] N. Tosi, M. Grott, A.-C. Plesa, and D. Breuer, "Thermochemical evolution of mercurys interior," *J. Geophys. Res. Plan.*, vol. 118, 2013, pp. 1–14, doi:10.1002/jgre.20168.

International Journal on Advances in Systems and Measurements, vol 9 no 1 & 2, year 2016, http://www.iariajournals.org/systems_and_measurements/

Performance Characterization of Multiprocessors and Accelerators Using Micro-Benchmarks

Javed Razzaq, Rudolf Berrendorf, Jan Philipp Ecker, Simon Eric Scholl
Computer Science Department
Bonn-Rhein-Sieg University of Applied Sciences
Sankt Augustin, Germany
e-mail: {javed.razzaq, rudolf.berrendorf, jan.ecker, simon.scholl}@h-brs.de

Florian Mannuss
EXPEC Advanced Research Center
Saudi Arabian Oil Company
Dhahran, Saudi Arabia
e-mail: florian.mannuss@aramco.com

Abstract—**In this paper, a set of micro-benchmarks is proposed to determine basic performance parameters of single-node mainstream hardware architectures for High Performance Computing. Performance parameters of recent processors, including those of accelerators, are determined. The investigated systems are Intel server processor architectures and the two accelerator lines Intel Xeon Phi and Nvidia graphic processors. Additionally, the performance impact of thread mapping on multiprocessors and Intel Xeon Phi is shown. The results show similarities for some parameters between all architectures, but significant differences for others.**

Keywords–Performance; micro-benchmarks; server processors; Intel Xeon Phi; Nvidia graphic processors; thread mapping

I. INTRODUCTION

For resource-intensive computations in High Performance Computing (HPC) on a single node level, a good performance can only be achieved if the performance characteristics of the processor, memory and core-core/core-memory interconnect architecture are understood. First investigations on that have been published in [1]. Finding and quantifying such characteristics for a certain system is motivated by the fact that, for most of their runtime, HPC applications stress only parts of the hardware in compute-intensive program kernels. Examples are compute-bound problems – such as direct linear solvers [2] that are bound by the floating point capability of a system, and memory-bandwidth-bound problems – such as the multiplication of a sparse matrix with a dense vector in iterative solvers [3], [4], [5]. Other application kernels may be bound differently.

This paper proposes a set of micro-benchmarks to characterize HPC hardware on a single-node level. The results of the micro-benchmarks are performance parameters related to performance bounds found in many computational kernels (see [6] for two such parameters). These parameters often allow conclusions to be drawn on the (at least relative) performance of real applications or performance critical application kernels of certain classes that are bound by one or few of those parameters. Additionally, if carefully chosen, architecture-bottlenecks can be revealed. The micro-benchmarks were chosen to allow conclusions on an application level rather than to evaluate deep structures in a processor architecture with sophisticated low-level programs, as for example in [7].

The proposed micro-benchmarks are applied to representatives of different classes of current hardware architectures. Results show similarities in performance between all architectures for some parameters (e.g., reaching near peak floating point performance for dense matrix multiply), but also significant differences between architectures (e.g., main memory latency and bandwidth). Consequently, only certain application classes are suitable for a specific architecture.

The paper is structured as follows. The following section discusses related work. Then, current mainstream HPC hardware architectures are briefly described, focusing on their differences. Section IV contains a description of the proposed micro-benchmarks. Section V describes our experimental setup and finally, in Section VI and Section VII, detailed evaluation results are presented and discussed, followed by a conclusion in Section VIII.

II. RELATED WORK

Benchmarks are widely used to evaluate certain performance properties of computer systems. A benchmark should thus be usable as an indicator that can support a decision, e.g., whether this system is feasible for a certain task or not. A multitude of different benchmarks exist, dependent on the question to be answered.

The Top500 list [8] uses the High Performance Linpack [2] to rank (very) large parallel systems. This benchmark produces only a single value, the Floating Point Operations per second (FLOP/s) for just one specific task, the direct solution of a very large dense linear system.

The widely used SPEC CPU benchmark [9] is a mix of several real world application programs for integer-dominant computations or floating point dominant applications. Running the benchmark on a system produces one number for each class, a performance factor. These two numbers then express a *relative* performance improvement compared to an older base system with respect to integer performance and floating point performance.

Williams et al. introduced the roofline model [6] to describe the expectable performance space in a resource-bound problem. The two resources in this model are computational density (operations per transfered byte) and peak floating point performance. This is an example where two limitating parameters on a system are used to show eligible perfomance values.

The NAS Parallel Benchmarks [10] are more application-oriented benchmarks. These benchmarks consist of larger compute-intensive kernels and were originally designed to test large parallel computers. Each of these applications in this benchmark represents a different computing aspect. The applications include, for example, Conjugate Gradient (irregular memory access), Multi-Grid (long- and short-distance communication), or fast Fourier Transform (all-to-all communication). These benchmarks have been, amongst others, implemented in OpenMP [11] and recently in OpenCL [12]. With the OpenCL extension they can be used to measure recent accelerators, such as Graphic Processor Units (GPUs).

While the Linpack and the NAS Parallel Benchmarks aim for rather scientific and computing intense applications, the Graph500 benchmark [13] aims for data intensive applications, which can arise in other fields such as social networks or cyber security. Here, graph operations such as parallel Breadth First Search or Single Source Shortest Path problems are considered. A sequential reference implementation and parallel implementations with OpenMP, XMT and MPI are given by the Graph500 committee [13]. Furthermore, various other implementations, e.g., with PGAS [14] or hybrid approaches [15], exist.

For a finer granularity, benchmarks that give individual results for several operational classes can be used. An example is the OpenMP micro-benchmark suite [16], [17] that gives a developer a measure of how well basic constructs of OpenMP [18] map to a given system. If a developer knows important parameters that mainly determine the overall performance of an application in this programming model, he is able to estimate how well his own application will perform on the system using these basic constructs.

In [19], Treibig et al. presented the likwid-bench micro-benchmark tool as part of the performance monitoring and benchmark suite likwid [20]. This benchmark tool works on an assembler level measuring streaming loop kernels. It consists of several default benchmarks and offers the possibility to add custom bemchmarks. The default benchmarks cover memory copy, load and memory bandwith. In [21], Hofmann et al. used the likwid-bench tool along with the performance counter tool of likwid, to give detailed insights on the current Intel Haswell CPUs. For this purpose, micro-benchmarks for the current instruction set of Haswell CPUs, e.g., fused multiply add (FMA), where added.

Lemeire et al. used micro-benchmarks and a modified roofline model to characterize current GPUs [22]. These benchmarks were tailored to address the specific architecture of GPUs. The benchmarks were implemented in OpenCL and results of a AMD Cayman GPU and a Nvidia Maxwell GPU where presented in the publication.

Other micro-benchmark suites, which aim for a finer granularity are proposed in [23], [24], [25]. These benchmark suites are based on OpenCL. Here, OpenCL is used to compare memory-related issues, low level floating point operations and real life applications on different hardware architectures, including accelerators.

Directly related to the memory performance are the well-known Stream benchmark for memory bandwidth [26] and papers that work on an even finer granularity taking coherence protocols in certain architectures into account [7], [27], [28].

III. Current Hardware Architectures

This section gives a very brief overview on current HPC processor architectures and memory technology. It is partitioned into sections on mainstream HPC processor architectures, HPC accelerator architectures and memory technologies.

A. Processor Architectures

We concentrate on the Intel Xeon EP line of current HPC relevant processors, as these processors are used in nearly all new systems in the HPC computer Top500 list [8]. Intel's recent micro-architectures are Sandy Bridge EP (SB), and its successor Ivy Bridge EP (IB). The lastest change in the architecture appeared late 2014 in the Haswell EP processors (HW). A detailed description of the architectures is given in the manufacturer's related literature [29].

Processors nowadays have several cores. In HPC clusters, multiprocessor nodes with 2 processors are often used. Keeping multiple core-private caches coherent is usually done in the hardware by cache coherence protocols. Keeping caches coherent costs latency, bandwidth and may also influence an architecture's scalability [7], [28].

B. Accelerator Architectures

Computations of certain application classes can be accelerated using special attached processors. Nvidia graphic processors (GPU) and Intel Many Integrated Core processors (MIC) of the Xeon Phi family are currently predominant in HPC [8].

A Nvidia GPU has a hierarchical design (CUDA architecture [30]) that differs from that of common CPUs. The execution units (SE, Streaming Processors) are organized in multiprocessors, called Streaming Multi-Processors (SM or SMX), and a GPU has several such multiprocessors. For example, the Kepler family of GPUs has up to 15 SMX and 192 SE per SMX, resulting in a total of 2880 SE in the largest device configuration. These execution units are always used by a group of 32 threads, called a warp. Such an architecture leads to several aspects that have to be respected in performance critical programs, e.g., coalesced memory access and thread divergence [4], [31].

An Intel Xeon Phi coprocessor [32] consists of multiple CPU-like cores. The current generation Xeon Phi Knights Corner (KNC) has between 57 and 61 such cores, which are connected via a bi-directional ring bus. To achieve good performance on a Xeon Phi, the application must use parallelism as well as vectorization. In [33], requirements for vectorization are specified for the usage of the Intel compiler, e.g., no jumps and branches in a loop.

Recent accelerators (i.e., GPU as well as Xeon Phi) are plugin cards connected to the host through a PCI Express (PCIe) adapter. This adapter is often a severe bottleneck, because the transfer rate through a PCIe connection is significantly lower (8 GB/s for PCIe 2.0 x16 and 16 GB/s for PCIe 3.0 x16) than, for example, memory transfer rates in a host system.

C. Memory Technologies

Memory Technologies are optimized for different aspects. DDR3 / DDR4 RAM, which is used in CPU-based systems, is optimized for a short latency time. However, GDDR5 memory, which is used in accelerators, is optimized for bandwidth. This difference is important, as the performance of accelerators mainly comes from Single Instruction Multiple Data (SIMD) parallelism [34], where the same instruction is applied concurrently to multiple data items. These data items have to be fed to the functional units in parallel, asking for high main memory bandwidth.

All processors discussed here, including recent GPUs, use caches to speed up memory accesses. While GPUs currently have at most a 2 level cache hierarchy, CPUs use 3 levels of caches with increasing sizes and latencies per level. Caches are only useful if data accesses initiated by the program instructions obey spatial or temporal locality [34].

TABLE I. OVERVIEW OF THE MICRO-BENCHMARKS.

Identifier	Benchmark	Category	Application
B1	Memory read latency	Memory access	Single-thread latency to main memory
B2	Memory bandwidth	Memory access	Bandwidth to main memory
B3	Atomic update	Synchronization	Multi-threaded atomic update of a shared scalar variable
B4	Barrier	Synchronization	Barrier operation of n threads
B5	Reduction	Synchronization	Parallel reduction of n values to a single value
B6	Communication	Communication	Data transfer bandwidth to/from an accelerator through PCI Express
B7	DGEMM	Computation	Parallel dense matrix multiply (compute-bound)
B8	SPMV	Computation	Sparse matrix multiplied with a dense vector (memory-bound)

IV. Proposed Micro-Benchmarks

We propose a set of 8 micro-benchmarks to determine performance critical parameters in single-node parallel HPC systems. Table I gives an overview of these benchmarks. Each single benchmark tests one specific aspect of a hardware architecture or parallel runtime system on that hardware. These aspects are performance critical for certain application classes. One or a combination of these parameters usually defines the performance bounds of the compute-intensive parts of an application. In real-life applications, it is possible that a combination of these parameters occurs with different factors/weights. It is up to the developer to use his knowledge of the application to weight these factors correctly. If the application is truly dominated by one of these parameters, the developers has an indication whether an architecture would be suitable for this application.

The presented set of micro-benchmarks were implemented in C with OpenMP for the use with Intel processors (including KNC). However, the OpenMP implementation could also be used for other shared memory architectures as well, such as Power 8, ARM, or AMD Processors. Moreover, widely used C compilers such as the Intel icc or the GNU gcc support this programming approach. Recently, the GNU gcc added support for OpenMP 4.0 constructs, which makes it possible to address future Intel Xeon Phi processors as well. For the usage with Nvidia accelerators, the commonly used CUDA programming approach was chosen, as this is the programming model delivering the best performance on these GPUs. Porting the CUDA implementation, for example, to OpenCL should be straightforward, because both programming platforms have similar concepts, although the syntax is quite different.

In the following, we describe the individual benchmarks and our reasons for using them.

A. Memory Performance

Memory accesses are often the main performance bottleneck in applications, for example in an iterative solver working on large sparse matrices [3] or graph processing [35]. The key performance parameters for memory performance are memory latency and memory bandwidth. An indicator of a latency-bound application are many accesses to different small data items (that are not cached). An indicator of a bandwidth-bound application kernel is a program kernel with low computational density, i.e., the ratio of the number of operations performed on data compared to the number of bytes that need to be transferred for that data is low.

1) Memory Read Latency (B1): Read latency can be determined by single threaded pointer chasing, i.e., a repeated read operation of type `ptr = *ptr` with a properly setup pointer table. If all accessed addresses are within an address space of size S (without associativity collisions in the cache) and S is smaller than the cache size, then all accesses can be stored in this cache.

2) Memory Bandwidth (B2): The Stream benchmark [26] is commonly used to measure main memory bandwidth. We adapted this freely available benchmark for the Xeon Phi using the OpenMP `target` construct [18] and for graphic processors using CUDA programming constructs [36], i.e., both are used in accerelator mode called from a host.

B. Synchronization Performance

Synchronization between execution units (threads, processes, etc.) is necessary at certain points during the program execution to ensure parallel program correctness. However, synchronization is often a very performance critical operation [37], because it requires serialization, e.g., atomic updates, or overall agreement, e.g., a barrier between the execution units. Moreover, reduction operations are another important and performance critical type of synchronization in real life parallel applications.

1) Atomic Updates (B3): In our atomic update benchmark, all participating threads perform an atomic increment operation on a single, scalar, shared, integer variable in parallel. As a side note, this operation also modifies the variable. Consequently, the coherence protocol initiates a cache line invalidation/update in a cache coherent multi-cache based system. The atomic increment operation is repeated by each thread many times during the benchmark. The benchmark then gives the time of one such operation performed by one thread. This operation is realized by the OpenMP atomic construct on the CPU/Xeon Phi and a Cuda atomic add operation on the GPU.

2) Barrier (B4): In the barrier benchmark, a barrier operation is carried out repeatedly. For multiprocessors, the benchmark uses an OpenMP barrier **`pragma`** inside a parallel region. For the Xeon Phi, this program kernel is surrounded by a `target` region. The CUDA execution model [36] does not support a barrier synchronization between all threads as such, because this would violate the basic concept of warp independence. In CUDA, a program with global steps is implemented using a sequence of multiple kernels. Therefore, the closest adequate comparison to a barrier is the kernel launch time (with an empty kernel), with the ensuing synchronization waiting for the kernel finalization.

3) Reduction (B5): In the reduction benchmark, a vector with n elements of type **`double`** is reduced to one **`double`** value summing up all vector elements. For a reduction, partial sums must be summed up in a synchronized way, which is additional work compared to a sequential implementation and needs some serialization between parallel entities. The program for the multiprocessors uses the OpenMP reduction clause in a parallel for-loop. On multiprocessor systems, the vector is initialized in parallel, such that parts of the vector are split over different Non-Uniform Memory Access [34] (NUMA) nodes

TABLE II. SELECTED HARDWARE PARAMETERS OF THE SYSTEMS USED.

Parameter	Processor Systems			Accelerator Systems			
Architecture	SB	IB	HW	KNC	M2050 (Fermi)	K20m (Kepler)	K80 (2 × Kepler)[4]
Clock [GHz] (with TurboBoost)	2.6 (3.3)	2.7 (3.5)	2.6 (3.6)	1.053	1.15	0.706	0.560 (0.875)
Peak double prec. perf.[1][GFlops]; 1 proc.	20.8	21.6	33.17	16.8	-	-	-
Peak double prec. perf.[1][GFlops]; all proc.	332.8	518.4	929	1010.8	515	1170	2× 935
Theor. memory bandwidth [GB/s][2]	102.4	119.4	136	320	148	208	2× 240
Main memory size [GB]	128	256	128	8	3	5	2× 12
Degree of parallelism [3]	32	48	56	240	448	2496	2× 2496

[1] In relation to baseclock
[2] ECC off for accelerators
[3] Including hyperthreads
[4] We used only one of the two processors

in a NUMA system. Such a distribution is performed internally by the operating system following the parallel memory access pattern. As CUDA does not provide reduction operations itself, the open source (CUDA-based) Thrust library [38] of Nvidia is used for this benchmark on the GPU systems.

C. Communication Performance (B6)

In the communication benchmark, we measure the transfer rate of a certain amount of data between a host and an accelerator device over PCI Express. This measurement is carried out for both directions (input data from the host to the accelerator and result data from the accelerator to the host).

D. Programming Kernels

For many scientific application fields, linear algebra operations are building blocks and often belong to the most time-consuming parts of a program. Depending on the problem origin, dense or sparse matrices occur. Operations on dense or sparse matrices stress different parts of a system. The following two evaluation benchmarks cover both matrix types and stress, therefore, different parts of a system. These are both performance limiting for many applications, also outside linear algebra.

1) Compute-bound application kernel – DGEMM (B7): For dense matrix multiply with a high computational density, many techniques are known (and applied inside optimized library functions) that allow this operation to be run near the peak floating point performance. Consequently, if implemented adequatly, dense matrix multiply evaluates in essence the floating point capability of a core/processor/multiprocessor system. This operation has been well researched and is implemented efficiently in the BLAS library [39] and vendor optimized libraries such as the Intel MKL [40] and Nvidia cuBLAS [41].

2) Memory-bound application kernel – SPMV (B8): In contrast, a sparse matrix multiplied with a dense vector (SPMV) stresses almost only the memory system, as it has a low computational density. The operation is available for multiple storage formats [3] and is, at least for larger matrices, memory bandwidth limited and *not* compute bound. SPMV is also available in the vendor optimized libraries Intel MKL [40] and Nvidia cuSPARSE [42], both with a small selection of supported storage formats for the sparse matrix. The CSR format [3] is a general format with good/reasonable performance characteristics for many sparse matrices on CPU-based systems. For appropriate matrices (that have a small and ideally constant number of non-zero elements per row), the ELL format is a favorable storage format on GPUs [43]. This difference is related to the different memory systems of CPU-multiprocessors and GPU systems. Nevertheless, in this benchmark we are not interested in the best possible performance for a specific matrix. We are more interested in relating the performance of different systems for this type of operation in a more general way.

V. Experimental Setup

In this section, we specify the parallel system test environment where the benchmarks were applied. Additionally, we discuss the bencmark parameter settings, because performance can be a parameterized function, e.g., dependent on the number of used threads or data items.

A. Test Environment

The used systems include the three latest generations of Intel server processors: Sandy Bridge-EP (SB), Ivy Bridge-EP (IB) and Haswell-EP (HW). All of the systems are 2-way NUMA multiprocessor systems with 2-way hyperthreading per processor. As representatives for accelerators the Intel Xeon Phi Knights Corner (KNC), with 4-way hyperthreading, as a many-core architecture and three most recent Nvidia GPU architechtures (M2050, K20m, K80) were examined. The tested accelerators use PCIe 2 x16 for KNC, M2050 and K20m (both Nvidia GPUs) and PCIe 3 x16 for the Nvidia K80 GPU. The new Nvidia K80 consists of two Kepler GPUs, which work as two single devices and have to be programmed seperately. Only one of the GPUs was used to perform the benchmarks. Table II summarizes key hardware parameters of the systems used.

B. Test Parameters

The benchmark tests were executed with the following parameter settings:

- *Memory latency (B1)*: Variable size of the pointer table with a single threaded run.
- *Memory bandwidth (B2)*: *a)* Fixed large vector size of `STREAM_ARRAY_SIZE=40000000` and a repeat factor of `NTIMES=1000` (all systems). *b)* Same, but different thread mapping (CPUs, KNC).
- *Atomic update (B3)*: *a)* Variable number of threads according to the systems used (all systems). *b)* Same, but different thread mapping (CPUs, KNC).
- *Barrier (B4)*: *a)* Variable number of threads according to the systems used (all systems). *b)* Same, but different thread mapping (CPUs, KNC).
- *Reduction (B5)*: *a)* Variable vector size with a full parallel run. *b)* Variable thread number with fixed vector size and different thread mappings (CPUs, KNC).
- *Communication (B6)*: *a)* Variable size of the transferred data (accelerators). *b)* Pinned and unpinned host memory (GPUs).

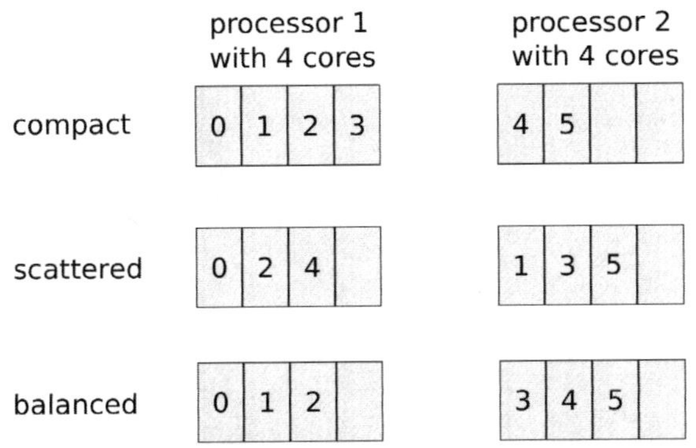

Figure 1. Strategies for thread mapping on CPUs. In this example 6 threads are mapped onto 2 processors with 4 cores each. Numbers in boxes are the thread numbers.

- *DGEMM (B7)*: *a)* Variable matrix size with a full parallel run (all systems). *b)* Fixed matrix size with a variable number of threads (CPUs, KNC).
- *SPMV (B8)*: Fixed test matrix according to the SPE10 problem [44]. *a)* SPMV implementation of MKL resp. cuSPARSE of CSR (all systems). *b)* Own implementation of ELL kernel with different thread mapping, ELL implementation of cuSPARSE (CPUs/KNC, GPUs).

C. Thread Mappings

Thread mapping/binding can be an important aspect achieving good performance. A thread mapping defines how application threads are mapped to hardware units, e.g., processor sockets, cores in a multi-core CPU, hardware threads in a hyperthreaded core. On a GPU, the definition of a grid size and block size defines a 1D-3D partitioning of the application data space (e.g., a 2D picture) to the hardware units. Thread mapping influences load balance, coherence issues, data locality and more.

Basic mapping strategies on a CPU-based system are (see Figure 1 for an example):

- *Compact*: keep consecutive threads as close as possible in the hardware, e.g., to exploit data locality between threads in a shared cache. Cores are filled up one by one with software threads.
- *Scattered*: spread threads to as many processors as possible in the hardware, e.g., to exploit as much memory bandwidth as possible from different CPU sockets in a NUMA system. If thread i was placed at processor p, then thread $i+1$ is placed at processor $p+1$ with a wrapping at the last processor. This means that all processors and the corresponding memory bandwidth is utilized if at least as many software threads are available as processors.
- *Balanced*: similar to scattered. Utilize as much processors as possible but fill nearby threads to the same core. This is a combination of locality utilization (nearby threads are mapped to the same processor with a unified last level cache for all cores on that processor) and memory bandwidth allocation (use as many processors as possible).

OpenMP defines appropriate environment variables to influence thread mapping strategies [18]. With the Intel icc compiler this can be accomplished by using the KMP_AFFINITY variable. This variable can be set to either compact or scattered (or balanced for KNC only) [45]. The names of the strategies are therefore different in OpenMP and the Intel specific KMP_AFFINITY variable, but the meaning is more or less the same.

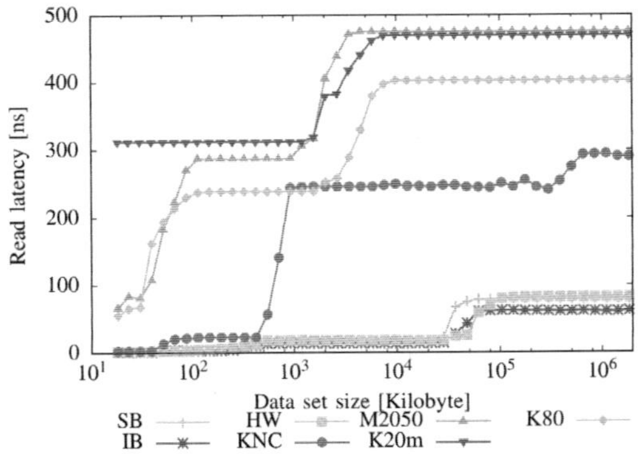

Figure 2. Memory latency results, absolute time.

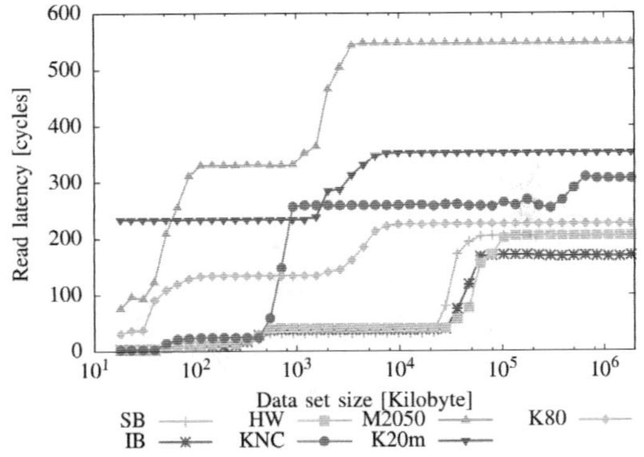

Figure 3. Memory latency results, relative cycles.

On GPUs the programming model is different to a CPU programming model. A thread mapping is done by specifying grid and block sizes. Different to a CPU-based system where usually a 1:1 mapping of software to hardware threads is established, on a GPU many more software threads are generated than hardware parallelism is available, with the aim to hide memory latency. If a hardware thread is blocked by a memory read operation, another runnable thread gets scheduled by the hardware scheduler to make the read latency tolerable. Specifying grid and block sizes partitions the space of software thread into up to 3 dimensions and these partition units get scheduled by the hardware scheduler on a GPU. While the thread mapping done by a programmer on CPU-based systems is optional, the thread partitioning on a GPU is an important part of GPU programming.

VI. Results

In this section, we discuss the main results of applying our proposed benchmarks to the different types of architectures described in Section V. We concentrate on the interesting

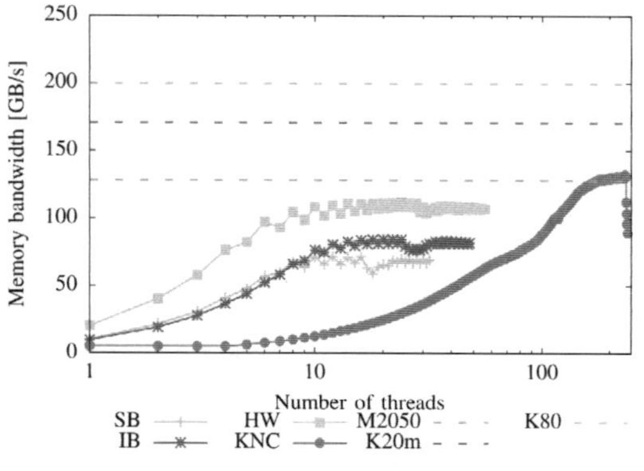

Figure 4. Memory bandwidth results.

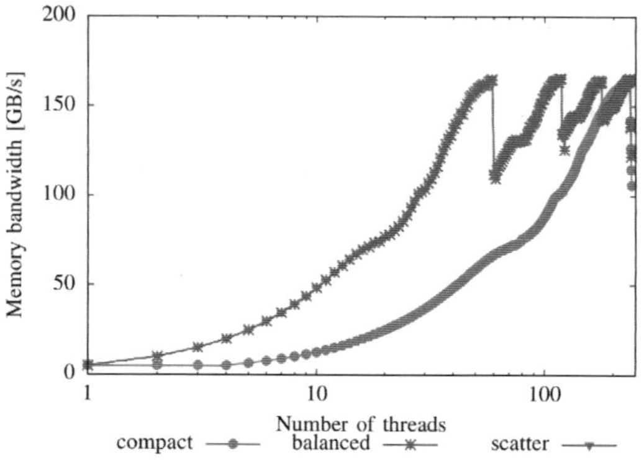

Figure 6. Memory bandwidth results on KNC, different thread mapping (balanced is nearly the same as scattered).

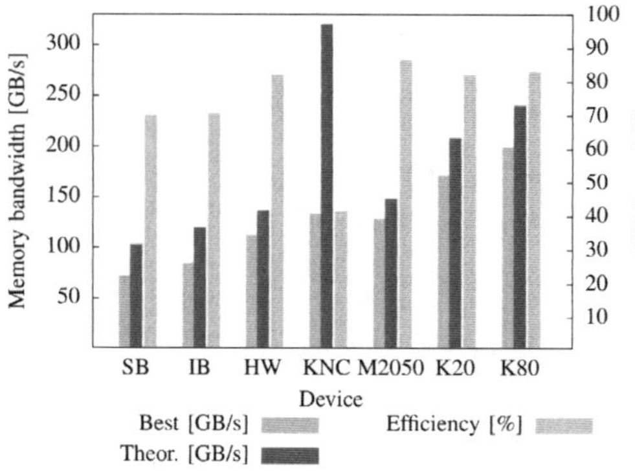

Figure 5. Memory bandwidth best results.

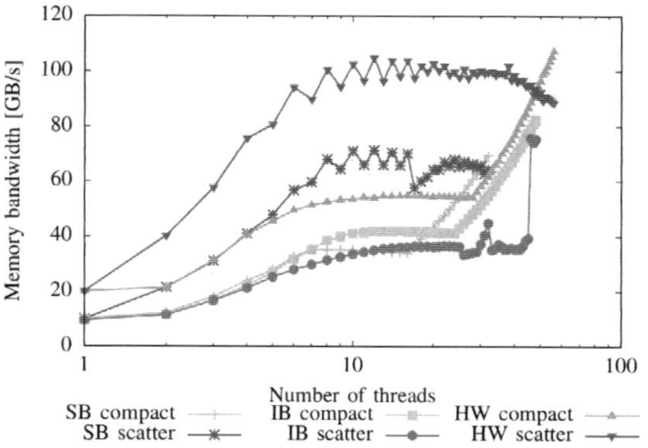

Figure 7. Memory bandwidth results on CPUs, different thread mapping.

aspects of the results. When performance data is plotted as a function of the number of threads, it is meant as number of thread blocks for GPUs, because the usage model for graphic processors differs from a multiprocessor system, as explained before. On GPUs, usually all stream processors of such a processor are used (with even more concurrency in the application to hide latencies) instead of specifying the exact number of threads, as it is usually done on a CPU.

A. Memory Read Latency (B1)

Figure 2 shows the results for the memory latency with an access stride of 256 byte in absolute times. Figure 3 shows these results in cycles relative to the respective base CPU/GPU clock. Clearly visible for all systems are the levels of the same latency induced by cache sizes of the different cache levels and the huge difference to a main memory access (the last step to the right). If only absolute times are considered, all accelerators have higher latencies than the processor architectures and the GPU-based Nvidia accelerators are slower than a CPU-based KNC. Moreover, there seems to be hardly any improvement between GPU generations. But, if relative latencies are considered, the GPUs improve over the generations quite significantly, as the base clock is much lower while the parallelism is higher. Related to relative cycles, the newest K80 outperforms the KNC and even gets close to the CPUs in access to the global/main memory.

The different cache levels show that the measurements on the M2050 and K80 GPUs have three different levels in access time, which can be explained by the L1/L2 caches and accesses to the main memory. On the K20m, only two levels of similar access times are visible. This is induced by different versions of the Kepler architecture in the K20m and the K80. The K20m does *not* cache global memory accesses in the L1 cache, but the newer generation K80 does.

On the CPU-based systems, the curves show first the smaller L1 and L2 caches, then the larger L3 cache and finally, in a fourth step, the access to the main memory. Access to the L1, L2, L3 caches is very fast, for L1 and L2 even on KNC. Altogether the processor systems still outperform the accelerators in latency time, although newer accelerator generations have improved (relatively). Therefore, applications that are already latency bound have a severe problem on accelerator systems if they cannot hide this latency, e.g., by allowing many read requests to be open at the same time.

B. Memory Bandwidth (B2)

The memory bandwidth performance is shown in Figure 4 as a function of used threads. For the processor systems, the default thread scheduling was used here. For graphic processors, the usage model is different to that of a multiprocessor system, because usually all stream processors of such a processor are used instead of specifying the exact number of threads. The

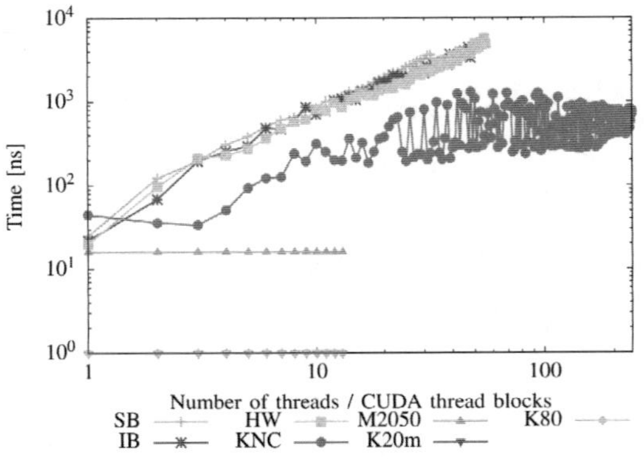

Figure 8. Atomic update results.

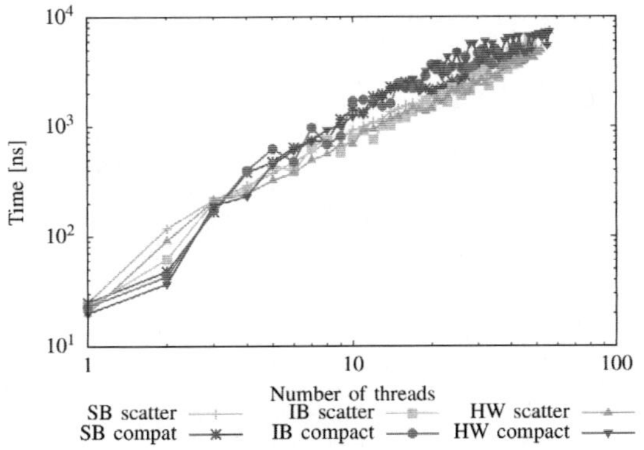

Figure 10. Atomic results CPU, different thread mapping.

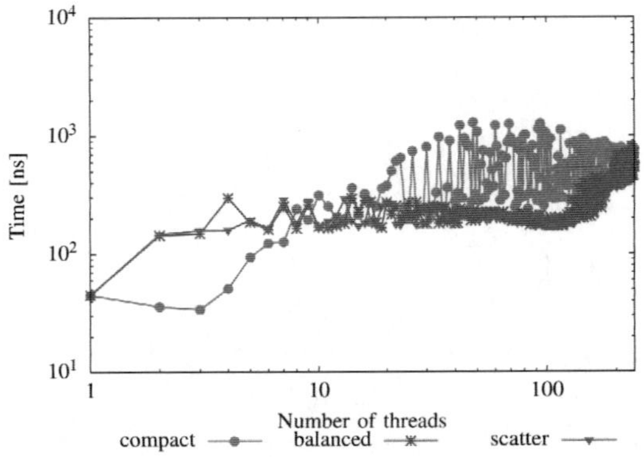

Figure 9. Atomic results KNC, different thread mapping.

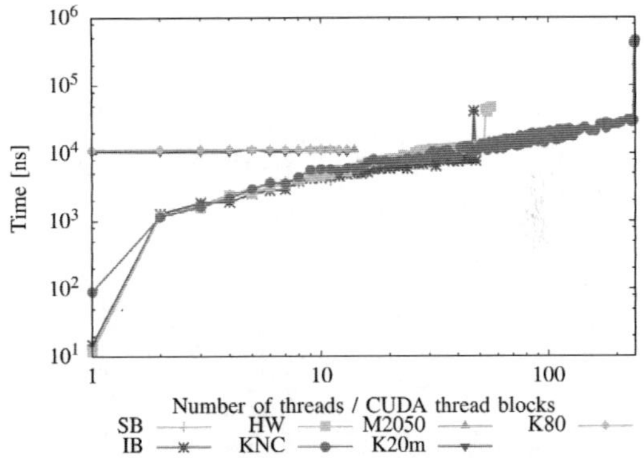

Figure 11. Barrier results.

performance number(s) for GPUs are therefore given as a dashed line with all stream processors used. In contrast to the results on latency, the accelerators perform better than the CPU systems. A summary and comparison to the theoretical bandwidth is given in Figure 5. It is noteable that the KNC performs relativly poorly here. Its measured bandwidth is comparable to the Haswell CPUs and the older Nvidia Fermi GPUs. Moreover, the KNC is not able to reach its theoretical bandwidth at all, though it has by far the highest theoretical bandwidth of all tested systems. For the CPUs, the efficiency within one similar microarchitecture (Sandy Bridge and Ivy Bridge) stays the same. A gain in performance is achieved with the new Haswell microarchitecture.

Figure 6 shows the bandwidth test for the KNC with different thread mapping in OpenMP. A significant difference can be observed when different thread mappings are used. If the compact thread mapping is used (same as in Figure 6), bandwith increases steadily with an increasing number of threads. The performance drops with the last four threads, because, at this point, the last core with its four hardware threads is used in the application, but that core is busy waiting for operating system tasks (communication with the host system).

When a scattered or balanced thread mapping is used, the impact of the four hardware threads per core can be seen. The performance increases until all cores are evenly utilized (one thread per core). Then, as soon as one core gets a second thread, the performance drops and increases again steadily. Again, the impact of the operating system core can be seen when all available threads of the KNC are used.

In Figure 7, similar to the KNC, changing the thread mapping for processor systems shows differences between compact and scattered thread mapping. When using a compact thread mapping on all three CPU architectures, the effect when the second CPU socket gets populated with threads is clearly visible. When only one socket is used, bandwith increases slowly to a point of saturation. Then, when the second socket is used, bandwith increases dramatically. This behavior is different to the KNC compact thread mapping, where a steady increase can be observed. This can be explained by the different layout of the memory connection in KNC (ring-bus) and the CPUs (cc-NUMA).

For the scattered thread mapping, the Ivy Bridge system behaves differently to the other CPU systems, because this node could not be used exclusively in our tests (some system services were active). For the Sandy Bridge and Haswell, results show similar behavior. First the bandwith increases steadily but oscilates. With an odd number of threads, the bandwith drops, and with an even number of threads, the bandwith rises again, because here the memory channels of both CPUs can be used evenly. Moreover, the overall bandwith drops when hyperthreads get used. This effect can be clearly

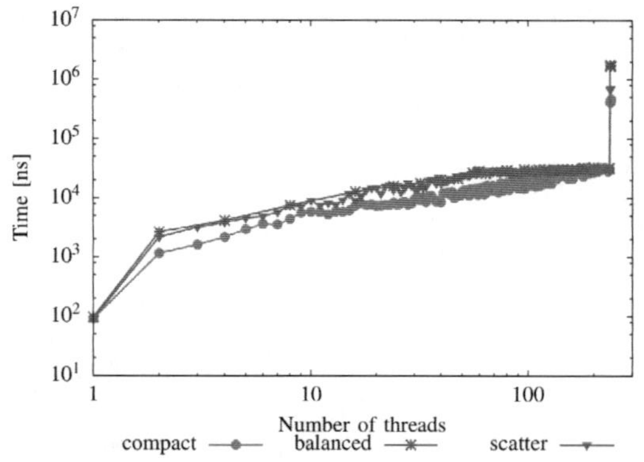

Figure 12. Barrier results on KNC, different thread mapping.

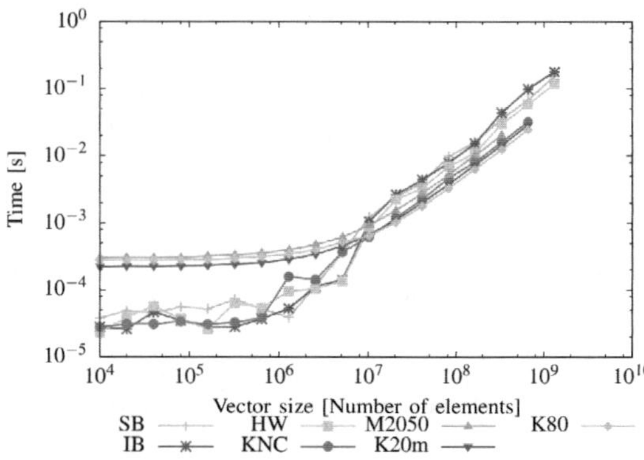

Figure 14. Reduction results, vector size variable.

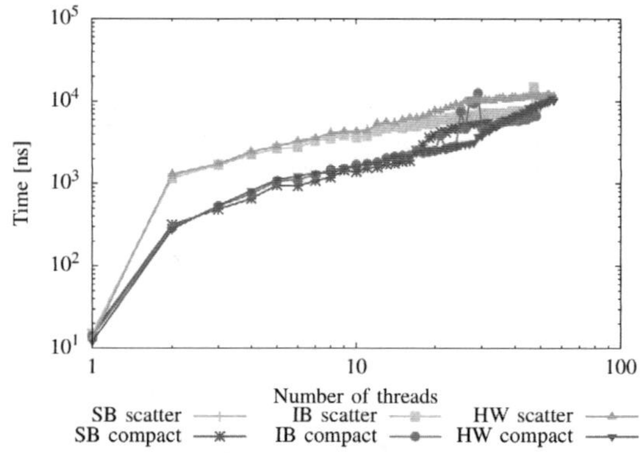

Figure 13. Barrier results on CPUs, different thread mapping.

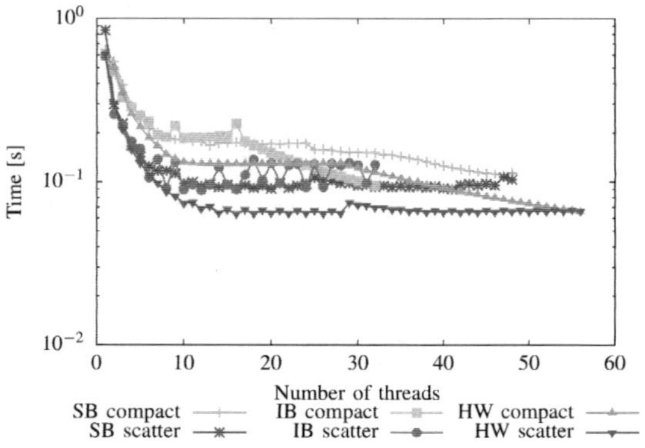

Figure 15. Reduction results on CPUs, thread number variable.

seen for Sandy Bridge with the strong drop in the curve. For the Haswell system, that drop is not as strong, but still the bandwidth decreases steadily from the point hyperthreads where are used. Furthermore, the bandwith drops even below the level of compact thread mapping at a certain point.

C. Atomic Updates (B3)

Figure 8 shows the performance results of the atomic operation on the different systems. On the multiprocessor systems, time increases linearly, proportional to the number of competing threads in use. Because the performance numbers show the normalized time for *one* operation of *one* thread, there is an increase in time *per operation* with the number of threads. This increase can be explained by the coherence and synchronization protocol, which is run by the processors/cores to ensure coherence and atomicity of such an operation. With more competing threads involved, the overhead increases [35]. For all three GPU systems, the time is constant, which can be explained by the use of the single unified L2 cache and the weak memory model without memory coherence. Moreover, the performance improvement for atomic operations from Fermi (M2050) to Kepler (K20m, K80) is clearly visible in this figure. For the KNC with compact thread mapping, quite large fluctuations can be observed (note the logscale of the plot).

Figure 9 shows the atomic benchmark for KNC with different thread mappings. When scattered and balanced thread mapping is used, the fluctuations become smaller, but the performance change with an increasing number of threads is still fairly unsteady. An explanation for this could be the ring bus of the KNC. The cache of *all* cores in the KNC have to be kept coherent via this ringbus. Moreover, from the time when one core is populated with all four hardware threads, the time for an atomic update increases significantly.

Figure 10 shows the results for changing the thread mapping for processor systems. The curves show the same linear behavior for compact and for scattered thread mapping.

D. Barrier (B4)

Figure 11 illustrates performance results of the barrier test with the default thread mapping. The barrier synchronization on the KNC shows a similar behavior to that on the multiprocessor systems with a linear increase with the number of used threads. Using the last core on KNC and on multiprocessors shows a large performance degradation. Again this can be explained by operating system tasks that perturb the (global) barrier operation, if the last available hardware thread is used.

For the Nvidia accelerators, the number of threads in the figure represents the number of used thread blocks (with 1024 threads per block used). The figure shows that the kernel launch time is nearly constant and equal for M2050, K20m and K80. Further, it does not depend on the number of blocks.

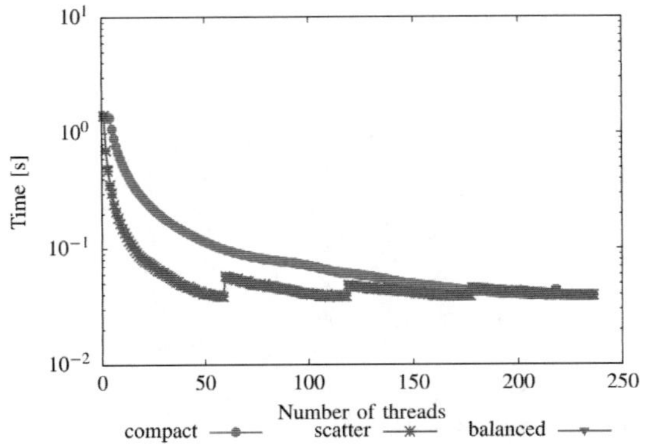

Figure 16. Reduction resultson KNC, thread number variable.

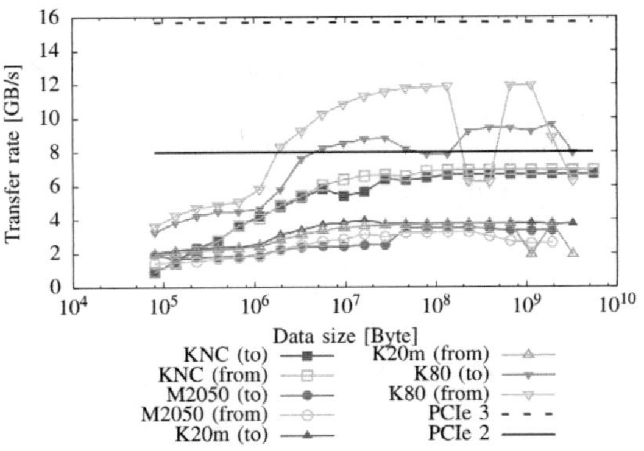

Figure 18. Communication performance results, unpinned memory.

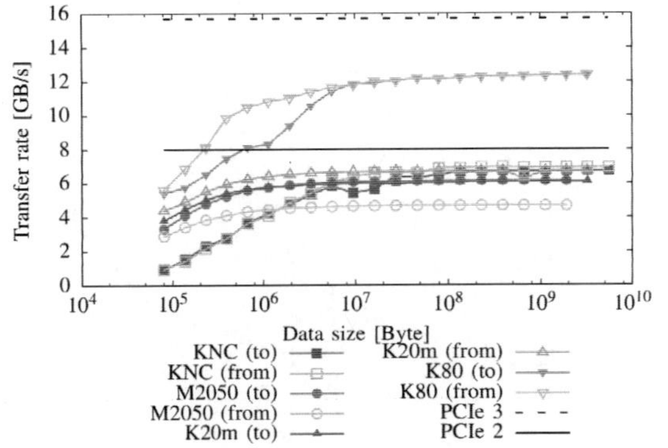

Figure 17. Communication performance results, pinned memory.

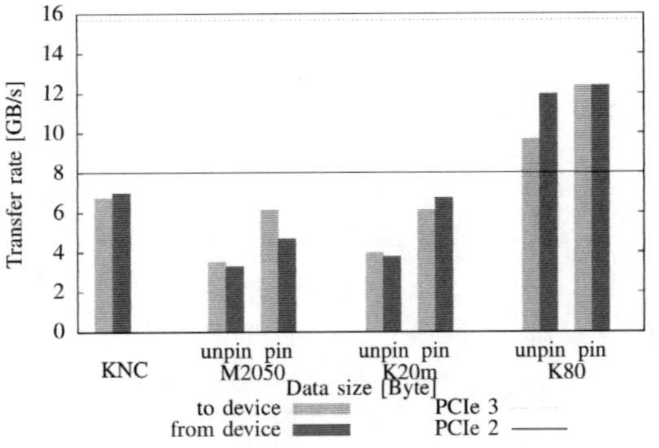

Figure 19. Communication performance best results.

The impact of different thread mappings for the KNC can be seen in Figure 12. The compact strategy is faster compared to scatter, because threads on the same core are synchronized faster than between cores. Therefore, utilizing as few cores as possible for a fixed thread count is the fastest strategy.

Figure 13 shows that, for the multiprocessor systems, the barrier operation is faster with few threads if the compact thread mapping is used (using less cores utilizing the hyper-threads on these cores) compared to the scatter strategy. When all threads are used, the performance is invariant of the thread mapping strategy.

E. Reduction (B5)

For the reduction test, Figure 14 shows the parallel run time using all available parallelism on each system with an increasing vector size. The M2050 card was limited by the available memory size, thus the largest vector size used on other systems could not be used on this system. The GPUs are slower than the multiprocessors for a smaller number of elements, and they are faster than the multiprocessors for large vectors, which corresponds to the usage model of GPUs.

In Figure 15, the results for the multiprocessors with varying thread numbers and different thread mappings are shown. Here, a sufficiently large vector with 10^9 elements was chosen. The figure shows that scattered thread mapping has a better overall performance than compact thread mapping. For a compact thread mapping, the time for the reduction decreases faster when the second CPU socket is used and both memory channels get used. However, times for compact and scattered thread mapping are equal when all threads are used. Furthermore, for scattered thread mapping, the effect of hyperthreads can be seen in the jumps of the execution time.

Figure 16 shows the results for a variable number of threads with a fixed vector size of 8×10^8 on KNC. Again the compact thread mapping shows an overall weaker performance than the scattered thread mapping due to memory bandwidth requirements. For a scattered thread mapping, the effect of the 4-way hyperthreading can be seen in the jumps of the execution time, too. Similar to the multiprocessors, compact and scattered thread mapping have equal results when all threads are used.

F. Communication Host-Device (B6)

For the communication benchmark experiments, the data transfer from the host to the device and back from the device to the host was considered. Moreover, we differentiated on the GPUs for the communication to/from a GPU between pinned and unpinned host memory. For GPUs, it is explicitly possible to allocate page-locked memory on the host using CUDA functions [36].

Figures 17 and 18 show data transfer rates in GB/s from the host to the attached accelerator and vice versa for pinned

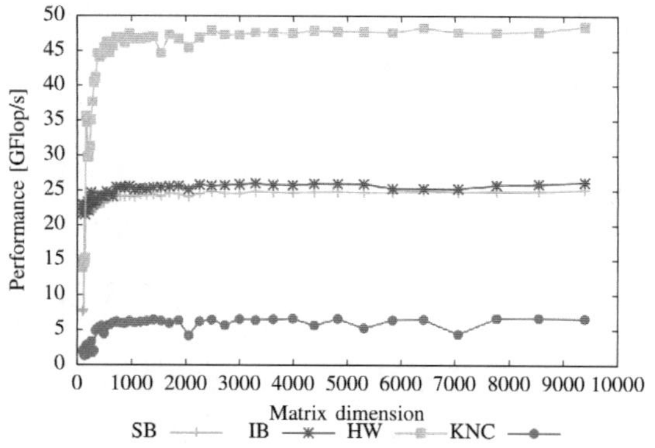

Figure 20. DGEMM results, single threaded.

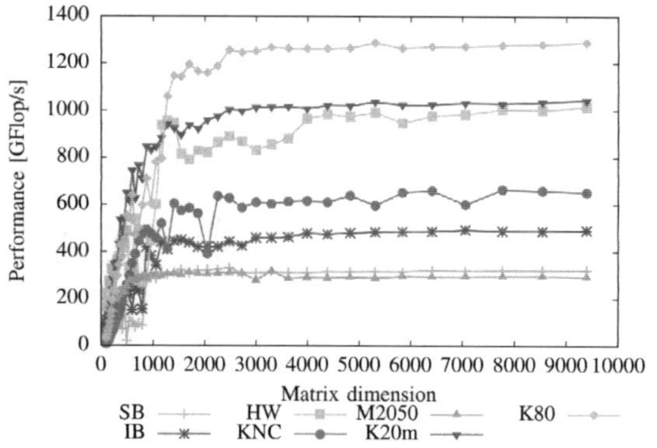

Figure 21. DGEMM results, full parallel.

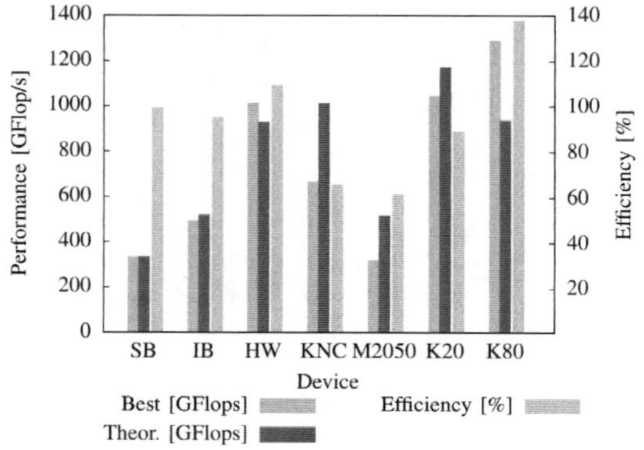

Figure 22. DGEMM best results, full parallel.

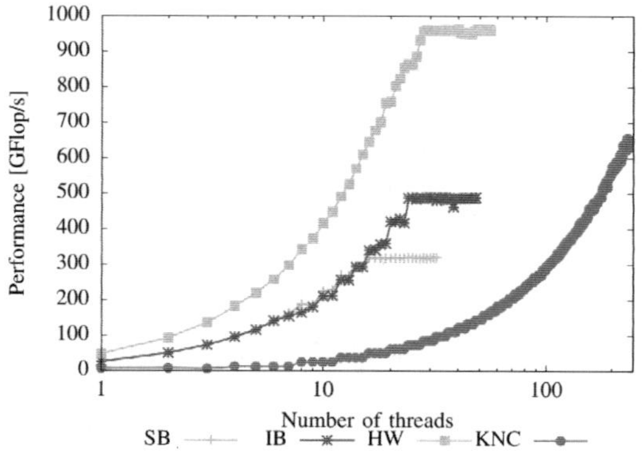

Figure 23. DGEMM results, thread number variable, n=5000.

and unppined memory. For KNC there is no such distinction. The figures show that, for a reasonably large data size, the communication links are used efficiently on the KNC, the theoretical data transfer rate of 8 GB/s for PCIe 2.0 minus protocol overhead can nearly be reached. Figure 17 shows that this is also true for the K20m and M2020 GPUs, when pinned memory is used. Here, the K20m and the M2050 perform similarly in data transfer to the device. For the transfer back from the accelerator to the host, there is a performance drop on the M2050, which reaches only approx. 5 GB/s instead of nearly 7 GB/s as on the other accelerators. The lower bandwidth seems to be a problem with our combination of host system and accelerator card.

On the K20m, the transfer from the device performs slightly better than to the device. For the K80, the transfer rate to and from the device is the same for larger data sizes, but this value does not reach the theoretical limit for the PCIe 3. Perhaps this limit could be reached if both GPUs of the K80 are utilized (as explained, we used only one of them). Moreover, for smaller data sizes, again transfer rates from the K80 are better than to the K80. The difference between host to device and device to host bandwidth for the GPUs could be due to the Direct Memory Access (DMA) initiator. When the DMA is initiated from the CPU, it has a better performance.

Figure 18 shows that not using pinned memory for GPUs deteriorates the transfer rate. The K20m and M2050 have almost completely lower transfer rates than the KNC and do not reach the theoretical limit at all. Moreover, in contrast to pinned memory, transfer rates from and to these GPUs show nearly the same behavior. The K80 is able to reach the pinned memory transfer rates only for larger data sizes.

Figure 19 summarizes the best communication results of the acclerators. It clarifies that there is only a minor difference between communication to or from the device. But there is a quite large difference in transfer rates between pinned and unpinned memory on GPUs.

G. DGEMM (B7)

In Figure 20, the results for a single threaded run with variable matrix dimension of the DGEMM benchmark are displayed. Here the GPUs are omitted, because a single threaded run does not correspond to the GPU usage model. It can be seen that, for an increasing matrix size, the perfomance quickly saturates.

The KNC has by far the weakest single thread performance of all CPU-like systems, because the single CPUs in the KNC have a rather limited performance compared to the other multiprocessors used. Moreover, Sandy Bridge and Ivy Bridge show nearly the same performance because they have more or less the same microarchitecture. The Ivy Bridge performs only a little bit better because of its higher clock. Finally, it can be seen that the new Haswell shows the best performance, twice

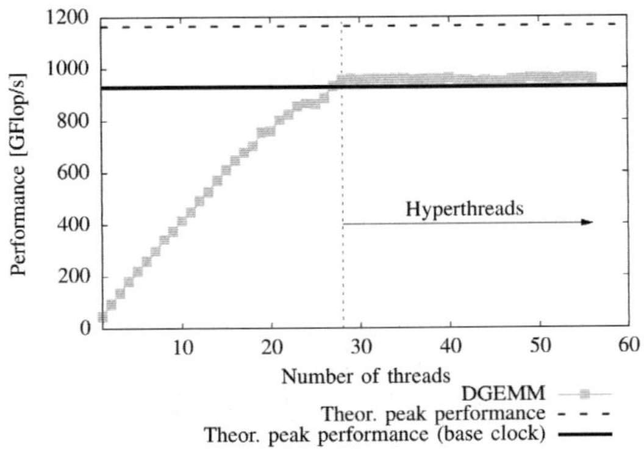

Figure 24. DGEMM on HW, thread number variable.

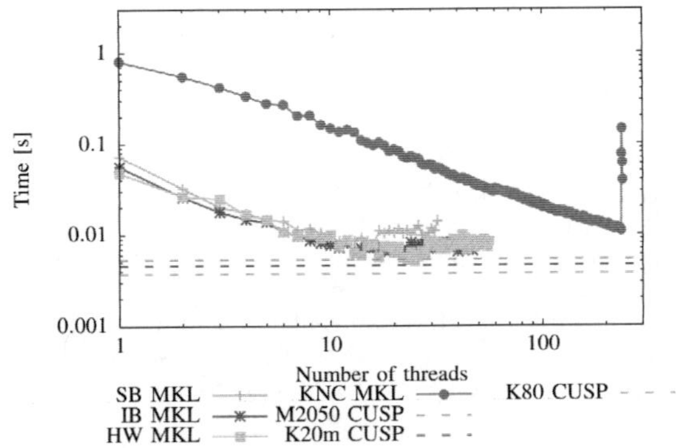

Figure 25. SpMV results, CSR format.

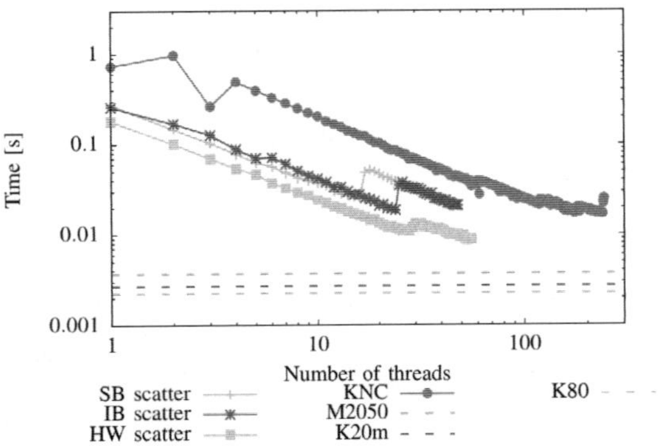

Figure 26. SpMV results, ELL format.

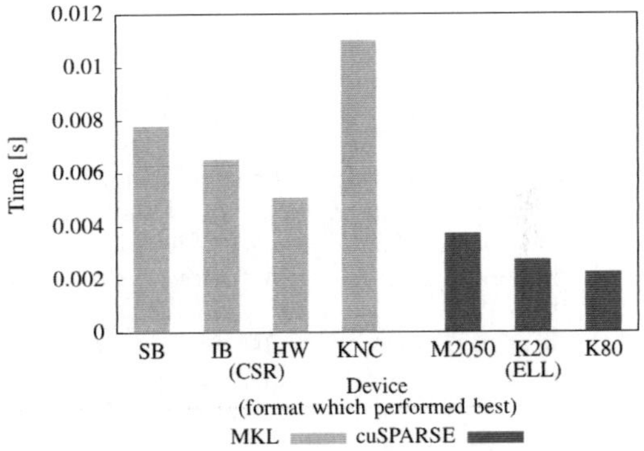

Figure 27. SpMV best results.

the performance of the older systems.

Subsequently, Figure 21 displays the results of the DGEMM benchmark for a full parallel run (now GPUs included) with variable matrix size. Again, on all systems, the perfomance rises quickly and reaches saturation for sufficently large matices. As one would expect, the K80 shows the highest performance, because it has the highest theoretical performance.

Figure 22 summarizes the performance results for the dense matrix multiply operation. Here, only the best performance over all matrix sizes is given. Moreover, the theoretical (base) performance and the efficiency (performance divided by theoretical (base) performance) for each system are shown. As expected, the operation has better performance on the accelerators due to their better raw floating point performance, which can be utilized in a DGEMM operation. It can be seen that, on the majority of the processor systems, almost peak performance is reached. The Haswell processor even shows better performance than the given theoretical peak performance in Table II (related to the base clock). This can be explained by the intelligent turbo boost and temporal overclocking of these processors. Moreover, the Haswell processors are the first CPUs that reach (nearly) one Teraflop performance. That makes them comparable to even recent accelerators. Haswell outperforms the older Fermi architechture and the KNC, which does not reach its theoretical performance at all. The Haswell results for matrix multiply are on nearly the same level as the recent Kepler K20m GPU and are only clearly beaten by the new Kepler K80 (with one GPU used). The K80 also shows better performance than its given theoretical peak performance based on the base clock. Again, this can be explained by the use of turboboost.

Furthermore, the number of threads on the CPU systems and KNC were varied for a dense matrix with a fixed size ($n = 5,000$) that is large enough to reach the compute performance limit. The results for that configuration are shown in Figure 23. For the KNC, the performance increases linearly (logscale used) until all threads are used. However, for all CPU systems, the performance increases linearly until a certain point (hyperthreads come into use) and then remains at that level. In Figure 24, this is shown for the Haswell architecture. Here, without the logscale, one can clearly see the linear increase in performance. Moreover, the figure clearly shows that the stagnation begins when hyperthreads are used. For the KNC this is different. Here, the hyperthreads have to be used to achieve performance [32].

H. SPMV (B8)

Figures 25 and 26 show the results for the SPMV benchmark using the CSR format and the ELL format, respectively. For the multiprocessors and the KNC, the number of threads was varied. For the GPUs the cuSPARSE library was used,

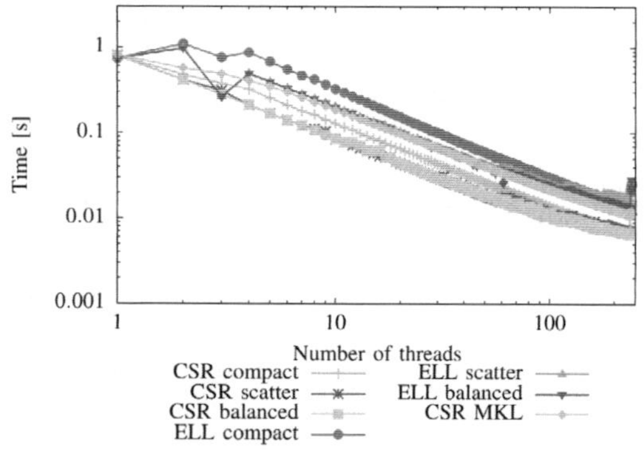

Figure 28. SpMV on KNC, CSR and ELL, different thread mapping.

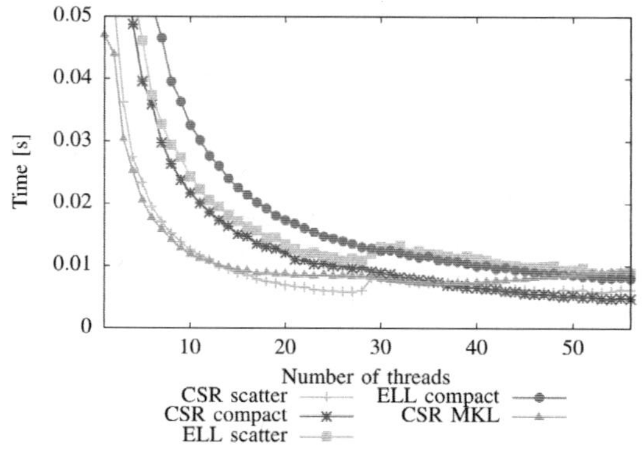

Figure 29. SpMV results on HW, CSR and ELL, different thread mapping.

consequently, the parallelism could not be explicitly controlled. Hence, in all SPMV figures, the GPU results are presented as a dashed line. In Figure 25, the results for the CSR format using the MKL and the cuSPARSE library are shown, because it is assumed that these highly optimized vendor libraries can achieve the best performance for the particular architectures. Overall, it can be seen that, for the test matrix in CSR format, the KNC shows the weakest performance, the Haswell CPU can compete with the older M2050 and K20m and the K80 shows the best performance. For the multiprocessors, it can be seen that the execution time first declines, but then rises again after a certain point (details see below). For the KNC, the execution time decreases steadily until all cores are used, again when the last core gets utilized there is a jump in the execution time because of the operating system administration.

Figure 26 shows the results for the ELL matrix format that is supposed to be a more suitable format for GPUs compared to the CSR format [43]. For the test matrix, this can indeed be verified, because here all GPU systems show relatively better performance than the multiprocessor systems and the KNC, which again has the weakest performance. Moreover, even the absolute execution times show an improvement for the GPUs and a degradation for the multiprocessors and the KNC. For the multiprocessors and KNC, the results of the scattered thread mapping are shown because this performed better on these system (again, for details see below).

As a summary, in Figure 27 only the best results for a system and a format are given. All GPU systems perform well, compared to the multiprocessors and KNC. The K20m performs around 26% faster than the M2050 using the ELL format. The low performance improvement of the K20m can be explained by the fact that the SPMV operation is memory bound and the memory bandwidth of the K20m is only around 25% higher compared to the M2050. Similar relations apply for K20m and K80. Surprisingly, the KNC shows the weakest performance in this test although this card has the highest nominal memory bandwidth of all used systems. The low performance is related to the bandwidth results, where the KNC reached only half of its peak memory bandwidth.

We investigated further the weak performance of the KNC. Figure 28 shows results on the KNC for the CSR and ELL format. Here a rather simple own OpenMP implementation with different thread mappings was used and performance compared to the Intel MKL version. The figure shows that our own CSR version with *all* thread mappings performs better than the Intel MKL version.

Figure 29 shows detailed results for the Haswell multiprocessor. Here the SPMV using CSR and ELL with different thread mapping and the implementation of the MKL for the CSR format are compared. The CSR format has an overall better performance for this matrix on the Haswell multiprocessors than the ELL format. Again, the curve for the execution time of the scattered kernels has jumps due to the use of hyperthreads.

Once more it should be pointed out that, as a common representative of memory bandwidth-bound application kernels, the SPMV benchmark should give a rather general view on these architectures. For detailed insights on computing techniques and further formats for sparse matrices see, for example, [3], [4], [43].

VII. Discussion

Characteristics of the examined architectures could be revealed using the proposed benchmarks. Additionally, the effect of different thread mappings for CPU based architectures was shown.

For memory latency, GPUs are still behind CPU-based systems in absolute times, but newer GPUs gain performance in terms of *relative* clock cycles, alleviating the effects of latency. However, on GPUs, latency time (and clock rate) is traded against parallelism, which follows the usage model of GPUs.

For the memory bandwidth benchmark, GPUs outperform multiprocessor systems and also the KNC. Moreover, the KNC shows a fairly weak memory bandwidth in practice, although it has the highest theoretical memory bandwidth. If on CPUs and KNC not all available hardware threads are used, scattered thread mapping should be used, to utilize as much bandwidth as possible.

For the atomic operations, it was shown that the strong cache coherence model in CPU based systems is disadvantegeous for the performance of that operation. This is especially true for the current MIC architechture of the KNC, where a lot of caches have to be kept coherent. The weak cache coherence of CUDA has clear performance advantages here.

Barrier operations are usually used to separate different program stages. The kernel launch time on a GPU (comparable to such a use) is independent of the number of used threads blocks. This is different on CPUs where the number threads and thread mapping have an impact on the performance of a barrier. The more threads, the longer the time for the barrier operation. But here a compact thread mapping is better for barrier operations if not all available hardware threads are used.

For the reduction operation, for a small amount of data, CPU-based systems with fast L1/L2 caches and a low latency have an advantage compared to GPUs. For a large amount of data, GPUs with the higher bandwidth outperform the CPUs.

For the communication between a host and an accelerator, it was shown that, for GPUs, pinned memory should be used to achieve good transfer rates. The accelerators generally reached their respective theoretical transfer rates via the PCI Bus for sufficiently large data packages. However, these PCI transfer rates of at most 8/16 GB/s (2nd/3rd generation PCIe) are still far behind memory transfer times of approx. 100 GB/s on two socket CPU systems. Therefore, the PCIe is still a severe bottleneck for accelerators. Particularly, the transfer of a small amount of data shows only low transfer rates. Consequently, the number of transfer packages should be reduced. Instead of many small transfers, a few large transfers should be preferred. Additionally, an asynchronous transfer should be used to hide the latency of such an operation. These aspects mean that accelerators are not appropiate for kernels that depend a lot on such a communication.

The DGEMM benchmark reached (near) peak floating performance on all systems, when it was executed with enough parallelism and sufficiently large matrices. For same generations, GPUs show a performance improvement compared to CPUs based on their better raw performance. On CPUs, DGEMM computations do not benefit from the use of hyperthreads due to way hyperthreads work (see, for example, [46]).

Generally, memory bandwidth-bound kernels such as the SPMV are far from reaching peak floating point performance on a system. However, these operations can benefit from the high memory bandwith of recent accelerators, especially on GPUs. The KNC shows severe problems here. This result reflects the result of the memory bandwith benchmark, where the KNC showed a weak performance, too.

VIII. Conclusions

This paper introduced a set of benchmarks to determine important performance parameters of single-node parallel systems. One or a combination of these parameters are often performance limiting in parallel applications. The benchmarks can easily be ported to other architectures.

The benchmarks were applied to systems of the same basic architecture but different processor generations (Intel Haswell, Ivy Brige, Sandy Bridge) as well as to different architectures (CPU, two different accelerator architectures).

It was shown that some parameters (e.g., the memory-related ones) show fairly different performance characteristics between the systems, qualifying or disqualifying a system for certain application classes. In contrast, all systems showed similar behavior for compute-dense problems reaching near-peak floating point performance, which is reasonably comparable between accelerators and latest generation multiprocessors. Due to design decisions in the processor architecture, graphic processors show a remarkable performance on some synchronization operations, operations that often limit the parallel performance.

For certain application classes, additional performance parameters might be important where appropriate benchmarks could be developed as well. This paper discussed only single-node parameters. An extension of this work would be to include cluster architectures, i.e., multiple-node architectures. Further investigation could include also the impact of different programming models such as OpenACC or OpenCL instead of CUDA on a GPU.

Acknowledgements

We would like to thank the CMT team at Saudi Aramco EXPEC ARC for their support and input. Especially we want to thank Ali H. Dogru for making this research project possible.

References

[1] R. Berrendorf, J. Ecker, J. Razzaq, S. Scholl, and F. Mannuss, "Using application oriented micro-benchmarks to characterize the performance of single-node architectures," in Proc. Ninth International Conference on Advanced Engeneering Computing and Applications in Sciences (ADVCOMP 2015), C.-P. Rueckemann, Ed. IARIA, 2015, pp. 31–38.

[2] A. Petitet, R. Whaley, J. Dongarra, and A. Cleary, "HPL - a portable implementation of the high-performance Linpack benchmark for distributed-memory computers," http://www.netlib.org/benchmark/hpl/, Tech. Rep., 2008, version 2.0, [retrieved: May 2016].

[3] Y. Saad, Iterative Methods for Sparse Linear Systems, 2nd ed. SIAM, 2003.

[4] J. Ecker, R. Berrendorf, J. Razzaq, S. E. Scholl, and F. Mannuss, "Comparing different programming approaches for SpMV-operations on GPUs," in Proc. 11th International Conference on Parallel Processing and Applied Mathematics (PPAM 2015), 2015, pp. 537–547.

[5] R. Berrendorf, M. Weierstall, and F. Mannuss, "Program optimization strategies to improve the performance of SpMV-operations," in Proc. 8th Intl. Conference on Future Computational Technologies and Applications (FUTURE COMPUTING 2016), 2016, to appear.

[6] S. Williams, A. Waterman, and D. Patterson, "Roofline: An insightful visual performance model for multicore architectures," Comm. ACM, vol. 52, no. 4, Apr. 2009, pp. 65–76.

[7] D. Molka, D. Hackenberg, R. Schöne, and W. E. Nagel, "Cache coherence protocol and memory performance of the Intel Haswell-EP architecture," in Proc. 44th Intl. Conference on Parallel Processing (ICPP 2015). IEEE, Sep. 2015, pp. 739–748.

[8] Top 500 List, http://www.top500.org/, [retrieved: May 2016].

[9] SPEC CPU 2006, Standard Performance Evaluation Corporation, https://www.spec.org/cpu2006/, [retrieved: May 2016].

[10] D. Bailey, E. Barszcz, J. Barton, D. Browning, R. Carter, L. Dagum, R. Fatoohi, S. Fineberg, P. Frederickson, T. Lasinski, R. Schreiber, H. Simon, V. Venkatakrishnan, and S. Weeratunga, "The NAS parallel benchmarks," NASA Ames Research Center, http://www.nas.nasa.gov/assets/pdf/techreports/1994/rnr-94-007.pdf, Tech. Rep., 1994, [retrieved: May 2016].

[11] H. Jin, M. Frumkin, and J. Yan, "The OpenMP implementation of NAS parallel benchmarks and its performance," NASA Ames Research Center, http://www.nas.nasa.gov/assets/pdf/techreports/1999/nas-99-011.pdf, Tech. Rep., 1999, [retrieved: May 2016].

[12] S. Seo, G. Jo, and J. Lee, "Performance characterization of the NAS parallel benchmarks in OpenCL," in Proc. International Symposium on Workload Characterization (IISWC). IEEE, 2011, pp. 137–148.

[13] R. Murphy, K. Wheeler, B. Barrett, and J. Ang, "Introducing the graph 500," Cray User's Group (CUG), http://www.graph500.org/, Tech. Rep., 2010, [retrieved: May 2016].

[14] N. Brown, "A task-oriented graph500 benchmark," in Proc. Intl.Supercomputing Conference (ISC 2014), ser. LNCS, no. 8488. Springer-Verlag, 2014, pp. 460–469.

[15] J. Jose, S. Potluri, K. Tomko, and D. K. Panda, "Designing scalable graph500 benchmark with hybrid mpi+openshmem programming models," in Proc. Intl.Supercomputing Conference (ISC 2013), ser. LNCS, no. 7905. Springer-Verlag, 2013, pp. 109–124.

[16] J. Bull and D. O'Neill, "A microbenchmark suite for OpenMP 2.0," SIGARCH Comput. Archit. News, vol. 29, no. 5, 2001, pp. 41–48.

[17] J. Bull, F. Reid, and N. McDonnell, "A microbenchmark suite for OpenMP tasks," in Proc. 8th Intl. Conference on OpenMP in a Heterogeneous World (IWOMP'12), 2012, pp. 271–274.

[18] OpenMP Application Program Interface, 4th ed., OpenMP Architecture Review Board, http://www.openmp.org/, Jul. 2013, [retrieved: May 2016].

[19] J. Treibig, G. Hager, and G. Wellein, "likwid-bench: An extensible microbenchmarking platform for x86 multicore compute nodes," in Tools for High Performance Computing 2011. Springer-Verlag, 2012, pp. 27–36.

[20] J. Treibig, G. Hager, and G. Wellein, "Likwid: A lightweight performance-oriented tool suite for x86 multicore environments," in Proceedings of PSTI2010, the First International Workshop on Parallel Software Tools and Tool Infrastructures, 2010.

[21] J. Hofmann, D. Fey, J. Eitzinger, G. Hager, and G. Wellein, "Analysis of intels haswell microarchitecture using the ecm model and microbenchmarks," in Architecture of Computing Systems – ARCS 2016, ser. LNCS, no. 3697. Springer-Verlag, 2016, pp. 210–222.

[22] J. Lemeire, J. G. Cornelis, and L. Segers, "Microbenchmarks for gpu characteristics: the occupancy roofline and the pipeline model," in 2016 24th Euromicro International Conference on Parallel, Distributed, and Network-Based Processing (PDP), 2016, pp. 456–463.

[23] P. Thoman, K. Kofler, H. Studtand, J. Thomson, and T. Fahringer, "Automatic OpenCL device characterization: Guiding optimized kernel design," in Proc. Euro-Par 2011. Springer-Verlag, 2011, pp. 438–452.

[24] A. Danalis, G. Marin, C. McCurdy, J. S. Meredith, P. C. Roth, K. Spafford, V. Tipparaju, and J. S. Vetter, "The scalable heterogeneous computing (shoc) benchmark suite," in Proceedings of the 3rd Workshop on General-Purpose Computation on Graphics Processing Units. ACM, 2010, pp. 63–74.

[25] X. Yan, X. Shi, and Q. Sun, "An OpenCL micro-benchmark suite for GPUs and CPUs," in Proc. 13th International Conference on Parallel and Distributed Computing, Applications and Technologies (PDCAT). IEEE, 2012, pp. 53–58.

[26] J. D. McCalpin, "Stream: Sustainable memory bandwidth in high performance computers," University of Virginia, http://www.cs.virginia.edu/stream/, Tech. Rep. TM-88, 1991-2007, [retrieved: May 2016].

[27] D. Molka, D. Hackenberg, R. Schöne, and M. S. Müller, "Memory performance and cache coherence effects on an Intel Nehalem multiprocessor system," in Proc. 18th Intl. Conference on Parallel Architectures and Compilation Techniques (PACT 2009). IEEE, Sep. 2009, pp. 261–270.

[28] D. Hackenberg, D. Molka, and W. E. Nagel, "Comparing cache architectures and coherency protocols on x86-64 multicore SMP systems," in Proc. 42th Annual IEEE/ACM Intl. Symposium on Microarchitecture (MICRO 42). IEEE/ACM, 2009, pp. 413–422.

[29] Intel® 64 and IA-32 Architectures Optimization Reference Manual, Intel, http://www.intel.com/content/www/us/en/architecture-and-technology/64-ia-32-architectures-optimization-manual.html, Sep. 2014, [retrieved: May 2016].

[30] Nvidia CUDA, https://developer.nvidia.com/cuda-zone, [retrieved: May 2016].

[31] M. Wolfe, Understanding the CUDA Data Parallel Threading Model. A Primer, pgiinsider ed., PGI, https://www.pgroup.com/lit/articles/insider/v2n1a5.htm, Feb. 2010, (Updated December 2012), [retrieved: May 2016].

[32] J. Jeffers and J. Reinders, Intel® Xeon Phi™Coprocessor High-Performance Programming. Morgan Kaufmann, 2013.

[33] M. Corden, Requirements for Vectorizable Loops, Intel, https://software.intel.com/en-us/articles/requirements-for-vectorizable-loops/, 2012, [retrieved: May 2016].

[34] J. L. Hennessy and D. A. Patterson, Computer Architecture: A Quantitative Approach, 5th ed. Morgan Kaufmann Publishers, Inc., 2012.

[35] R. Berrendorf and M. Makulla, "Level-synchronous parallel breadth-first search algorithms for multicore- and multiprocessors systems," in Proc. Sixth Intl. Conference on Future Computational Technologies and Applications (FUTURE COMPUTING 2014), 2014, pp. 26–31.

[36] Nvidia, CUDA C Programming Guide, pg-02829-001_v6.5 ed., http://docs.nvidia.com/cuda/pdf/CUDA_C_Programming_Guide.pdf, Aug. 2014, [retrieved: May 2016].

[37] R. Berrendorf, "A technique to avoid atomic operations on large shared memory parallel systems," Intl. Journal on Advances in Software, vol. 7, no. 7&8, 2014, pp. 197–210.

[38] Nvidia, Thrust, https://developer.nvidia.com/thrust, [retrieved: May 2016].

[39] BLAS (Basic Linear Algebra Subprograms), http://www.netlib.org/blas/, [retrieved: May 2016].

[40] Intel® Math Kernel Library, https://software.intel.com/en-us/intel-mkl, [retrieved: May 2016].

[41] Nvidia cuBLAS, https://developer.nvidia.com/cublas, [retrieved: May 2016].

[42] Nvidia cuSPARSE, https://developer.nvidia.com/cusparse, [retrieved: May 2016].

[43] N. Bell and M. Garland, "Efficient sparse matrix-vector multiplication on CUDA," Nvidia Corp., Tech. Rep. NVR-2008-004, Dec. 2008.

[44] SPE Comparative Solution Project, Society of Petroleum Engineers, http://www.spe.org/web/csp/, [retrieved: May 2016].

[45] User and Reference Guide for the Intel C++ Compiler 15.0, https://software.intel.com/en-us/ ed., Intel Corporation, 2014, [retrieved: May 2016].

[46] G. Hager and G. Wellein, Introduction to High Performance Computing for Scientists and Engineers. CRC Press Taylor and Francis Group, 2011.

International Journal on Advances in Systems and Measurements, vol 9 no 1 & 2, year 2016, http://www.iariajournals.org/systems_and_measurements/

Smart Factory Systems - Fostering Cloud-based Manufacturing based on Self-Monitoring Cyber-Physical Systems

Simon Bergweiler

German Research Center for Artificial Intelligence (DFKI)
Kaiserslautern, Germany
Email: simon.bergweiler@dfki.de

Abstract—**This paper describes the concept and realization of an architecture using cloud-based smart components to achieve a more responsive production system that provides a modular and re-configurable production framework. For each important part of the plant and the manufactured product, digital virtual copies are created and stored in active digital object memories, a unified structured format for data access and further processing. Cyber-Physical Systems act as intelligent nodes within the cloud-based network and guarantee the function of technical communication and data exchange. Moreover, these systems continuously perform and execute almost autonomous simple state and feature checks, up to a certain level of complexity. In various points of the production process these simple checks can ensure or even optimize the quality of the product. An assistance system makes use of these technical solutions and manages and monitors the distributed components and their responsibilities for quality assurance during the whole production process. In compliance with prescribed quality characteristics and the situational context necessary processing steps are defined or rearranged.**

Keywords–active digital object memory; cyber-physical systems; cyber-physical production system.

I. INTRODUCTION

The present approach of intelligent manufacturing, called cyber-physical Production Assistance System (cPAS), shows the realization and implementation of a concept of networked autonomous devices, sensors and machines that monitor themselves and perform condition-based, decentralized small tasks for continuous monitoring and self-diagnosis by simple state checks. The crosslinking is carried out by upstream Cyber-Physical Systems (CPS) and the data storage and the extended decentralized monitoring is realized by Active Digital Object Memories (ADOMe) [1].

The industry is facing a change and needs improved production system efficiency and robustness through more flexible, automated production, because it will no longer be sufficient to produce good products in high quality. The current order of the market is shifting more and more towards the idea of contemporary customer-specific individual production, combined with the shortest possible cycles for development and processing, different product variants need to be made in almost no time [2]. However, this flexible approach also requires that future factories must be easily adapted and converted to the order situation, but this is time-consuming and costly. To make such a complex task more manageable, parts of the plant, e.g., sensors, machinery and products need to be developed that will make a flexible and modular engineering possible. Through the application of innovative self-monitoring techniques for manufactured products and field devices the efficiency in production will be increased [3]. Nowadays, as a general trend, the focus shifts from pure engineering, which is based on mechanical processes, to software-controlled processes that offer potential for further optimization [4].

The evolution of the Internet to the Internet of Things (IoT) corresponds to the fusion of the real and the virtual world. When considering this trend, CPS play a main role by coupling the different scientific worlds - mechanical engineering, electrical engineering and computer science. This trend reveals the German industry that it stands on the threshold of the fourth industrial revolution (*Industrie 4.0*) [3]. Future production processes are characterized by specific requirements to the individual manufacturing of products. This opens up new requirements for highly flexible production systems, and increasing efficiency in industrial production processes will become a significant competitive factor. CPS form a solid basis for *Industrie 4.0* [5], and this approach shows the integration of these systems in a real production environment. The vision of *Industrie 4.0* describes the digital transformation of industry and the networking of production and products. With the development of *Industrie 4.0*, machinery, equipment and sensors are communicating with each other and exchange data. This leads to a combination of the physical and the virtual world [2], [3].

The development of component-based machine-to-machine (M2M) communication technologies enable field devices to exchange information with each other in an autonomous way without human intervention. The concept of IoT extends this M2M concept by the possibility to communicate and interact with physical objects, which are represented by CPS. These CPS provide the necessary computing power, storage, sensors and ubiquitous access to the functionality of the instrumented machines and field devices [6], [7]. In this approach, all major field devices are equipped with CPS and installed in spatially separated production lines. The idea goes here towards the concept of "retrofitting" [8]. Retrofitting means the advanced equipment of existing facilities through additional hardware: function-enhancing modules for communication and distributed processing. With this instrumentation, it is possible that individual field devices and the manufactured products communicate with each other, until the industrial plant meets the standards and directives of future factories and principles of *Industrie 4.0* [9].

In Section II, this paper gives an overview of used technologies and introduces the terms field devices, IoT, CPS, automation pyramid, active digital object memories, smart factories and smart products. It closes with a with a brief summary that addresses the importance of networking in the industry and manufacturing domain. Section III describes the concept of cloud-based manufacturing, the modeling, and distributed decentralized CPS and corresponding locally and globally stored data structures. Section IV describes the scenario and application domain and shows how the approach and the developed framework can be used in this industrial environment. In the following Section V, the technical realization of an infrastructure for distributed CPS-based product memories and the upstream assistance system of the CPPS is shown. Section VI gives a conclusion and an outlook on future work.

II. Background

A. Field Devices

Field devices are electronic devices that are located at the field level, the lowest level in the hierarchical level model for automation. They are associated with sensors that, on one hand, detect the data of the measuring points and on the other pass the control data to the actuators. At certain time intervals, field devices continuously supply measured data for process control and receive control data for the actuators.

B. Internet of Things

The inexorable growth and innovation diversity of information and communication technologies leads to a fundamental change in daily life. Computers are becoming smaller and can be used almost anywhere. They are built almost inside of all of our technical equipment, e.g., smart watches that track bio-physical data. These devices provide a wide range of technical capabilities that can be used quite comfortable and allow individual components to communicate and cooperate by constantly exchanging sensor information. Following this future trend it can be expected that all utensils of our daily life are turning into smart nodes within a global communication network: this is called the IoT [10], a trend that will also find its way into domains such as consumer electronics and also industrial production.

The term *Internet of Things* was coined and popularized by the work of the Auto-ID Center at the Massachusetts Institute of Technology (MIT), which in 1999 started to design and propagate a cross-company RFID infrastructure. In 2002, its co-founder and former head Kevin Ashton was quoted in Forbes Magazine as saying, "We need an internet for things, a standardized way for computers to understand the real world" [11]. This article was entitled "The internet of things", and was the first documented use of the term in a literal sense [12].

C. Industrial Internet

The idea of the Industrial Internet, also known as the Industrial Internet of Things (IIoT), is a network of physical components, systems and applications that contain embedded technology to communicate. The term is coined by the company Frost & Sullivan and refers to the integration or union of physical machines with their networked sensors and actuators with complex software technologies, like Machine Learning, Big Data, IoT, and Machine-to-Machine communication. Machines are talking to machines and analyze and optimize data to perform better. Different components, like sensors or actuators, share intelligence and solve complex problems in combination with a CPS.

For a better coordination, acceleration, and development of Industrial Internet technologies the Industrial Internet Consortium (IIC) was founded by AT&T, Cisco, General Electric, IBM, and Intel, in 2014. This consortium of industry players from multinational corporations attempts to establish a comprehensive application of the identified technologies.

The focus of the IIoT is on improving efficiency, safety, productivity of processes in the field of production. Optimized machine-to-machine communications, efficient parametrization, easier monitoring, and a better planning of capacities leads to a significant cost reduction in production and to a quick return on invest [13].

D. Cyber-Physical Systems

In the fields of agriculture, health, transport, energy supply and industry, we are facing a revolution, a new era, and the IoT will open up new ways and possibilities in the upcoming years. Modern information technologies connect data out of different areas and bring them together. This works, if there is a virtual counterpart for every physical product, that can reproduce, by means of sensors and cameras, the environment and the context to combine simulation models and predictive models.

Therefore, the paradigm of the IoT describes distributed networks, which in turn are composed of networks of smart objects. As a technical term for such smart objects, the term Cyber-Physical System (CPS) was coined [14]. The main feature of a CPS is that the information and communication technologies were developed and finely tuned to create virtual counterparts to physical components. CPS link data of the real world and this increases the effectiveness and does not encapsulate computing power in an embedded system. Over the communication channel available distributed computing power can be used to solve problems within a network.

The IoT and CPS are not fundamentally new concepts. Indeed, Simon [15] already identified the importance and benefits of combining both, physical and virtual domains. His approach was presented many years ago, when not all embedded platforms and manufacturing techniques were developed as today. In fact, the possibility to develop and use a mature platform and techniques are nowadays widely accepted by the industry. Production processes in the context of the initiative "Industrie 4.0" of the federal German government can be fine-grained equipped with sensors and deliver real-time internal and external production parameters in an very high level of detail [3], [16].

These following four features typically characterize CPS [17]:

- A physical part, e.g., sensors and actuators capture physical data directly. This allows a direct influence on physical processes.
- A communication part, e.g., connected to digital networks: wireless, bound, local, global. This allows the use of globally available data and services.
- A computation part, e.g., save and evaluate data and interact on this basis, active or reactive with physical and digital worlds.
- An interaction-layer for HMI, e.g., feature a range of interfaces for multi-modal human-machine interaction.

This provides dedicated facilities for communication and control, like control by speech and gestures.

In this approach, CPS are embedded micro-controllers installed either inside or outside of physical objects, responsible for the connection and communication over a network, e.g., the Internet. The technical aspect of classical embedded systems is extended by the idea of *Real World Awareness* and tight integration in digital networks. In the context of this implementation, CPS act as digital counterpart and couples the real and the virtual worlds [5], [18]. Furthermore, the "Real World Awareness" and dynamic integration of CPS is based on three basic principles: self identification (*Who am I?*), service exploration (*What do I offer?*) and active networking (*Where are my buddies?*).

E. Cyber-Physical Production Systems

The application of CPS in production systems leads to the Cyber Physical Production Systems (CPPS), in which products, machines and other resources are represented by CPS sharing information and services across the entire manufacturing and value network. Future factories use CPPS, semantic machine to machine communication (M2M) and semantic product memories to create smart products [19]. These smart products are the basis for smart services that use them as a physical platform.

Overall, a CPPS, which is based on decentralized production logic and networked principles, offers advantages in terms of transparency, adaptivity, resource efficiency and versatility over traditional production systems. In the context of CPPS, CPS are fundamental units that have almost instant access to relevant information and parametrization of machines, production processes and the product itself. On the automation level of a CPPS all these information out of the CPS-network is needed to run the manufacturing process successfully and to make strategic decisions. For decision making and control of the manufacturing processes, consistent and coherent information of the "real" world is needed [20].

F. Automation Pyramid

Today's conventional automation pyramid consists of three clearly separated levels, see Figure 1. The automation level, where sensors, actuators and in general field devices are located, the Manufacturing Execution System (MES) level, and the Enterprise Resource Planning (ERP) level. In each of these levels, different planning and construction processes take place. A new control paradigm, based on CPS and Service-Oriented Architectures (SOA) that interact in an automation network, and the direct communication and administration of field devices puts a question mark on the strict separation of the automation pyramid. The digital transmission and permeability of the engineering is in the focus of current factories of the future and softenings up the concept of the strict separation in encapsulated automation levels, where a strong vertical and horizontal communication of field devices within automation systems is not considered [3], [21].

Through the vision of networking of Industrie 4.0 this strict separation of the levels and the top-down approach of the information flow is mixed. Intelligent networked devices can operate independently and communicate with each other via

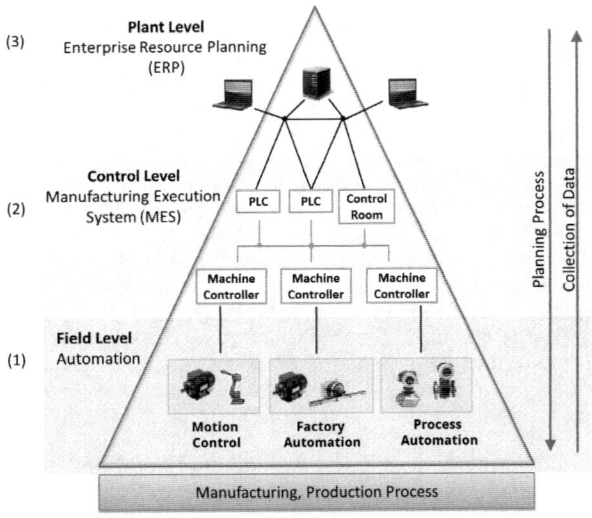

Figure 1: Conventional automation pyramid.

services that in turn can be used flexibly to support value-added processes [22].

G. Active Digital Object Memories

The development of the IoT makes it possible to assign a digital identity to physical objects [23], [24]. Paradigms, such as human-machine interaction and machine-to-machine communications are implemented by the use of clearly identifiable markers, so-called smart labels. However, the identification is not only bound to those labels, it can be also achieved by integrated sensors or by providing identification methods.

These developments pave the way for the concept of Active Digital Object Memories (ADOMe), which extend the usage of smart labels by additional memory and processing capabilities [25]. By the use of the product memory concept all data in the life cycle of a product (manufacturer information, suppliers, dealers and users) can be added, and furthermore, the data exchange can be made over this specific memory model. Also, memory-related operations can be performed by small scripts in a local runtime environment directly on the ADOMe [26]. According to the functionality of these scripts it is possible to closely monitor decentralized production processes and resource consumption, to impove the quality of the products [27].

These innovative technologies and techniques are crucial parts and the further development is highly supported in national research initiatives, such as *Smart Manufacturing Leadership Coalition* in the US [28] and *Industrie 4.0* in Germany [3].

The next step in the development and to establish new technologies is to evaluate, process and merge data from existing enterprise resource planning systems (ERP) [29] and data from different ADOMes. Both sources, considered as a single unit, offer comprehensive access to domain knowledge and contextual information. A more concrete description of the industrial environment and the running manufacturing processes enables a better user assistance to automatically recognize intentions and activities of the worker. Recommendations for improvements of the current activity of the worker can be presented proactively by the system. The approach of Haupert et al. [30] refers to a system for intention recognition and recommendation that shows an example scenario also based on ADOMes.

Furthermore, the concept of digital product memories still has an active part. This activity is realized in the form of small embedded scripts that can be run in a separate runtime environment on the specific CPS. Thus, according to the computing power and storage capacity autonomously simple tasks can be executed independently in a decentralized way. In a certain interval or linked to events, deployed scripts are executed and perform small tasks such as storage cleaning, threshold value monitoring or target/actual-value comparisons.

The present work uses the idea of the Object Memory Modeling (OMM) [31] and implemented an Application Programming Interface (API) on this basis. OMM is an XML-based object memory format, which can be used for modelling events and it also defines patterns, so called block structures, to store information about individual physical objects. Moreover, this format is designed to support the storage of additional information of physical artifacts or objects.

H. Fields of Application - Smart Factories and Smart Products

Powerful computers are becoming smaller, inexpensive and energy efficient and suitable for the integration in devices, the instrumentation of everyday objects and integration in clothes - *smart products*. Tiny CPS-adapted sensors and actuators are able to perceive and respond to their environment and interact with connected services in the network. These sensor networks are an essential piece of the foundation for future factories - *smart factories*. Software-defined platforms, like CPPS, make sensor data available and processable, enriched with intelligence by integrated analysis methods for monitoring and controlling. CPS-enabled factory modules or factory parts and the produced smart products communicate and interact with each other. In this context, ADOMes provide a way to collect and analyze structured data and gives an answer to the question in which format the obtained data sets of all connected CPS could be stored. A smart service uses a smart product of the smart factory, to use smart data as an asset, linked via semantic technologies, see Figure 2 [32].

Smart factories and smart products characterize a generation change to new, highly flexible and adaptive manufacturing technologies for the production.

- More computing power in many small devices - extend functionality of existing industrial plants with several CPS.
- Better networked via Cloud-services.
- Gathering and fusion of information - local and global data processing (sensors, actuators).
- Create object memories, and store product/object-specific data.

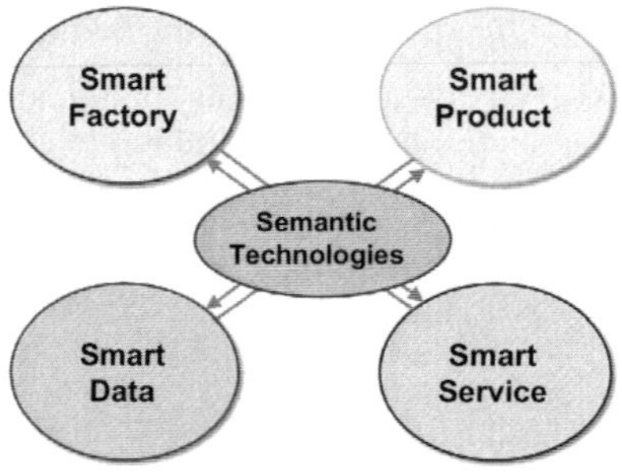

Figure 2: Customization based on semantic technologies [32].

I. Summary

Goal of research in this field is the virtualization of the traditional automation pyramid from sensor control to the ERP level to achieve the synchronization of the digital and the real world, as well as the integration of novel distributed architectures into existing production systems. Mechatronic and logical hierarchies must be decoupled and the turn to service orientation leads to an adjustment of the existing hierarchical layer structure. In our point of view, a production line, of a Smart- or Future Factory, consists of many autonomous CPS-enabled modules, which in turn could be composed of several CPS. Only with the appropriate infrastructure it is possible to create hybrid products, combinations of goods and services.

The IIoT uses the embedded technology of CPS to communicate and share intelligence within a network of physical objects. It connects platforms, applications sensors, and devices and enables improved availability and affordability of sensors, devices, processors and other infrastructure components that facilitate and provide a stable access to real-time information.

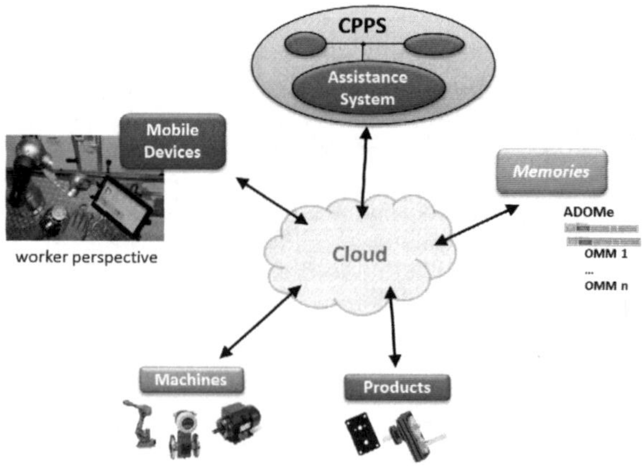

Figure 3: Cloud infrastructure.

Figure 3 shows the cloud that connects and combines

infrastructure components, like the assistance system and the ADOMes, the interaction layer via mobile devices (from the perspective of the worker), the manufactured products, and the field device level, e.g., sensors and machines. Based on a systematic monitoring of all components intelligent data analysis (data mining) can help to detect early signs of problems or uncover impending problems on device level. This saves maintenance costs and avoids a system break down.

III. Concept of Distributed Manufacturing Data

This concept is based on the idea of distributed manufacturing data across a network. This distributed functionality forms the basis for the independent configuration of system components and the context-specific consideration by analysis tools. In the implementation, we use the vision of agile automation systems that is based on distributed CPS and SOA. This vision defines a new control paradigm to improve traditional control structures in the domain of industrial automation [21], [33] and puts focus on the four-stage concept of intelligent behavior of production systems [5]:

1) Communication and distributed functionality
    - Factory as a network of mechanical parts
    - Resolution of the communication hierarchy
    - Horizontal and vertical integration
2) Adaptivity and autonomy
    - Independent configuration of the system control at run-time
    - Autonomous control of machining processes by target
3) Context-sensitive cognitive machine systems
    - Dynamic adjustment of production parameters is determined by environmental influences
    - Consideration of knowledge of products and systems to optimize production by target
4) Self-optimizing production systems
    - Independent setting of production targets of the individual process steps for the comprehensive optimization of the value chain

Today's efforts tackle the challenges, described at the first stage *communication and distributed functionality*, with focus on the horizontal and vertical integration and the communication without hierarchical restrictions. This work exactly aims on this aspect and considers a production line of a smart factory as a sum of several autonomous CPS. In addition to these aforementioned smart products, there are also intelligent CPS-enabled ADOMes that structure the accruing data of field devices and produced objects and make them accessible. Accordingly, each of these systems is able to act self-regulating and self-monitoring as autonomous factory component, consequently they are able to communicate with each other.

To get a higher impact and more context-sensitive adaption of the production system, the heterogeneous environment of a production line must be virtually mapped and formalized. In this concept we use the ADOMe-approach in combination with suitable models that describe resources and the situational context. These models minimize the dependencies between technologies providing flexibility and individual adaptability. The creation, maintenance, evaluation and handling of the models require a series of processing steps that have been merged into one production system to achieve a combination of decentralized control, data storage, and access.

A. Cloud-based Manufacturing

This approach makes use of the potential of a cloud-based networked service platform to improve the manufacturing process, information sharing, and quality management. The advantages of the IoT and information technology, that everything is linked via network, promote the combination and conversion of manufacturing and service, to integrate new resources or orchestrate existing resources in the manufacturing process in a new manner [34], [35]. Figure 4 shows the focus on SOA and services, which means that the existing hierarchical level structure needs to be adjusted. Tasks and functions of individual systems will be divided and provided by services. Functionalities of the MES level are split up and different parts are assigned to the CPPS and the field device level. Basic services describe field device functionality and each device also addresses dedicated requirements and complex dependencies. In addition, the services provide convenient access to their knowledge sources and the parametrization of dedicated field devices and sensors. Thus, it is possible to adjust a device for the purposes of configuration or optimization within the cloud.

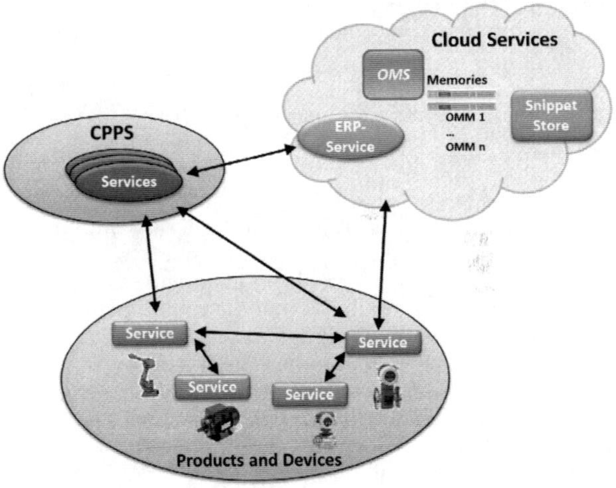

Figure 4: Cloud-based automation network.

Within the cloud network different resources, such as processing power, memory or software, in the form of little scripts, are provided dynamically and appropriately. In this approach, small decentralized scripts perform simple comparison tasks, like state monitoring and value checks, and the result is reported to an upstream assistance system. In same cases a reaction, like a rework task for drilling a whole again with another drill, can be immediately triggered in the process.

The Object Memory Server (OMS), described in detail in Section V-B, is a decisive infrastructure component that stores ADOMes, according to the model of an application server to serve a large number of users.

B. Smart CPS-enabled Field Devices and Active Digital Object Memories

In this approach, each field device has an upstream CPS, described as CPS-enabled, but in the future existing micro controllers and CPS merge to a smart system and take over the tasks of networking and automation control. The specific functionality of each the field device is offered by a service description, e.g., Web Service Description Language (WSDL) [36], in a SOA, shown in Figure 5. The networking of the individual devices is carried out in accordance with an IP network.

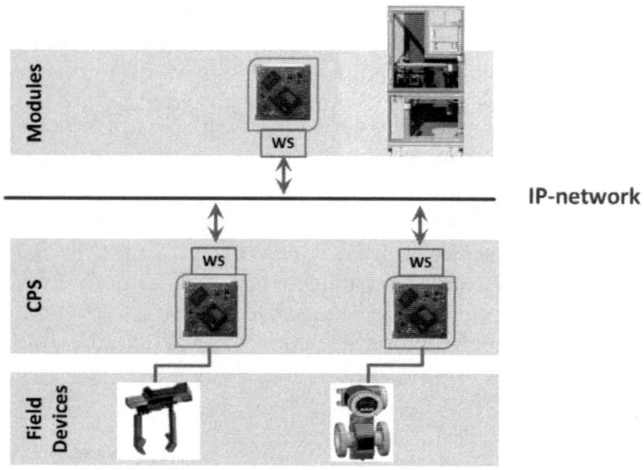

Figure 5: Smart CPS-enabled field devices.

From the user perspective it is absolutely essential to save the production data both locally and globally in a respective ADOMe. This is intended for safety reasons in case of failure or network problems to provide additional security and another possible way to access the production data. Whereby both versions differ from each other, the local memory represents only a subset of the global memory. Because large amounts of data or storage-intensive data types (e.g., CAD drawings, manufacturer documentation and other internal company documents, videos and examples, electrical wiring diagrams, data history) must be stored in the global version of the ADOMe, because the storage capacity of embedded systems is usually tight. Taking into account these memory restrictions, the local version is an adaptation or filtered version of the global ADOMe, only the necessary information, required for operation and production are stored here. But to accomplish this and to create a special limited local version of an ADOMe, there exist synchronization points and communication structures to ensure the correct synchronization when modifying local or global variables or parameters. Nevertheless, the specific parametrization of field devices should be done first on the unit's local ADOMe and shall be directly accessible. For the fine tuning of dedicated field devices, it is to complex and not practicable to access the central CPPS or global ADOMe. This decentralized parametrization can also be advantageous by setting up a new plant whose infrastructure is also still under construction, or when plant parts are reconstructed and quick compatibility checks must be performed using local data access. Moreover, by the idea that the data is available on the produced object, the ability is given to access these information, just in other factory halls or other companies without access to the central network. Due to the possibility, to keep only certain production data locally in the product's object memory, no sensible production data leaves the factory.

C. Data Modeling and Interpretation

Modeling is an aim to make a feature or part easier to understand, define, monitor, and analyze by referencing on common knowledge. Modelling processes using semantic technologies provide machine- and as well as human-readable descriptions. Such descriptions give more control on the defined processes compared to syntactic technologies in terms of meaningful relations, reusability, and interoperability.

Within complex processes of modern production facilities information from different sources of knowledge are used to monitor and analyze the expiring manufacturing processes. A simplified representation of complex processes and data structures by special classification structures or taxonomies of categories and concepts can contribute added value, because problems, e.g. of field devices or machines, can be detected in an early stage of production. Figure 6 shows needed parts for a uniform description of field device functionality.

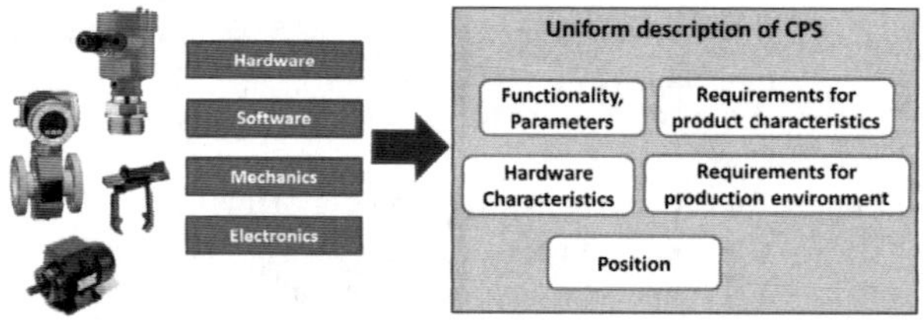

Figure 6: Uniform description of field device functionality.

As a solution of this project, we created semantic models of the different application domains that represents the properties and characteristics of the factory environment, sensors, processes, products and field devices and describes them formally and unambiguously. To bind all of these different application models via one situational base model allows drawing connections, so-called implicit dependencies, e.g., of certain groups of devices or users and processes.

The situational model represents the data structures from all connected application domains, see Figure 7. The user model gives a personalized view on handling user roles and skills. Whereas the device and resource model creates a semantic description for the whole factory view. This includes large amounts of sensor and field device data as well as the functionality parametrization of these different devices. The process and the product model handle large amounts on process or product data. One goal of this approach is to examine technical specifications and dependencies of products and their quality characteristics and create a specific model, in order to make a discovery or usage in the production process possible.

Through the use of such a device model, neighboring CPS-enabled devices can communicate with each other. This allows

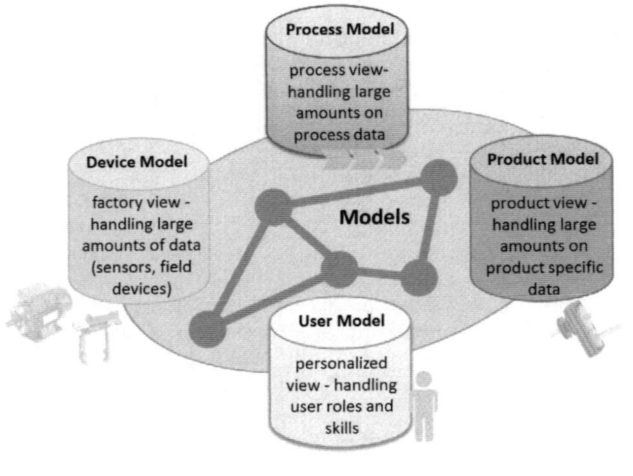

Figure 7: Models of different application domains.

a better coordination of relevant dependencies of field devices with encapsulated functionality, e.g., just to define the transfer points of a workpiece or the conveyor belt height and speed. Furthermore, this model also allows the aggregation of field devices within a production line. Specific manufacturing steps can be carried out in encapsulated manufacturing steps of a CPS-enabled field device, but all processes are effectively planned, managed, and overall controlled by inference mechanisms at CPPS-level.

Involving semantic technologies in the industrial domain of manufacturing requires a comprehensive analysis of existing approaches, standards and guidelines. The examination, analysis and evaluation of existing research approaches and standards, currently used in the field of automation and process industry, leads to the conclusion that there exists no model for the description of field devices which could be taken without any change or adaptation. To find or develop an existing approach, an analysis and assessment has been carried out, describing how semantic technologies in exactly this areas are used. Private domain models, e.g., to describe field devices of specific plant parts in detail with information classes and concepts have been build on this consideration. Furthermore, this model formally represents encapsulated specific control knowledge and concrete parametrization of field devices in machine-readable structures. This is also important for further processing of the data in order to use background, environmental or implicit knowledge by inference mechanisms.

IV. Scenario

In our scenario, depicted in detail in Figure 8, we take the specific case of the production of a gearbox that should be improved or modified during the manufacturing stage. The focus is on the milling of the base plate and the subsequent process of assembling the individual parts. First, the bottom plate is milled and verified by camera, before in a second production step, the product is assembled. These processes take place in different production lines, which are coupled via a workpiece carrier (WPC). The WPC accompanies the product through the milling, assembling and processing cycle and carries the product physically. The WPC is also equipped with a CPS-enabled ADOMe, which couples the physical product part with its virtual counterpart, which represents all product-specific data. Within this interconnected infrastructure, the WPC has access to all information of the product, to provide relevant and necessary data at the respective part of the industrial plant. The WPC communicates with the ADOMe of the respective object, to provide information for the next production step. Thus, produced objects can be registered early in the process flow.

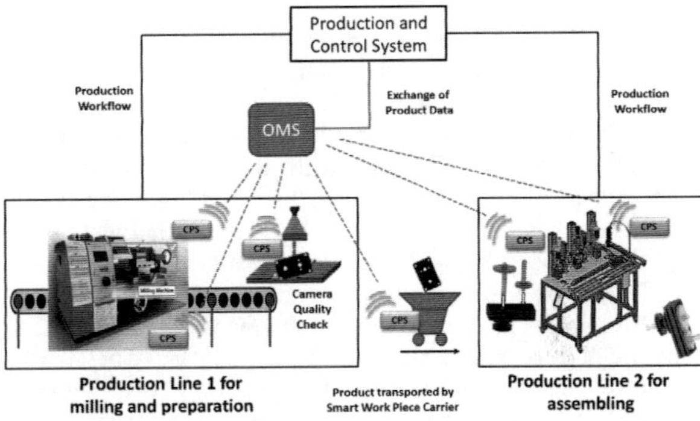

Figure 8: Production scenario.

Beside the idea to structure information in a unified structured format, another goal of this approach is the decentralized autonomous processing of information and immediate derivation of a solution on a CPS-enabled ADOMe. After milling a small script, which has already be embedded to the local ADOMe of the product, checks in a comparison task, whether the actual values match to the specified target values, which are also stored in the same ADOMe. This review will determine, whether the product is fine and meets the quality requirements for the production order, if rework is necessary or it is a faulty product. If reworking is required for that workpiece, a note is stored in the product's memory and the product can be supplied to the production cycle again, when a correctable deviation can be solved directly in the production line. The delayed delivery of produced products, because of reworking, can bring the production process to a standstill. Such bottlenecks can be identified and communicated early enough, so that the overall system is able to reschedule the production workflow.

The smart product knows the sequence and which operations a machine did during the production cycle. Each action is stored by timestamp in an ADOMe. In this assembling scenario of a gearbox, many parts exist that look very similar and have to be prepared and assembled in a certain order. In many cases, it is difficult or not possible to distinguish the material characteristics and the suitability of the gear parts with the naked eye, or depending on the order specification materials of different quality, e.g., stainless steel, titanium or steel, are used and incorporated in the gearbox. In this special case, every produced part has its ADOMe that allows access to the data, which are needed for the next processing or assembling step and for reasons of quality assurance. Furthermore, every single processing step is registered and must be compared with the desired processing steps, defined in the detailed construction phase of the product. Furthermore, also the quality of products varies depending on the customer different dimensions of the gaps are tolerated.

In order to deploy and synchronize a global ADOMe, an server platform was created, the Object Memory Server (OMS), which provides service functionality in the cloud or the local network. This component is described in detail in Section V-B, cloud-based manufacturing.

V. Technical Components of the Framework

The approach can be subdivided into three processing areas that need to interact with each other. Figure 9 shows the actual products and field device level, represented by each CPS and the associated ADOMe, furthermore, the supply level, where services, snippets and ADOMes are hosted as cloud-based networked solutions, and the assistance level for decision support and knowledge acquisition of the *CPPS*. Decision making is based on the dedicated processing steps and the context-adaptive provision of information of field devices and manufactured products stored in their ADOMes. Each product or field device has both a local and a global ADOMe. The local ADOMe is stored directly on the CPS with limited memory, and the global ADOMe, for storage-intensive data types, is stored by a central server, the OMS.

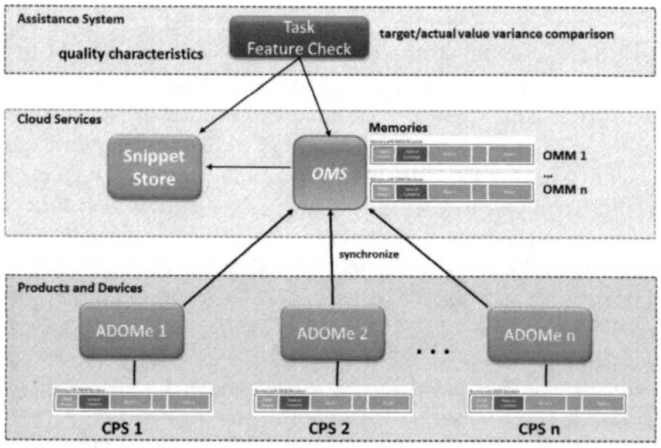

Figure 9: Interaction of the individual components of the framework.

A. Production Assistance System

In a CPPS with many decentralized CPS-enabled modules, condition reports to the overall system are very important. The adopted assistance system for CPPS acts as logical parent unit and is based on managed information out of individual product ADOMes. As presented in Figure 10, the contextual evaluation and context-specific management of processes and procedures is based on facts about the manufactured products (ADOMe), the factory parts (factory model) and the current situation, influenced by the manufacturing process and the skills and role of the user (user model, situational model). The assistance system monitors and supervises the course of production based on process data of the production cycle, and it also monitors and supports the decisions taken by the decentralized scripts. If an intervention in the workflow of the current manufacturing process is needed, based on all converging information here, it generates precise instructions for handling and rescheduling of the production order, or triggers actions, such as maintenance, alteration, or replacement of system components. These reactions of the system are defined in context-dependent rules based on described models, which represents the domain knowledge and the special vocabulary and terminology. The system decides, whether the manufactured parts are ready for further processing, if they must be revised or if it is rejected goods. These actions are transferred to and processed by the module for output presentation and communicated to the registered clients and subsequent actors. [30]

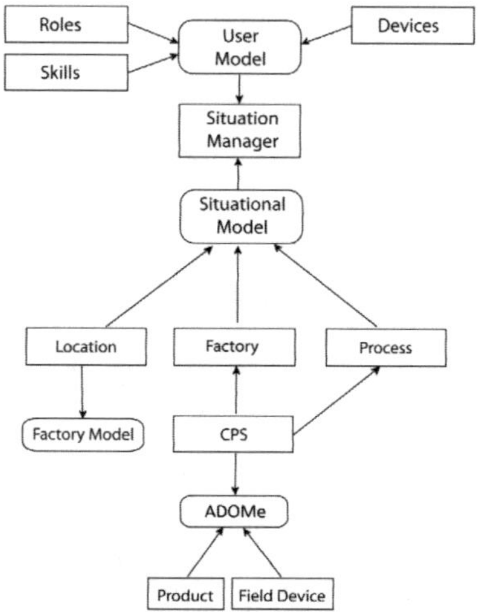

Figure 10: Contextual management based on a situational model.

However, the focus of this approach is not on the consideration and evaluation of complex relationships, for which this assistance system has been designed, but first on simple evaluation purposes, such as self-monitoring and the self-check of quality parameters of a manufactured object or a single field device within its ADOMe and its aligned embedded system. Each distributed ADOMe performs its individual quality checks and returns the data to the assistance system. For example, when a field device is re-parametrized, recommendations are formulated that rely upon the data stored in the history of the memories of this device.

Within the system infrastructure, the tiny scripts, we named them snippets, will be hosted in a central cloud-based *Snippet Store*, see Figure 9. Moreover, based on the task description of the assistance system, e.g., "quality control by target value comparison", concrete recommendations for scripts are given which adequately provide the required skills. An appropriate matching script is installed in the local ADOMe, when it is compatible with the existing combination of hardware and software of the CPS. The assistance system administrates the runtime of the local ADOMe and sets the execution interval of the script. This scheduling job of the script runs the small tasks, like memory operations or maintenance procedures, based on necessary boundary parameters made dynamically available on the product memory. Moreover, the assistance system must react according to the notification or event mechanism and create a listener functionality for this device configuration. This means that the overall CPPS must check within a time interval, whether the message or event status of an ADOMe has changed. In accordance to these message or event types a recommendation is triggered of the CPPS, which may affect the current production process.

The component is used for decision support and the derivation of recommendations. The structure and the data flow of the assistance system with its input and output channels is shown in Figure 11. Several information sources, like products and machine parts, and also the decentralized working small scripts report data in certain time intervals. All these information are classified and evaluated by the assistance system using the situational model and the models of the different application domains. To evaluate the inputs, a rule system is used that operates on a set of predefined rules, adapted to the present compilation of the plant. The results of the evaluation process are delivered to the presentation manager, which prepares them for the respective user and his device.

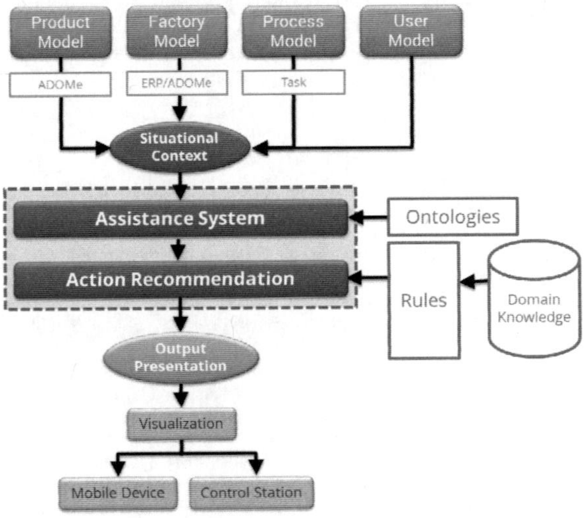

Figure 11: Assistance system and data flow.

B. Object Memory Server

OMM-based object memories can be created and stored as XML-file or binary block, but this is no longer practical for a large number of memories. For this reason, the OMS has been implemented, which can be embedded as a service in the cloud infrastructure and manages all ADOMes. Figure 12 shows the architecture and dedicated modules of the OMS that can be orchestrated on demand, depending on the intended application scenario. This server component allows the deployment and undeployment of ADOMes at runtime and uses for protection of the stored contents a role based authentication module for restricted access. Currently, three different modes are supported for data access: passwords, certificates and electronic ID cards [37].

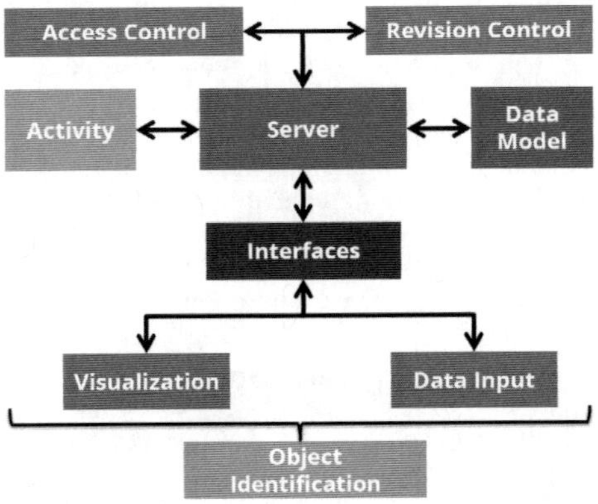

Figure 12: Server-based OMM Architecture [37].

Via a RESTful Web service interface the OMS permits access to process data of each manufacturer and provides the functions to create, store, replace, and modify the data structures in a uniform and consistent manner. Figure 13 shows the interaction of the CPS' client layer with the OMS. The OMS uses an generic software library to handle XML-based OMM representations to structure and represent the delivered data in an appropriate format. This entails the creation of OMS-records, all communicated data are checked and traceably documented at the time the information was accepted and inserted in the CPS' ADOMe [25]. But upon closer examination of the data structures from different manufacturers, it becomes evident that no approach is suitable for all requirements, hence the OMS will always be characterized by a certain heterogeneity.

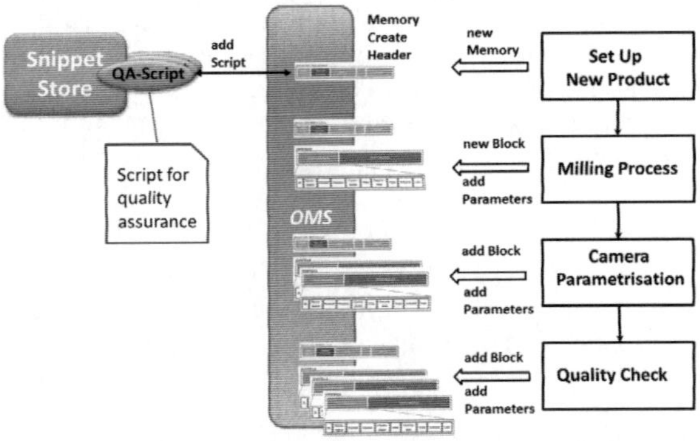

Figure 13: OMS creates ADOMe in production.

C. Interaction and Output Presentation

A smart factory can never operate without human employees, so one key issue is the human to machine interaction. In a production process, a lot of information passes from monitoring and control, but the problem usually lies in the overview and the appropriate visualization. When people work together with self-learning and self-adapting systems like CPS-based systems, they need to understand each other and which processes are internally occurring. Therefore, the user interface for technical experts or operators is dynamically adapted by a personal assistance system and its module for situational management. This system creates specific UI-layouts or templates for the presentation of contents for diverse mobile devices of the workers (notebooks, smartphones, tablets, smart watches). Currently available monitoring data are presented in adaptable views in form of a curve visualization as depicted in Figure 14. This overview allows the trained experts to draw conclusions about the manufacturing process and possible bottlenecks.

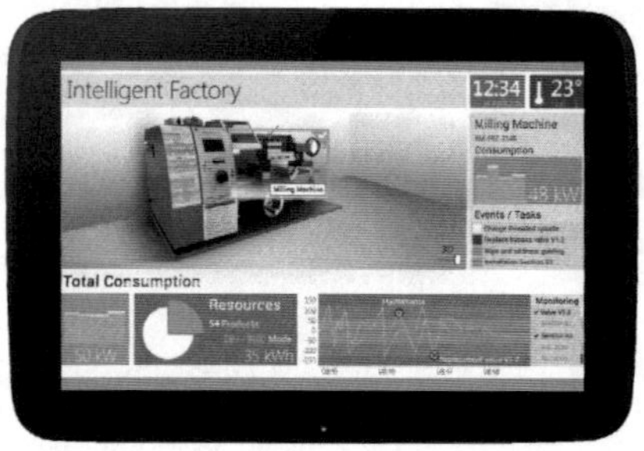

Figure 14: Worker performing a maintenance task with a mobile device.

First, the situational management component selects the appropriate visualization for a registered device. This selection is based on the situational model, that provides all gathered information about the present situational factors (e.g., user model, parametric influences of the location, factory and production process). According to specific predefined inference rules, which are applied to this model, a visualization pattern is determined and prepared for different devices. In this consideration, the special privileges and responsibilities play a major role for an adaptive intelligent visualization, because a technician requires a different view in error or maintenance purposes, as a machine operator who inspects the up and running plant.

VI. Conclusion and Outlook

This article described the conceptualization and implementation of a cyber-physical industrial environment and the use of virtual counterparts of real physical objects, whose data is stored in active digital object memories (ADOMe), hosted on a dedicated Object Memory Server. The described Cyber-Physical Systems (CPS) enable these memories to communicate over the network and to fulfill small tasks in a decentralized autonomous way, which contribute to the production cycle, like storage cleaning, threshold value monitoring or target/actual-value comparisons. The expertise of a fully fitted and configured production line is now available and formalized in the dedicated ADOMes of each plant part. Based on this data an assistance system can easily assist in the configuration or reconfiguration of new devices, machine parts, and CPS. Furthermore, the permanent monitoring of the data generates a large amount of data that can be used to improve the early detection of errors and feedback loops, as well as for functional testing. This could even reach a stage, referred to the case of maintenance, in which production systems autonomously order spare parts long before a component fails. With these interconnected CPS, it will be possible to implement further product requirements, such as the efficient use of energy and raw materials in production. Moreover, it will be possible to personalize products and adapt product features in regards to local needs and their individual manufacturing process. According to the product lifecycle management (PLM) and the deposited history in the active digital object memories, it is easily possible to draw conclusions from the product to the plant parts, which has manufactured the product. This could be advantageous in cases of warranty claims.

A smart factory can never operate without human employees, so one key issue is the visualization of the stored contents of a dedicated ADOMe. Future work will cover this topic and will further develop strategies that will help to identify and visualize important key values and how these should be presented to the worker (e.g., via tablets or smart watches).

VII. Acknowledgment

This research was funded in part by the German Federal Ministry of Education and Research under grant number 02PJ2477 (project CyProS), 01IA11001 (project RES-COM), and the EIT project CPS for Smart Factories. The responsibility for this publication lies with the authors.

References

[1] S. Bergweiler, "Intelligent manufacturing based on self-monitoring cyber-physical systems," in The Ninth International Conference on Mobile Ubiquitous Computing, Systems, Services and Technologies. International Conference on Mobile Ubiquitous Computing, Systems, Services and Technologies (UBICOMM-15), 9th, located at located at NexTech 2015, July 19-24, Nice, France, C. B. Westphall, J. L. Mauri, and P. Pochec, Eds., International Academy, Research, and Industry Association (IARIA). IARIA, 2015, pp. 108–113.

[2] S. Russwurm, "Digital Factory: Why the Digital Transformation Offers a World of Opportunities," Magazine for Research and Innovation, 2015, [retrieved: May 2016]. [Online]. Available: https://www.siemens.com/innovation/en/home/pictures-of-the-future/industry-and-automation/digital-factory-chances-of-digitalization.html

[3] H. Kagermann, W. Wahlster, and J. Helbig, Eds., Securing the future of German manufacturing industry - Recommendations for implementing the strategic initiative INDUSTRIE 4.0, Final report of the Industrie 4.0 Working Group. Berlin: acatech National Academy of Science and Engineering, 2013, [retrieved: May 2016]. [Online]. Available: {http://www.acatech.de/fileadmin/user_upload/Baumstruktur_nach_Website/Acatech/root/de/Material_fuer_Sonderseiten/Industrie_4.0/Final_report__Industrie_4.0_accessible.pdf}

[4] M. Loskyll, I. Heck, J. Schlick, and M. Schwarz, "Context-based orchestration for control of resource-efficient manufacturing processes," Future Internet, vol. 4, no. 3, 2012, pp. 737–761.

[5] J. Schlick, P. Stephan, M. Loskyll, and D. Lappe, "Industrie 4.0 in der praktischen Anwendung [Industrie 4.0 implemented in practical applications]," in Industrie 4.0 in Produktion, Automatisierung und Logistik, T. Bauernhansl, M. ten Hompel, and B. Vogel-Heuser, Eds. Springer Fachmedien Wiesbaden, 2014, pp. 57–84.

[6] S. Weyer, M. Schmitt, M. Ohmer, and D. Gorecky, "Towards industry 4.0-standardization as the crucial challenge for highly modular, multi-vendor production systems," IFAC-PapersOnLine, vol. 48, no. 3, 2015, pp. 579–584.

[7] J. Manyika et al., "The internet of things: Mapping the value beyond the hype," McKinsey Global Institute Report, 2015, p. 131.

[8] A. Gontarz, F. Hänni, L. Weiss, and K. Wegener, Sustainable Manufacturing: Shaping Global Value Creation. Berlin, Heidelberg: Springer Berlin Heidelberg, 2012, ch. Machine Tool Optimization Strategies: Evaluation of Actual Machine Tool Usage and Modes, pp. 131–136.

[9] S. Russwurm, Industrie 4.0: Beherrschung der industriellen Komplexität mit SysLM [Industrie 4.0: Control of industrial complexity with SysLM]. Berlin, Heidelberg: Springer Berlin Heidelberg, 2013, ch. Software: Die Zukunft der Industrie [Software: The future of the industry], pp. 21–36.

[10] J. Höller, V. Tsiatsis, C. Mulligan, S. Karnouskos, S. Avesand, and D. Boyle, From Machine-to-Machine to the Internet of Things: Introduction to a New Age of Intelligence. Elsevier, 2014.

[11] C. R. Schoenberger, "The internet of things," 2002, [retrieved: March 2016]. [Online]. Available: http://www.forbes.com/global/2002/0318/092.html

[12] F. Mattern and C. Floerkemeier, "From the internet of computers to the internet of things," in From Active Data Management to Event-Based Systems and More, ser. Lecture Notes in Computer Science, K. Sachs, I. Petrov, and P. Guerrero, Eds. Springer Berlin Heidelberg, 2010, vol. 6462, pp. 242–259.

[13] P. C. Evans and M. Annunziata, "Industrial Internet: Pushing the Boundaries of Minds and Machines," General Electric, Tech. Rep., 2012, [retrieved: May 2016]. [Online]. Available: http://www.ge.com/docs/chapters/Industrial_Internet.pdf

[14] E. Lee, "Cyber physical systems: Design challenges," in Object Oriented Real-Time Distributed Computing (ISORC), 2008 11th IEEE International Symposium on, 2008, pp. 363–369.

[15] H. A. Simon, The Sciences of the Artificial (3rd Ed.). Cambridge, MA, USA: MIT Press, 1996.

[16] M. Broy, Cyber-Physical Systems: Innovation durch softwareintensive eingebettete Systeme [Innovation through software-intensive embedded systems], ser. acatech Diskutiert. Springer, 2010.

[17] B. Vogel-Heuser, "Automation als enabler für industrie 4.0 in der produktion auf basis von cyber physical systems [automation as an enabler for industrie 4.0 in production on the basis of cyber physical systems]," Engineering von der Anforderung bis zum Betrieb, vol. 3, 2013, p. 1.

[18] F. Hu, Cyber-Physical Systems: Integrated Computing and Engineering Design. Taylor & Francis, 2013.

[19] W. Wahlster, Ed., SemProM: Foundations of Semantic Product Memories for the Internet of Things. Heidelberg: Springer, 2013.

[20] G. Reinhart, B. Scholz-Reiter, , W. Wahlster, M. Wittenstein, and D. Zühlke, Eds., Intelligente Vernetzung in der Fabrik: Industrie 4.0 Umsetzungsbeispiele für die Praxis [Intelligent networking in the factory: Industrie 4.0 application examples for use in practice]. Stuttgart: Fraunhofer Verlag, 10 2015.

[21] D. Zühlke and L. Ollinger, "Agile automation systems based on cyber-physical systems and service-oriented architectures," in Advances in Automation and Robotics, Vol.1, ser. Lecture Notes in Electrical Engineering, G. Lee, Ed. Springer Berlin Heidelberg, 2012, vol. 122, pp. 567–574.

[22] M. Kleinemeier, "Von der automatisierungspyramide zu unternehmenssteuerungsnetzwerken," in Industrie 4.0 in Produktion, Automatisierung und Logistik, T. Bauernhansl, M. ten Hompel, and B. Vogel-Heuser, Eds. Springer Fachmedien Wiesbaden, 2014, pp. 571–579.

[23] L. Atzori, A. Iera, and G. Morabito, "The Internet of Things: A survey," Computer Networks, vol. 54, no. 15, 2010, pp. 2787–2805.

[24] H. Chaouchi, Ed., The Internet of Things: Connecting Objects. Hoboken, NJ, London: Wiley-ISTE, 2010.

[25] J. Haupert, "DOMeMan: A framework for representation, management, and utilization of digital object memories," in 9th International Conference on Intelligent Environments (IE) 2013, J. C. Augusto et al., Eds. IEEE, 2013, pp. 84–91.

[26] A. Kröner, J. Haupert, C. Hauck, M. Deru, and S. Bergweiler, "Fostering access to data collections in the internet of things," in UBICOMM 2013, The Seventh International Conference on Mobile Ubiquitous Computing, Systems, Services and Technologies, W. Narzt and A. Gordon-Ross, Eds. IARIA, 2013, pp. 65–68, best Paper Award.

[27] L. Abele, L. Ollinger, I. Dahmann, and M. Kleinsteuber, "A decentralized resource monitoring system using structural, context and process information," in Trends in Intelligent Robotics, Automation and Manufacturing. Intelligent Robotics, Automation and Manufacturing (IRAM-2012), vol. 330. Springer Berlin Heidelberg, 2012, pp. 371–378.

[28] "SMLC Forum: Priorities, Infrastructure, and Collaboration for Implementation of Smart Manufacturing: Workshop Summary Report," Workshop Summary Report, 2015, [retrieved: March 2016]. [Online]. Available: https://smartmanufacturingcoalition.org/sites/default/files/smlc_forum_report_vf_0.pdf

[29] L. Wylie, "A Vision of Next Generation MRP II," Gartner Group, 1990, pp. 300–339.

[30] J. Haupert, S. Bergweiler, P. Poller, and C. Hauck, "IRAR: Smart Intention Recognition and Action Recommendation for Cyber-Physical Industry Environments," in Intelligent Environments (IE), 2014 International Conference, 2014, pp. 124–131.

[31] A. Kröner et al., "Object Memory Modeling," Worldwide Web Consortium, Tech. Rep., 2011, [retrieved: May 2016]. [Online]. Available: http://www.w3.org/2005/Incubator/omm/XGR-omm/

[32] W. Wahlster, "Semantic Technologies for Mass Customization," in Towards the Internet of Services: The THESEUS Research Program, ser. Cognitive Technologies, W. Wahlster, H.-J. Grallert, S. Wess, H. Friedrich, and T. Widenka, Eds. Springer International Publishing, 2014, pp. 3–13.

[33] D. Zuehlke, "SmartFactory - Towards a Factory-of-Things," Annual Reviews in Control, vol. 34, no. 1, 2010, pp. 129 – 138. [Online]. Available: http://www.sciencedirect.com/science/article/pii/S1367578810000143

[34] T. Song, H. Liu, C. Wei, and C. Zhang, "Common engines of cloud manufacturing service platform for smes," The International Journal of Advanced Manufacturing Technology, vol. 73, no. 1, 2014, pp. 557–569.

[35] L. Zhang et al., "Cloud manufacturing: a new manufacturing paradigm," Enterprise Information Systems, vol. 8, no. 2, 2014, pp. 167–187.

[36] E. Christensen, F. Curbera, G. Meredith, and S. Weerawarana, "Web Services Description Language (WSDL) 1.1," W3C, W3C Note, March 2001, [retrieved: May 2016]. [Online]. Available: http://www.w3.org/TR/wsdl

[37] A. Kröner, J. Haupert, M. Deru, S. Bergweiler, and C. Hauck, "Enabling data collections for open-loop applications in the internet of things," International Journal on Advances in Internet Technology, vol. 7, no. 1+2, 2014, pp. 75–85. [Online]. Available: http://www.iariajournals.org/internet_technology/inttech_v7_n12_2014_paged.pdf

International Journal on Advances in Systems and Measurements, vol 9 no 1 & 2, year 2016, http://www.iariajournals.org/systems_and_measurements/

Person Re-Identification for Non-overlapping Cameras in Multimodal Person Localization

Thi Thanh Thuy Pham*†, Thi-Lan Le*, Trung-Kien Dao*
*International Research Institute MICA, HUST - CNRSUMI-2954 - GRENOBLE INP, Vietnam
†Faculty of Information Technology, University of Technology and Logistics, Bacninh, Vietnam
Email: {Thanh-Thuy.Pham;Thi-Lan.Le;Trung-Kien.Dao}@mica.edu.vn

***Abstract*—Person re-identification is a crucial step in an indoor human localization system. It is a problem of person identity association at different locations and times. This paper presents a method for person re-identification in the context of multi-modal person localization using WiFi and camera. From the human region of interest determined by human detection, our method builds a visual signature of the person based on kernel descriptor and performs person re-identification by applying ranking Support Vector Machine. The evaluation results on several benchmark datasets as well as our dataset built in the context of multimodal person localization confirm the robustness of the proposed method.**

Keywords–Multimodal person localization; Person re-identification; Human detection.

I. INTRODUCTION

Person re-identification (Re-ID) and positioning are two key problems in a typical human localization system. In case of multi-object localization, we need to identify the person who is localized, therefore, we know the determined positions belong to which objects. Person Re-ID in camera network is a hard problem and has increasingly attracted many researchers. Three basic steps need to be done for vision-based person Re-ID problem. Human detection in consecutive frames is firstly executed, then feature extraction within the detected regions and feature descriptor is generated, finally object matching is done for Re-ID. Each step has its own challenges and these strongly affect to the system performance. In general, they include (1) illumination conditions that are different by time and space; (2) pose, scale and appearance variation of person at distinctive camera FOVs (Fields of View). This is considered as the most challenging, because human appearance features are mainly used in human re-identification systems; (3) occlusions in which people are obscured by each other or obstacles in the environment; (4) Re-ID scenarios involving closed set Re-ID (the identified objects are included in both gallery and probe sets) or open set Re-ID (the objects may not be contained in the gallery set).

Many approaches are proposed for vision-based person Re-ID problem, however, most of them are oriented to (1) build a distinctive feature descriptor for each object and then apply an effective object classifier for that or (2) design potential distance metrics from data. In our previous work [1], we concentrate on establishing a robust feature descriptor that improves the original KDES (Kernel Descriptor) of [2], and applying multi-class SVM as relative ranking for person Re-ID in camera networks. The proposed method is evaluated on two benchmark datasets (CAVIAR4REID and iLIDs) and our own dataset named MICA1. With these datasets, the person ROI (Region Of Interest) is manually determined. We extend our previous work with two main contributions. First, in order to make a fully-automated person Re-ID system, in the detection step, we propose to use a fusion method based on GMM (Gaussian Mixture Model) and HOG (Histogram of Oriented Gradients) along with SVM (Support Vector Machine). Second, we evaluate the proposed method on a dataset which is built in the context of multi-modal person localization, with both cases of automatic and manual person detection are considered.

The rest of the paper is organized as follow. In Section II, the related works on vision-based human Re-ID are presented. Section III indicates a combined system of WiFi and visual signals for human localization, in which appearance-based person Re-ID problem in camera network is solved by improved KDES. Some experimental results on benchmark datasets and our dataset are shown in Section IV. Conclusion and future directions will be finally denoted.

II. RELATED WORK

Design of a robust person descriptor is the most decisive step for vision-based person Re-ID problem. Many kinds of features are utilized for this, in which human body appearance is the simplest and the most popular one. Color, texture, and shape are features that can be extracted for human appearance. In [3][4], color histogram is used for feature descriptor. There are two ways to represent the image of detected people with color histogram: global color histogram and local color histogram. A single histogram is used in the first method for the whole image, while in the second way, image is divided into some parts and concatenating the part-based color histograms is done to give a final result. Most reported person Re-ID works pay attention on the second solution, such as in [5], a weighted color histogram derived from MSCR (Maximally Stable Colour Regions) and structured patches are combined for visual description. In [6][7], color histogram on different color models is calculated and syndicated with texture features to make person descriptor more robust. Shape features are also extracted for appearance model. However, they are unstable because of non-rigid objects as people; so, in [8], color and texture features are associated with shape feature to enhance the effectiveness of person descriptor. Local region descriptors, such as SIFT (Scale-Invariant Feature Transform), SURF (Speeded Up Robust Features) and GLOH (Gradient Location and Orientation Histogram) are evaluated in [9] for person Re-ID in image sequences. The results show that GLOH and SIFT outperform both shape context and SURF descriptor. Additionally, a large number of visual features are exploited for person Re-ID problem, such as Haar-like features, HOG

(Histogram of Oriented Gradients), edges, covariance, interest points, etc.

The next step in human Re-ID process is classification, with two scenarios of single-shot and multi-shot being reported. The first case is simpler with one-to-one matching between a pair of probe and gallery image for each person, whereas in the second scenario, each object has multiple images, either in the gallery or the probe set. In general, the purpose of classification in person Re-ID is finding out the most similar candidate for a target or ranking the candidates based on a standard distance minimization strategy, which is known as distance metric. This metric can be chosen independently (non-learning based method) [10] or learned from the data (learning-based method) [11] in order to minimize intra-class variation whilst maximize extra-class variation. They typically include histogram-based Bhattacharyya distance, K Nearest Neighbor classifiers, L1-Norm, diffusion distance [12]. Additionally, some later proposed methods, such as LMNN-R (Large Margin Nearest Neighbor) distance metric in [13] or PRDL (Probabilistic Relative Distance Learning) in [14] are more robust.

To get an ID ranking list, distance scores between true and wrong matches can be compared directly or relatively (ranking the scores that show the correspondence of each likely match to the probe image). The relative ranking treated by either Boosting as RankBoost in [15] or kernel-based learning, such as RankSVM [16], primal-based RankSVM [17] or Ensemble RankSVM [7].

III. Proposed System

In this section, we propose a fused system of WiFi and camera for person localization. In this system, the important role of person Re-ID based on the human appearance images extracted from a combined detector of adaptive GMM and HOG-SMV is analyzed. Thence, a new appearance-based model based on KDES is build for each individual and based on this, multi-class SVM is applied for person classification.

A. *Overview of multimodal person localization system*

Object localization is known as a problem of determining the object position in the environment. For each user in multi-user localization system, two problems of positioning (where the user is) and identifying (who the user is) must be solved simultaneously. A general diagram for object localization is illustrated in Figure 1. In this figure, the input cues can come from different sensors, such as optical, radio frequency, ultra sound, inertia, DC Electromagnetic sensors, etc. From the input cues, localization and Re-ID are executed simultaneously to give the output for object position and ID. Multimodal object localization is defined as a problem of multi-cue combination for input or fusion of different positioning methods. As proven by Vinyals et al. [18] and Dao et al. [19], compounding of different models gives better positioning results than applying a single model. Teixeira et al. [20] proposed to use the motion signature taken from wearable accelerometer for identifying people in camera network.

Our research aims at developing a multimodal person localization system by using both WiFi and camera systems. This offers some benefits in comparison with single-method systems. (1) System setting cost is limited because of available WiFi infrastructure and uncrowded-deployed cameras. (2)

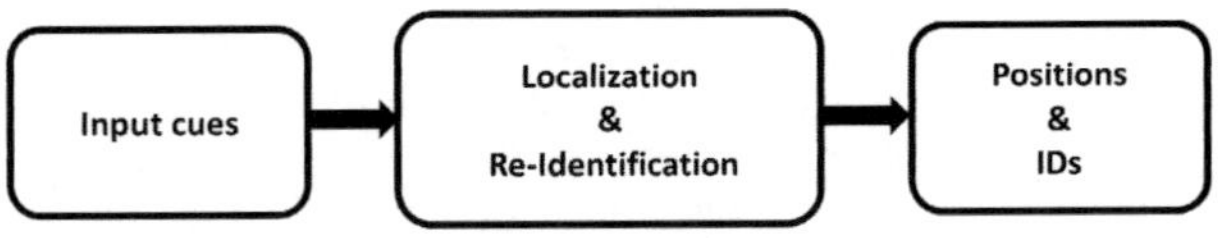

Figure 1. Flowchart of object localization system.

Positioning range is easily broaden by simply adding more APs (Access Point) in the environment. (3) Computational expense is much lower for WiFi-based than vision-based positioning system. (4) The positioning accuracy is provided in accordance with the application-specific demands. Although the camera-based system brings more impressed positioning results, but not every where in building needs high localizing accuracy. (5) Sampling frequency is improved for the WiFi-based system, because it has lower sampling rate (about one signal measure per second) than vision-based system (approximately 15 fps). (6) The information for person Re-ID becomes richer. One object can be identified simultaneously by both WiFi and camera systems. These ID cues can be used in the way of supporting one another in multi-model object localization system. For example, at a certain time, one object is localized and identified by WiFi system, with the position of P_{WiFi} and the identity of ID_{WiFi} (the MAC address of mobile device), respectively. At the same time, this object is also determined by P_{cam} and ID_{cam} from camera system. However, P_{WiFi} is not as accurate as P_{cam}, whilst ID_{WiFi} is clearer than ID_{cam}. Therefore, by using both of these systems, the object can be localized by P_{cam} and identified by ID_{WiFi}.

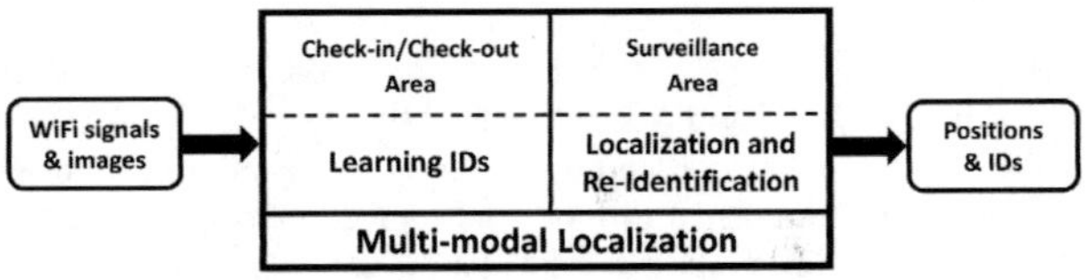

Figure 2. Multimodal localization system fusing WiFi signals and images.

Figure 2 shows a framework for our multi-model human localization system using both WiFi signals and camera network. The framework indicates that the proposed system is implemented in two subregions of the whole positioning area: check-in/check-out region and surveillance region. In the first region, learning ID cues is executed. Person holding a WiFi-integrated device will one by one come in and come out of the first region. At the entrance of the first region, the person's ID will be learned individually by the images captured from cameras and MAC address of WiFi-enable equipment held by that person. One camera, which is in front door of check-in gate, captures human face and then a face recognition program is executed. Another camera acquires human body images at different poses and learning phase of appearance-based ID is done for each person. In short, in the first region, we get three types of signature for each person (N_i): face-based ID (ID_F^i), WiFi-based ID (ID_{WF}^i), and appearance-based ID (ID_{Apr}^i). Depending on different circumstances, we can map among signatures of (ID_F^i, ID_{WF}^i), (ID_F^i, ID_{Apr}^i), (ID_{Apr}^i, ID_{WF}^i) and utilize them for person localization and identification in the surveillance region. The user will end up his route at the exit gate and he will be checked out by other camera. This camera acquires human face for person Re-ID, and based on this, the user will be removed from the localization system. By using check-in/check-out region, we can (1) control the human appearance changes (the difference in cloth colors) at each time people come in the positioning area, (2) decrease the computing cost by eliminating the checked-out users from the system, (3) map between different ID cues for the same person.

In the surveillance region, two problems of person localization and Re-ID will be solved concurrently by combining visual and WiFi information. Figure 3 demonstrates a surveillance region which contains WiFi range and camera FOVs. In this region, the WiFi range covers some visual ranges (the camera FOVs: FOV of C_1, FOV of C_2,..., FOV of C_n). This means the user always move within WiFi range but switch from one camera FOV to others.

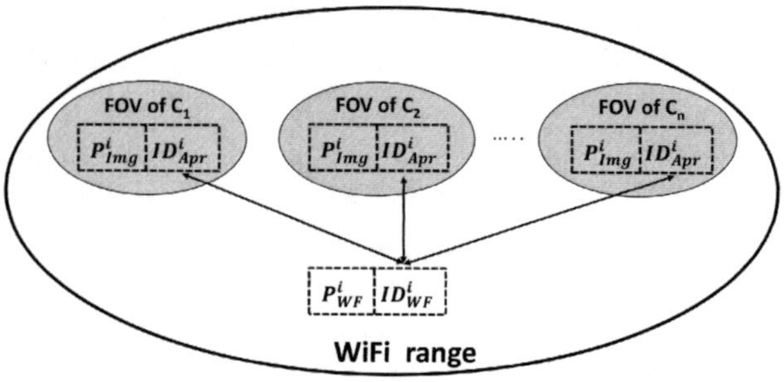

Figure 3. Surveillance region with WiFi range and disjoint cameras' FOVs.

In each camera FOV and for an individual, we calculate image-based and WiFi-based positions (P^i_{img}, P^i_{WF}) and ID^i_{Apr}. From ID^i_{Apr}, we know ID^i_{WF} correspondingly by ID mapping result taken from the first region. Outside the camera FOV, there only exits the information of P^i_{WiFi}, ID^i_{WF}, and ID^i_{Apr}, respectively. When people switch from one camera FOV to others, their positions and IDs will be updated in the WiFi-available region. The localization accuracy then be tuned by combination of WiFi-based and vision-based systems.

From the above analysis, we see that finding ID^i_{Apr} plays a key role in the proposed multimodal person localization system. It is used to link the object trajectories from one camera range to others through the intermediate positioning range of WiFi. Therefore, ID^i_{Apr} must be shown at each frame captured from different cameras in the surveillance area. That means the appearance-based person Re-ID problem needs to be solved. In this circumstance, it belongs to multi-shot person Re-ID problem, with multiple images for each detected person at different resolutions, lighting conditions, and poses are processed.

B. *Vision-based person re-identification*

1) The system overview: The flowchart of vision-based person Re-ID system is illustrated in Figure 4. It includes three stages of (1) person detection, (2) feature extraction, and (3) classification. Human ROIs (Region of Interest) are extracted from the first stage and based on this, in the second stage, feature extraction is done to build a feature descriptor for each individual. A classifier is then applied to learn the person model and predict the corresponding ID.

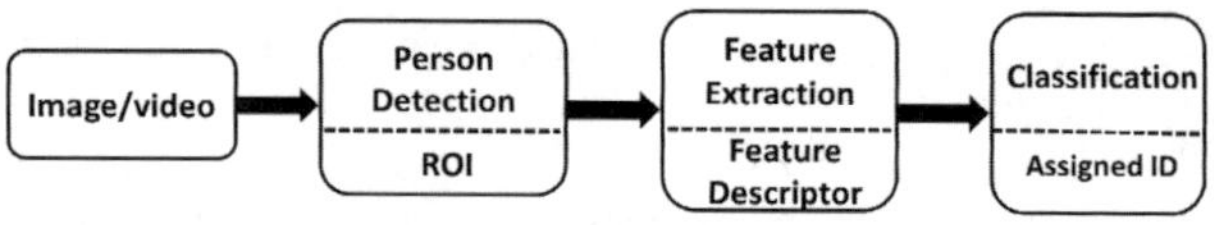

Figure 4. A diagram of vision-based person Re-ID system.

In the first stage, a popular background subtraction technique of adaptive GMM [21] and HOG-SVM [22] are combined for human detection. GMM is suitable method for real-time applications, but in case people are in close proximity or occlusion, it can not give the separated human ROIs for each individual. This can be partially solved by applying a HOG detector. However, the computation time for HOG-SVM is higher than most other background subtraction methods. The fusion of these two methods can help to achieve both accuracy and real-time demands for human detection, as proved in [23].

In adaptive GMM method, K Gaussian distributions are used to model the recent history $\{X_1, .., X_t\}$ of each pixel X. The probability of the pixel value is then defined by a sum of weighted Gaussian distributions as follows:

$$P(X_t) = \sum_{i=1}^{K} w_{i,t} * g(X_t|\mu_{i,t}, \Sigma_{i,t}) \quad (1)$$

where K is the number of distributions, $w_{i,t}$ are the mixture weights, $g(X_t|\mu_{i,t}, \Sigma_{i,t})$ are the component Gaussian densities, with mean vector $\mu_{i,t}$ and covariance matrix $\Sigma_{i,t}$ of the ith Gaussian component in the mixture at time t. When the new pixels are matched with the model, the mean and the variance values are updated using:

$$\sigma_t^2 = (1-\eta)\sigma_{t-1}^2 + \eta(X_t - \mu_t)^T(X_t - \mu_t) \quad (2)$$

$$\mu_t = (1-\eta)\mu_{t-1} + \eta X_t \quad (3)$$

where σ_{t-1}, μ_{t-1} are the previous mean and variance of the matched Gaussian, X_t is new pixel value and η is a learning rate. Conversely, when no ones are matched, the least probable component of the mixture is replaced by a new one modeling the incoming pixel.

In the proposed fusion method of human detection, from an input frame, if the human region is extracted by HOG-SVM, this region will be taken for final human detection result, otherwise the result of adaptive GMM is used. In case of having the human detection results from both methods, the area of the detected overlapping region between them will be checked. If it is bigger than a threshold τ, then the matching region is found and HOG-based result will be chosen as the final one for human detection, whilst a false positive of HOG-SVM or adaptive GMM is detected.

The second stage is done based on the results of human detection in the first stage. In the second stage, the features are extracted from the human ROIs and feature descriptors are created for each individual. The details of a new person appearance representation model based on KDES of [2] will be shown in the next subsection.

2) KDES-based person representation: The basic idea of the representation based on kernel methods is to compute the approximate explicit feature map for kernel match function (see Figure 5). In other words, the kernel match functions are approximated by explicit feature maps. This enables efficient learning methods for linear kernels to be applied to the non-linear kernels. This approach was introduced in [2]. Given a match kernel function $k(x, y)$, the feature map $\varphi(.)$ for the kernel $k(x, y)$ is a function mapping a vector **x** into a feature space so that $k(x, y) = \varphi(x)^\top \varphi(y)$. Given a set of basis vectors $B = \{\varphi(v_i)\}_{i=1}^{D}$, the approximation of feature map $\varphi(x)$ can be:

$$\phi(x) = Gk_B(x) \quad (4)$$

where G is defined by: $G^\top G = K_{BB}^{-1}$ and K_{BB} is a $D \times D$ matrix with $\{K_{BB}\}_{ij} = k(v_i, v_j)$, and k_B is a $D \times 1$ vector with $\{k_B\}_i = k(x, v_i)$.

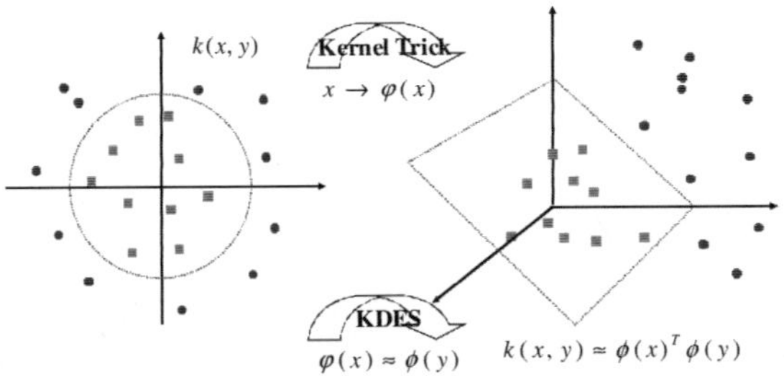

Figure 5. The basic idea of representation based on kernel methods.

Like in [2], in this work, three match kernel functions of gradient, color and shape are built from different pixel attributes of gradient, color and local binary pattern (LBP). For each match kernel, feature extraction is done at three levels: pixel, patch and whole detected human region.

First, gradient match kernel K_g is computed from three kernels of normalized gradient magnitude kernel $k_{\widetilde{m}}$, normalized orientation kernel k_o, and position kernel k_p. At pixel level, a normalized gradient vector is constructed for each pixel z. It is defined by magnitude $m(z)$ and normalized orientation $\omega(z) = \theta(z) - \overline{\theta}(P)$, where $\theta(z)$ is orientation of gradient vector at the pixel z, and $\overline{\theta}(P)$ is the dominant orientation of the patch P that is the vector sum of all the gradient vectors in the patch. This normalization is unlike the approach in [2] which presents $\theta(z)$ as orientation of gradient vector, and it will make patch-level features invariant to rotation. In practice, the normalized orientation of a gradient vector is:

$$\widetilde{\omega}(z) = [sin(\omega(z))\ cos(\omega(z))] \quad (5)$$

At patch level, the image with different resolutions will be divided into a grid of a fix number of cells, instead of size-fixed cells as in [2]. A patch is then set by 2×2 cells and two adjacent patches along x axis or y axis are overlapped at two cells. This division results in size-adaptive patches to the different image resolutions, and nearly the same feature vectors for the scale-varied images of intraclass are created (see Figure 6). In this work, this technique is utilized for KDES extraction because of a large variation in human size caused by different distances from pedestrian to the stationary camera. From this remark, the gradient match kernel K_g is constructed as follows:

$$K_g(P, Q) = \sum_{z \in P} \sum_{z' \in Q} k_{\widetilde{m}}(z, z') k_o(\widetilde{\omega}(z), \widetilde{\omega}(z')) k_p(z, z') \quad (6)$$

where P and Q are the patches of two different images needed to measure the similarity, z and z' denote the 2D positions of a pixel in the image patches P and Q, respectively, $k_{\widetilde{m}}(z, z') = \widetilde{m}(z)\widetilde{m}(z')$ is a positive definite kernel with the normalized gradient magnitude $\widetilde{m}(z) = m(z)/\sqrt{\sum_{z \in P} m(z)^2 + \epsilon_g}$, ϵ_g is a small constant, $k_o(\widetilde{\omega}(z), \widetilde{\omega}(z')) = exp(-\gamma_o \|\widetilde{\omega}(z) - \widetilde{\omega}(z')\|^2)$ is Gaussian kernel over normalized orientation, $k_p(z, z') = exp(-\gamma_p \|z - z'\|^2)$ is a Gaussian position kernel.

The approximate feature $\widetilde{F}_g(P)$ over the image patch P is constructed in Eq. (7) with normalized gradient magnitude $\widetilde{m}(z)$ and the feature maps of $\varphi_o(.)$ and $\varphi_p(.)$ for the gradient orientation kernel k_o and position kernel k_p, respectively.

$$\widetilde{F}_g(P) = \sum_{z \in P} \widetilde{m}(z) \phi_o(\widetilde{\omega}(z)) \otimes \phi_p(z) \quad (7)$$

where $\otimes$ is the Kronecker product, $\phi_o(\widetilde{\omega}(z))$ and $\phi_p(z)$ are approximate feature maps (Eq. (4)) for the kernel k_o and k_p, respectively.

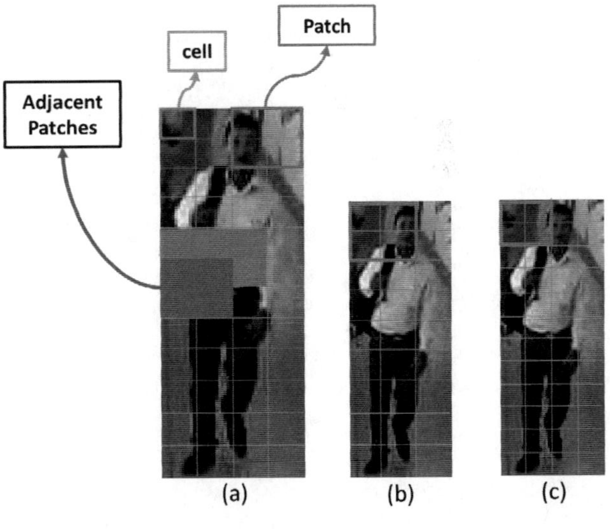

Figure 6. Illustration of size-adaptive patches (a, c) and size-fixed patches (a, b) which is mentioned in [2].

Second, the color match kernel K_c is computed over color pixels (RGB values) at position z as in [2] as follows:

$$K_c(P, Q) = \sum_{z \in P} \sum_{z' \in Q} k_c(c(z), c(z')) k_p(z, z') \quad (8)$$

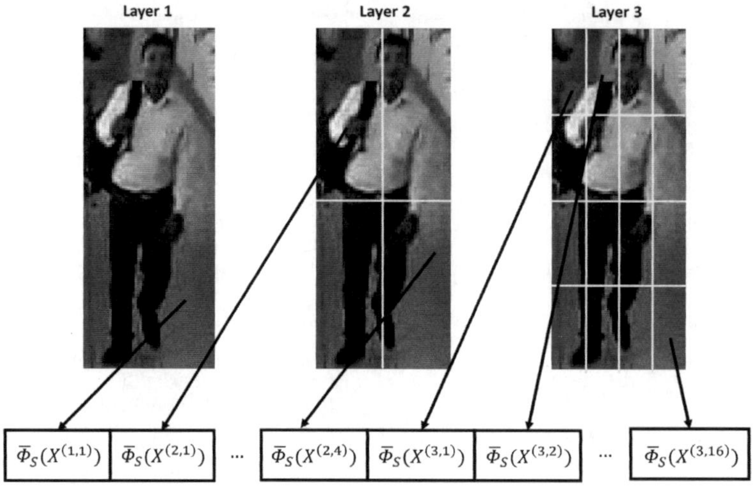

Figure 7. Image-level feature vector concatenated by feature vectors of blocks in the pyramid layers.

where $c(z)$ is the color value at pixel z, and the Gaussian color kernel $k_c(c(z), c(z')) = exp(-\gamma_c\|c(z) - c(z')\|^2)$ shows the similarity between two color pixels z and z'.

Similar to the calculation of $\widetilde{F}_g(P)$, the approximate color feature over patch P is defined by:

$$\widetilde{F}_c(P) = \sum_{z \in P} \phi_c(c(z)) \otimes \phi_p(z) \tag{9}$$

Finally, the shape match descriptor K_s is built from local binary pattern (LBP) attributes.

$$K_s(P,Q) = \sum_{z \in P} \sum_{z' \in Q} k_{\widetilde{s}}(z,z') k_b(b(z), b(z')) k_p(z,z') \tag{10}$$

where $k_{\widetilde{s}}(z,z') = \widetilde{s}(z)\widetilde{s}(z')$, and the standard deviation of pixel values in the 3×3 pixel block around z is $\widetilde{s}(z) = s(z)/\sqrt{\sum_{z \in P} s(z)^2 + \epsilon_s}$, and $b(z)$ is a vector of binary codes which label the pixel value differences in a local window around z. The similarity of LBP features is measured by the Gaussian kernel $k_b(b(z), b(z')) = exp(-\gamma_b\|b(z) - b(z')\|^2$.

The shape feature over image patch P is then derived as follows:

$$\widetilde{F}_s(P) = \sum_{z \in P} \widetilde{s}(z) \phi_b(b(z)) \otimes \phi_p(z) \tag{11}$$

The last level is achieved by creating a complete descriptor for the whole image. As in [24], a pyramid structure is used to combine patch features. Given an image, the final representation is built on the basis of features extracted from lower levels using EMK (Efficient Match Kernels) proposed in [2]. First, the feature vector for each cell of the pyramid structure is computed. The final descriptor is then the concatenation of feature vectors of all cells.

Let B be a block that has a set of patch-level features $\mathbf{X} = \{\mathbf{x}_1, ..., \mathbf{x}_p\}$, then the feature map on this set of vectors is defined as:

$$\overline{\phi}_S(X) = \frac{1}{|X|} \sum_{x \in X} \phi(x) \tag{12}$$

where $\phi(x)$ is the approximate feature map defined in Eq. (4) for the kernel $k(x,y)$. The feature vector $\overline{\phi}_S(X)$ on the set of patches is extracted explicitly. Given an image, let L be the number of spatial layers to be considered. In this case, $L = 3$ (see Figure 7). The number of blocks in the lth layer is n_l, $X(l,t)$ is a set of patch-level features that fall within the spatial block (l,t) (the tth block in the lth layer). A patch falls in a block when its centroid belongs to the block. The feature map on the pyramid structure is:

$$\begin{aligned} \overline{\phi}_P(X) \quad = \quad & [w^{(1)}\overline{\phi}_S(X^{(1,1)}); ...; w^{(l)}\overline{\phi}_S(X^{(l,t)}); \\ & ...; w^{(L)}\overline{\phi}_S(X^{(L,n_L)})] \end{aligned} \tag{13}$$

In Eq. (13), $w^{(l)} = \frac{\frac{1}{n_l}}{\sum_{l=1}^{L} \frac{1}{n_l}}$ is the weight associated with level l.

The final feature vector is then concatenated from three image-level feature vectors of gradient, color and shape.

Once KDES descriptor is computed, a multi-class SVM is applied to train the model for each person. For each detected instance, a list of ranked objects will be generated on the basis of the class probabilities returned by SVM classification.

IV. EXPERIMENTAL RESULTS

This section presents the testing datasets and the comparative results of person Re-ID obtained by using the proposed method and some other state-of-the-art methods. The CMC (Cumulative Match Curve) is employed as the performance evaluation method for person Re-ID problem. The CMC curve represents the expectation of finding correct match in the top n matches.

A. Testing datasets

In our experiments, two multi-shot benchmark datasets of CAVIAR4REID and i-LIDS for person Re-ID are chosen for evaluating the proposed KDES descriptor. These datasets contain the manually-extracted human ROIs and most of the state-of-the-art methods for person Re-ID are evaluated on these. In order to evaluate the person Re-ID performance in real scenarios of vision-based human localization system, the automatically-detected human ROIs should be considered. A new dataset with the human ROIs resulted from auto human detector (as mentioned in Section III-B1) and manual cropping is built for the person Re-ID evaluation.

The CAVIAR4REID dataset includes 72 pedestrians, in which 50 of them are captured from two camera views and the remaining 22 from one camera view. i-LIDS dataset contains 119 individuals, with the images captured from multi-camera network. In ETH dataset, multiple images of diverse human appearances are captured by a moving camera.

Concerning to our dataset, we build it for multimodal person localization evaluation. A database for testing appearance-base person Re-ID is also established in this. Figure 8 shows a floor plan of the office building. It is set as the testing environment for our combined person localization system. At the entrance, people hold smart phones or tablets go one by one through the check-in gate, then move inside the surveillance area, and finish their routes by going out check-out gate.

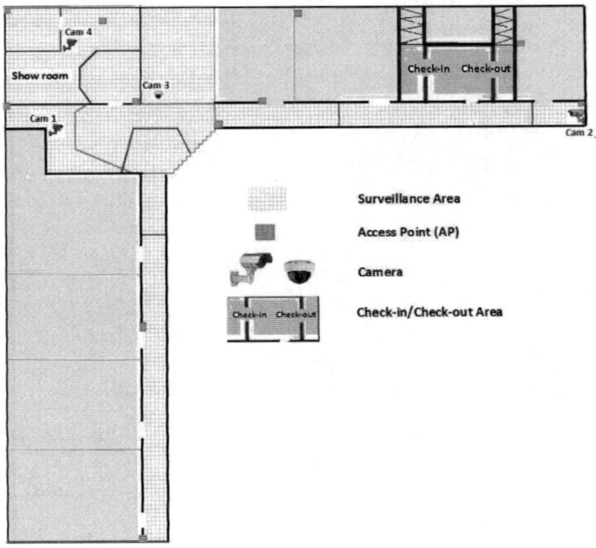

Figure 8. Testing environment.

In the check-in and check-out area, we set three cameras. Two of them are used at the entrance. One camera captures human face in order to check-in user by face recognition. The remaining camera acquires human body images at different poses. This will help the system learn appearance-based signature of the checked-in user. The third camera is used to capture human face at the exit, and based on this, the system will check out or release the user from its process. In the surveillance area, four cameras with non-overlapping FOVs are deployed along the hallway and in a room. People are detected, localized, and re-identified at each frame captured from these cameras. Besides this, 11 APs are established throughout the testing environment. RSSIs (Received Signal Strength Indicators) and the MAC address are consecutively scanned and sent from mobile device to the server to calculate the position and ID of the device holder.

In short, a total of seven AXIS IP cameras and eleven APs are deployed throughout the testing environment. These cameras and APs are fixed at certain distances from the floor ground (about 1.6 m - 2.2 m for cameras and 2 m - 2.8 m for APs). They are configured with static IP addresses. The camera frame rate is set to 20 fps and image resolution is 640x480.

Two scripts are proposed for building the human Re-ID datasets. The first script, namely MICA1 [25], includes 25 people and the second script called MICA2 [25] contains 40 people moving in different routes in the testing environment. Each person spends from 3 to 5 minutes for his route. An approximation of 800 values of RSSIs are scanned, about 3000 frames are captured for each camera in the surveillance area. All acquired frames are processed as real Re-ID scenario of multimodal pedestrian localization system.

In the MICA1 dataset, the human ROIs are manually extracted from video sequences acquired by the cameras. The training images are captured from the entrance camera so that they present the variety of human poses at different viewpoints. The images captured from four cameras (Cam1, Cam2, Cam3, Cam4 in Figure 8) in the surveillance area are processed for testing phase of person Re-ID. Examples in the MICA1 dataset are shown in Figure 9, with the images on the top are used for the training phase of the appearance-based human descriptor and the images for the testing phase are shown at the bottom.

In the MICA2 dataset, the training images are captured from Cam2 and the testing images are acquired from Cam1, Cam3, Cam4. Unlike the MICA1, the training images in the MICA2 dataset are nearly taken from two viewpoints of front and back (see the images on the top of Figure 10). The testing phase is done with the human ROIs extracted both manually and automatically from the images captured by Cam1 and Cam4. The examples of manually-cropped and automatically-detected human ROIs used for testing phase are shown respectively in the middle and at the bottom of Figure 10.

In comparison with other person Re-ID datasets, such as iLIDS, CAVIAR4REID, our datasets have more variations for intra-class images in terms of resolution, illumination, pose, scale, and occlusion. In our datasets, the human ROIs are not only extracted manually, but also automatically from the frames captured by many cameras at distinctive FOVs. Table I shows the summary of these datasets.

B. Person re-identification results

The person Re-ID performance of the proposed descriptor is compared with some other state-of-the-art methods in two situations of human detection: manually-cropped and automatically-detected human ROIs.

In the first situation, the benchmark datasets of CAVIAR4REID and i-LIDS are used. These datasets contain the human ROIs extracted manually from the captured frames. In addition, the manually-cropped images in the MICA1 and MICA2 datasets are also utilized in this evaluation. The

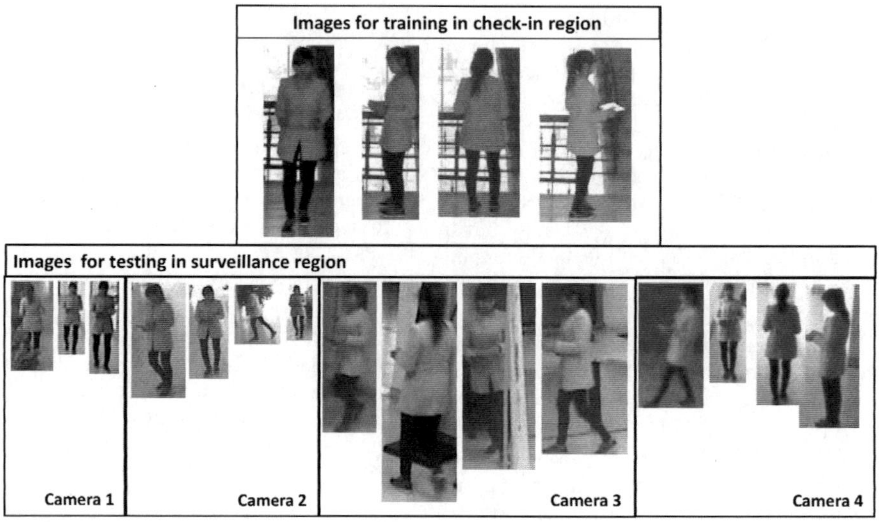

Figure 9. Examples in the MICA1 dataset. The images on the top are captured from a camera at check-in region and used for training phase. The images at the bottom are the testing images which acquired from 4 other cameras (Cam1, Cam2, Cam3, Cam4) in surveillance region.

Figure 10. Examples in the MICA2 dataset. The images on the top are captured from Cam2 and used for training phase. Images of human ROI with manual and automatic detection are shown on the left and right groups, respectively.

TABLE I. Datasets for person re-identification testing. In the last column, the number of sign (√) shows the ranking for intra-class variation of the datasets.

Dataset	Release time	# identities	# cameras	Label method	Crop size	Multi-shot	Tracking sequences	Intra-class Variation
iLIDS	2009	69	1	Hand	Vary	Yes	Yes	√
CAVIAR4ReID	2011	72	2	Hand	Vary	Yes	No	√√√
MICA 1, 2	2015	25, 40	5, 3	Hand, Auto	Vary	Yes	Yes	√√√√

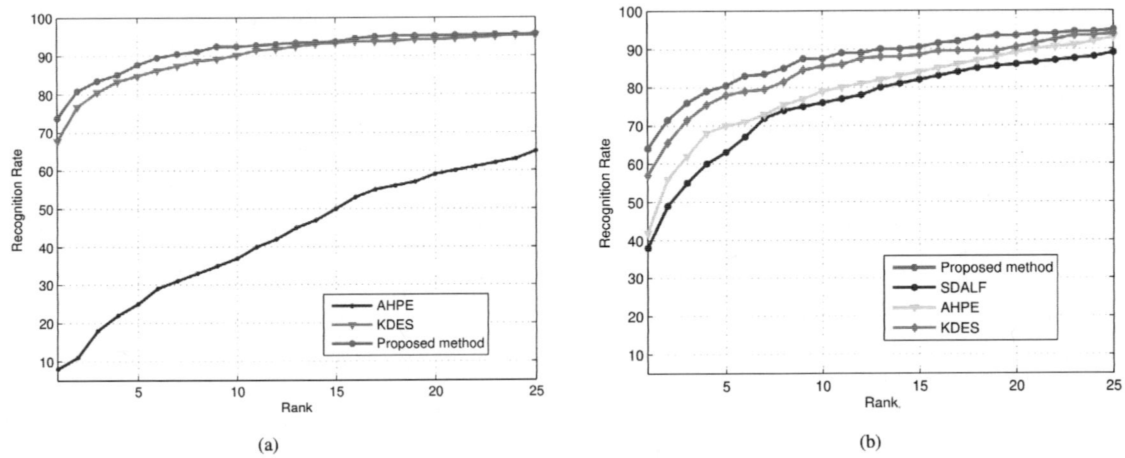

Figure 11. The results of proposed method against AHPE [26], SDALF [27] and KDES [2] on (a) CAVIAR4REID dataset and (b) iLIDS dataset.

automatically-detected human ROIs in the MICA2 dataset are used in the evaluations of the second situation to give the comparative results for person Re-ID in real scenarios of human detection and localization.

The person Re-ID results of the proposed method are compared with the original KDES [2] and other state-of-the-art approaches reported in [26]. In [26], multi-shot datasets of CAVIAR4REID and a modified version of iLIDS are used. The same experimental settings as in [26] are used in this paper for evaluation the performance of person Re-ID. The outperforming results of the proposed method are shown in Figure 11. For CAVIAR4REID dataset, the recognition rate of Rank 1 for AHPE (Asymmetry-based Histogram Plus Epitome) in [26] is much lower than the proposed method. It is only about 8 % compared with 67.76 % of the original KDES in [2] and 73.81 % of the proposed method. However, both KDES and the proposed methods gain nearly the same figures from Rank 13 and backward.

For iLIDS dataset, the gap of Rank 1 between the proposed method with AHPE in [26] or SDALF (Symmetry-Driven Accumulation of Local Features) in [27] is approximately 20 %, and about 7 % with the original KDES in [2]. This gap is slightly decreased for KDES but significantly reduced for AHPE and SDALF after Rank 15.

Other experiments with iLIDs dataset are presented in Figure 12-a in comparison with other methods reported in [28]. In [28], the highest result for Rank 1 belongs to RDC (Relational Divergence Classification), but it is roughly 14% lower than the proposed method with 66.18%. The method of KDES in [2] is tested on this dataset with 61.76% for Rank 1, which is approximately 5% smaller than the proposed method at the first 7 ranks.

The state-of-the-art SDALF reported in [26] and the proposed method for person Re-ID are also tested on MICA1 dataset. Figure 12-b shows the testing results, with 73.13% at Rank 1 for the proposed method compared with the original KDES of 67.16% and 30% of SDALF. The deviation between two recognition rates of the proposed method and the original KDES gradually declines and almost reaches to the same value as SDALF after Rank 21.

All of the above person Re-ID evaluations are done on the manually-cropped human ROIs, with the outperforming results obtained from the proposed KDES descriptor in comparison with the original KDES and some other state-of-the-art methods.

In order to show the comparative results between the manually-cropped and automatically-detected human ROIs, an experiment on MICA2 dataset is done. As indicated in Figure 13, when the human ROI images are gained by manual cropping, the recognition rate of Rank 1 is 33.25% by applying the proposed KDES descriptor. However, this figure falls sharply to 18.47% when the human ROIs are detected automatically. Clearly, the person Re-ID performance based on the proposed descriptor depends strongly on the human detection results. The well-aligned bounding boxes of the manually-extracted human ROIs give the better person Re-ID results than the automatically-detected ones because of occlusion, shadow phenomenon or background clutter appeared in the phase of human detection.

Some examples of automatic human detection results are shown in Fig. 14. We can see that the human detection is far from perfect. The human ROIs are sometimes false positive, mis-aligned or contain multiple persons. These can strongly affect the results of human re-identification.

V. Conclusion and Future Work

In this paper, person Re-ID problem in camera network achieves state-of-the-art performance on the benchmark datasets and our dataset by applying a robust person appearance representation based on KDES. Unlike some other state-of-the-art methods which are tested on the benchmark datasets with the manually-cropped human ROIs, in this paper, the person Re-ID performance is evaluated on the results of automatic human detector. Our experiments show that the proposed method gives an acceptable result for person re-identification in case of perfect human detection (74% for

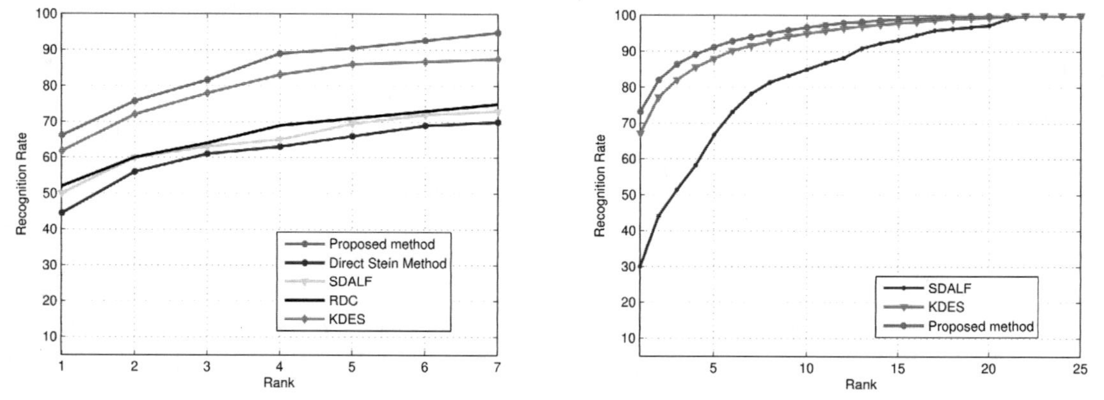

(a) (b)

Figure 12. The comparative results with (a) reported methods in [28] with iLIDs dataset and (b) the results are tested on our MICA1 dataset.

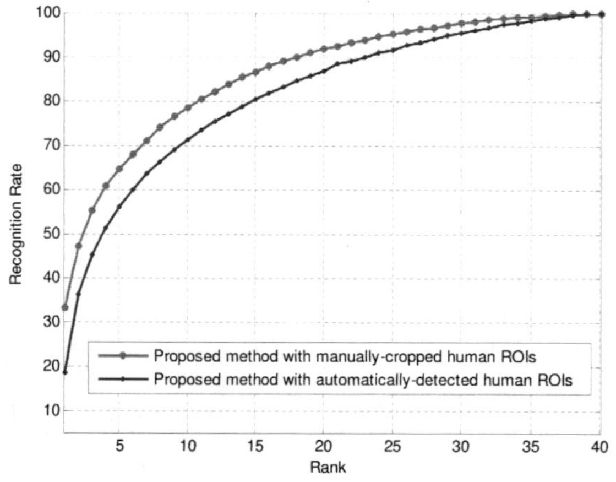

Figure 13. The recognition rates of the proposed KDES on the MICA2 dataset with manually-cropped and automatically-detected human ROIs.

CAVIAR4REID dataset). However, with the automatic human detection, it needs more works in order to reach the requirement. The vision-based person ID can be used in connective and complementing manner of different types of information in the proposed multimodal pedestrian localization system. The experimental results are promising, and based on this, a multimodal method, which uses particle filter and integrated data association algorithm, will be promoted in the future work to increase the performance of the combined person Re-ID and localization system.

ACKNOWLEDGEMENT

This research is funded by Vietnam National Foundation for Science and Technology Development (NAFOSTED) under grant number 102.04-2013.32.

REFERENCES

[1] T. T. T. Pham, T. L. Le, T. K. Dao, and D. H. Le, "A robust model for person re-identification in multimodal person localization," in The Ninth International Conference on Mobile Ubiquitous Computing, Systems, Services and Technologies (UBICOMM), 2015, pp. 38–43.

[2] L. Bo, X. Ren, and D. Fox, "Kernel descriptors for visual recognition," in Advances in Neural Information Processing Systems (NIPS), Vancouver, Canada, 2010, pp. 244–252.

[3] L. F. Teixeira and L. Corte-Real, "Video object matching across multiple independent views using local descriptors and adaptive learning," Pattern Recognition Letters, vol. 30, no. 2, 2009, pp. 157–167.

[4] D. N. T. Cong, C. Achard, L. Khoudour, and L. Douadi, "Video sequences association for people re-identification across multiple non-overlapping cameras," in Image Analysis and Processing (ICIAP). Springer, 2009, pp. 179–189.

[5] D. S. Cheng, M. Cristani, M. Stoppa, L. Bazzani, and V. Murino, "Custom pictorial structures for re-identification," in The British Machine Vision Conference (BMVC), vol. 2, no. 5, 2011, p. 6.

[6] D. Figueira, L. Bazzani, H. Q. Minh, M. Cristani, A. Bernardino, and V. Murino, "Semi-supervised multi-feature learning for person re-identification," in 10th IEEE International Conference on Advanced Video and Signal Based Surveillance (AVSS), 2013, pp. 111–116.

[7] B. Prosser, W.-S. Zheng, S. Gong, T. Xiang, and Q. Mary, "Person re-identification by support vector ranking." in The British Machine Vision

Figure 14. Results of automatically-detected ROIs for 10 people in MICA2 dataset.

Conference (BMVC), vol. 2, no. 5, 2010, p. 6.

[8] N. Martinel, C. Micheloni, and C. Piciarelli, "Learning pairwise feature dissimilarities for person re-identification," in Distributed Smart Cameras (ICDSC), 2013 Seventh International Conference on. IEEE, 2013, pp. 1–6.

[9] M. Bauml and R. Stiefelhagen, "Evaluation of local features for person re-identification in image sequences," in 8th IEEE International Conference on Advanced Video and Signal-Based Surveillance (AVSS), 2011, pp. 291–296.

[10] S. Bak, E. Corvee, F. Brémond, and M. Thonnat, "Person re-identification using spatial covariance regions of human body parts," in Seventh IEEE International Conference on Advanced Video and Signal Based Surveillance (AVSS), 2010, pp. 435–440.

[11] W. Zheng, S. Gong, and T. Xiang, "Person re-identification by probabilistic relative distance comparison," in IEEE Conference on Computer Vision and Pattern Recognition (CVPR), 2011, pp. 649–656.

[12] D. Figueira and A. Bernardino, "Re-identification of visual targets in camera networks: A comparison of techniques," in Image Analysis and Recognition. Springer, 2011, pp. 294–303.

[13] M. Dikmen, E. Akbas, T. S. Huang, and N. Ahuja, "Pedestrian recognition with a learned metric," in Asian Conference on Computer Vision (ACCV), 2011, pp. 501–512.

[14] W.-S. Zheng, S. Gong, and T. Xiang, "Reidentification by relative distance comparison," IEEE Transactions on Pattern Analysis and Machine Intelligence, vol. 35, no. 3, 2013, pp. 653–668.

[15] Y. Freund, R. Iyer, R. E. Schapire, and Y. Singer, "An efficient boosting algorithm for combining preferences," The Journal of machine learning research, vol. 4, 2003, pp. 933–969.

[16] D. Simonnet, M. Lewandowski, S. A. Velastin, J. Orwell, and E. Turkbeyler, "Re-identification of pedestrians in crowds using dynamic time warping," in European Conference on Computer Vision (ECCV), 2012, pp. 423–432.

[17] O. Chapelle and S. S. Keerthi, "Efficient algorithms for ranking with svms," Information Retrieval, vol. 13, no. 3, 2010, pp. 201–215.

[18] O. Vinyals, E. Martin, and G. Friedland, "Multimodal indoor localization: An audio-wireless-based approach," in Fourth International Conference on Semantic Computing (ICSC), 2010, pp. 120–125.

[19] T. K. Dao, H. L. Nguyen, T. T. Pham, E. Castelli, V. T. Nguyen, and D. V. Nguyen, "User localization in complex environments by multimodal combination of gps, wifi, rfid, and pedometer technologies," The Scientific World Journal, vol. 2014, 2014.

[20] T. Teixeira, D. Jung, G. Dublon, and A. Savvides, "Identifying people in camera networks using wearable accelerometers," in Proceedings of the 2nd International Conference on PErvasive Technologies Related to Assistive Environments, 2009, p. 20.

[21] Z. Zivkovic, "Improved adaptive gaussian mixture model for background subtraction," in Proceedings of the 17th International Conference on Pattern Recognition (ICPR), vol. 2, 2004, pp. 28–31.

[22] N. Dalal and B. Triggs, "Histograms of oriented gradients for human detection," in Conference on Computer Vision and Pattern Recognition (CVPR), vol. 1, 2005, pp. 886–893.

[23] W. Bing-Bing, C. Zhi-Xin, W. Jia, and Z. Liquan, "Pedestrian detection based on the combination of hog and background subtraction method," in International Conference on Transportation, Mechanical, and Electrical Engineering (TMEE), 2011, pp. 527–531.

[24] L. Bo and C. Sminchisescu, "Efficient match kernel between sets of features for visual recognition," in Advances in neural information processing systems, 2009, pp. 135–143.

[25] "http://mica.edu.vn/perso/Le-Thi-Lan/ReID.html, last access date is 4th may 2016."

[26] L. Bazzani, M. Cristani, A. Perina, and V. Murino, "Multiple-shot person re-identification by chromatic and epitomic analyses," Pattern Recognition Letters, vol. 33, no. 7, 2012, pp. 898–903.

[27] M. Farenzena, L. Bazzani, A. Perina, V. Murino, and M. Cristani, "Person re-identification by symmetry-driven accumulation of local features," in IEEE Conference on Computer Vision and Pattern Recognition (CVPR), 2010, pp. 2360–2367.

[28] A. Alavi, Y. Yang, M. Harandi, and C. Sanderson, "Multi-shot person re-identification via relational stein divergence," in 20th IEEE International Conference on Image Processing (ICIP), 2013, pp. 3542–3546.

Multiple Faults Simulation of Analogue Circuits

Eduard Weber, Klaus Echtle
University of Duisburg-Essen
Dependability of Computing Systems
Essen, Germany
e-mail: (echtle, weber)@dc.uni-due.de

***Abstract*—Software-based fault simulation can support all abstraction levels, is flexible and allows reliability assessment at different stages in the design process. Fault diagnosis and reliability analysis are increasingly important in circuit design and determine the product's time-to-market. In this paper, we provide a new efficient method and systematic scheme for reducing the time for simulation of multiple simultaneous faults and/or multiple failure modes per element in an analogue circuit. By arranging similar multiple faults in groups, some so-called failure classes can be interpolated with an adequate precision rather than being evaluated by time-consuming simulation. The technique can be used to perform efficient multiple fault diagnosis based on multiple fault injection. Finally, the implemented procedure is validated with some simulation results.**

Keywords*—*Fault simulation; fault modeling; multiple fault injection; fault diagnosis; reliability prediction

I. Introduction

Fault diagnosis of circuits is a well-developed research field with a long tradition. The first scientific publications are from early 1960s. Circuit simulation is nowadays an accepted standard in the development of electronic circuits. Small to complex analogue, digital and mixed-signal circuits can be tested and verified with appropriate simulation software. A lot of progress has been made in the development of software tools for the design and verification of analogue and/or mixed-signal circuits, both in the open-source and in the commercial sector. Already two decades ago the method of analogue fault modelling has been suggested to enable both fault diagnosis and reliability evaluation. Different approaches have been developed for fault simulation of analogue and mixed-signal circuits. Previous work on analogue fault modelling focuses on parametric defects (soft faults) and catastrophic defects (hard faults). Parametric faults are typically simulated with parameter modifications, while open and short defects are dealt with via injecting a high or low resistance on transistor level, respectively.

Fault simulation is generally done by injecting a fault on transistor level and analysing the circuit's behaviour by applying single DC, transient or AC simulation for linear or nonlinear circuit models. Also, software tools for automatic fault injection and efficient test generation have been developed. However, mostly single faults have been considered in the past.

Test cases for fault injection have been generated often by hand from an understanding of the design and fault expectations of major circuit elements (components). Most of the fault simulators for analogue circuits presented in the literature cover only parameter or catastrophic faults. Some tools have attempted to automate test generation and the fault simulation process for analogue circuits. The runtime problem of analogue circuit simulation also needs to be addressed, and advanced simulation techniques are required to accelerate the simulation to an acceptable proportion [1].

Most existing fault simulators use the Simulation Program with Integrated Circuits Emphasis (SPICE), and modify SPICE net lists to represent faults [2] - [3]. The fault simulation software [4] used for the work presented in this paper defines circuit faults in Visual Basic (VB-Script) language and allows flexible and very accurate fault modelling. The main goal of this paper is to speed up the simulation for multiple faults.

II. Diagnosis of Analogue Circuits

Test and fault diagnosis of analogue circuits are necessary despite the ongoing digitalization. Analogue circuits are always required to form the interface to the physical environment. Analogue signals do not consist of just "low" or "high" values like in the digital field. In principle, infinite numbers of signal values are conceivable. The time and frequency characteristics of analogue signals bring another dimension, and are an additional issue within circuit assessment. The propagation of faults is more difficult than in the digital field. Typically, it does not occur in just one direction, but could be from any element in all directions towards neighbour elements within the circuit. A particular fault in an element (like resistor, capacitor, transistor, etc.) does not provide explicit information about the resulting signal values. Therefore, a calculation of signal values (done by circuit simulation) is always necessary.

Nonlinear models, parasitic elements, charges between elements or energy-storing elements make diagnosis and reliability analysis more complex [5]. Because of these reasons, the automation level of fault diagnosis procedures for analogue circuits has not yet achieved the development level realized in the digital field. The reason for the limited automation is simply due to the nature of analogue circuits. The predominant design methodology for analogue circuits is still the individual design based on the designer's experience.

The simulation of multiple simultaneous faults is even more complex. The consideration of multiple faults is important for the following reasons. Different fault modes can be present in the elements of complex circuits. Their occurrence increases even more in rough environments. Also, multiple parametric faults can be present in the field as a result of ageing, environmental stress and design errors. Moreover, multiple fault diagnosis is relevant when a new circuit design is introduced and a high failure density exists. The restriction to single fault simulation only can lead to incorrect evaluation results.

One of the main issues in software-based fault simulation is the relatively long runtime in case of complex analogue circuits. In general, the runtime increases rapidly with the simulated circuit size, the number of faulty elements (fault depth or multiple fault simulation) and the failure modes per element. When performing fault simulation, the runtime is mostly determined by the number of fault injections. Each injection of a multiple fault has to be simulated separately. Usually, the simulation time for single faults (at transistor level) is tractable because of available computer performance. Also, the performance of Electronic Design Automation (EDA) tools has been increased during the last decade. However, multiple fault injection is a challenge with respect to runtime.

The fault simulation framework [4] used for the work presented in this paper can deal with several fault modes injected simultaneously into elements of a circuit. We consider permanent hard (open and short circuit) and soft faults (parametric faults). Please note, that even shorts and opens are dealt with as analogue (not digital) faults, because the simulator generates the analogue signal throughout the complete circuit in the case of these faults.

Figure 1 shows how the total simulation time (here number of simulation runs) is influenced by the number of multiple faults and the failure modes per element. The diagram shows a medium-sized circuit example composed of 20 elements where faults are injected, each of which leads to two different failure modes. The solid line represents the number of simulation runs for all necessary test cases. This quantity increases rapidly with the number of multiple faults.

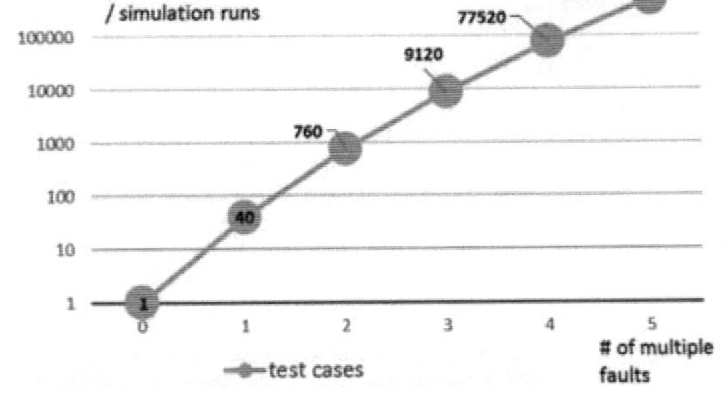

Figure 1. Complexity of fault simulation for an example medium-sized circuit (20 elements with two fault modes per element).

III. FAULT SIMULATION FRAMEWORK

The starting point of EDA-based fault simulation is the circuit's schematic model. The designer can construct a circuit with all available elements by using some circuit design tool. A wide variety of measurements and graphical data representation (also denoted graphs) can be utilized. NI AWR Microwave Office® (National Instruments) [6] features broad post-simulation capabilities, allowing displaying of computed data (measurements, such as gain, noise, power, or voltage) on rectangular graphs, polar grids, Smith Charts, histograms, tabular graphs, and 3D graphs, etc. Every defined measurement point is associated with a particular graph.

The fault simulator [4] uses the graphs to check the circuit's behaviour after fault injection by defining tolerance bands and success areas. The defined tolerance bands and success areas are stored as parts of so-called goals. The circuit under diagnosis (CUD) and its success can be measured in detail by inspection of multiple graphs. After each simulation run the deviation between the fault-free and faulty response is computed for preselected measurements. If the difference exceeds the tolerance band, the injected fault is declared as not being tolerated by the circuit.

The general process of fault simulation is depicted in Figure 2. In the first step the fault-free circuit is simulated. Fault modes for circuit elements are defined within the GUI of the implemented fault simulator (implemented on top of the NI AWR Microwave Office simulator [6]). Usually, several fault modes are possible for each element. Faults are injected into the user-defined circuit via predefined fault modes. The fault injection is done automatically and is undone after every fault simulation run. This means a direct fault modification inside the original circuit within the EDA environment. In addition to the hard faults (open or short circuit) also soft faults (mostly parameter faults that provide a flexible parameter variation of the models of circuit elements) are possible. Faults may change the electrical values (increase or decrease) permanently or for a short time (e.g., temperature), and modify the behaviour of the individual elements which can also lead to a global malfunction of the circuit. After each simulation, measurement data are compared with user-defined goals specified by the tolerance bands. Multiple faults are considered to increase testing quality and enable better reliability analysis. Obviously, the quality of fault simulation highly depends on a realistic set of faults. The fault simulator can automatically generate hard faults (open-circuit, short-circuit) depending on the elements utilized in the circuit. Additionally, parameter faults can be generated automatically or specified by the user.

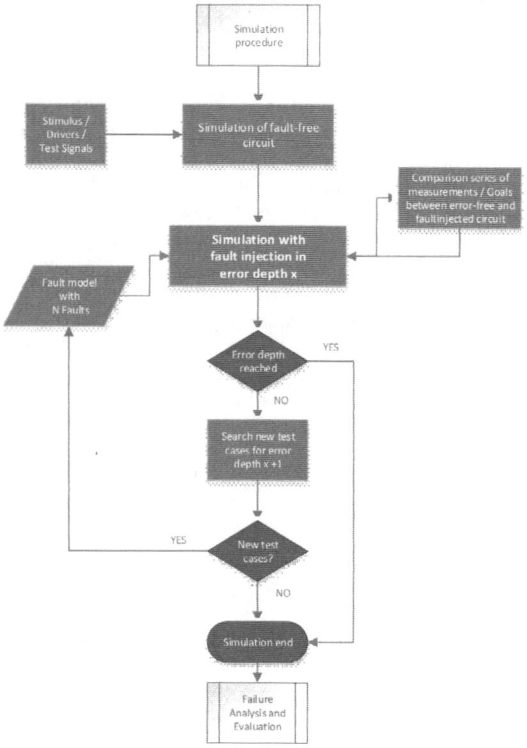

Figure 2. General process of fault simulation.

IV. DEFECTS AND ANALOGUE FAULT MODELING

Fault simulation can only work effectively when the fault model corresponds as closely as possible to the real physical defects. One common approach is the usage of inductive fault analysis (IFA) [7]. The circuit layout and statistical selection among production errors form the basis for IFA. Physical defects of the circuit can be modelled by fault models at the transistor level or at higher abstraction levels. Finally, the fault list will be developed and adapted by the probability of occurrence. Due to the characteristics of analogue circuits, infinitely interim parameter values are possible, so there are an infinite number of analogue errors and, therefore, indeterminable fault models. Therefore, an optimal subset of faults must be selected to do fault simulation with realistic simulation duration and sufficient accuracy. The defined fault list at the transistor level serves as input for the sequential or concurrent fault simulation. The generation of the fault list is therefore a very important step of fault simulation, since it directly determines the quality of the simulation results and time of the analysis. The modelled defects or error types are simulated with test stimuli according to the profile of circuit's application. The results of fault simulation are used to validate its fault tolerance, fault detection and the circuit's quality in general. In other words, Fault simulation reveals the redundancy of a circuit (whether implemented in the circuit intentionally or just by chance).

The physical types of defects can be distinguished into two basic classes. Either a fault has arisen from neighbourship according to the layout, or from an element itself.

Layout-based faults include defects that are only possible in special layout configurations (e.g., placement of elements). In particular, shorts are only possible between neighbouring elements (with very few exceptions). Shorts between distant elements need not be considered in the fault model. Accordingly, parasitic capacitances arise when two electrical connection lines are close enough to each other and the frequency is in the respective range. Trivially, open faults can only occur where a connecting line exists in the layout.

Element-based fault types are defects, which arise within an element. Typically, the model of these faults expresses the element's behaviour between its terminals (e.g., emitter, base and collector of a bipolar transistor, connection pins of resistors, capacitors, diodes, etc.). Six primary error types (three shorts and three opens) can be defined for elements having three terminals and at least two types for passive elements with two pins. Traditionally, opens and shorts are modelled in form of resistors with high or low resistance, respectively. Open defects have a value greater than 1 GΩ and shorts between 0 and a few ohms, within chips up to 500 ohms [8]. If the resistance of a short is relative small, we speak of a strong short, otherwise of a weak short. Analogously, we define a strong open by an almost infinite resistance, and a weak open by a resistance of some 100 MΩ or GΩ. Real analogue circuit's faults have ideal shorts and opens only in rare cases. Therefore, a set of appropriate parameter values must be chosen.

TABLE I. PHYSICAL DEFECTS AND ELECTRONIC FAULT MODELS FOR OPEN ERRORS.

Physical defect open defect	**Electronic fault model**
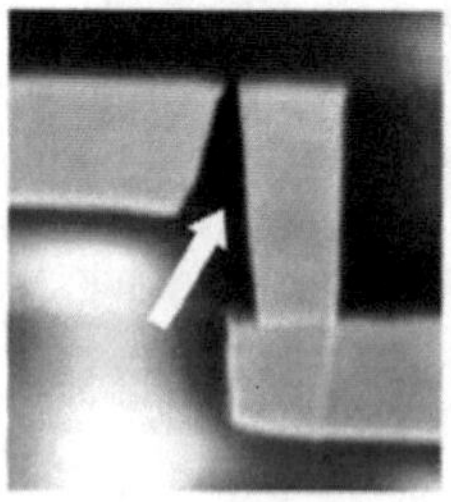 Open circuit [9]	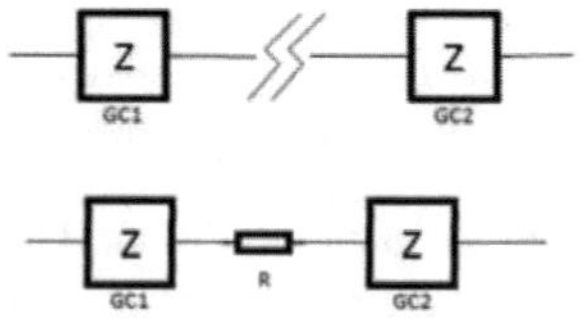 The resistance value (R) has a high value (> 100MΩ). An open defect can have multiple subtypes: • Complete (strong) open, without any electrical connection • Partial (weak) open, variates the line resistance

TABLE II. PHYSICAL DEFECTS AND ELECTRONIC FAULT MODELS FOR SHORT ERRORS.

Physikal defect bridging defect / short	**Electronic fault model**
 Short circuit with low resistance [9]	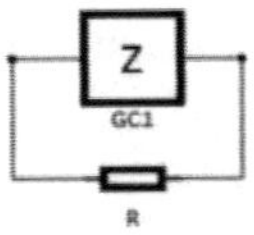 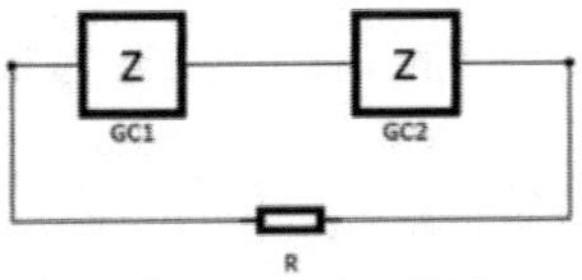 The resistance value (R) has a low value (< 500Ω).
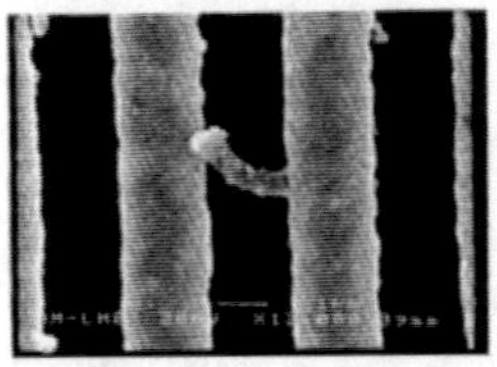 Short circuit with high resistance [9]	A short circuit can at least be assumed between the pins of elements or generally between each connection line. Real shorts have rarely a resistance value of exactly 0 ohms, most shorts are in the range between 0 and 500 ohms.

To describe fault models precisely, the cause and the appearance of errors must be understood. Especially for analogue circuits, the circuit layout and the element's parameters influence the possible errors and the effect on the circuit's performance. Defects or undesirable characteristics can sneak up not only during manufacturing, but can also arise at the utilization phase. In Table I and Table II the reader will find general physical defects and the equivalent electronic fault models.

The following Tables III, IV, and V provide an overview of the basic types of analogue elements and error models. We show the simplest errors at first, i.e., shorts by lines and, therefore, without a resistance value or a capacitance. Complete interruptions (i.e., opens) of elements are modelled by disabling the elements (i.e., switching the respective element OFF). Parameter errors, interruptions and weak shorts can be expressed by variation of the respective parameter values. Basically, the implemented fault simulator can be applied to all assigned elements and circuit models in the EDA environment. All types of faults are described by a script language (VBScript) and applied directly to the circuit schematics before each fault simulation.

TABLE III. SELECTION OF FAULT MODELS FOR A RESISTOR

Element with fault injection

Resistor

Strong short

Strong short

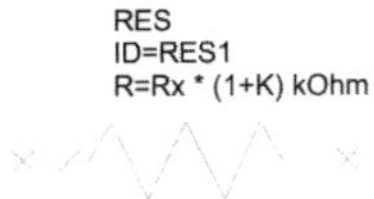

Parameter fault (Depending on model)

Strong open

TABLE IV. SELECTION OF FAULT MODELS FOR A TRANSISTOR.

Element with fault injection

Transistor

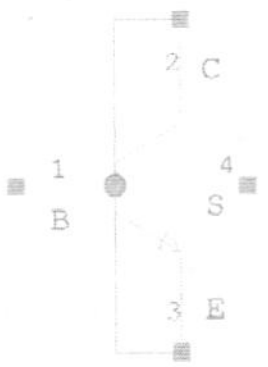
Strong short

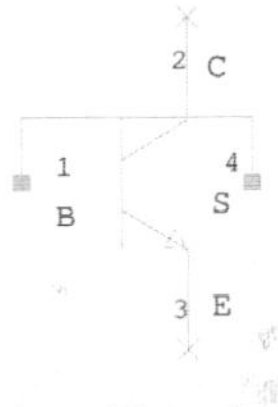
BS short (S = substrate)

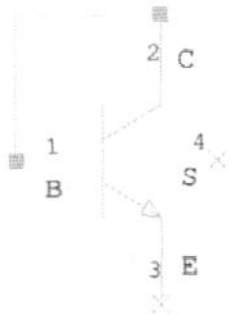
BC short

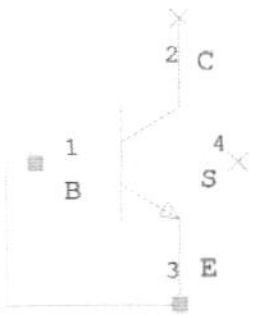
BE short

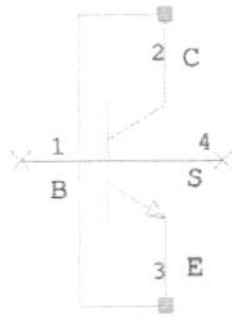
CE short

Faults of any combination of the ports are possible.

TABLE V. SELECTION OF FAULT MODELS FOR A DIODE AND CAPACITOR.

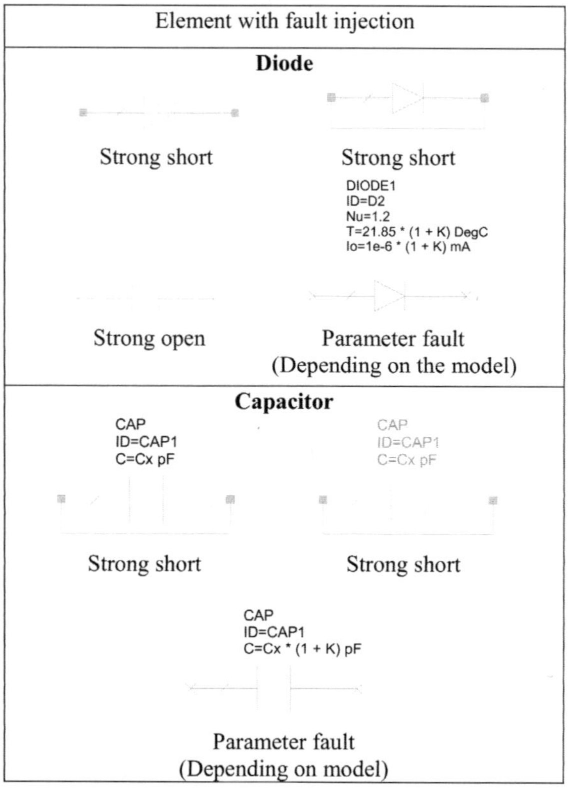

V. STRATEGIES FOR REDUCING SIMULATION TIME

One of the main problems in analogue fault simulation is the relatively long simulation time. Acceleration of fault simulation / reducing the simulation duration is an important goal. To reduce the runtime of simulation with fault injection the following two general approaches are feasible: reduce the amount of fault injections (simulation runs) or speed up the simulation procedure for every fault injection. Several approaches are described in the literature to speed-up the simulation process, including fault or test case ordering [10–13] and distributed fault simulation [14][15]. Several approaches for multiple fault generation [16][17] and simulation [18][19] for reliability analysis are described in the literature as well. In the following, the reader can find an overview of several techniques on how the simulation duration can be reduced.

A. *Concurrent or parallel fault simulation*

Simulation by using multiple physical or logical CPU cores can accelerate the circuit or fault simulation, respectively. Multiple CPU cores can simulate parts of a single circuit, and collect the results at the end. Then the faster simulating cores wait for the final part of the simulation and can then move on to the next fault simulation. In the general case of fault simulation, the different injected faults can be simulated independently. For this reason, the fault simulation can be performed very efficiently because each CPU core simulates a different fault. If one CPU core finishes earlier, it starts immediately with the next fault simulation. Parallel fault simulation can also be processed on independent workstations that are connected over a network, see [20].

B. *Random fault simulation*

Simple random sampling is a widely known test method for selecting errors in digital systems. It is a classic approach, where a small subset of errors out of the large set of errors is selected to determine certain characteristics of the system. The achieved accuracy depends on the size of the selected subset. For example, if the number of potential or possible errors is 5,000 and 500 errors have been selected and simulated, then the reduction in simulation time is a factor of 10.

C. *Fault models on higher level of abstraction (e.g., for elements not being subject to fault injection)*

A widely known method to speed up the fault simulation is partial simulation on a higher level of abstraction. Parts of the circuit can be simulated, for example, in the form of an analogue description language (Verilog-AMS or VHDL-AMS) or by simplified SPICE models. The fault simulator can thereby accelerate simulation runs by replacing all elements without fault injection through behavioural models which are on a higher level and more efficient to simulate. In most cases, this reduces the simulation time significantly.

TABLE VI. IMPORTANT PARAMETERS THAT INFLUENCING ELEMENT FAILURE RATE. BASED ON [21].

D is a symbol for dominant parameter and x for important parameter.

Stress parameters	Hybrid circuits	Bipolar transistors	FETs	Diodes	Resistors	Capacitors	Coils, transform.	Relays, switches	Connectors
Ambient temp.	D				D	D	D	D	D
Junction temp.	D	D	D	D					
Power stress	D	D	D	x	D		x		
Voltage stress	D	x	x	x		D	x	x	
Current stress	D			x				x	x
Breakdown voltage	x	x	x	x					
Technology	x	x	x	x	x	x	x	x	x
Complexity	x							x	
Package	x	x	x	x		x		x	x
Application	x	x	x	x		D		x	x
Contact construction	x	x	x	x				D	D
Range	x	x		x	x	x			x
Production maturity	x	x	x	x	x	x	x	x	x
Environment	x	x	x	x	x	x	x	x	x
Quality	x	x	x	x	x	x	x	x	x

D. Probability of occurrence of element defects

Some studies have examined the probability of occurrence of individual element fault types. In Table VI, the reader will find the most relevant stress parameter types that influence the failure rate of analogue electronic elements. Table VII provides an overview of statistical distributions of faults for different electronic elements. It can be noted that 60% to 100% of analogue element's defects are some kind of shorts and opens. The remaining faults are mainly drifts of parameter values. The fault simulation can be performed only on the most likely types of element faults (e.g., 70%). The less likely faults can be omitted.

TABLE VII. STATISTICAL INDICATOR VALUE FOR FAILURE MODES BASED ON [21].

Element		Shorts	Opens	Drift
Bipolar transistors		80	20	
Field effect transistors (FET)		80	10	10
Diodes (Si)	general purpose	80	20	
	Zener	70	20	10
Resistor,	fixed (film)		60	40
Capacitors	foil	15	80	5
	ceramic	70	10	20
	Ta (solid)	80	15	5
	Al (wet)	30	30	40
Coils		20	80	
Quartz crystals			80	20

E. Early abortion of a simulation run

The values of element parameters and the tolerance bands are specified before fault simulation starts. This can be done by simulating the fault-free circuit and determining the allowed deviations of the measures values. During the fault simulation procedure, the measured values can be compared with the predetermined tolerance range. If some value is above or below the specified limits of fault-free circuit, then it is immediately clear that the injected fault has not been tolerated. Consequently, further simulation of this injected fault can be skipped. The reduction in simulation time depends on the amount of faults that allow early abortion of simulation and, moreover, the point in time when the tolerance band is violated. This method has already been used in transient analogue fault simulation, see [10, 22] for example.

F. Leave out elements outside the test object

Circuit may include some "additional elements" that are not of interest because they are outside the test object. They should be excluded from simulation.

G. Leave out unrecognizable defects

In special cases, it may be clear that some faults of an element do not cause an effect that can be recognized. Examples are unconnected elements, special types of elements, or elements that fulfil some protection functionality. Since the simulator would not notice any effect of an injected fault, the respective fault case can be omitted.

H. Monotonicity assumption

A basic rule (if applicable) is the assumption of monotonic behaviour. Two joint faults will not be tolerated, if at least one of them is not tolerated when injected as single fault. By "tolerated" we mean that the circuit under diagnosis (CUD) is still providing its function according to a given maximum deviation from the expected behaviour. The monotonicity assumption has the advantage that many irrelevant multiple fault combinations can be discarded before being simulated. The effect to the number of test cases (= simulation runs) is quite substantial. Discarding dual faults will also result in a smaller number of considered triple faults, and so on. The simulation time is reduced for all multiple fault combinations (see Figure 3). The dashed line shows that the quantity of simulation runs can be reduced significantly by assuming monotonic behaviour as follows: When a set F of multiple simultaneous faults is not tolerated, then also a superset of F will not be tolerated. Consequently, the superset needs not be simulated. The assumption of monotonic behaviour is slightly pessimistic. In practice there are rare exceptions. Think of two resistors in series, each of 1 kΩ. If both of them are parametrically faulty and half their resistance down to 500 ohms, then the voltage at the point between them does not necessarily change. It may still be correct. Monotonicity does not always exist. However, we have observed that it exists in an overwhelming majority of cases with only very few exceptions. In general, the monotonicity assumption reduces the number of both considered circuit elements and failure modes per element.

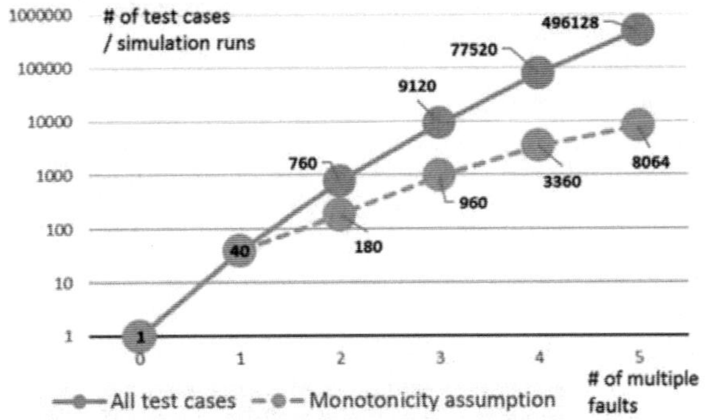

Figure 3. Complexity of fault simulation for an example medium sized circuit (20 elements with two fault modes per element). Only ten elements are considered at monotonicity assumption for multiple faults (≥ 2).

I. Standardized input parameters

During fault simulation, a circuit simulation is made for every fault injection. Repetitive parts of the circuit simulation, such as DC analysis (steady-state) can be conducted only once by simulation of the fault-free circuit. Thus, the fault simulations finish earlier and reduce the total simulation time.

J. Measurement-based simulation

Once the measurement point within the circuit have been defined, one may identify parts of the circuit that do not exercise an influence to these measurement points. Consequently, the non-relevant parts can be excluded from simulation to achieve an overall acceleration. The exclusion does not affect the checks whether or not the tolerance bands are violated. Note that the decision on an exclusion is more complicated in analogue circuits compared to digital circuits, because there may be no clear input and output pins of an element. In a bipolar transistor, for example, the base current determines the collector current. However, depending on the operation conditions, there may also be an influence from the collector to the base.

K. Faults classes (focus of this paper)

In the remainder of the paper, we present a further method how the number of simulation runs can be reduced, see Sections IV and V. Before we describe the method we will formalize the selection of test cases to achieve a better precision in the description of the fault classes (= sets of fault cases) the new method is making use of.

Formally, the relationship between faults, elements of the circuit, injections and simulation runs is defined by the following tuples and functions:

1) $C = \{c_0, \dots, c_m\}$ is the set of circuits to be evaluated, $c_0 \in C$ is the fault-free circuit.
2) E = {transistor1, transisitor2, ..., resistor1, ..., …} is the set of elements of the circuit c_0.
3) F = {short_circuit, open_circuit, parameter_mod., ...} is the set of considered fault modes of the circuit c_0.
4) $I = \{ (f, e) \in F \times E$: probability of fault f in element e} is the set of potential injections.
5) $I^* = \{ i^* \subset I : (x \in i^*, y \in i^*, x \neq y) \Rightarrow x|E \neq y|E \}$ is the set of potential multiple injections. I* is a subset of the power set of I. By $x|E$ and $y|E$ we denote the element of injection x or injection y, respectively. The inequality $x|E \neq y|E$ excludes joint injection of different faults to the same element of the circuit.
6) $Q : F \times E \rightarrow [0, 1]$ is the probability of fault $f \in F$ in a <u>faulty</u> element $e \in E$. If a fault $f \in F$ is not applicable to an element $e \in E$ then $Q(f, e) = 0$. For a given faulty element $e \in E$ the sum of fault probabilities is always 1: $\Sigma_{f \in F}$: $Q(f, e) = 1$.

Example: If we assume only two fault modes F = {open, short} and only two elements $E = \{R_1, R_2\}$, there may be four injections $I = \{(open, R_1), (open, R_2), (short, R_1), (short, R_2)\}$ and four double injections. In all we obtain:

$I^* = \{ \{(open, R_1)\}, \{(open, R_2)\}, \{(short, R_1)\}, \{(short, R_2)\}, \{(open, R_1), (open, R_2)\}, \{short, R_1), (short, R_2)\}, \{(open, R_1), (short, R_2)\}, \{short, R_1), (open, R_2)\} \}$.

If shorts are more likely for R_1 and opens are more likely for R_2 we may get, say,
$Q(open, R_1) = 0.2$, $Q(short, R_1) = 0.8$ $(0.2 + 0.8 = 1)$.
$Q(open, R_2) = 0.4$, $Q(short, R_2) = 0.6$ $(0.4 + 0.6 = 1)$.

$P : E \rightarrow [0,1]$ is the function indicating the probability that element $e \in E$ is fault-free.

Function R: $I^* \rightarrow \{0,1\}$ is a simulation run with joint injection of all faults from $i \in I^*$. The method returns 1 if the injected faults are tolerated according to the tolerance criterion, otherwise 0. In the following, the fault simulation procedure is described for single, double, triple fault injection.

<u>Single faults:</u>

$I_1 = I$ is the set of single fault injections to be evaluated by simulation.

$T_1 = \{ i \in I_1 : R(\{i\}) = 1 \}$ is the set of single injections that have been tolerated. The function

$P_1 = \sum_{i \in I_1} R(i) \cdot (1 - P(i|E)) \cdot Q(i|F) \cdot \prod_{y \in (I_1 \setminus i)} P(y|E)$

expresses the probability of tolerated single injections.

<u>Double faults:</u>

$I_2 = \{\{(f, e), (f', e')\} : (f, e) \in T_1, (f', e') \in T_1, e \neq e' \}$ is the set of double injections to be evaluated by simulation. I_2 has been defined on the basis of T_1, not I_1, because the non-tolerated injections from the complement $I_1 \setminus T_1$ are excluded due to the assumption of monotonicity.

$T_2 = \{i^* \in I_2 : R(i^*) = 1\}$ is the set of double injections that have been tolerated.

$P_2 = \sum_{i^* \in I_2} R(i^*) \cdot \prod_{x \in i^*} (1 - P(x|E)) \cdot Q(x|F) \cdot \prod_{y \in (I_2 \setminus i^*)} P(y|E)$

expresses the probability of tolerated double injections.

<u>Triple faults:</u>

$I_3 = \{\{(f, e), (f', e'), (f'', e'')\} : \{(f, e), (f', e')\} \in T_2, (f'', e'') \in T_1, e \neq e', e \neq e'', e' \neq e''\}$ is the set of triple injections to be evaluated by fault simulation. Again, the non-tolerated previous injections have been excluded due to the assumption of monotonicity.

$T_3 = \{i^* \in I_3 : R(i^*) = 1\}$ is the set of triple injections that have been tolerated.

$P_3 = \sum_{i^* \in I_3} R(i^*) \cdot \prod_{x \in i^*} (1 - P(x|E)) \cdot Q(x|F) \cdot \prod_{y \in (I_3 \setminus i^*)} P(y|E)$

expresses the probability of tolerated triple injections.

The injections of higher numbers of joint faults are defined accordingly.

VI. FAULT CLASS ALGORITHM

The algorithm is an heuristic approach that is based on an observation of simulation results [4] of so-called fault classes. A fault class is a set of test cases (series of fault injections) all of which have the same number of faults and the same types of fault modes, independent of the element where the faults are injected.

Experimental results show that three fault classes FC1, FC2 and FC3 for multiple faults mostly exhibit a monotonically increasing degree of tolerance, when the fault distance between FC1 and FC2 is 1, and also the fault distance between FC2 and FC3 is 1. By a fault distance d(FC, FC') (similar to the Hamming distance), we understand the number of fault modes that differ between FC and FC'. The degree t of tolerance is defined by the number of tolerated test cases divided by the number of all test cases of a fault class.

The case d(FC1, FC2) = d(FC2, FC3) = 1 means that each pair of fault classes differs by just one fault mode. For example, consider the following fault classes:

FC1 (open, open, open),
FC2 (open, open, short),
FC3 (open, short, short).

The fault distances are d(FC1, FC2) = d(FC2, FC3) = 1 and d(FC1, FC3) = 2. Typically this leads to
either $t(FC1) \leq t(FC2) \leq t(FC3)$
or $t(FC1) \geq t(FC2) \geq t(FC3)$.
From this observation we developed an algorithm that can be characterized as follows:

- Search for fault classes FC1, FC2, FC3 satisfying the condition above – or search for even longer chains (>3 multiple faults) of fault classes with this property.
- Determine which of the chains will typically lead to an ascending or descending degree of tolerance. To decide that, analysing the fault classes of the previous fault depth is necessary, see Step 2 of this section below.
- Quantify the tolerance of the first and the last fault class of a chain by simulation.
- Quantify the tolerance of the remaining fault classes of a chain by interpolation.

Fault classes are defined by the modes of the injected faults and their number of simultaneously injected faults. $FC_2(x, y)$ denotes a fault class for two joint injections, namely fault modes x and y. Since the fault classes $FC_2(x, y)$ and $FC_2(y, x)$ are identical, we enforce a unique notion by assuming an order among the fault modes. Since fault modes x and y may be identical (injection of two faults of identical mode into different elements), we require $x \leq y$ for $FC_2(x,y)$. For an arbitrary fault class $FC_n(x_1, x_2, \dots, x_n)$ we require $x_1 \leq x_2 \leq \dots \leq x_n$. Then, a fault class for double fault injection is defined as follows:
$FC_2(x, y) = \{ \{(f, e), (f', e')\} \in I_2 : f = x, f' = y \}$
A fault class for the injection of n faults is defined accordingly: $FC_n(x_1,\dots, x_n) = \{\{(f_1, e_1),\dots, (f_1, e_1)\} \in I_n : f_i = x_i\}$.

The subset of test cases in a fault class $FC_n(x_1,\dots, x_n)$ that has been tolerated is called tolerance class $TC_n(x_1,\dots, x_n)$. The following holds: $TC_n(x_1,\dots, x_n) \subset FC_n(x_1,\dots, x_n)$. Moreover, $TC_n(x_1,\dots, x_n) = FC_n(x_1,\dots, x_n) \cap TC_n$. The quotient of the cardinality of $TC_n(x_1,\dots, x_n)$ and the cardinality of $FC_n(x_1,\dots, x_n)$ is called tolerance degree $t_n(x_1,\dots, x_n)$. Thus

$$t_n(x_1, \dots, x_n) = \frac{|TC_n(x_1, \dots, x_n)|}{|FC_n(x_1, \dots, x_n)|}$$

The heuristic approach is defined in the following steps and the algorithm is shown in Figures 4 and 5. We assume that the tolerance classes $TC_1(\dots)$ and $TC_2(\dots)$ have already been generated by the respective fault simulations. Consequently, the tolerance degrees $t_1(\dots)$ and $t_2(\dots)$ are known. Then the following steps describe how the fault classes $FC_3(\dots)$ for triple fault simulation – or interpolation! – are formed.

A. *Step 1 – Generation Of Fault Classes*

A fault class $FC_3(x, y, z)$ with 3 faults is generated by combining all test cases of TC_2 with all test cases of TC_1 in the following way: Each union of a test case $tc_2 \in TC_2(x,y)$ and a test case $tc_1 \in TC_1(z)$ form a test case $tc_3 \in FC_3(x,y,z)$ provided x, y and z inject faults into different elements. Since we avoid double injections into a single element, the respective combined injections {x, y, z} are filtered out. The corresponding algorithm is shown in Figure 4. In the algorithm we denote the fault mode of injection x by x|F.

Procedure 1 Generate Fault Classes

```
for all test cases tc₂ ∈ TC₂ do
  for all test cases tc₁ e TC₁ do
  { test case {x, y, z} = i ∪ j;
    if x|E ≠ y|E and x|E ≠ z|E and y|E ≠ z|E then
      FC₃(x|F, y|F, z|F) = FC₃(x|F, y|F, z|F) ∪ {x, y, z}
  }
```

Figure 4. Generate Fault Classes.

B. *Step 2 – Search Fault Class Chains*

The search of fault class chains starts with a search in TC_2. We inspect all pairs of tolerance classes $TC_2(x, y)$ and $TC_2(x', y')$ and filter out those with a fault distance of 1 and, moreover, with "significantly unequal" tolerance degrees (the difference should be at least Δ). Formally:
$d(TC_2(x, y), TC_2(x', y')) = 1$ and $|t_2(x, y) - t_2(x', y')| \geq \Delta$
where Δ may be in the range of 5% of the absolute values.
From the fault distance 1 we can conclude that either $x = x'$ or $y = y'$. In the following, we assume $x = x'$ and $y \neq y'$ without loss of generality.

From the two tolerance classes $TC_2(x, y)$ and $TC_2(x, y')$ we derive the following chain of three fault classes:
$< FC_3(x, y, y),\ FC_3(x, y, y'),\ FC_3(x, y', y') >$
According to the observation of likely monotonicity (see Section II and Section IV) we only simulate the test cases of the first and the last fault class in the chain to obtain the tolerance degrees $t_3(x, y, y)$ and $t_3(x, y', y')$, respectively. The tolerance degree $t_3(x, y, y')$ of the inner fault class in the chain is obtained by interpolation:
$t_3(x, y, y') = (t_3(x, y, y) + t_3(x, y', y')) / 2.$
The algorithm can be seen in Figure 5.

TABLE VIII. COMPARISON OF SOME FAULT SIMULATION RESULTS

Circuit name	No. of simulation runs			Speed-up factor	Error
	Number of simulation runs for all possible fault combinations	Number of simulation runs with monotonicity assumption	Number of simulation runs for the new approach with fault classes	Our approach over simulation with monotonicity assumption	Our approach over fault simulation with monotonicity assumption
Two stage BJT amplifier with feedback (Fault depth 1-4)	22422	356	284	1.25	5.4 %
LM741 AMP [23] (Fault depth 1-4)	3923175	2090	1718	1.22	0.5 %
Broadband VHF/UHF amplifier [24] (Fault depth 1-3)	695525	18187	10928	1.66	1.8 %
Limiter BSP [25] (Fault depth 1-4)	1045256	1208	858	1.40	0.2 %
Voltage stabilizer circuit I (Fault depth 1-3)	8358	4088	2688	1.53	0.15 %
Voltage stabilizer circuit II (Fault depth 1-4)	317248	11173	5209	2.14	0.10 %
				Average: 1.53	Average.: 1.28 %

Procedure 2 Search Fault Class Chains

```
for all pairs (TC2, TC2') of tolerance classes with two injections do
  if d(TC2(x, y), TC2(x', y')) = 1 and |t2(x, y) – t2(x', y')| ≥ Δ then
  { fault class FC = FC3(x, y, y),
    fault class FC' = FC3(x, y, y'),
    fault class FC'' = FC3(x, y', y');
    t3(x, y, y) = simulation of FC3(x, y, y);
    t3(x, y', y') = simulation of FC3(x, y', y');
    t3(x, y, y') = (t3(x, y, y) + t3(x, y', y')) / 2;
  }
```

Figure 5. Search Fault Class Chains.

C. *Step 3 – Calculation of Probabilities*

The simulations of $FC_3(x, y, y)$ and $FC_3(x, y', y')$ deliver the set of all tolerated test cases, this means the two tolerance classes $TC_3(x, y, y)$ and $TC_3(x, y', y')$. The probability of tolerating the respective triple faults can be calculated by the formula presented in Section III. When this formula is applied to tolerance class $TC_3(x, y, y)$ we obtain

$$\sum_{i^* \in TC_3(x,y,y)} \prod_{x \in i^*} (1-P(x|E)) \cdot Q(x|F) \cdot \prod_{y \in (TC_3(x,y,y) \setminus i^*)} P(y|E)$$

For tolerance class $TC_3(x, y', y')$ we obtain:

$$\sum_{i^* \in TC_3(x,y',y')} \prod_{x \in i^*} (1-P(x|E)) \cdot Q(x|F) \cdot \prod_{y \in (TC_3(x,y',y') \setminus i^*)} P(y|E)$$

The probability of tolerating the triple faults of the interpolated fault class cannot be obtained directly, because the test cases of this class have not been simulated. For this reason, we approximate the probability by multiplying the respective formula with the tolerance degree:

$$t3(x,y,y') \cdot \sum_{i^* \in TC_3(x,y,y')} \prod_{x \in i^*} (1-P(x|E)) \cdot Q(x|F) \cdot \prod_{y \in (TC_3(x,y,y') \setminus i^*)} P(y|E)$$

The tolerance class of the non-simulated fault class is generated by selecting a portion of $t_3(x, y, y')$ test cases at random. For the injection of more than three joint faults, steps 1 to 3 can be applied accordingly.

VII. EXPERIMENTAL RESULTS

In this section, the efficiency of the proposed solution to reduce the simulation time is evaluated. The fault simulation framework [4] is used to evaluate the dependability of five example electronic circuits. It should be noted that for the used circuits only permanent faults (e.g., short, open or parameter deviations) have been considered. The simulation time (fault injection and simulation) depends on the number of elements, the number of injected faults per element and the fault depth. Appropriate fault tolerance criteria have been defined on circuit outputs.

All of the circuits have been evaluated in two ways. The first evaluation was without generation of fault classes (all multiple fault combinations have been simulated with the monotonicity assumption). The second evaluation applied the new method with fault classes (therefore, only a portion of the test cases needed to be simulated). The remaining fault classes (which have not been simulated) have been evaluated by interpolation according to the algorithm in steps 1 to 3. This way the new method can be compared directly to the solution without using fault classes.

The result of the comparison of some simulations results is shown in Table VIII. The second to last column shows that the speedup achieved by the new approach is 50% in the average (see bottom line of Table VIII: "Average 1.53"). It has to be paid by an error in the results (see last column). The error refers to the absolute value of the fraction "result with new method" / "result without new method". A deviation around 1.3% is noticed in the average (see bottom line of Table 8: "Average 1.28 %").

VIII. CONCLUSION

Fault simulation of analogue circuits with multiple faults is an important problem to deal with, since their appearance is unavoidable in real systems. In this paper, we have introduced the fault class concept for our approach to reduce the simulation time for multiple fault analysis. We discussed the idea of fault classes, providing conditions that ensure chains of fault classes with ascending or descending degree of tolerance. We implemented the procedure and evaluated it experimentally. In this paper, we have successfully reduced the duration of software-based fault simulation for multiple faults and different fault modes. In the evaluated example circuits, our methodology shows that the number of simulation runs is significantly lower while preserving the precision quite well.

REFERENCES

[1] E. Weber and K. Echtle, "Efficient Simulation of Multiple Faults for Reliability Analysis of Analogue Circuits," in *DEPEND 2015. The Eighth International Conference on Dependability*, 2015, pp. 23–28.

[2] Z. R. Yang and M. Zwolinski, "Fast, robust DC and transient fault simulation for nonlinear analogue circuits," in *Design, Automation and Test in Europe Conference and Exhibition 1999. Proceedings*, 1999, pp. 244–248.

[3] H. Spence, "Automatic analog fault simulation," in *Conference Record. AUTOTESTCON '96*, 1996, pp. 17–22.

[4] E. Weber and K. Echtle, "Simulation-Based Reliability Evaluation for Analog Applications," in *2014 IEEE International Reliability Physics Symposium (IRPS)*, The Institute of Electrical and Electronics Engineers, 445 Hoes Lane, Piscataway, NJ 08855, USA, 2014, 4B.2.1-4B.2.6.

[5] P. Kabisatpathy, A. Barua, and S. Sinha, *Fault Diagnosis of Analog Integrated Circuits*. Boston, MA: Springer, 2005.

[6] *Microwave Office | NI AWR Design Environment.* Available: http://www.awrcorp.com/de/products/microwave-office (2016, Feb. 01).

[7] J. Shen, W. Maly, and F. Ferguson, "Inductive Fault Analysis of MOS Integrated Circuits," *IEEE Des. Test. Comput*, vol. 2, no. 6, 1985, pp. 13–26.

[8] R. Rodriguez-Montanes, Bruls, E. M. J. G, and J. Figueras, "Bridging defects resistance in the metal layer of a CMOS process," *J Electron Test*, vol. 8, no. 1, 1996, pp. 35–46.

[9] H.-J. Wunderlich, Ed, *Models in Hardware Testing: Lecture Notes of the Forum in Honor of Christian Landrault*. Dordrecht: Springer Science+Business Media B.V, 2010.

[10] J. Hou and A. Chatterjee, "Concurrent transient fault simulation for analog circuits," *IEEE Trans. Comput.-Aided Des. Integr. Circuits Syst*, vol. 22, no. 10, 2003.

[11] P. N. Variyam and A. Chatterjee, "FLYER: fast fault simulation of linear analog circuits using polynomial waveform and perturbed state representation," in *Tenth International Conference on VLSI Design*, 1997, pp. 408–412.

[12] A. V. Gomes, R. Voorakaranam, and A. Chatterjee, "Modular fault simulation of mixed signal circuits with fault ranking by severity," *IEEE International Symposium on Defects and Fault Tolerance in VLSI Systems*, 1998, pp. 341–348.

[13] H. Hashempour *et al.*, "Test time reduction in analogue/mixed-signal devices by defect oriented testing: An industrial example," *Design, Automation & Test in Europe*, 2011.

[14] T. Markas, M. Royals, and N. Kanopoulos, "On distributed fault simulation,", *Computer*, vol. 23, no. 1, 1990.

[15] C. P. Ravikumar, V. Jain, and A. Dod, "Faster fault simulation through distributed computing," *Tenth International Conference on VLSI*, pp. 482–487, 1997.

[16] S. Kajihara, T. Sumioka, and K. Kinoshita, "Test generation for multiple faults based on parallel vector pair analysis,", *International Conference on Computer Aided Design (ICCAD)*, 1993, pp. 436–439.

[17] H. H. Zheng, A. Balivada, and J. A. Abraham, *A Novel Test Generation Approach for Parametric Faults in Linear Analog Circuits: Proceedings / 14th IEEE VLSI Test Symposium, Princeton, New Jersey*. Los Alamitos, Calif: IEEE Computer Society Press, 1996.

[18] K. Saab, N. Ben-Hamida, and B. Kaminska, "Parametric fault simulation and test vector generation," *Meeting on Design Automation*, 2000, pp. 650–656.

[19] Y. C. Kim, V. D. Agrawal, and K. K. Saluja, "Multiple faults: modeling, simulation and test," *7th Asia and South Pacific Design Automation Conference*, pp. 592–597, 2002.

[20] S. Spinks, "ANTICS analogue fault simulation software," in *IEE Colloquium on Testing Mixed Signal Circuits and Systems*, 1997, p. 13.

[21] A. Birolini, *Reliability engineering: Theory and practice*, 7th ed. Heidelberg, New York: Springer, 2014.

[22] Junwei Hou, *CONCERT: a concurrent transient fault simulator for nonlinear analog circuits*. New York, NY: Association for Computing Machinery, 1998.

[23] National Semiconductor, *LM741 Operational Amplifier.* Available: http://web.mit.edu/6.301/www/LM741.pdf (2015, Mar. 05).

[24] C. G. Gentzler and S. K. Leong, "Broadband VHF/UHF amplifier design using coaxial transformers," *High Frequency Electronics*, pp. 42–51, http://www.polyfet.com/HFE0503_Leong.pdf, 2003.

[25] AWR Corporation, *Bipolar Limiting Amplifier Circuit.* Available: https://awrcorp.com/download/faq/english/docs/Getting_Started/Tonal_Analysis.html (2015, Mar. 05).

COTS or Custom Made?

A Multi-Criteria Decision Analysis for Industrial Control Systems

Falk Salewski

Department of Electrical Engineering and Computer Science
Muenster University of Applied Sciences
Germany
Email: falk.salewski@fh-muenster.de

Abstract—**The choice between *custom made* electronics and the use of *commercial of the shelf* (COTS) components is often not trivial for industrial control systems. The selection is particularly challenging, when required quantities or specific requirements do not give a clear sign for the one or the other approach. While a consideration of the resulting costs (development costs and product costs) gives some indication, only a broader view helps to perform a sound decision. In this work, a set of decision criteria (targets to be reached by the control unit) and a decision method based on *multi-criteria decision analysis* are presented for industrial control systems. The presented approach is considering COTS devices, custom made devices as well as a combination of both. Moreover, a case study with three industrial control systems is presented showing the application of the approach.**

Keywords–commercial of the shelf; electronic design decisions; industrial control units; MCDA

I. INTRODUCTION

This article is extending previous work on design decisions for industrial control units presented at CENICS 2015 [1]. The most important extensions are the inclusion of further decision criteria, iterations in the specification phase, as well as a proposal for the selection procedure itself.

Commercial of the shelf (COTS) components as programmable logic controllers (PLCs) and industrial PCs (IPCs) are widely used as control units in industrial automation (For this article, we follow the following definition for COTS: A COTS device can be bought from a catalog without modifications [2]). In some applications, companies are faced with the decision if a *custom made* (CM) design of a control unit might be beneficial for their products and systems. Such a CM design includes the development of the control electronics, the corresponding software as well as mechanical parts as the housing and the user interface. In other applications, a change from a custom made design of control units to COTS components is discussed (mostly with the idea of cost reduction in mind).

Both approaches have their specific advantages and disadvantages. A custom made device often comes with an optimized functionality and an attractive price of the final product, but involves much more effort than the required development activities. Especially in case of safety or mission critical systems, it has to be assured that specific requirements (temperature range, failure rate, electrical robustness, etc.) are met over the complete product life cycle (and not only with a prototype during development). While a custom made design allows full control of the final product, all relevant aspects have to be verified. These activities are performed on basis of prototypes and first series devices, but also have to be reconsidered in case of all changes (e.g., if obsolete memory chips require replacement, at least an impact analysis is required but often several verification, validation and certification activities have to be redone).

On the other hand, the use of COTS devices often requires more than applying a plug and play procedure. Depending on the application, the selection of a suitable device could be challenging. And also systems based on COTS devices have to undergo verification, validation and certification activities. Moreover, it could be required to establish specific relationships with the suppliers and/or to perform additional tests on the COTS components if they are applied in critical applications (examples can be found in [2]).

In both cases, the complete life cycle of the product has to be considered for a sound selection. An approach for such a selection is the so called Total Cost of Ownership (TCO) [3] that aims to consider all cost factors of a product during product life. To supplement existing approaches with the required technical data, this article deals with the differences of the following approaches for industrial control units:

1) COTS - *commercial of the shelf*
2) CM - *custom made*
3) Combination of 1 and 2.

The main focus of this article is on electronic control units (including their software), but not on pure software products as discussed for example in [4].

As a basis for a systematic selection procedure, we collect relevant selection criteria (targets) in the following Section II. Next, the specialties of the three approaches are analyzed based on their product life cycle in Section III. Based on these two sections, a selection procedure is presented in Section IV, followed by a case study in Section V. After a discussion in Section VI, this article ends with a conclusion.

II. TARGETS FOR SELECTION

For any selection procedure, it is necessary to define the key targets to be fulfilled by the devices. Common targets often cited are fast time to market, improved costs and competitive advantages [5]. These competitive advantages describe product properties beside the price and differ between application domains. In previous work, we already identified a set of impact factors for hardware platforms [6]. For this work, we take a system view on the control units (electronics + software + mechanical). Moreover, we assume that the functional requirements are fulfilled for industrial environments in case of all candidates. The resulting set of targets is presented in Figure 1 and will be further described below.

A. Time to Market

A fast *time to market* is an obvious target. As soon as the product is on the market, amortization of non-recurrent costs can start. Moreover, a fast *time to market* can be a competitive advantage to competitors.

B. Costs

As with *time to market*, it is an obvious target to keep the *costs* low. However, several aspects have an impact on the overall costs for a product.

In case of *recurrent costs*, it is the cost of purchasing or manufacturing the product itself. In addition, license costs for software (drivers, operating systems, etc.) and/or hardware modules (e.g., inclusion of externally developed modules in custom made products) as well as costs resulting from later maintenance activities have to be considered.

The *non-recurrent costs* for a custom made control unit include development costs (including costs for prototypes and test activities during development) as well as costs for the preparation of the series production (creation and test of tooling, as soldering frames, adapters for automatic assembly, programs for test equipment as automated optical inspection (AOI), in circuit tester (ICT), and/or functional tester, test adapters and specific test electronics). Further non-recurrent costs that also appear for COTS systems are the costs of integration of the electronic control system into the target system as well as those for verification, validation and certification activities (performed before and/or after integration in target system). Often, at least certification activities are executed on system level, but benefit from pre-certified components. Finally, costs resulting from required documentation activities (product + development process) have to be considered.

C. Product Properties

While we assume that all candidates can fulfill the specified functional requirements, further properties could make a difference.

A first important property is the *availability* of the product (availability in this context is not the operational availability but the possibility to purchase or manufacture the product). For any application, it is important that the required control electronics are available for new products and the replacement of defect units.

As many industrial control electronics perform safety and/or mission critical tasks, their *reliability* and *functional safety* is another important factor. As evaluated in previous work, the choice of the hardware platform has impacts on the safety properties of the overall system [7]. The specific needs have to be analyzed for each application individually.

Security is another important property. Especially the increasing interconnection of industrial automation systems via the internet requires corresponding measures [8], [9], [10]. Additionally, a protection of the *intellectual property* (IP: firmware, electronics, design, etc.) is often desirable to protect own products from plagiarizing. As with functional safety and reliability, the requirements depend on the individual application.

For applications that evolve during their life time (e.g., an industrial plant undergoing modernization) or those in which a control unit should be applied in several different target applications (perhaps not all of them defined today), it is desirable to work with systems that can be *adapted* to different or changing requirements. Examples are modular PLCs which allow to add a variety of different plug-in modules (analog and digital I/O, communication interfaces, special function modules). Another approach is to define major parts of the product via software or reconfigurable hardware (e.g., FPGAs).

While *energy efficiency* of control units was predominantly an issue in mobile and battery powered devices in the past, it is now also an issue in all industrial application (especially if a high number of control units is applied). Additionally, *size* and/or *weight* is an issue in several applications.

Sustainability in this context describes environmental aspects in the life cycle of the product. The increasing number of electronics produced every day comes with an urge to think about resources and recycling. In the area of resources, relevant questions are for example the following: Is it feasible to reduce the amount of energy needed for the creation of a product? Is it possible to use sustainable resources (e.g., material of natural origin, as described for example in [11]) and to avoid critical materials (an example is the ROHS directive [12]). Recycling on the other hand deals with options to reuse parts and materials from old electronics at the end of their life-time.

D. Customer Perception

Another target that could be important is the customer perception. While a decision could not be the optimum choice, it still might be the optimum solution from the customers perspective. As an example, the use of a COTS device with a good reputation might increase customer's confidence in the product although it does not differ from alternatives from a technical point of view.

E. Legal and Regulatory Requirements

Finally, legal and regulatory requirements have to be considered for every product. These requirements have effects on product properties (for example on safety properties) as well as on the overall development and production process (e.g., safety standards require certain development processes). To follow all given requirements becomes especially critical if the product should be sold in several different countries (e.g., Europe, US, and India). There is strong effort to harmonize the different standards and regulations present all over the world, but today one still has to deal with differences between countries. Thus, at least the selection of countries in which the product should be sold later on has to be considered as a target in the selection process.

III. PRODUCT LIFE CYCLE

In this section, a typical product life cycle is presented for a design based on COTS control units, a design with CM control units and a combination of COTS and CM components.

Following accepted processes, the product life cycle starts with a specification. While the creation of a sound specification

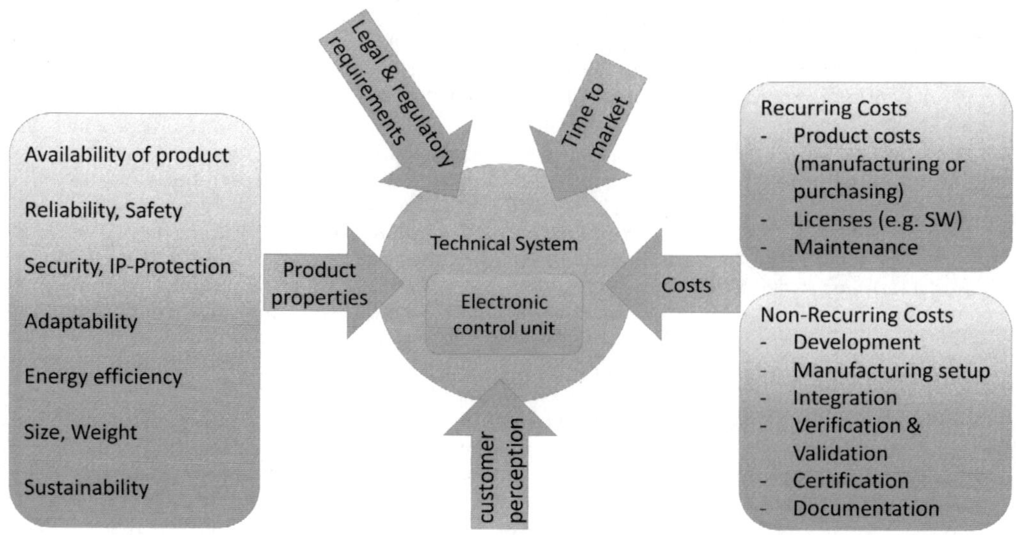

Figure 1. Targets for selection of electronic control units

is a major task, we assume it is already existent for the next step. Nevertheless, it has to be noted that specifications are often not fixed in early phases. While a first approach typically includes the complete "wish list", first concepts based on the early specification often show that targets (mostly costs) cannot be reached. Therefore, typically several iterations of specifications and corresponding concepts are required to create a practicable specification (see Figure 2), especially if new and unfamiliar approaches and techniques are applied. It is expected that also in this phase of creating the specification, differences between COTS and CM components are present (for example, concepts for first estimations are probably easier to establish with COTS components than on basis of a CM design). While the impact on the specification might be a further interesting difference between COTS and CM approaches, it is outside the scope of this article. Therefore, it is assumed that a suitable specification is present for the remaining article.

Based on the specification, an implementation could be realized in the three ways presented in Figure 3.

1) For a CM approach, development activities are required followed by integration, verification, validation and certification. In parallel, the manufacturing set-up has to be established and verified.
2) In case of a COTS approach, development activities are replaced by a selection and qualification of suitable COTS devices. In this case, no production activities take place.
3) A combination of COTS and CM devices includes the elements of both life cycles, CM and COTS.

In all three cases, the aforementioned activities are followed by operation, maintenance and repair activities.

Industrial control systems have a long useful life that requires *life cycle services* (examples are maintenance, modifications and retrofit). According to a publication by the international society of automation, only 20-40% of the investment for an automation systems is spent on the purchasing of the system while the remaining 60-80% are required for life cycle services [13]. Accordingly, these activities are of great importance for industrial applications and should be kept in mind during the selection process.

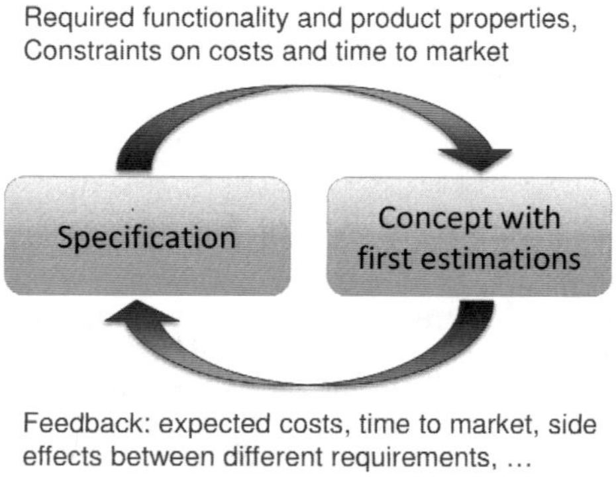

Figure 2. Typical iterations during creation of the specification

Finally, each product life cycle ends with some *end of life* activities, typically decommissioning. As the impact of this phase is considered low for the selection process, end of life activities are not considered in this article. The following subsections deal with the specific characteristics of the three approaches.

A. COTS

In case of a COTS design, a suitable device has to be selected. The aim is to identify an existing product that fulfills the requirements given in the specification. Moreover, further aspects as those presented above could be important for the selection, although often not explicitly stated in the specification. Depending on the application, it might be useful to reconsider the specification, if no suitable COTS device could

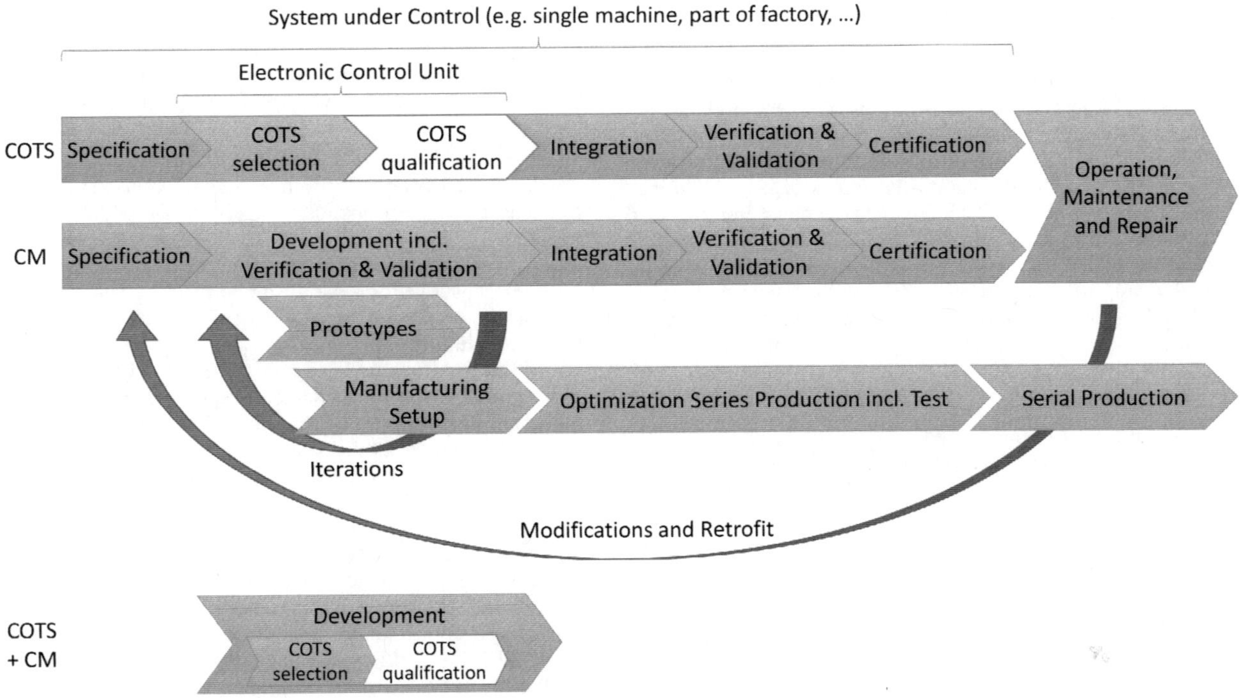

Figure 3. Product life cycle for different approaches (length of phases does not necessarily reflect the effort required for this phase)

be identified. Moreover, the fulfillment of the requirements is often not only determined by the product itself and related aspects (e.g., documentation), but also by the relationship to the supplier of this device (support during integration, operation, maintenance, long time availability, insight into verification and validation activities, willingness to perform further verification and validation activities if needed, etc.). Especially for critical applications, additional verification activities could be required to apply COTS devices (see [2] as an example for military applications). If these verification activities are required and cannot be performed by the supplier, own verification activities have to be performed with the COTS device.

In the next phase, the selected COTS device has to be integrated into the application (for this approach, we assume that no modifications are required to integrate the COTS device). In this phase, the knowledge of the COTS device's properties is of great importance. Gaining this knowledge could be time consuming, but could be eased by support given by the supplier (good documentation, qualified hotline support, tools supporting integration, etc.).

While verification and validation of the control unit itself has already been targeted, it is the overall system that has to fulfill the requirements. Thus, verification and validation activities have to be performed also on system level. Based on the application, also certifications are required or recommended (e.g., functional safety applications). Several COTS devices come with some pre-certification for certain applications (as the mentioned safety applications). These pre-certifications typically ease the certification activities on system level.

B. Custom Made

The CM approach requires development (including all design, implementation and test activities to reach a suitable prototype) and manufacturing activities. During development, prototypes are implemented and verified on basis of the specification. Design decisions have to consider functional aspects, as well as further impacts (see Figure 1). Some aspects for COTS apply here for specific integrated circuits used in the design. They can simplify design and verification activities, but also lead to the challenges listed in the COTS section (e.g., availability). Especially in complex designs, often several prototype stages are required until verification and validation activities are passed successfully.

Additionally, an ideal design is optimized for later manufacturing as these optimizations can significantly reduce manufacturing times and tooling costs. Generally speaking, the aim is to deal with the complexity in development and manufacturing [14]. For optimum time-to-market, the preparation for manufacturing is started before the development activities are finished. The required synchronization between development and manufacturing activities are often challenging [15]. Moreover, to determine the start time of preparation activities, the following tradeoff is necessary. On the one hand, the risk of changes in the product that are relevant for production has to be kept low (ideal: wait until everything is definitely working as specified). On the other hand, a late start of preparation activities is resulting in negative impacts on the time to market and/or a reduced preparation time.

In the following steps, optimizations of the manufacturing process take place, mostly to optimize manufacturing time and quality. Integration, verification and validation activities can start with prototypes, but final tests and certification typically require first samples from the serial manufacturing process.

In case of a COTS product, analysis of defect products, obsolete components or changes in regulatory requirements (e.g., EMC requirements) are typically performed by the supplier. Also in case of a CM design, this analysis has to be performed periodically to check if changes in the product are required. While these activities could be outsourced, the effort for these activities has to be considered. Moreover, required changes could result in costly redesign activities (new verification, validation and certification activities might be needed), a risk worn by the supplier in case of COTS components.

C. Combination

The process of combining COTS components with a CM design follows a combination of both processes. Typically, the product core is implemented with a COTS component and the interfaces are custom made, but also other parts as interfaces or power supplies can be implemented with COTS parts. Thus, during development all aspect of a CM design have to be followed in addition to a selection of suitable COTS components (lower part of Figure 3, only the differences to the CM process are displayed).

While the use of COTS components comes with some challenges to be considered (see section above), it can simplify the remaining development significantly. An example is the use of a COTS single board PC on a custom made printed circuit board (PCB) populated with interface and power supply circuits (and some application specific functions if needed, see also Section V). This combination can simplify the manufacturing process if the main PCB is populated with comparatively simple components only (e.g., easy assembly, no extra small structures on PCB). Furthermore, PC parts as memory chips tend to become easily obsolete, a problem now covered by the supplier of the PC board. For the supplier of the PC board this problem is less critical, as he typically benefits from higher production volumes (boards are sold to many customers). Thus, the resulting price of buying the PC modules could be lower than to manufacture low quantities in house.

IV. Selection Procedure

The combination of the targets presented in Section II and the product life cycles presented in the preceding Section III provide the basis for a systematic selection. The consideration of the many factors presented above leads to a so called *multi-criteria decision analysis* (MCDA) [16], [17]. MCDA offers several different approaches for a systematic decision, one will be described in the following. For all approaches, it is necessary to establish an objective evaluation. Therefore, it is recommended to evaluate each factor in a team (at least technical and sales representatives) to consider different viewpoint in the decision process.

An example for a decision procedure is displayed in Figure 4. Each selection procedure should start with a sound requirements analysis. As a result of this analysis, functional requirements should be defined as well as **all** required targets (see Figure 1 for detailed targets). The following analysis of design alternatives is then based on these requirements as well as on the corresponding life cycles (see Figure 3).

In case a CM design might be the desired choice, experts from the area of electronic development and manufacturing should be consulted (internal or external partners). This way, quantitative data can be achieved for costs and time-to-market aspects. However, for reliable data, a sound specification and "trustworthy" experts are required.

Besides costs and time to market, the targets are of qualitative nature. While a qualitative analysis is probably sufficient in many cases, a rating system can be applied in case of all qualitative aspects (e.g., rating of products availability from 1 to 10) if needed, for example in form of a decision matrix. Rating can be agreed on in the team or it can be build from a set of individual ratings. An example for such a decision matrix can be found in Figure 5. On the left, quantitative aspects of three different devices are evaluated. On the right, the qualitative aspects are rated based on the rating proposed above. It is important that a consensus should be found within the decision team for each result. In Figure 5, all targets are considered as equally important and no weighting has been applied. In the case that differences in the importance of the targets exist, a weighting can be applied as presented in Figure 6. In this extended approach, the rating of each target is multiplied with the weighting factor (with 1 for the lowest importance and 9 for the highest importance) in the column W·R. Obviously, this weighting can have a significant effect on the result (in the given example, the COTS approach now outperforms the CM approach). The impact of the importance of the different targets is further discussed in Section VI.

During the evaluation, it will become obvious that the results within the targets have dependencies with the costs (e.g., reliability can be typically approved by additional measures. However, these measures typically have an impact on the costs). Thus, every change in the concept should be evaluated concerning it's impact on other factors (especially cost). If a consensus is found on the results for all targets, a sound decision is possible between design alternatives.

V. Case Study

In this section, three existing control units are evaluated based on the criteria defined before. The emphasis of the following description is on the properties of the selected system and not on the selection process (devices already exist).

A. Three Control Units

The following control units are considered for the presented case study:

1) A machine for sorting metal parts: The control unit is required to switch electric motors and pneumatic valves and read several position sensors and an analogue input for measuring the metal parts. Moreover, the status of the machine has to be displayed on a screen. The expected volume required of this machine is ≤ 50 units per year.
2) A user terminal for an embroidery machine: The control unit has to read the required embroidery pattern from a USB stick and display it on the screen of the terminal. Moreover, user commands have to be read from the terminal. A set of commands is computed and send to the embroidery machine via a proprietary interface. The expected volume is 800 units per year.

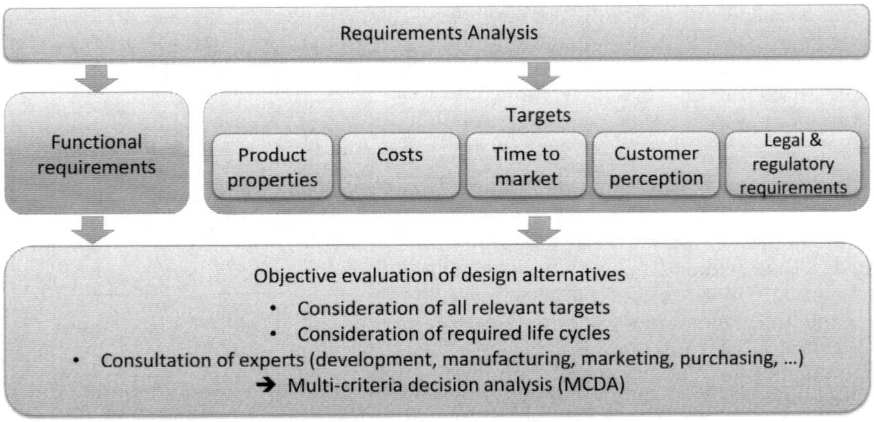

Figure 4. Proposed selection procedure

	Alternatives :	A	B	C
	Type :	CM	CM+COTS	COTS
	Targets ↓			
Costs Recurring	Product	100	250	500
	Licenses	0	0	0
	Maintenance	0	0	0
Costs Non-Recurring	Development	150000	50000	0
	Manufacturing Setup	50000	30000	0
	Integration	3000	4000	5000
	V&V	10000	10000	5000
	Certification	7000	7000	4000
	Documentation	2000	2000	1000
	Σ	*222000*	*103000*	*15000*
Σ	100 units	232000	128000	65000
Σ	500 units	272000	228000	265000
Σ	1000 units	322000	353000	515000

	Alternatives :	A	B	C
	Type :	CM	CM+COTS	COTS
	Targets ↓			
Product Properties	Availability of product	9	6	5
	Reliability & Safety	6	6	6
	Security & IP-Protection	7	7	7
	Adaptability	9	9	7
	Energy efficiency	8	8	8
	Sustainability	8	7	7
	Size & Weight	8	7	7
time to market		4	6	9
legal & regulatory requirements		8	8	9
customer perception		8	8	7
Σ		75	72	72

Figure 5. Example for MCDA based on decision tables

		Alternatives :	A		B		C	
		Type :	CM		CM+COTS		COTS	
Targets ↓		Weighting ↓	Rating	W ·R	Rating	W ·R	Rating	W ·R
Product Properties	Availability of product	7	9	63	6	42	5	35
	Reliability & Safety	8	6	48	6	48	6	48
	Security & IP-Protection	7	7	49	7	49	7	49
	Adaptability	4	9	36	9	36	7	28
	Energy efficiency	8	8	64	8	64	8	64
	Sustainability	8	8	64	7	56	7	56
	Size & Weight	1	8	8	7	7	7	7
time to market		9	4	36	6	54	9	81
legal & regulatory requirements		9	8	72	8	72	9	81
customer perception		4	8	32	8	32	7	28
Σ			*75*	**472**	*72*	**460**	*72*	**477**

Figure 6. Example decision table with weighting of targets

3) A control unit for automatic domestic windows: This electronic unit has to control a DC motor (PWM, encoders) based on sensor information and information received via a proprietary bus interface. Moreover, the available space for this device is limited to 100x40x18mm. The expected volume here is ≥ 1000 units per year.

B. Evaluation

An overview of the evaluation can be found in Figure 7 while details will be described below. The target *sustainability* as well as *legal and regulatory requirements* were not formulated at the time of this case study and are not considered for this reason. Nevertheless, no changes in the results are expected (no specific requirements for sustainability or legal and regulatory requirements to be covered by the product are given). A general discussion of potential impacts of these two targets can be found in Section VI.

1) Case A: The low quantity of required products indicate a COTS device as best choice. However, a conflict could arise from the remaining targets which are evaluated in the following.

The non recurrent costs, as well as the required time to market clearly benefit from the use of a COTS component. The recurrent price is probably higher than a CM approach, but a quantity of 50 units in most cases does not allow to amortize non recurrent costs for a custom made design including verification.

In addition, product properties have to be considered. Size and weight targets, which could be a tough challenge for COTS approaches, are not critical in this application. The same is true for the energy efficiency of the control unit.

For this application, a modular programmable logic controller (PLC) has been chosen. This approach allows to adapt the control units in case of later changes (e.g., by changing or adding I/O modules or special function modules). Moreover, this approach allows to use similar approaches in different machines (same core unit but differences in modules used).

During the selection of the device, the availability of this device or potential replacements is crucial. Well established systems as well as individual contracts can mitigate the risks. Additionally, the use of standardized components (including the programming languages) ease the migration to alternative systems when needed.

Finally, no specific safety, security or reliability requirements were given in this application. Nevertheless, specific PLC systems targeting these requirements are available.

Based on this brief evaluation, a COTS approach is the optimum solution for this application.

2) Case B: In this application, the need for a proprietary interface requires at least some CM design. Moreover, the visualization requirements for the terminal screen require a certain amount of processing power.

In this application, a combination of a COTS processor board was chosen in combination with a custom made main board implementing the power supply and required interfaces. The use of the COTS board was driven by the following aspects:

- This approach simplifies the design and the manufacturing of the main board (no fine pitch components and less high speed design required o this board).
- For the required quantities, the COTS board has an attractive price compared to the CM approach.
- Components as memory chips change frequently. In the COTS approach, the qualification of new chips is done by supplier.
- An approach of a complete COTS user terminal in combination with an interface converter (required for the proprietary interface to the machine) was resulting in a significantly higher product price.

Furthermore, the remaining cost related factors show no disadvantage of this approach compared to a full custom made design. With respect to time to market, this approach benefits from the COTS components in comparison to the CM approach, as a major part of the design could be implemented as a pretested module. The product properties are influenced as follows:

As the COTS board has a major impact on the availability, a long term contract was set up with the supplier. Nevertheless, a migration to another processor board is possible (probably involves redesign).

Reliability analysis is possible as the complete design including all components is known. Optimizations in the architecture or the applied components could have been performed if required, as well as the implementation of safety functions on the main board.

A protection of the program memory is supported by the processor, no further security or IP protection requirements exist. Adaptability can be achieved by modifications of the main board. However, this approach requires redesigns (incl. verification activities). In this application, it is expected to handle all modifications via SW.

Customization allows optimization of energy, size and weight properties. However, none of these are considered as critical for this application.

Finally, a CM design allows significant separation from competitors (customers perception). In summary, the application benefits from the chosen combination of COTS and CM components.

3) Case C: Size and product price restrictions are major impacts for this application and could not be fulfilled with available COTS components.

The non-recurring costs for the required design and manufacturing activities are significantly higher than with a COTS approach, but could be amortized by the expected quantity in an acceptable period. Costs for verification and certification activities could be held on a moderate level as the complete system was already undergoing sufficient procedures.

With full control of HW and SW design, specific project properties (e.g., proprietary bus interface, protection of firmware, emergency stop, life beat) could be fulfilled. Finally, the time to market was (with almost a year) long compared to a COTS approach, but not critical as the development of the complete system took a similar amount of time.

	Case :	Case A	Case B	Case C
	Description :	Machine for sorting metal parts	User terminal for embroidery machine	Window control unit
	Assumed annual quantity :	≤ 50	800	≥ 1000
Targets ↓	**Choice →**	**COTS**	**COTS + CM**	**CM**
Costs Recurring	Product	high, but according to low quantity best with COTS device (here PLC)	combination of a COTS processor board with a custom made main board allows a competitive product price	custom made design allows cost optimized approach (for given constraints)
	Licenses	no licence for operation	open source operating system	none
	Maintenance	diagnosis features supported by PLC, modular PLC allows replacement/ repair of modules	individual repair/replacement of processor and main board possible, maintenance features have to be custom made	diagnosis features implemented via bus interface
Costs Non-Recurring	Development	HW: only selection & integration SW: based on PLC operating system => application only	HW: only main board + selection processor board & integration SW: operating system has to be adapted to custom design + application SW	full development of electronics and software
	Manufacturing Setup	none	manufacturing of main board + integration processor board + test in manufacturing; separate processor board, no fine pitch devices on main board => simplifies manufacturing process	full manufacturing setup incl. test required
	Integration	HW setup with COTS IDE + wiring of sensors and actuators	1) main and processor board 2) operating system and HW 3) application	HW/SW integration in development, integration with remaining system via bus interface
	V&V	focus on SW + overall system	complete system	complete system
	Certification	not required for control unit	EMC test for CE marking	EMC test for CE marking, further tests with complete system
	Documentation	SW + wiring (hardware configuration saved in project data)	full documentation, exisiting documentation for processor board and operating system can be included	full documentation
Product Properties	Availability of product	depends on PLC supplier, long term industrial availability provided	depends on supplier of processor board (long term contract), processor board can be replaced (redesign main board + comparable alternative processor board)	depends only on components used, obsolences can be handeld with 2nd source components, if needed in combination with redesign (HW or HW+SW)
	Reliability & Safety	no specific requirements, COTS HW is assumed to be well tested, COTS devices typically = black box, but reliability and safety data is available for certain devices	complete reliability analysis possible for main board, data für processor board available from supplier. No specific safety requirements. (implementation on main board could be an option if required)	complete reliability analysis possible for electronics. Specific safety requirements could be implemented in SW and HW (emergency stop, life beat)
	Security & IP-Protection	supported, setting via COTS IDE	processor supports protection of program memory	processor supports protection of program memory
	Adaptability	modular PLC systems allows to add further modules (I/O, special function, ...), other devices can be added via bus interface	full control of SW, custom main board allows adaptations, but these changes require redesigns of the hardware (incl. verification and certification)	full control of SW, full control of HW, but changes require redesign (incl. verification and certification)
	Energy efficiency	COTS devices with acceptable energy efficiency are available	the custom made design and the selection of a suitable processor board allows an optimized design	stand by <0,4W => low power controller in combination with suitable HW and SW design (sleep modi)
	Size & Weight	no specific requirements	size of PCB determined by 10" screen (not critical) no specific weight requirements	critical => only achievable with custom design
time to market		fast (weeks)	medium (months), with COTS processor board, the SW development can start before custom made HW is ready, risk of design iterations	medium-high (months), with evaluation board, the SW development can start before custom made HW is ready, risk of design iterations
customer perception		selected brand of COTS device supports image of high quality product	customized solution allows separation from competitors	customized solution allows to meet the targets for size and product price

Figure 7. Case Study

VI. Discussion

In the presented case study, the emphasis is on the differences of the three approaches presented. However, even the simplified description of the selection performed for these case studies shows the advantages compared to an unsystematic approach. The collection and evaluation of the proposed targets in combination with the consideration of the complete product life cycle prevent that important factors are neglected during the decision process. In addition, quantitative approaches as described in Section IV can be applied to further formalize the selection.

Moreover, one could argue that the decision for or against COTS devices is solely driven by the quantity of the required units. For sure, in extreme cases (less than 10 units, more than 100000 units) the decision is probably simple. However, for medium numbers and depending on further targets to be fulfilled by the control unit, the decision process differs. As an example, a product with a quantity of 1000 units/year could be better implemented with COTS (high volume product that perfectly matches requirements) and a unit only needed a few 100 times a year might be better in CM (e.g., when other targets do not allow a pure COTS approach).

Furthermore, it has to be noted that the importance of the different targets could be rated very differently for different applications (An example for a weighting of targets in the decision process has been presented in Figure 6). As the result of the overall analysis depends a lot on this rating, it has to be performed precisely. If, for example, the following targets are rated very high compared to other targets, this rating can have a major impact on the decision:

- *availability of the product:* if a CM design is possible with standard components (all with at least 2nd source), a high independence from suppliers can be achieved by a CM design. This independence could result in a major advantage compared to a COTS approach. However, it has to be noted that it is often not possible to find suitable 2nd sources for all components of a product. Examples for critical components are microcontrollers and all other specific integrated circuits, displays and specific connectors. Nevertheless, an option to reduce the risk of unavailability for the components without a suitable 2nd source is to set up delivery contracts with the suppliers of these components.
- *safety and adaptability:* if a control unit including safety functions should be open to later adaptations, the effort for later changes (concept, implementation, verification, validation and certification) could be significantly lower in case of a well supported COTS device.
- *legal and regulatory requirements - device should be sold worldwide:* Depending on the product, this requirement could result in a high effort, especially in case of certification activities. If COTS devices with the required certifications are available (or can be made available by the COTS supplier), this target can be met easily by choosing the COTS approach.
- *sustainability:* If specific sustainability requirements are given (e.g., high percentage of the material used in a control system should be recycled at the end of product life, overall energy footprint of the manufacturing of the device should be below a certain threshold), the set up and implementation of the recycling concept can be challenging. As with the requirement above, a COTS approach can simplify the effort to reach this target IF a COTS device with the required properties is available.

VII. Conclusion

The comparison of COTS and CM approaches (or combinations of both) requires more than just an analysis of cost and time to market. In addition, the overall costs (recurring and non-recurring) are compiled from several aspects and not only the cost of the control system itself. Therefore, a set of important targets to be considered in the decision process has been presented in this work. These targets include different types of costs, time to market, legal and regulatory requirements, customer perception as well as large set of product properties. The considered costs are compiled from recurring costs (for product, licenses and maintenance) and non-recurring costs (for development, manufacturing setup, integration, verification, validation, certification and documentation). The presented product properties include availability, reliability, safety, security, IP-protection, adaptability, energy efficiency, sustainability, size and weight. Moreover, impacts on the product life cycles of the different approaches have been discussed. Based on these two aspects (targets and impacts on life cycles), a systematic selection process for industrial control systems has been proposed. The proposed process includes MCDA and allows to apply quantitative approaches to further formalize the selection. Finally, the selection process has been demonstrated in a case study with three industrial control units.

References

[1] F. Salewski, "COTS or custom made? Design decisions for industrial control systems," in Proc. of the Eighth International Conference on Advances in Circuits, Electronics and Micro-electronics (CENICS 2015). IARIA, 2015, pp. 7–12.

[2] J. Hall and R. Naff, "The cost of cots," in Proceedings of the Digital Avionics Systems Conference. IEEE, 2000, pp. 20–24.

[3] F. Wynstra and K. Hurkens, "Total cost and total value of ownership," in Perspektiven des Supply Management, M. Eig, Ed. Springer Berlin Heidelberg, 2005, pp. 463–482.

[4] K. Megas, G. Belli, W. B. Frakes, J. Urbano, and R. Anguswamy, "A study of cots integration projects: Product characteristics, organization, and life cycle models," in Proceedings of the 28th Annual ACM Symposium on Applied Computing, ser. SAC '13. New York, NY, USA: ACM, 2013, pp. 1025–1030.

[5] E. R. Hnatek, Practical Reliability Of Electronic Equipment And Products. Marcel Decker, 2003.

[6] F. Salewski and S. Kowalewski, "Hardware platform design decisions in embedded systems - a systematic teaching approach," in Special Issue on the Second Workshop on Embedded System Education (WESE), vol. 4, no. 1, SIGBED Review. ACM, Jan. 2007, pp. 27–35.

[7] ——, "The effect of hardware platform selection on safety-critical software in embedded systems: Empirical evaluations," in IEEE Symposium on Industrial Embedded Systems (SIES'07). IEEE, July 2007, pp. 78–85.

[8] E. Byres and J. Lowe, "The myths and facts behind cyber security risks for industrial control systems," in Proceedings of the VDE Kongress, vol. 116, 2004, pp. 213–218.

[9] K. Stouffer, J. Falco, and K. Scarfone, Guide to industrial control systems (ICS) security. National Institute of Standards and Technology, 2011, Special Publication 800-82.

[10] C. Alcaraz, R. Roman, P. Najera, and J. Lopez, "Security of industrial sensor network-based remote substations in the context of the internet of things," Ad Hoc Networks, vol. 11, no. 3, 2013, pp. 1091–1104.

[11] M. Irimia-Vladu, "green electronics: biodegradable and biocompatible materials and devices for sustainable future," Chemical Society Reviews, vol. 43, no. 2, 2013, pp. 489–736.

[12] EU, "2011/65/EU RoHS (restriction of certain hazardous substances)," Directive of the European Parliament and the Council, June 2011.

[13] L.Poulsen, "Life-cycle and long-term migration planning," InTech (isa.org), January/February 2014, pp. 12–17.

[14] W. ElMaraghya, H. ElMaraghy, T. Tomiyamac, and L. Monostorid, "Complexity in engineering design and manufacturing," CIRP Annals - Manufacturing Technology, vol. 61, no. 2, 2012, pp. 793 – 814.

[15] E. Puik, P. Gielen, D. Telgen, L. van Moergestel, and D. Ceglarek, "A generic systems engineering method for concurrent development of products and manufacturing equipment," in Precision Assembly Technologies and Systems, ser. IFIP Advances in Information and Communication Technology, S. Ratchev, Ed. Springer Berlin Heidelberg, 2014, vol. 435, pp. 139–146.

[16] E. Triantaphyllou, "Multi-criteria decision making methods: A comparative study," Applied Optimization, vol. 44, 2000.

[17] E. Jacquet-Lagrze and Y. Siskos, "Preference disaggregation: 20 years of {MCDA} experience," European Journal of Operational Research, vol. 130, no. 2, 2001, pp. 233 – 245. [Online]. Available: http://www.sciencedirect.com/science/article/pii/S0377221700000357